Continuity and Change

A Festschrift in Honor of
Irving Greenberg's 75th Birthday

Edited by
Steven T. Katz
Steven Bayme

UNIVERSITY PRESS OF AMERICA,˙ INC.
Lanham • Boulder • New York • Toronto • Plymouth, UK

Copyright © 2010 by University Press of America,® Inc.

4501 Forbes Boulevard
Suite 200
Lanham, Maryland 20706
UPA Acquisitions Department (301) 459-3366

Estover Road
Plymouth PL6 7PY
United Kingdom

British Library Cataloging in Publication Information Available

Library of Congress Control Number: 2010926360

ISBN: 978-0-7618-5145-5 (paperback : alk. paper)
eISBN: 978-0-7618-5146-2

∞™ The paper used in this publication meets the minimum requirements of American National Standard for Information Sciences—Permanence of Paper for Printed Library Materials, ANSI Z39.48-1992

Contents

Acknowledgments

The idea for a Festschrift in honor of Yitz Greenberg initially occurred during a phone conversation between the two editors early in 2008. We both realized that Yitz was about to celebrate his 75th birthday, and we thought it reasonable that his many students, colleagues, and long time admirers would welcome the opportunity to express their appreciation for all that he has contributed to many different areas of contemporary Jewish life and thought. Having quickly come to this decision, we immediately consulted with Blu Greenberg, who urged us to contact two younger scholars, Elli Stern and Daniel Septimus, who had been thinking along similar albeit different lines, and with their agreement the project became a reality.

Soon the concept of the *Festschrift* began to take shape. The editorial team identified approximately twenty individuals, who by dint of their long-term association with Yitz and their distinguished reputations, seemed a rich pool of potential contributors to begin with. Almost every scholar contacted happily agreed to participate. As a result the roster of contributors to the present volume includes many of the leading intellectuals in contemporary Jewish life. This in and of itself is a powerful testimony to Yitz's broad influence and high regard in which he is held by his peers.

A number of individuals and institutions have helped make this volume possible. Blu Greenberg served as a marvelous resource and constant source of encouragement. Elli Stern and Daniel Septimus assisted in multiple ways, providing invaluable technical, editorial, and research assistance. Each of the contributors we solicited graciously shared not only their expertise and scholarship but also their enthusiasm for the project. As the project neared completion, one of the contributors, Prof. Benny Kraut, passed away tragically and suddenly. At the time of his passing, he was working on a longer history of *Yavneh*, the Orthodox college student association. Both the organization itself and Professor Kraut's research on it were profoundly inspired by Yitz Greenberg. Sadly, the extremely rich article he prepared for the *Festschrift* is being published posthumously.

The financial assistance of three foundations made the publication of the volume possible. They are The Andrea and Charles Bronfman Philanthropies, the Harold Grinspoon Foundation, and the Charles and Lynn Schusterman Family Foundation. We thank, in particular, Jeff Solomon, President of The Andrea and Charles Bronfman Philanthropies; Joanna Ballantine, Executive Director of the Harold Grinspoon Foundation; and Sanford Cardin, President of the Charles and Lynn Schusterman Family Foundation, for their assistance in securing these grants. The American Jewish Committee (AJC) and Boston University's Elie Wiesel Center for Judaic Studies both provided a home, and various types of support, for this project from its gestation. The editors are particularly indebted to Ms. Pagiel Czoka, the Administrator of the Elie Wiesel Center, for managing the production of the volume. Once the volume was completed, Judith Rothman, Vice President and Director of University Press of America, graciously agreed to accept it for publication.

On a different level, both of the editors wish to express their deep admiration for and appreciation of Dr. Yitz Greenberg who has served the Jewish community so well as intellectual leader, teacher, and professional mentor over many decades. We, therefore, gratefully dedicate this volume to our distinguished colleague who has provided outstanding intellectual leadership and Jewish public service for nearly the past half -century.

Steven Bayme
(AJC)

Steven Katz
Boston University

1

Dr. Irving Greenberg:
A Biographical Introduction[1]

Steven Bayme

My first encounter with Yitz Greenberg occurred during my high school years in Brookline, Massachusetts in the mid 1960s. A high school associate principal, charged both with teaching Talmud and college guidance, suggested to me that I would profit from studying with Dr. Irving Greenberg, already a renowned professor of history at Yeshiva University. Knowing of my fascination with history, the administrator wisely explained that Yitz, along with Charles Liebman, Eliezer Berkovits, Emmanuel Rackman, and David Hartman constituted the leading lights of what was then termed the "Orthodox Left." To be sure, he added that personally he had striven to remain in the "center," aligning himself with the teachings of Rabbi Joseph B. Soloveitchik. However, he conceded, recognizing my leanings, and perhaps subconsciously giving voice to a few of his own, that in all likelihood I would find the Orthodox Left far more compelling and attractive.

Soon I discovered how prescient my high school administrator had been. Yeshiva University in the 1960's indeed was an exciting place that captured the ethos of a dynamic and vibrant Modern Orthodoxy, best expressed in Yitz Greenberg's courses and public lectures. Correctly, Greenberg judged that YU students had unlimited potential, and that the university provided an ideal venue to train a distinctive Modern Orthodox leadership for the future. His courses constituted models of synthesis probing the relevance of Jewish teaching to modern culture and challenging students to assess areas of conflict between these two realms. In his view a true Modern Orthodoxy did not connote weakness or concession to the pleasures of modernity but rather an incredible opportunity to wed the best values of the modern world with those of Jewish tradition.

Needless to say, many found this vision inspiring. Others, however, expressed considerable dismay. For the Talmud faculty, Greenberg's curriculum constituted, at best, unproductive use of time stolen away from the exclusive study of rabbinic text. At worst, his program constituted an invitation to engage in heresy. An in-depth interview of Greenberg printed in the undergraduate student newspaper in 1966 reverberated nationally and may well have diverted Greenberg's then-ascending career at Yeshiva.[2] In the interview, Greenberg specified three areas where he maintained contemporary Orthodox leadership had failed to respond to the challenges of modernity. The areas in question concerned pre-marital sexual contact, biblical criticism, and relations with the non-Orthodox movements.

Naturally, all attention focused on the first of these areas, notwithstanding that the latter two were in all probability of considerably greater significance. As one might imagine, students were far more titillated by the pleasures of the flesh than by the intellectual challenges to contemporary Orthodoxy. More to the point, by focusing on pre-marital sexual contact, Greenberg was wading into an area of Halakha, albeit one often observed more in the breach than in reality. Many Orthodox students at that time prioritized the imperative of developing a long-term relationship with a would-be partner over certain dictates of Halakha. (One might add that the then-nascent practice of a year in Israel following high school eventually transformed the dating practices of Modern Orthodox young people so that by the late 1970s, most YU students adhered to more restrictive modes often neglected in the 1960s.)

Claiming he had been misunderstood, Greenberg chose to retreat. By his own admission some 40 years later, he immediately realized that the interview had been an error.[3] Sadly, his two other tropes, the challenge of Biblical scholarship and Orthodoxy's isolation from the non-Orthodox movements, attracted comparatively little attention. In right-wing Orthodox circles, however, Greenberg now was seen as someone who embodied all the ills of Modern Orthodoxy.

Yet Greenberg retained considerable Orthodox supporters, especially among Orthodox laity. Gratifyingly for him, Greenberg's own congregation, the Riverdale Jewish Center, stood by him and continued to encourage his teaching. Long-time congregation members to this day fondly recall the intellectual excitement in the community over Yitz's teachings. One prominent family even claims to have chosen to reside in Riverdale because they found the controversy so interesting! YU students continued to flock to Greenberg's courses and claimed him as one within a diverse range of views on what constituted a true synthesis of Torah and western culture.

To his credit, Greenberg persevered in his teaching. His courses on intellectual history challenged students to explore new vistas on Christianity and its relationship to Judaism. He promoted a pluralistic model for relations between differing religious groupings, and a reformulation of Jewish theology given the challenges of contemporary scholarship. Few, even among Greenberg's most vigorous critics, denied either the intellectual demands of his courses or the rewards for fulfilling them.[4]

Within the Orthodox rabbinate Greenberg continued to take outspoken positions that he believed to be correct. He was willing to court controversy within the pulpit by speaking out on Vietnam, Soviet Jewry, New York City mayoral politics, and even made the *New York Times* list of Ten Top Sermons by speaking about the New York Mets. The congregation served as a forum for him to develop his ideas. His first book, *The Jewish Way*, emanated from pamphlets on the history and meaning of the Jewish holidays developed within the Riverdale Jewish Center.[5] Publicly he called for new liturgies to commemorate the two seminal events of the modern Jewish experience—the Holocaust and the birth of Israel.

Yet Greenberg's optimism, so present in the 1960's, faded somewhat in subsequent decades, particularly given his despair at Orthodoxy's turn to the right and its growing isolationism from the broader Jewish community. Modern Orthodoxy appeared to forfeit its verve and independence, constantly fearing ever more bold criticism emanating from the Orthodox Right. At Yeshiva University, Greenberg's base for many years, at which his affiliation terminated in 1972, attention turned to how the university could best position itself so as to attract the growing number of students from right-wing family backgrounds. The concern, of course, reflected a growing Haredi demographic ascendancy at the expense of Modern Orthodoxy. The reasons for this Orthodox shift to the right were complex, emanating from a combination of political, educational, and general religious currents. Put more specifically, the transformational impact of the near-universal practice of post-high school study in Israel for Orthodox students coupled with a rise in absolutist thinking generally shifted profoundly the balance of relations between Modern and Haredi Orthodoxy—with the full implications for the future of American Jewry still to be fathomed.[6] More generally, the Greenberg-Lichtenstein debate in effect heralded the rightward shift within Orthodoxy. Modern Orthodoxy redefined itself as "Centrist"—a necessarily vague formulation that ceded far too much ideological power to the Orthodox Right.

For Greenberg personally, this right-ward shift connoted his marginalization within Orthodox circles. His career at YU, once so promising, had been diverted by the aforementioned interview and, subsequently, by his public dissent from Rabbi Joseph B. Soloveitchik's opposition to interfaith theological dialogue.[7] Although he never surrendered either his aspirations or his willingness to battle on behalf of a truly *modern* Modern Orthodoxy, he began to cast his net more broadly upon the Jewish community generally, which he hoped to transform in a more positively Jewish direction.

Already in the mid 1960's at Yeshiva University Greenberg had introduced one of the first university-level courses on the Holocaust. The university's administration, failing to realize how path-breaking Yeshiva might be in introducing such a course, urged that the course be titled "Totalitarianism and Ideology."[8] To be sure, within a decade, the undergraduate dean acknowledged that he had approved the course primarily in order to expose students to Greenberg's thinking and that the somewhat mystifying name was meant essentially for external consumption. In fact, the course heralded the introduction of Holocaust courses in universities across the country.

In introducing the course into the curriculum, Greenberg was both signaling his shift of academic interests from American history to Jewish theology and identifying the Holocaust as seminal event of the 20th century. To be sure, the Eichmann trial had already penetrated the communications barrier concerning the Holocaust in public discourse, and the fears generated by the isolation of Israel politically in May 1967 brought Holocaust awareness to the forefront of Jewish public consciousness. But it was Greenberg, notwithstanding the opposition of many academic colleagues, who advocated successfully for the place of the Holocaust in Jewish and American higher education.

Understanding the Holocaust as a "central orientating event" in Jewish historical memory on par with the Exodus and the destruction of the Second Temple must be regarded as one of Greenberg's greatest historical and theological breakthroughs.[9] The Holocaust became central to both formal and informal Jewish education. Holocaust commemoration became an ongoing theme on the Jewish communal calendar, particularly in relationship to Yom Ha-shoah.[10] Most strikingly, and to the dismay of many, on campuses around the country, the Holocaust by 1980 had become perhaps the most popular course in Judaic studies departments. Or, as Prof. Arnold Eisen, then of Columbia University and today Chancellor of the Jewish Theological Seminary, put it cogently, "I am afraid that we're educating a generation of students whose only knowledge of Jews is how they died."[11]

These efforts culminated in the opening of the Holocaust Museum in Washington in May 1993. Yitz's dedication, perseverance, and personal leadership helped facilitate the creation of what would become one of the most important American cultural institutions, attracting over two million visitors each year. For two years he served as Executive Director of the President's Commission on the Holocaust, which developed the initial blueprints for the institution and its educational mandate and functions.[12]

In subsequent years he served on the Museum's governing board, chairing it in the opening years of the 21st century. Although the Museum has often been the focus of political and cultural controversy, few today deny its significance as primary vehicle for communicating the story of the Holocaust to American society at large and as permanent memorial of what occurred and reminder of human capacity for evil in the face of public indifference.[13]

To be sure, this successful initiative to stimulate Holocaust awareness became subject to the "law of unintended consequences." Few in fact predicted the extent of the initiative's success. The Holocaust became perhaps the most dominant aspect of Jewish identity, repeatedly trumping in surveys items such as Jewish holidays, family and peoplehood. For Jews, the Holocaust often became the primary lens through which to view the collective Jewish experience. For many, the richness of Jewish history gave way to a return of the "lachrymose conception of Jewish history" soliciting memories of persecution as central to Jewish self-image and identity.[14]

The success of the Holocaust Museum gives voice to its status as perhaps the most dominant expression of Jewish history and memory in American public space. Over 80% of the Museum's visitors have been non-Jews, exceeding even the most optimistic expectations of the Museum's founders. Clearly these successes enabled the Museum to fulfill its vision of creating a permanent memorial. One wondered, however, whether such successes meant that the primary image through which Gentiles viewed the Jewish people was one of a persecuted people. It was as if the Jewish community had been given a magic wand enabling it to teach America one and only one chapter of Jewish history, which would it choose? Rather than privileging the Exodus, the birth of Israel, the richness and creativity of Jewish literature, or other Jewish success narratives, the Jews had chosen to teach the narrative of Jewish destruction.

Greenberg defended this focus upon the Holocaust as both necessary and desirable. The Holocaust represented the most horrendous chapter of Jewish history if not of all human history. Over the years many have sought either to deny its proportions or to relativize them as one tragedy among others. We need not only to answer these voices but to preserve the story and its lessons for future generations.

Greenberg's primary interest in teaching the Holocaust lay less in its historical dimensions, notwithstanding their importance, and more in its theological ones. Despairing of the traditional "punishment for sin" theology, Greenberg sought alternate models within Jewish tradition to explain the problem of evil – the Book of Job, anger at God as affirmation of Him as reflected in the third chapter of Lamentations, and even kabbalistic *tzimtzum* or contraction of the Deity. What Greenberg refused to do was to justify Divine inaction by claiming the Jews had sinned. As he put it in a memorable phrase, "No statement, theological or otherwise, should be made that would not be credible in the presence of the burning children."[15]

These theological explorations led Greenberg into uncharted waters. Given the reality of the Holocaust, he argued that the Holocaust had shattered God's covenant with the Jewish people. Post-Holocaust Jewry constituted a "wounded people" for whom the covenant had become voluntary. In turn, it was now up to the Jews to assume responsibility for their own history. Far from being a victimized people, the Jews in fact now had to take responsibility for the wise uses of power in a world in which Jews alone were responsible for their fate.[16]

In some respects, Greenberg was boldly reconceptualizing Jewish theology in the aftermath of the Holocaust. The Holocaust constituted a unique event shattering the dominant paradigm of Jewish modernity and modern culture generally by demonstrating human potential for the demonic and the limits of Jewish emancipation as safeguard of Jewish security. Yet Jews were now called upon to reaffirm the Covenant. The State of Israel, although hardly a theological response to the Holocaust, provided an opportunity both to rebuild Jewish life and to reaffirm Judaic principles of "living in the image of God" in a modern secular society. That the Jewish people, broken by the Holocaust, could take the opportunity to rebuild a Jewish state upon principles of human rights and democracy constituted a compelling statement of the ongoing vitality of the Covenant in a post-Holocaust world.

Reactions to these theological explorations varied. Some claimed that the Holocaust in fact had posed no novel theological questions. The problem of theodicy had originated as far back as the Books of Jeremiah and Job. Others claimed that there were no real answers in any case and that only questions remained. Still others, particularly on the Haredi right, which in fact had suffered the greatest human losses, persisted in the claim of "punishment for sin."

Yet others, particularly within Modern or "Centrist" Orthodoxy feared the radicalism of Greenberg's theology. In their view Greenberg implicitly, and at times explicitly, advocated specific changes in Jewish law. If Jews now were responsible for renewing the covenant, did they not have the authority to make changes when necessary? Greenberg certainly had implied as much and in fact had utilized considerable precedents in Jewish tradition for change. Moreover, the non-Orthodox movements had been advocating changes in Jewish law for the past 150 years. By calling for relatively modest changes, Greenberg was again goring a sacred cow of contemporary Orthodoxy—namely, that in an age of widespread assimilation, Orthodoxy must insist upon the immutability of halakha and the exclusive halakhic authority of rabbinic scholarship rather than meet the needs of the moment, however worthy they might appear. Moreover, by advocating the possibility of change, Greenberg was aligning himself with social movements, e.g., Jewish feminism, which the Orthodox right opposed on cultural and religious grounds.

Last, some remained unconvinced by Greenberg's theological justifications for change. For one thing, a shattering of the covenant and its replacement by a "voluntary covenant" constituted a leap of faith that could not be proven empirically. In turn, Greenberg's historical precedents for halakhic change were often dismissed as too glib and as "telescoping of history." Most importantly, the community of halakhic authorities, temperamentally alien to Greenberg's models of thinking in any case, maintained that he had failed to provide sufficient grounds to justify a theory of halakhic change, much less the authority upon which changes might be based. The end result, of course, was that Greenberg became even more marginalized within his own community.

By the late 1970's, Greenberg was retreating from the front lines of Orthodox communal dynamics and found his natural constituency among the leadership of Jewish federations. As early as the 1960's he had electrified audiences at federation and UJA events. Within a decade he had become the most popular and sought after speaker on the federation lecture circuit. Together with Elie Wiesel and Steven Shaw, as well as academic associates including Reuven Kimelman and Steven Katz, he positioned CLAL—the National Jewish Center for Learning and Leadership, which he founded and served as president for twenty years--as a critical Judaic resource for Jewish leadership. Teaching across the country, serving as scholar in residence, Greenberg challenged Jewish leaders to think more Jewishly.

More specifically, Greenberg underscored the "holy secularity" of federations. He believed strongly, perhaps following Rav Kook, that sparks of Jewish holiness permeated every Jew and that the ostensibly secular work of federation leaders to enhance the Jewish people reflected that holiness. Some criticized this notion as validating "checkbook Judaism". Others, including Greenberg himself, defined federation work as laying building blocks of Jewish identity but by no means a substitute for serious Judaism.[17]

At its inception, CLAL aspired to become a think tank and retreat center for American Jewry. Through various CLAL programs and venues—classes, retreats, publications, etc,-- it became primarily a vehicle for adult Jewish education. Federations across the country enrolled current and future leaders in CLAL programs and classes. Greenberg attracted a faculty which sought to demonstrate the power and excitement in Jewish learning and in effect say to Jewish leadership, "Here at your fingertips lies a marvelous treasure underlying all the work you do for the Jewish people, why not turn to it and probe it for its contemporary wisdom?"

In the eyes of many, Greenberg and CLAL were virtually inseparable. CLAL's projected image was that of Yitz Greenberg teaching and lecturing to Jewish leadership. CLAL classes sought to impart his theological teachings –

post-Holocaust, renewal of covenant, third era of Jewish history and, most importantly, Jewish leadership taking responsibility for molding Jewish destiny. This theology in turn was translated as the Jewish communal agenda of pro-Israel political activism, philanthropic support for Jewish causes, and renewal of Jewish identity. In effect, Greenberg became a national rabbi for federation leadership providing Jewish content at federation events and anchoring federation activity in Jewish teachings.

Overtly, Greenberg captured the communal ethos and agenda of Jewish survivalism – a federation fundraising slogan had once stated simply, "Survival demands sacrifice." One CLAL publication equated fundraising with "Jew raising". More subtly, however, Greenberg was engaging in a far more transformative initiative to re-shape the map of Jewish communal priorities. The net effect of his teachings and influence upon federation leadership was to challenge Jewish organizations to take tradition seriously, think in Jewish terms, and, most important, to raise the profile of Jewish education among communal priorities. In that respect, Greenberg's strongest impact was in creating a more Jewishly-grounded Jewish leadership, one which would think beyond survivalist terms and towards a Jewish community worth preserving. In effect, Greenberg's challenge lay in harnessing the blessings of American freedom and affluence to create a Jewish community so compelling as to retain current members and attract new adherents.

It would be difficult to over-state Greenberg's personal impact upon Jewish leaders. His lectures and classes were a natural drawing card, and his personal attention to every student endeared him to legions of supporters. Individual communal leaders internalized his message of Jewish renewal and acknowledged how deeply his theology based upon Israel and the Holocaust had shaped their "civic Judaism." The world of Jewish federations and most particularly the General Assembly, the key gathering on the Jewish communal calendar, were transformed gradually into profoundly Jewish entities.

While CLAL's distinctive achievement lay in education of Jewish leadership, Greenberg also hoped to create a retreat center and think tank under CLAL's auspices. As a teacher, he understood the power of a Shabbat retreat as an opportunity to live the full Jewish experience—intellectual learning, shared rituals, and common Jewish family. At one point plans were advanced to merge CLAL with the Brandeis-Bardin adult camp on the West Coast. For multiple reasons the planned merger did not materialize, and the retreat center remained a visionary dream rather than a reality.[18]

CLAL, however, had greater success in its think tank efforts to catalyze Jewish leadership thinking on critical issues. Greenberg pioneered the field of intra-Jewish relations, hoping to engender sustained dialogue between Jews of differing religious movements and persuasions. Greenberg called for the same perseverance, patience, and dedication that Jewish leaders had given to inter-faith dialogue to the ascending field of intra-Jewish relations.

Greenberg summarized the case for such an effort in a 1985 essay, provoca-tively titled, "Will There Be One Jewish People by the Year 2000?" He pre-dicted that given widening chasms over issues of personal status and incipient tensions over communal and political issues between the religious movements that the flag of Jewish unity would be threatened over the long term. His solu-tion lay in underscoring repeatedly one of his favorite themes—religious pluralism among Jews.[19]

Again, Greenberg encountered opposition from Orthodox precincts. The very term pluralism became taboo within Orthodox circles. Orthodox leaders equated religious pluralism with religious relativism claiming that Jewish lead-ers speaking in the name of Judaism cannot sanction whatever it is that Jews happen to be doing. Greenberg's phrase, "Jewish is as Jewish does" perhaps unwittingly fed this misconception even though he himself continued to un-derscore both the limits of pluralism and the dangers of relativism.[20] More generally, Orthodox leaders dismissed the message of pluralism as an attempt to pander to the natural proclivities of Jews. Unfortunately, the real message of pluralism and the need for intra-Jewish dialogue as a corrective to extremist tensions on both left and right fell on deaf ears in the Orthodox community.

On other issues Greenberg encountered more positive reactions. His pow-erful intellectual defense of Israel in the face of unfriendly criticism evoked great admiration even from his critics.[21] Yet he was by no means impervious to problematic aspects of Israeli policy in the occupied territories, and he criticized some of the support given to West Bank settlers and the Gush Emu-nim movement.[22] He best articulated his message on Israel in a stimulating essay in which he argued that the uses of power must be tempered by ethical considerations, but there can be no Jewish ethics when Jews are powerless.[23] Perhaps his finest piece emanating under CLAL auspices consisted of a mov-ing and penetrating essay written in the aftermath of the Rabin assassination. The essay summarized many of Greenberg's themes concerning polarization, pluralism, and the ethics of power. In a Jewish world saddened and perplexed by an act of political murder, Greenberg provided considerable wisdom, per-spective and analysis.[24]

To be sure, Greenberg's optimism about Jewish power, influence, and afflu-ence was tempered not only by the failure of Oslo but also by the continuing data concerning Jewish assimilation. Perhaps he had too easily embraced the sense of Jewish empowerment and renewal, so current in the 1980's and best articulated by Charles Silberman's 1985 volume, *A Certain People*. Silberman had celebrated Jewish affluence and power and boldly predicted that no crisis of assimilation threatened the future of the American Jewish community.[25]

Greenberg had shared some but by no means all of these assumptions and was shaken by the release of the 1990 Jewish population study. The study demonstrated that intermarriage had risen significantly and that conversion to Judaism occurred only in a relatively small minority of cases. Jewish renewal, to be sure, did coexist alongside the specter of continued erosion.[26] But Jewish forebodings and anxieties about the future could by no means be dismissed as excessive Jewish worrying.

In this context Greenberg attempted to channel the resources of Jewish wealth towards programs of Jewish renewal. Joining forces with mega-philanthropist Michael Steinhardt, a committed secular Jew, appeared an odd match for Greenberg, a deeply religious man fascinated by theology and questions of belief. Yet philanthropy offered new opportunities to implement Greenberg's long-term thinking. As far back as 1965, in one of his earliest published articles, Greenberg had taken note of both the opportunities and risks provided by America.[27] Having succeeded by American social and economic standards, Jews now possessed the resources to forge their own destinies. The question was whether the wise uses of philanthropy could shape the Jewish future in positive ways. The question confronting Greenberg in this phase of his career was, assuming money were not an obstacle, what could be done to strengthen Jewish life?

Moreover, Steinhardt invited new and unconventional thinking. He was also prepared to risk failure—a trait all too often absent from a Jewish community which consistently touted its successes but only rarely recorded failures. Together, he and Greenberg explored whether American Jewry was ready for a secular high school – perhaps an elite boarding school along the model of Exeter as a training ground for future Jewish leaders. Steinhardt was also keen to learn from other philanthropists and to join forces when possible in partnerships so as to broaden the pool of resources. Clearly the most successful and far-sighted of these coalitions was a partnership of philanthropists, Jewish federations and the Government of Israel in creating the Birthright program, offering an expense-paid trip to Israel to every American Jew aged 18-26.

Philosophically, Birthright articulated several profound messages. First, it signaled that 1948 had changed the map and meaning of Jewish peoplehood in irrevocable ways. After 1948 our relationship with Israel constituted a critical aspect of Jewish identity so as to be part of the "birthright" of every American Jew. Second, Birthright connoted a profound statement of Israel-Diaspora relations by dint of the Israel experience and the partnership with the Israeli government. Thus Birthright signaled a statement about contemporary Zionism—that it was a responsibility of the State of Israel to ensure the future of Jewish life and continuity in North America. Last, Birthright signaled a statement by mega-philanthropists concerning the priorities of Jewish life—namely that for Jewish philanthropists the key priority had become securing Jewish continuity.

To date Birthright appears to have succeeded beyond expectations. Over its first decade, Birthright enrolled in excess of 150,000 young people. The program in turn has expanded to include other Diaspora communities. To be sure, questions of follow-up remain and long-term impact may be measured only longitudinally. By helping to forge the Birthright partnership, however, Greenberg helped create one of the most exciting initiatives to transform the Jewish scene in decades and one that reflected the new realities of 21st century Jewish history.[28]

A second partnership brought Greenberg full circle to Jewish education. In the 1960's he had established the SAR Academy in Riverdale as a leading Jewish day school. Together with Steinhardt, he and other philanthropists now helped to establish PEJE, the Partnership for Excellence in Jewish Education. PEJE held out the promise of providing Jewish education with top quality Jewish leadership. It focused on creating and nurturing elite Jewish day schools as the jewel and the crown of the Jewish educational system and the most effective vehicle of securing long-term Jewish identification.

Over a twelve-year period, Greenberg and Steinhardt had in effect challenged the Jewish community to go about its business differently. Their partnership reflected Greenberg's longstanding hypothesis that Jews can succeed only if they take responsibility for their destiny. The blessings of power and affluence that American Jewry had attained now would be tested in terms of the capacity of Jews to build a Jewish future.

How, then, may we assess Greenberg's impact? Although least appreciated within the Orthodox world, Greenberg greatly influenced an entire generation of Modern Orthodox intellectuals. For many, he modeled a way to live within two cultures, weighing the areas of consonance and dissonance between them. Whether the issues were religious Zionism, feminism, contemporary scholarship, or intra-Jewish relations, Greenberg provided a lens through which Modern Orthodox Jews perceived a difficult yet highly rewarding path to navigate the claims of each without negating either. Some of his most outstanding students, as evidenced by this volume, went on to leadership positions in academic Jewish studies and Jewish public service—two areas where Modern Orthodoxy continues to thrive.

In concrete terms, Greenberg was responsible for creating new Jewish institutions, many of which prospered subsequently. The SAR Academy in Riverdale stands as a shining example of Jewish day school education at its finest and as an enormous tribute to Greenberg as founder and initial dean. In the 1960s Greenberg also helped establish the Student Struggle for Soviet Jewry (SSSJ), which played a catalytic role in raising the plight of Jews in the Soviet Union and in effect galvanizing the Jewish establishment to take action in one of the most heroic undertakings of 20th century Jewish foreign policy and diplomacy. The United States Holocaust Museum, contrary to many predictions, has become one of the most important of American cultural institutions to focus upon a clearly Jewish theme. As described elsewhere in this volume, Greenberg was instrumental in creating Yavneh as an intellectual organization for Jewish college students, in some respects supplementing and going beyond Greenberg's intellectual influence at Yeshiva University. Last, as noted, Greenberg rightly merits a place among the founders of the Birthright Israel program.[29]

Yet Greenberg's most widespread following lay among federation leadership. For federations he was both instrumental in raising Jewish consciousness and in supplying the Judaic base and content in Jewish communal life. By necessity his tones here were considerably milder rarely challenging federation leadership to the degree he challenged Orthodoxy. Yet he did sensitize federation leadership to prioritizing Jewish concerns and taught an entire generation of federation activists to think and visualize themselves in more Judaic terms. In the constant tension between universal and particular philanthropic needs, Greenberg argued successfully that Jewish philanthropy must become more focused on Jewish causes.

In so doing Greenberg provided much of the vocabulary of contemporary Jewish thinking. He consistently underscored the Judaic teaching that the purpose of the mitzvot was "to live by them" interpreting tradition as teaching to advance human life. He helped capture the transformation in Jewish self-image from one of weakness and vulnerability to one of asking how best to harness Jewish power and strength for ethical and just purposes.

As an assertive and self-confident "ambassador" of the Jewish people, Greenberg helped shape and transform the nature of Jewish-Christian relations in the decades following Vatican II. Partially influenced by the writings of Franz Rosenzweig, he daringly went so far as to proclaim multiple covenants—to the Jews via Moses and to Christians via Jesus.[30] Yet he spared Christians no false consolation or sympathy in response to unfair Christian attacks upon Israel following the collapse of Oslo in 2000.[31] In effect, Greenberg claimed sincere friendship and dialogue with Christians, taking Christian theology seriously yet offering honest rebukes to Christian leaders when warranted.

Theologically, Greenberg appreciated perhaps most keenly the power of the critical events in modern Jewish history—the Holocaust and the birth of Israel. The Holocaust for him possessed revelatory significance as seminal event of our time. In Greenberg's language, the Jewish covenant after the Holocaust now was re-framed by Jews reclaiming a national Jewish homeland and promoting Jewish life in the Diaspora. Greenberg acutely understood the manner in which the Holocaust was re-shaping Jewish memory and what that memory might mean in terms of Jewish renewal. In so doing he sought new paradigms of man's relationship to God in a post-Holocaust world.

For Greenberg Jewish identity could not be "business as usual" after 1948. The birth of Israel embodied Jewish perseverance and willingness to continue in the face of catastrophe. Israel symbolized Jews taking responsibility for their own destiny. Heavily influenced by a 1950s essay by Joseph B. Soloveit-chik, Greenberg identified the birth of Israel as a major revelatory event of no less momentous consequence than the Holocaust.[32] Both events, in his view, would capture their place on the Jewish calendar and in the historical memory of the Jewish people of the 21st century.

For these reasons Greenberg emerged in the 1970's as a rabbi and theologian of the "civic Judaism" of Jewish leaders. If the Holocaust and Israel constituted the twin symbols of Jewish identity, Greenberg gave voice to their theological significance. For an entire generation of Jewish leaders, he epitomized their quest for Jewish meaning, helping them to channel their resources towards the strengthening of the Jewish people.

To be sure, as profound as this impact was, it had its limitations and came at a price. Greenberg did lead his constituency into uncharted waters yet at times found himself too far ahead of some constituents. Many federation activists, attracted to his vision of civic Judaism, in turn found his program of Jewish renewal too demanding. Conversely, those who had resonated to his vision of Modern Orthodoxy now found themselves theologically homeless in the contemporary Orthodox world that had rejected Greenberg while sidelining his brand of Modern Orthodoxy.

More generally one should acknowledge Greenberg's intellectual contributions to modern Jewish thought. Notwithstanding the time-honored approach of "we were punished for our sins," an approach even sanctified by the Shabbat liturgy, Greenberg courageously challenged this model as both morally repulsive and theologically inadequate. He understood that this classical approach emanated from Jewish perceptions of powerlessness in exile and the well-intentioned desire to regain control over Jewish destiny by attributing tragedy to Jewish misdeeds. Last, he understood the model as one seeking to justify God rather than a more forward-looking approach to re-thinking Jewish belief in the light of tragedy. In his view, no human sin could possibly justify punishment of such proportions.

Ingeniously, Greenberg combed Judaic scriptures for alternative models. He found particular inspiration in Job's model of debate with God and refusal to admit sin. Similarly, he pointed to Isaiah:53, the "Suffering Servant," widely identified with the Jewish people suffering vicariously for all of humanity. Following this model, the Holocaust served as warning to humanity at large of our capacity for evil, perhaps even a foreshadowing of possible nuclear

exchange. The third chapter of the Book of Lamentations also spoke to Greenberg invoking controlled anger at God as affirmation rather than rejection of
the Deity. Neutrality towards God connoted denial, but casting God as a foe,
"a lurking bear to me, a lion in hiding" (Lamentations 3: 10), enabled one to
maintain belief even while giving voice to disappointment.

Greenberg did not treat these models as conclusive. The overall context of
his response remained dialectical, focusing on the aspects of awe and silence
in the face of the catastrophe. Yet the models did offer avenues of possible
theological affirmation even while absorbing the reality of radical evil and
acknowledging the sincerity of disbelief. In effect, Greenberg's theological
response to the Holocaust illustrated the time-honored Jewish capacity to rebuild and renew while permanently absorbing the reality of the tragedy into
Jewish historical memory, practice and thought.

Over time, Greenberg came to understand the Holocaust as a statement of
human responsibility for human destiny. He began to look for allies among
Christian theologians. Here he encountered an enthusiastic audience among
those prepared to acknowledge Christian misdeeds in treatment of the Jews
and who were prepared to join hands with Jews in a battle against unbridled
secularism. In effect Jews and Christians could become partners in continuing
the work of the "voluntary covenant" in which humanity had increasingly
become the senior partner.

Greenberg's positions on Christianity were quite advanced, going far beyond
"tolerance" or perceiving Christianity as "a step in the right direction." By
granting Christianity theological validity and revelatory power, he was according Christianity "full partner" status in on-going covenantal work. In so doing
he challenged Jews to rethink inherited images of Christianity as historically
false and theologically untenable. Whether that theological pluralism would
over time become a mainstream position within Jewish thought will require
extended and longitudinal observation and testing. For the present, however,
Greenberg had raised new theological possibilities approaching Christians
with a willingness to both embrace and critique on a basis of mutual equality.

Greenberg's theology underscoring human dignity and power in turn readily
translated into support for a bold yet traditionalist Jewish feminism. Heavily
influenced by his spouse and intellectual partner Blu Greenberg, he praised the
empowerment of women as giving voice to the Divine image within all of us
and as illustrating the power of modern values to join forces with those of tradition in enhancing that Divine image.[33] At the same time, he underscored the
tensions between tradition and modernity in confronting feminism. He urged
feminists to preserve traditional values of family and volunteerism, even at the
risk of conflict with immediate feminist aspirations. For him, there could be no
finer example of "tikkun olam" than restoration of the ideals of family.

Today Greenberg remains an Orthodox intellectual with doubts about the course Orthodoxy was taking, a theologian wrestling with the impact of the Shoah and the birth of Israel, a teacher and rabbi of Jewish leaders, and an ambassador of the Jewish people and defender of the collective Jewish narrative. Never one to shy away from intellectual combat, he perhaps serves best as public Jewish intellectual and as revered rabbi. This volume constitutes a modest statement of appreciation on behalf of the literally thousands of individuals whose lives he has touched and who have benefited from his wisdom.

November 2008

NOTES

1. This introductory essay is based largely on my personal contact with Dr. Greenberg over four decades and my understanding of his career over that span of time. I benefited greatly from the comments of my co-editor, Dr. Steven Katz, and our two editorial assistants, Dr. Elli Stern and Mr. Daniel Septimus. They are, of course, in no way responsible for any errors or misunderstandings.

2. The best analysis of this controversy, albeit limited to the exchange between Greenberg and leading Talmud scholar Rabbi Aharon Lichtenstein, may be found in David Singer, "Debating Modern Orthodoxy at Y.U.: The Greenberg-Lichtenstein Exchange of 1966," *Modern Judaism*, Vol. 26 No. 2 (May 2006), pp. 113-126.

3. See Greenberg, "Yeshiva in the Sixties", in Menachem Butler and Zev Nagel eds., *My Yeshiva College* (New York: Yashar Books, 2006), pp. 184-186, with subsequent comments by Lichtenstein and Greenberg's reply, pp. 375-377, 379-381.

4. For Greenberg's reminiscences on his career at Yeshiva University, see Irving Greenberg and Shalom Freedman, *Living in the Image of God* (Northvale: Jason Aaronson, 1998) pp. 8-10.

5. Greenberg, *The Jewish Way* (New York: Summit Books, 1988), passim.

6. Samuel Heilman, *Sliding to the Right* (Berkeley, University of California Press, 2006), pp. 112-126. For a considerably more benign view of the study programs in Israel, see Shalom Berger et al., *Flipping Out?* (New York: Yashar Books, 2007), section 1. The data in this latter volume, although useful, are far too limited in the time span studied to reach longitudinal conclusions.

7. Soloveitchik had limited interfaith dialogue to social and political matters, excluding theological ones. See his essay, "Confrontation" *Tradition*, Vol. 6 No. 2 (Spring-Summer 1964) pp. 5-29. For Greenberg's dissent, see Greenberg, *For the Sake of Heaven and Earth* (Philadelphia: Jewish Publication Society, 2004), pp. 12-16.

8. Greenberg and Freedman, *Living in the Image of God* pp. 10-11. Greenberg did in fact first propose introduction of the course in 1962, when, to his knowledge, only one such course existed anywhere in the country. See Paula Hyman, "New Debate on the Holocaust," *New York Times Magazine*, Sept. 14, 1980, p.86.

9. See the important essay by Greenberg, "Cloud of Smoke, Pillar of Fire: Judaism, Christianity and Modernity After the Holocaust", in Eva Fleischner ed., *Auschwitz:*

Beginning of New Era?, (New York: Ktav, Cathedral Church of St. John the Divine, and ADL, 1977), pp. 7-55. See also Greenberg, "The Third Great Cycle in Jewish History," *Perspectives*, National Jewish Resource Center, 1981.

10. Greenberg, *The Jewish Way*, Ch. 10.

11. Cited in Hyman, p.109

12. Greenberg and Freedman, *Living in the Image of God* p. 21.

13. The story of the Museum and its creation is best chronicled in Edward T. Linenthal, *Preserving Memory* (New York : Viking, 1995).

14. Hyman, p.78

15. Greenberg, "Cloud of Smoke, Pillar of Fire", in *Auschwitz: Beginning of New Era?*, p. 23..

16. Greenberg, "Voluntary Covenant", *Perspectives*, National Jewish Resource Center, 1982.

17. Greenberg and Freedman, p. 59. See also Jonathan Woocher, *Sacred Survival* (Bloomington: Indiana University Press, 1986), pp. 193-198. Kook's views on "holy secularity" focused upon the work of secular Zionists in Palestine. See Arthur Hertzberg, *The Zionist Idea* (New York: Atheneum, 1971), p. 430. In later years Greenberg acknowledged the possible influence of Christian theologians Dietrich Bonhoeffer and Harvey Cox in developing the concept of "holy secularity." See Greenberg, *For the Sake of Heaven and Earth*, p. 29.

18. Greenberg and Freedman, *Living in the Image of God*, pp. 14-15.

19. Greenberg, "Will There Be One Jewish People by the Year 2000?", *Perspectives*, CLAL, 1986. See also the essay by Jacob Ukeles, this volume.

20. Greenberg, "Towards a Principled Pluralism", in Ronald Kronish, ed., *Towards the 21ˢᵗ Century*, (Hoboken: Ktav, 1988), esp. pp 190-193, and Greenberg, *For the Sake of Heaven and Earth*, pp. 202-208.

21. David Berger, "Covenant, Messiahs, and Religious Boundaries" *Tradition*, vol. 39 No. 2, (Summer 2005), p. 75.

22. Greenberg and Freedman, *Living in the Image of God*, pp. 184-192.

23. Irving Greenberg and David Elcott, "The Ethics of Jewish Power: Two Views" *Perspectives*, CLAL, 1988, pp. 1-28.

24. Greenberg, "Yitzhak Rabin and the Ethic of Jewish Power", *Perspectives*, CLAL, 1995.

25. Charles Silberman, *A Certain People* (New York: Summit Books, 1985), Chs. 5-7. For a critique, see Steven Bayme, "Crisis in American Jewry?", *Jewish Arguments and Counterarguments,* (New York : Ktav and AJC), pp. 415-418.

26. Barry Kosmin et al., *National Jewish Population Survey,*(New York: Council of Jewish Federations, 1991)

27. Greenberg, "Adventure in Freedom or Escape from Freedom?", *American Jewish Historical Quarterly*, Vol. 55 no. 1 (September 1965), pp. 5-21.

28. Leonard Saxe and Barry Chazan, *Ten Days of Birthright Israel*, Waltham: Brandeis University Press, 2008, esp. pp. 116, 121, 183, for Greenberg's involvement.

29. Greenberg and Freedman, *Living in the Image of God* p. 219. See also essay by Benny Kraut, this volume.

30. Greenberg, *For the Sake of Heaven and Earth*, esp. pp 64-69, 187-197. It should be noted that Rosenzweig limited the respective covenants to Judaism and Christianity alone. Greenberg's focus remained primarily Judaism and Christianity, but he was

prepared to consider further expansion, including Islam and other faiths. Greenberg's differences with Rosenzweig centered on the latter's positioning of Judaism beyond the historical framework, which, for Greenberg, writing a generation after the Holocaust, implied a call for continued Jewish powerlessness. *Ibid*, pp. 39-40.

31. David Berger, "Covenant, Messiahs, and Religious Boundaries," p.75.

32. Soloveitchik, *Kol Dodi Dofek* (New York: Yeshiva University, 2006). Greenberg, "On the 45th Birthday: An Assessment of Israel's Religious Significance", *Reflections*, CLAL, April 1993, p. 3.

33. Blu Greenberg's views may be found in her *On Women and Judaism* (Philadelphia: Jewish Publication Society, 1981). In later years she founded JOFA, the Jewish Orthodox Feminist Alliance.

2

Intra-Aggadic Control of Theological Freedom: A Speculation

Eugene B. Borowitz

Fifty years ago, in my first book on Jewish theology (A New Jewish Theology In The Making, Westminster, 1958) I defined my task as seeking to speak as much out of the Judaism which grounded my existence as from the contemporary intellectual climate which structured my mentality. How to do that while remaining true to each of the sources of my being was clearer as my project than as a method of executing it. As the decades have passed, I have had some useful insights into what may help me reach my goal, but the enterprise still resists unitary formulation. Nonetheless, I persist in the inquiry and it seemed to me that I might contribute a proper tribute to Yitz's admirable pursuit of a similar if more traditionalistic goal, if I added to this volume a small study of aggadic self-restraint. Since it involves taking a comprehensive vision of honored Jewish opinion on a given theological theme, I have permitted myself the privilege of speaking in generalizations rather than in the minutiae that normally attest to scholarly reliability. What follows, then, is an account of significant Jewish views of God's nature which turned out to be a case of aggadic self-restraint whose contents surprised and enchanted me. A major reason for that was that the limitation arose not from required practice—the halakhah often setting limits to Jewish theological freedom—but, as it were, from aggadic self-limitation.

THE THEME IN QUESTION

My inquiry began, as often happens, as a result of an apologetic encounter. Modern Jews often, albeit unconsciously, enthusiastically follow Rene

Descartes' advice that proper thinking should begin from the stance of doubt. In the case of doubt about God's reality people have suggested that if they could only get some idea of what God is like they might then be able to fit God into their basic understanding of what is real. Thus, though none of us have ever seen a live Pterodactyl, we have seen birds. So when researchers have come across certain bones from the days of the dinosaurs, they have been able to convince us otherwise skeptical moderns that there once were very large creatures that flew. That suggests that if we had some indication of what God is like we would certainly find it easier to accept God's reality.

When the challenge to Jewish belief is put in something like those terms it does not require esoteric research to realize that, in diverse ways, it has been something of a constant in the Jewish response to God. Thus the spiritual geniuses who contributed their insights to what became the Bible and rabbinic literature did not hesitate to speak of what God was like in God's momentary interactions with people or the world. Later, in medieval times, when philosophy and mysticism made their appearance in Jewish thinking, some writers sought to explicate more encompassing views of God's nature. Indeed, in modern times Jewish thinkers have in their own intensely self-conscious ways, sought to provide rather comprehensive statements on the topic. In what follows I propose a quick survey of this theme in these three periods.

GOD'S NATURE IN THE BIBLE

In all the diverse books of the Bible, only once do we find the text directly speaking of what God is like. After the Golden Calf incident, there is a mystifying story in which Moses, God's incomparable intimate (Ex.33:11), suddenly asks God, "Let me, please, see k'vodecha." (v. 18, literally, "Your glory," but, more likely, an honorific for "Your Self," as when we call a judge, "your Honor," or various high officials, "Your Excellency"). To this, God replies that Moses may see God's goodness and hear God's personal name, Yud-Heh-Vav-Heh (for which later custom requires that we substitute Adonai, "my Lord"). But then God adds, "But you cannot see panay (literally, "My face," which is the Hebrew euphemism for "Me-as-I-am") for no human may see Me-as-I-am and survive" (v. 20). Note how the two Hebrew terms themselves deflect us from God's selfhood and thus indicate the Bible writers' sensitivity to the unbridgeable gap between even the holiest of humans and Adonai. (The astonishing conclusion of this encounter in Ex. 33:21-34:7 involves God inserting Moses in a cleft in the mountain, putting God's hands over the opening and when God goes by [proclaiming God's policy toward humans], God removes God's hands so Moses may see God's achoray, God's "back" [? or perhaps the consequences of God's deeds] but not, says God, "panay." That is as close as we come to a direct biblical revelation of God's fundamental nature but there are many partial indications by the Bible's writers of what God is sometimes like. I often find it helpful to discuss this aspect of the topic by reference to biblical verses which are familiar from the siddur, the Jewish prayer book.

Many worshippers report being deeply moved by the personal prayer moments which conclude the *amidah,* the collection of prayers whispered while "standing," that are the heart of each Jewish service. That silent period concludes with the saying or singing of Psalms 19:15, "May the words of my mouth and the meditations of my heart be acceptable to You, *Adonai,* my rock and my redeemer." This oft-recited, much beloved biblical verse unabashedly describes God in contradictory ways. A "rock" does nothing; it just stays in its place, which is good if you do not want to be moved from where you are. A "redeemer," on the other hand, is someone who acts to extricate you from a difficulty. Why have Jews over the centuries found themselves moved by a sentence that describes God in such incompatible ways? Because, without having to say so, we know that sometimes we experience God as the solid, unchanging foundation of our existence and yet at other times we feel God has helped us surmount some recent trouble. As the Bible's almost endless descriptive terms for God testify, sometimes God is our judge, sometimes God is our forgiving father or, more rarely, our suckling mother; sometimes God is an "ancient of days," sometimes God is a dashing lover or an invincible young warrior; sometimes God is a harsh ruler and sometimes a caring shepherd or even a bird whose wings shelter the trembling chicks. But because we mostly think of God as the One who creates, maintains and orders the universe, who controls its forces, both the terrifying and the life-enhancing, who calls us to righteousness and forgives us when we repent our sins, our ancestors most frequently addressed God by the most powerful term they knew, "king"—and on special days, "Our Father, Our King."

JEWISH FAITH DOES NOT CLAIM TO KNOW EVERYTHING

The root of the old Jewish insight that we only know aspects of what God is really like is the Hebrews' insight that God is One, and thus Unique and Incomparable. In their thoroughgoing prohibition of idolatry the biblical authors and then the Rabbis asserted their conviction that any effort to indicate what God was like was not only sinful but an intolerable affront to the Unique and Incomparable One, the ultimate Singularity. However, when speaking situationally, that is, of the same God whom people sometimes meet in suffering and sometimes in celebration, sometimes in judgment and sometimes in forgiveness, these same teachers used an extraordinary variety of terms from their experience to describe the One who meets us where we are. Confusing these two levels of description—of God as God-truly-is with our sense of God as God-sometimes-appears has caused even otherwise thoughtful people much confusion about the God of whom the best that we can truly say is that God is One.

The Hebrews, after a thousand years or so of living their uncommon monotheistic faith, encountered a series of Greco-Roman sects that claimed to know what God was truly like. Their priests promised to reveal to their initiates the true "God" who ruled above the "god" who had so botched the creation of our world. Modern scholars have called these sects "Gnostics" ("gno"="know," as in the word "agnostic"). The Rabbis of the early Common Era condemned this teaching and carried on a strong polemic against all those who asserted that there were "Two Powers" ('god" and "God") in heaven.

Monotheism was so firmly set in the minds of believing Jews that early in rabbinic times the prayers after the declaration of God's unity, the *Sh'ma*, were climaxed by a telling citation from the ancient song celebrating the miracle at the Sea of Reeds. Exodus 15.11 seems to shout exultantly, *"Mi chamochah ba-elim Adonai,"* "Who is like you among the [so-called] 'gods' *Adonai*?" It is a boast, not an inquiry, the truth being so obvious that the song had no need to provide an answer. Another biblical poet, however, provided a positive statement of the obvious truth. It occurs in Psalm 86:8, *"Eyn kamochah baelohim, Adonai,"* "There is none like You among the [so-called] 'gods' *Adonai,"* a verse often chanted in Jewish services before the Torah scroll is taken from the Ark.

Here the logic of Jewish faith asserts itself. "God is one" means there really is nothing like God. So as much as we'd like to equate God with something else we know, we can't do it. What we can know about God is that God exists and that God wants us to live righteously, truths that have shaped and reshaped Jewish existence over the centuries.

THE MEDIEVAL EFFORTS TO GO
BEYOND MERE ASPECTS OF DIVINITY

Two innovative Jewish ways of understanding God more comprehensively emerged in the Middle Ages. The philosophic one resulted from the Moslem conquest of many lands bordering the Mediterranean Sea and then bringing with them some wonderful booty: philosophy, the old Hellenic approach to reality. Scholars are less certain about the origins of the second development in which the old rabbinic mysticism rather suddenly began teaching dazzlingly detailed descriptions of God, a doctrine that came to be called "Kabbalah."

Radically different as these rationalistic and mystic approaches to God were, both sought to move substantially beyond the old "aspect" understanding of God's nature.

As so often in matters of medieval Jewish philosophic developments, we can turn to the thought of Maimonides for a précis of what transpired. Utilizing Aristotle's view of the orderliness of nature, Maimonides clarified how God, the Epitome of wisdom, *chochmah*, brought an ordered uni-verse out of chaos by means of God's Active Intellect. When people utilize their own intellect, they may become attuned to God's own ordering intelligence and thereby increasingly understand God's purposes in structuring reality and, especially, the standards of proper human and Jewish behavior. Although Maimonides gloried in the wisdom that God and humankind shared, he emphasized that the rational mind could not vault over its human limitations to know God's essence. Thus the greatest Jewish rationalist of his era—and perhaps any era—forthrightly affirmed the logic of classic Jewish monotheism that God is incomparable.

Though mysticism promises personal intimacy between people and God its mature form reached a similar outcome. Its doctrine of the ten *sefirot*—the nodes of God's being and functioning (of which more below)—made possible an inexhaustible variety of depictions of aspects of God's nature. However, this data rested on a prior and overriding understanding that God was *Eyn Sof*, the One of No Limits, of whom, therefore, ~~nothing~~ could properly be said, including this. Thus despite their multiple certainties about God, kabbalists realized that they had to be dumb when it came to saying anything truly substantive about God.

ENVISIONING GOD'S NATURE TODAY 1: WHEN CLARITY IS PARAMOUNT

Contemporary Jewish philosophers and others who value intellect continue to seek a rational understanding of God's nature. Their strategy in this quest generally begins by clarifying the limits of what a rational mind might logically say and then describing God within these bounds.

The earlier of the two most widely accepted Jewish versions of this position illuminated non-Orthodox Jewish lives well past the first half of the twentieth century. Hermann Cohen, the great German reviver of the philosophy of Immanuel Kant, followed that master by creatively speaking of God as the most basic and integrative idea of the human mind. Where Kant had specified and analyzed the three fundamental logics by which a rational mind operated— science, ethics and aesthetics—Cohen argued that the unity of consciousness required a transcending concept to ground and integrate them into a rational consciousness. Cohen's unifying God-concept was not only an insightful re-statement of Jewish monotheism but, he argued, that its pre-modern state-ment of human duty, *halakhah*, Jewish law, anticipated Kant's insistence that ethics, to be rational, had to take the form of Moral Law. Though Kant's phi-losophy no longer commands the widespread allegiance it once had, most of the Jewish community today still resonates to Cohen's rational insistence that God and ethics are inseparable.

Some decades later when science replaced philosophy as the epitome of ra-tionality, Mordecai Kaplan, following the lead of some American philosophers, boldly asserted that Jews should think of God in terms of a natural force. Even as gravity and electro-magnetism function universally, so God could be under-stood as effectively omnipresent. However, Judaism could not tolerate a God who, like these forces, was value-free. So Kaplan, basing himself on the anthro-pologists' judgment that religions are human constructs created in response to human needs, daringly proposed that Jews now understand God in this fash-ion. Here is his exact definition of God–the only one ever given in Jewish his-tory—"God is the [natural] Power that makes for Salvation [human flourish-ing]." Note, how, by limiting God to just this positive function, Kaplan resolved the old problem of how a good God could tolerate evil (although he never ex-plained who or what was responsible for the evil in the universe).

Contemporary Jewish philosophers are still setting forth other clear and logical ways of thinking about what God is like but none has yet received the communal acceptance that these two proposals once did. Nonetheless, our present-day rationalists would most likely answer the question of what God is like in terms of how they believed the mind can most effectively operate. Thus many of them still conceive of God not as God may be said to be real in absolute reality but only as some version of our Most Fundamental Idea, or as the Goodness in Nature. As valuable as such descriptions may be, they testify to what a rational human mind can assert about God, not about what God, in fact, is.

ENVISIONING GOD'S NATURE 2: OUR UTMOST INTIMATE

As the twentieth century matured a major change in thinking about the meaning of life swept through western culture. Its central theme was that a person is more than a mind and that human existence ought to involve far more than ideas and ethics. Early on, two German Jews, Franz Rosenzweig and Martin Buber, created, in somewhat different ways, a radically new manner of thinking about life and religion that continues to inform many lives. Buber's explanation being far more accessible, what follows uses his terminology.

People naturally, though quite unconsciously, confront the world in one of two ways. Buber called the usual style "I-it" and in that mode we are essentially observers—detached, analytic, judging. But on occasion, quite spontaneously, we move beyond the common stance and become personally involved, a relation he called "I-thou." Think back to a moment in a supermarket or at an Oneg Shabbat when a casual exchange has for some brief moments opened up you and someone else to one another. Recalling it later you now realize that your former casual acquaintance is "a real person" and you now relate to them somewhat differently than before. Should this encounter be with someone with whom you've had such exchanges before, the new I-thou experience comes as a confirmation of your old friendship or love.

I-thou moments are generally fleeting but they are what give life its fullest value. The world's many religions—for I-thou experiences occur universally—are efforts to renew and be rededicated to the God one has met this way before. Such encounters yield us no data about what God is like for description always turns a "thou" into an "it." Only poets, musicians or others who can transcend descriptive prose, may hope to communicate something about a friend or a love. The rest of us stammer, inevitably unable to describe them as we have come to truly know them.

We have special difficulty talking intimately about God, Buber says, because God, unlike all others we know, never reverts to being an "it." God, the Unique One, is the Eternal Thou. So after we have proclaimed God's one-ness in the *Sh'ma* we are not called on to cogitate about God but to love God with all our heart and soul and being.

All genuine faith originates in an encounter with the Eternal Thou and when that happens to a group in an especially moving historical experience a new religion may come into being. The Bible reports that the Hebrews experienced this century after century and these continual encounters engendered this people's determination, unique in human history, to make their national existence a faithful response to their ongoing involvement with the Eternal Thou.

We who share in our people's millennia-old relationship with God come to know our covenant Partner very well but we also know that try as we may, all efforts to describe our precious Intimate are doomed to superficiality. God is never an "it" as all other realities are most of the time.

ENVISIONING GOD'S NATURE 3: FEMINIST EXPLORATIONS

As feminists have been rethinking Jewish belief some have charged that the rather rigidly ordered style of argument that characterizes many male Jewish theological works is the antithesis of how women should speak about their faith, particularly when the topic is God. This demanding standard of openness and spontaneity may be the reason that few extended Jewish feminist statements about God have appeared and none has captured the allegiance of many feminist thinkers. In contrast, feminists almost universally condemn the classic Jewish practice of depicting God as a paragon of masculine severity: king, not queen; father, not mother; warrior, not nurse; judge, not teacher; denouncer not comforter. Abiding by this ancient cultural sexism deprived the Jewish people of the many ways in which traits more commonly associated with women—nurturing, inspiring, loving, guiding and much else—are features of our Jewish nearness to God. Feminist Judaism has taught us all that our monotheism belittles God when it substantially symbolizes God as mono-gendered.

The very term "God"—not "Goddess"—itself subtly arouses masculine associations with the One who is the focus of our worship and the standard of our way of life. In that spirit, all of us should be troubled about what we should call the One who, in many ways, ought to be the chief focus of our lives. Even the suggested substitute terms for "God" like "the Eternal" or "*Adonai*," or others, always seem to subtly create limited or otherwise misleading senses of Israel's Ultimate One. Every thoughtful Jew must now hope that some gifted souls among us will one day provide us with terms that more fully express our expanded sense of Divinity.

Some feminists have responded to this issue by trying to create an understanding of Divinity as thoroughly feminine as the biblical one is masculine. Others have gone further and created or re-created Goddess worship of various kinds where an exclusively feminine clergy leads a community which sometimes includes men. Most feminist thinkers, including those still loyal to Judaism, have rejected this reaction as gross over-compensation. They deny that women's individuality is restricted by their femininity, an error they call "essentialism." In their eyes, gender, while highly significant in one's character, is only one factor in that mysterious mix we call existence.

An instructive sisterly exchange clarifies some of the difficulties Jewish feminists face as they seek to clarify what God is like. The accomplished poet, Marcia Falk, particularly in her magisterial volume of poem-prayers, *The Book of Blessings*, has sought to clarify the nature of the God she addresses. Her awe and thanks are directed to the beneficent forces in nature, particularly those which ennoble humankind. Though she largely arrived at her views on her own she has come to realize how close she is to the God-concept of Mordecai Kaplan. His intention may only have been to gain the clarity of scientific language and to avoid the problem of theodicy. This naturalistic characterization of God also appeals to Falk as a feminist because it immediately rules out the problems of God's gender which are so obtrusive in classic Jewish liturgy and elsewhere. Her warm poetic appreciation of the daily wonder of nature and its nurturing of our humanity makes possible a newly loving relationship for all genders.

Her friend, the eminent feminist thinker Rachel Adler, while appreciating her accomplishment, has questioned the adequacy of her vision of God. The central problem with characterizing God as a force of nature is that such entities are indifferent to human values. They react alike to saint and sinner, and if we are exhorted to model ourselves after God's image surely we should not now seek to live conscience-free. Falk and others respond to this challenge by emphasizing that it is only the beneficent forces in nature that these "impersonalists" connect with their notion of God. They further charge that to suggest that God is the source of our values effectively implies God is somehow personal, thus returning us to the evils of associating God with gender. These responses are in turn rebutted by Adler and others as avoiding the issue of inquiring whence, other than arbitrary personal choice, those who speak of "beneficent natural forces" derive their standard of goodness.

This question of the ground of our values bedevils much of contemporary philosophy and will not easily be settled. Feminist Jewish theology being so young and vigorous a movement, we may hope that in due course it will yield one or more creative responses to this and other issues.

ENVISIONING GOD'S NATURE 4: MYSTICISM AND KABBALAH

While feminist Judaism is multi-faceted because of its newness, the many spiritualities speaking of Jewish inwardness not only speak in recent accents but draw on the centuries old variety of Jewish esoteric teachings. Two venerable themes predominate among them. The one, common to many world mysticisms, is that merger with God, temporary though it must be, is the goal of Jewish religiosity. The other, the central insight of Kabbalah, is that God is a dynamic structure of ten sefirot, a doctrine requiring even brief explication.

The esoteric Jewish teaching about God and our access to God that emerged in the Middle Ages centered on a breathtaking contradiction about God's nature. God was simultaneously *Eyn Sof*, the Unlimited about whom ~~nothing~~ could be said, including this, and a dynamic structure of ten inter-related nodes of God's power and functioning called *sefirot*. Taken singly or in combination, one could say a bewilderingly unlimited number of things about them and what God is "sometimes" like. At the same time, the mystic adept could use the diagram of the order in which they were arrayed as a mystic ladder by which one might experience God's reality. Mystic practices--often

Jewish observance accompanied by mystic intent or various exercises of one's consciousness—were the means of accomplishing this and another exalted goal. As one linked one's soul with ever higher rungs on the sefirotic ladder, one helped rectify the present incoherence among the *sefirot* which is responsible for the misery of our post-Edenic world. (This is the medieval version of *tikkun olam*, the mending of the world, which has in recent years come to mean ethical social action.) Most kabbalists were monists, asserting that as one's consciousness expanded, one realized there was only God and nothing else. Our everyday experience of other realities, they believed, is a function of our presently clouded consciousness—as, they insist, is our question of what God is like.

Numerous variations on these themes all call themselves "Kabbalah."

The teachings and practices being so diverse, I suggest that present-day Jewish mysticisms may be characterized in terms of the level of truth they attach to the classic doctrines of Kabbalah.

At the simplest level, much contemporary writing about Jewish mysticism echoes the language of American New Age spirituality. It teaches the meditative practices—breathing, posture, concentration—which expand one's consciousness and enable one to feel God's presence within. The Jewish groups also commend ritual observance, social action, and some familiarity with Kabbalah. However, the emphasis on this level is largely upon the single self and its way to God. It is difficult to estimate the place of marijuana and other psychodelics in bolstering such mysticism (or those that follow) but its users may find some prior Jewish model in the unprotested use of *hashish* among North African Jews in years gone by.

In the more textually oriented groups the expanded consciousness is closely linked to the classic doctrine of the *sefirot* and the guidance for life and inwardness that it offers. Contemporary teachers have added their modern insights as to how our relationship with given *sefirot*, can expand our mystic existence today and bring us to ever closer identification with God. However, on this level Kabbalah is essentially treated as midrash, as imaginative Jewish guidance rather than as literal truth.

As a result of their mystic experiences some Jews have come to accept the Kabbalah as essentially factual. They are convinced that as they can identify with ever higher levels of the *sefirot* they will personally participate in God's all encompassing reality. Here, union with God is not merely theory but a life goal. Only the rarest exemplars of such monism will seek to describe their mystic experience or speak of their spiritual attainment. The goal is too rarified and God is indeed utterly ineffable, *Eyn Sof*. So if the teaching is put into words, it is largely allusive; or, since it is beyond words, one is expected to gain it from the person and presence of one's mystic guide.

DIVERSITY AND ITS LIMITS

In practice, to the extent that most believing Jews think about God's nature, they tend to be eclectics. At times they may feel that God is the idea of all ideas while at other times they experience God as personally available or then again as the utterly remote one with whom, however, they can be quite intimate. Other people mix these and other ideas into a shifting vision of That Remoteness which touches them in moments of belief. Moreover, they tend to feel quite justified in taking such theological liberties because, though their Jewish knowledge may be limited, they feel reasonably confident that different opinions about God's nature have long been tolerated in our community.

The ultimate coherence of the diverse theological positions we have traced above raises an intriguing question. Structurally, how did the life of Torah keep Jews faithful to the old insight that, speak about God as we will, we all believe that God's nature is, for all God's accessibility, beyond description?

The traditional answer would seem to be that as long as one's ideas lead one to be properly observant—that is, abide by the *halachah*—the idea will be tolerated in the Jewish community. The obverse is probably more significant practically, that is, to the extent that an idea might lead people to violate the accepted halachic norms—on which, I shall add a clarifying qualification below—it will be treated with suspicion if not outright opposition. However, this standard is of limited help in our case which has to do with thinking rather than acting. To be sure, were any of these formulations seen as inducements to idolatry or as defamations of God's name, they would be Jewishly decried. The most that can be said of the function of the halachic standard in this essentially aggadic area is that it hovers in the background of our theologizing, something like a warning system whose sensors define the area forbidden to us but allowing us freedom of movement within its bounds.

In addition to this indirect limitation on Jewish religious thinking, I want to suggest two somewhat indeterminate non-halachic "norms" which reciprocally constrain the exercise of aggadic freedom. The first of these is time. That is, an idea is not likely to be taken seriously in the learned Jewish community—see below—unless for some years, perhaps decades, it has been found convincing. It is tempting to see, in this the pragmatist's assertion, that this is our best means of ascertaining certain kinds of truth. However I do not see any clear indications that the Jewish concern with the long-term vitality of ideas has focused on their practical effects rather than their spiritual appeal.

Closely connected with the issue of time is the attitude toward the idea of the Jewish learned community. There is clearly nothing institutional about this standard, say an ongoing Sanhedrin or Curia. Nonetheless, in some non-organized way, thoughtful, scholarly Jews will react to ideas which have been

put before the community, particularly if they have been of interest to informed thinkers of prior generations. While the standard cannot be made
precise, the more these earlier thinkers have been halachically significant, the
more their opinions of various ideas will have significance to believing Jews of
later times. This describes, I believe, the traditional attitude and practice down
to our own day.

It seems to me something like this interplay of law, time and informed response can is also true of Jewish religious thought in today's largely non-Orthodox community. In any case, I have raised this issue about the inner limits
of aggadic speculation as a tribute to Yitz whose ideas have brought him to a
unique place in the traditional Jewish community and have also been richly
meaningful to many less observant Jews as well.

3

Has the Holocaust Been a Turning Point in Christian Theology about Judaism?

Alice L. Eckardt

"Good theology cannot be based on bad history."

—*James Parkes*

"The Holocaust is an abyss which never cries 'Enough!'" . . .

—Robert Reeve Brenner

"Neither [Judaism nor Christianity] can confront the Holocaust without in some way being transformed [for] the event forever precludes easy faith in God or faith in humanity."

—Robert McAfee Brown

"Christianity will not be able to overcome its legacy of guilt for the Holocaust without a major purging of its sources of Jew hatred. . . . [This] can come only from recognition that the Holocaust is an orienting event in Christian history."

—Irving Greenberg

Over many decades Dr. Irving "Yitz" Greenberg has played a significant role in the rethinking of Christian faith which my husband and I undertook. This essay focuses on issues that in particular challenge Christians but are necessarily of concomitant concern to Jews.

"There is a dimension to the *Endlösung* [The "Final Solution of the Jewish Question"] that the Christian must know, and from which the Jew is spared . . . .[T]he dark night that surrounds the Christian soul is the night of objective guilt . . . . because here in this event, . . . 'the theological negation of Judaism and the vilification of the Jewish people' within the Christian tradition were, at last, translated in the genocide of the Jews. . . . the final logic and application of nineteen hundred years of Christian teaching respecting the Jewish people."[1]

Such radical judgment of Christianity is inescapable once the churches' open and often vehement and violent hostility to Jews and their faith, particularly in central and eastern Europe where the Catholic Church predominated, is recognized. The judgment is further reinforced by viewing foundations laid by the centuries'-long renunciation of Judaism and denunciation of its people from at least as early as the 2nd century.[2] Early "Church Fathers" pronounced that Judaism and its people had been cast off by God because of crucifying God-in-Jesus, thus becoming the Devil's spawn.[3] Christian theological insistence from the 4th century that Jews would live forever in homelessness because of putting the Lord to death[4] led to a whole range of legal decrees ensuring their subjection. In this way they became a visible testimony to their replacement by Christianity in God's plan. Papal documents and teachings of Protestant Reformers, particularly Martin Luther,[5] added further animus. Thus the church and its community was embedded in anti-Judaism right into modern times.

In the years 1933 to1945 all of the foregoing was carried to finality in the Third Reich's calculated murder of some six million Jews. By engrafting and propagating its "Final Solution" onto these early Christian roots of anti-Judaism Nazism undercut church resistance to National Socialism's actions against the Jewish people and even gained enthusiastic followers.

While liberal Protestants in the West optimistically believed that the modern world was free of much of the previous centuries' beliefs and actions, their churches also faced a fundamental test of their theology. Even so, there was a significant difference in the responses of many western churches from those of central and eastern European Catholic and Orthodox churches. The Reformed (Calvinist) churches in The Netherlands, France, and Belgium, and the Lutheran churches of Denmark and other Scandinavian countries showed significant concern and tried to help Jews (though not necessarily successfully). But also Catholics in Italy and Orthodox Christians in Bulgaria resisted their government's antisemitic policies.

In Britain and the United States (both unoccupied) Protestant churches and clergy along with Catholic Church leaders actively voiced extensive criticism of Germany's policies but were unable to rouse their governments to offer direct assistance to the endangered Jews.[6] Yet some of America's Catholic community accused the Jewish community of lack of concern for Catholic suffering in Mexico and in Spain's Civil War but demanding aid for Germany's Jews. Father Charles Coughlin's radio preaching endorsing Nazi principles and spouting from the spurious *Protocols of the Elders of Zion* attracted 15 million listeners.

What made the difference in Christian communities? How much of pre-Holocaust Christianity can remain unchallenged? What needs to be seriously, even radically, reconsidered? And how are churches responding to new manifestations and forms of antisemitism and anti-Judaism in the 21st century, as well as to anti-Israelism?

I write as a post-Holocaust Christian. Not because of being born after that time; quite the contrary. But because I join others who are convinced that the "Kingdom of Night" moved history into a radically changed era in which all religious beliefs that were held before the Holocaust must be closely reexamined and retested.

THE GERMAN CHURCHES

The churches of Germany faced the greatest challenge for they were part and parcel of the nation and its people, deeply wedded to the country's place in the world, influenced and tested at every step. Most Germans were so desperate for something new to replace the ineffective regimes prior to 1933 that they welcomed a strong new government. They refrained from objecting to the Nazi regime's actions and laws against German Jews due to the long-standing general Christian emphasis on the curse upon Israel. In addition, Protestants in particular had been influenced theologically by a number of leading German theologians of the preceding six decades who had emphasized "reverence for (the Germanic) race, the German people as the "people of God," and "justifiable antisemitism" in their arguments against the Jewish "menace," Jews' corrupting influence, and the "cancerous sore" which Jews represented in the national body.[7] Both Protestant and Catholic churches refrained from objecting to the Nazi regime's actions against German Jews: the initial boycott of Jewish businesses in April 1933, the Nuremberg racial laws of 1935, and the violent destructions of Kristallnacht in November 1938. The churches focused their relatively few protests on internal matters, unsuccessfully.[8] Only the State's euthanasia of "life unworthy of life" elicited sermonic attacks in late 1940-41, successfully, at least on the surface.

Most *Protestant* churchmen enthusiastically supported the New Order and the new national awakening. Dietrich Bonhoeffer epitomizes Protestant difficulty in expressing any opposition to the Hitler regime. Early on he held the traditional Lutheran position affirming the State as "God's order of preservation in a godless world"; it was "justified in adopting new methods of dealing with the 'Jewish Question.'" The church, as spiritual guide for its people, "had no right to address the State directly" on political matters. However, when the "Aryan Paragraph" was applied to non-Aryan pastors and theological students Bonhoeffer joined Martin Niemöller in seeing this as an infringement of the church's function[9] and the Confessing Church came into being. Yet it did not concern itself with the Jewish issue. Only the Old-Prussian Union's Confessing Synod in 1935 openly professed that when racial and nationalistic ideology replace God as source of authority the state is undermined. Five hundred pastors were arrested. Not until October 1943 did that same Synod make another public protest when it insisted that one's neighbor is "always the one who is helpless and who especially needs him, and [the Christian] makes no distinction between races, nations or religions [for] all life is sacred to [God], *even that of the people of Israel.*" Also in `43 Lutheran Bishop Meiser of Bavaria received a number of private letters protesting the systematic murders of Jews and Poles as contrary to God's commandments. One lengthy letter from a group of Christians spoke against the church's silence, and their own, regarding Jewish persecution. The church should testify to the State about Israel's place in the plan of salvation and should resist all attempts to "solve the Jewish Question."[10] Bishop Wurm made three private protests during `43: the killing of people simply on the basis of their race contradicts divine commandments; the annihilation of Jews was a terrible injustice, *"fatal to the German people"*; and people viewed the German setbacks on the Russian front as a sign of German guilt. He saw retribution as inevitable and the people saw it being enacted in the enemy air attacks.[11]

Robert Ericksen insists that *the Confessing Church never worked on behalf of the Jews.*[12]

The *Catholic Church* opposition to National Socialists' ideology ceased once the Party took power. The Vatican's Concordat with the Third Reich (initiated by Hitler for his own purposes) undercut any remaining German Catholic protest. Gordon Zahn believes that the Catholic church "contributed more in the way of effective support than in effective opposition."[13] No Catholic protests were made even to Nazi attacks on German Catholic institutions, and on priests and nuns. Once war began even the excesses of Nazi brutality, including wholesale attacks on Polish Catholic clergy, religious orders and churches, the concentration camps, and the "Final Solution," elicited no public outcries from the Roman church. Cardinal Bertram and most of his fellow bishops resolved to *"protect the church by not protesting injustice,"*[14] and consistently prayed for the Reich's military victory.

Richard Rubenstein and John Roth note that all the German churches found "some reason why silence was more important than protests. Thus, religion was neither able to prevent nor even to express verbal opposition to . . . the assembly-line, depersonalized, mass extermination camp."[15]

POST-WAR CHURCHES

The first significant church response to the Holocaust and Christian behavior was made less than a year after the war ended in Europe by leaders of The Netherlands' Reformed Church who recognized that a new confessional statement was essential. They insisted that the divine covenant with the Jewish people had never been revoked and Jews "remain the people of the promise." Any who are offended by this "take offense at God's sovereign action, to which they themselves owe their salvation."[16] Few other churches followed the Dutch church in recognizing the need to go beyond condemning antisemitism, as the World Council of Churches, meeting in Amsterdam in 1948 demonstrated: "No people in [God's] world have suffered more bitterly from the disorder of man than the Jewish people" which the churches had failed to fight. Nevertheless, it continued to insist on the Gospel's commission to convert Jews.[17]

One would not expect, nor will one find, a dramatic turnaround in the German churches. Both Protestantism and Catholicism continued to express theological antisemitism with its reflections of Nazism even while they sought to exonerate themselves from complicity in the Nazi crimes.

When world church representatives visited Germany in October 1945, leaders of the *German Protestant* church confessed their "oneness with our nation in a great community of suffering, but also in a solidarity of guilt" because of the unending suffering imposed on "many peoples and countries" – but they did not mention Jewish suffering. While claiming to have fought against the evil National Socialist tyranny in Christ's name, they admitted to not having done enough.[18] Bishop Marahrens reflected a common view when he said Jews should not have been attacked so grievously, yet he still spoke about them in negative terms. The Oldenburg church insinuated that behind the Nazi measures lay God's judgment against Israel for its rejection of God's Messiah.[19] An April '48 "Statement on the Jewish Question" reiterated the traditional view that Israel, by crucifying its Messiah, had counteracted its election and rejected salvation. One year later the Darmstadt Declaration (of the Confessing Church's Council) saw the Holocaust murders as God's wrath against Jewish disobedience.[20] A recent study of the post-war bishops and theologians finds them failing to show repentance and contrition or helping fellow Germans to understand Judaism in a new way. Instead they decried post-war hardships born by the German people and the expellees from the east, but said nothing about the terrible suffering of Germany's victims, especially Jews.[21]

By contrast, in 1950 the Protestant Synod of Berlin-Weissensee rejected self-pity and admitted German guilt. It opposed the traditional rejection theology and affirmed that God's Promises to "His Chosen People Israel" remained in force after the Crucifixion of Jesus Christ."[22]

In August `45 Germany's *Catholic* bishops rejected collective guilt for the war and its atrocities, and Pope Pius XII underscored this with his commendation of German Catholic martyrdom and opposition to Nazism. Only at Bishop Preysing's insistence did the bishops' letter allow for *some* individual guilt by *some* Germans including *some* Catholics. The1950s is seen as an "era of Catholic triumphalism *par excellence*," ending only after the death of Pope Pius XII in `58.[23]

One exception was the statement of the Catholic Conference in Mainz which contritely admitted crimes against "people of Jewish stock."[24] A number of German Catholics also were ready to accept collective guilt and had urged (unsuccessfully) the bishops to do the same. Walter Dirks insisted that widespread German antisemitism was the beginning of the road to Auschwitz. When Ida Friedricke Görres's published letter in `46 charged the church with insensitivity to the wartime atrocities, and triumphalism for having survived the Nazi regime, many readers wrote to agree.[25]

The turnabout in the German Catholic stance came about in 1959 when a new group of bishops reversed the church's exculpatory stand of preceding years and acknowledged German guilt for the Holocaust, blamed "Catholic Germans and *especially church leaders* for not having spoken out against the murderous Nazi regime," and expressed "profound sorrow for the Jewish people.[26]

Unfortunately national cohesion free of remorse replaced public discourse about the Nazi era when the "cold war" with the Soviet Union set in. Most of the mid-level Nazi officials returned to normal civilian life in law, business, education, and medicine, while thousands of Jewish survivors continued to languish in DP camps.

It is essential that Christians remember what Jews faced *after* the Nazi killings were stopped.

THE JEWISH SITUATION AND EFFORTS AFTER THE WAR

Even after the last of the camps were liberated thousands of Jews continued to die. And when survivors returned to their former homes in Eastern Europe seeking relatives, they often were met with local hostility and violence.[27] During the first post-war year Poles killed more than a thousand Jews in various places. Then on July 4,1946 Polish residents of Kielce carried out a pogrom against Jewish returnees killing forty-two and wounding many more. Jews fled en masse to the western DP camps or sought to reach Palestine by whatever means possible. Yet Britain used its naval power to keep ships from reaching Palestine,[28] re-interning Jewish survivors in new camps on Cyprus. And the United States continued to refuse visas to them for several years. Jewish hopes for new lives anywhere but in the graveyard of Europe seemed doomed.

From the late 19th century on the Vatican had steadily opposed Jewish efforts to establish a homeland in Eretz Israel. In 1943 just shortly before the Warsaw Ghetto uprising and decimation, Cardinal Spellman while visiting Palestine insisted that the Holy Land was a place for Catholic pilgrimage. Jewish possession of a portion of it would be "a severe blow" to Catholic attachment, and would "interfere with the peaceful exercise" of the Catholic rights vested in Catholic institutions. In any case, a "Hebrew home" could be found "in a more fitting territory. . . without too much difficulty."[29]

Nevertheless, only two years after the end of the war the United Nations voted to partition Palestine[30] into a Jewish and a Palestinian Arab state. Britain began removing its troops even while clandestine fighting was going on. When the Governor General left on May 14, 1948 Israel proclaimed its independence and Arab forces attacked the next day. Ultimately the small Jewish community of approximately 543,000 faced five Arab armies plus Palestinian units. By war's end thirteen months later 4,000 Israeli military and 2,000 civilians were dead (out of a population then numbering 650,000). Many Holocaust survivors who had finally reached their wanted destination perished in the fighting. No nation had come to Israel's defense.[31] By 1951 antisemitic actions in Arab countries forced 684,000 Jews of centuries-old communities to flee to Israel.[32]

SOME CHANGING CHRISTIANS THEOLOGIES

Slowly western churches began to recognize that the Holocaust was a Christian problem. After almost two millennia tentative new steps had to be taken, daunting as that was.[33]

Some groundwork had been laid for a different theology during the 1930s by James Parkes' work which undercut much of the mythology underlying Christian anti-Judaism, though it was largely ignored at the time. In the United States during the `40s Roy Eckardt carried Reinhold Niebuhr's theological support for Judaism further with a thorough critique of various Christian theologies about Judaism.[34]

Recognition that the church's replacement theology was at least partly responsible for the Jewish tragedy led to some acknowledgments that Israel remains God's beloved people (as the Dutch church had affirmed in `46) How could that be united with affirmation of faith in Jesus Christ?

Most *Protestant* churches continued to deny God's covenant with the Jewish people as valid. A 1970 lengthy statement by the Dutch Reformed Church insisted that Jews "have continued on the course of alienation which they had already taken before" Jesus. Yet the Dutch church also held that Jews are "still the chosen people, destined to fulfill a lasting and separate role." *If* God's covenant still includes the Jewish people, *then* their role must call for their behaving more righteously than other peoples. This led to special demands being made on the State of Israel by many churches.[35]

The World Lutheran Federation's series of conferences have been wrestling since 1964 with the question of whether God still remains in covenant with the Jewish people. The struggle between the theology of replacement and the theology of recognition has persisted, with each position being dominant at different times. The initial `64 Løgumkloster document contains notable ambiguities: The church remained committed to carrying on mission to the world, and to Jews; and even dialogue did not assume an equating of the two religions. The Lutherans confessed their own role in the long history of antisemitism, which they asserted is a "demonic form of rebellion" against God; "'Christian' antisemitism is spiritual suicide." While the accusations of deicide and God's rejection of the Jewish people were rejected, the section dealing with the theological relationship of the church and the Jewish people could not be issued until 1969 and then only by finding that both traditional and revisionist theories have their place within Lutheranism.[36] The inability to resolve this difference still continues.

The Evangelical Lutheran Church in the United States has taken steps to reverse the long-standing negative Lutheran-Jewish relationship. The theology of revisionism, or recognition, has been dominant, though not exclusive. Of particular consequence is their assertion that the imperative for moral behavior is not effective when accompanied by a theology of replacement.[37] In 1974 the church affirmed the two faiths' worship of the same God with whom both are in covenant, though differences of biblical interpretation were acknowledged. Deicide was specifically rejected, and Christian participation in persecution of Jews was confessed and repented. "Lutherans bear a special responsibility" since Nazism found a church foundation for its racial program of destruction in the preceding Lutheran denunciations of Jews. A significant step was taken in 1994 with its Declaration to the Jewish Community. It forthrightly rejected "Luther's anti-Judaic diatribes and violent recommendations," and further deplored the use of Luther's words by today's antisemites to teach hatred toward Judaism and its people.

Most other American *Protestant* documents from `64 to `75 were not prepared to give up the eventual necessity of Jewish acceptance of Jesus Christ as their messiah. But all rejected antisemitic accusations against Jews. Questions regarding the State of Israel in some cases received lengthy, and often critical, consideration, while in one case the link between covenant and the gift of the land was seen as incontrovertible. Since survivors overwhelmingly sought their own country the churches' response the State of Israel cannot be separated from their response to the Holocaust.

There were almost no *Catholic* statements until 1965 when the Second Vatican Council produced (among many others) the initial and foundational Catholic document on the Jewish issue, *Nostra Aetate*. Yet it was disappointingly tentative: Even though "Jerusalem did not recognize the time of her visitation . . . . God holds the Jews most dear" for the "sake of their [biblical] Fathers"; nor does God "repent of the gifts He makes . . ." Because the "beginnings of her faith and her election are found among the Patriarchs, Moses and the prophets," and is "foreshadowed by the chosen people's exodus," the Council recommended "mutual understanding and respect" and rejection of hatred and antisemitism.[38]

The strongest Catholic statement following the Vatican II document again emanated from The Netherlands. Speaking from of its own experiences the church in 1970 insisted that "the horrifying persecution" and destruction of most of the European Jewish communities during 1940-45 "still calls for reflection" in order to uphold the "living remembrance of the courage and faith-inspired power" so many demonstrated under "privation and torture." Christians need to remember the centuries of Christian anti-Semitism which led to "vast numbers of Christians and their Churches hardly [raising] their voices against a massacre of the Jewish people which exceeds all imagining . . . ." Jewish people have "their special place in the Church's faith" and the Church cannot be "the Church for all Nations without being connected to the living Jewish people of today." That "unbroken link" between Church and Jews "must be a determining factor in the Church's own mission. . . ."[39]

STATEMENTS AND THOUGHT SINCE 1970

From the late 1970s into the present at least 30 Protestant statements have been issued in Europe (especially in Germany), the U.S., and Australia, most all indicating significant and positive theological changes such as affirmation of the continuing Jewish covenant with God, rejection of supersessionism, confession of Christian silence during the Holocaust, Christian obligation to correct historical and theological teachings and end pejorative representations of Judaism. Out of the many let me cite a few of the outstanding ones.

In 1970 the Protestant Church of the Rhineland had led the way when it insisted on the permanent election of the Jewish people as the people of God, into which, through Jesus Christ, the church is taken into the covenant with his people. The 1981 joint statement of the Catholic and Reformed churches' in The Netherlands affirmed God's unfailing faithfulness to the Jewish People which has all too often been "forgotten or even denied." And Christianity's role in preparing the way for the annihilation camps was confessed. The United Church of Canada not only undertook a several year program of consultations with their congregations as their document was being drafted, but produced accompanying study programs for congregational use.

Churches are on their way to removing theological *adversus judaica*. Further steps may well be needed. But the urgent question is: How many of the Christian laity and clergy are aware of, no less in rapport with, these momentous changes?

The only way to teach congregations is to include these statements with readings from Scripture on a regular basis. For, like Paul's letters to the early churches, these are letters from fellow Christians speaking about the further light and truth breaking forth about God's word for our world. Christians also need to recognize a parallel to Jesus' experiences of birth, life, death, and resurrection in the Jewish peoples' "birth," life, mass death, and rebirth in the State of Israel.

SETBACKS AND NEW DANGERS

There are setbacks to the progress of converting Christianity away from its triumphalist past. In the late `90s and into the new century more negative voices have been raised. In 1999 the Protestant Church Council in Germany voted down a resolution that would have rejected mission work among the Jews, and a student gathering in Tübingen shortly thereafter repeated that vote. The Presbyterian Church (USA) voted in 2004 to withdraw church investment funds from companies doing business in Israel, along with voting not to end missions to the Jewish people.[40] At the same General Assembly other documents submitted for adoption denied the Jews were still in covenant with God, and blamed Jews for Jesus' crucifixion (though they were not accepted).

In 2002 when the document "Reflections on Covenant and Mission" was published by Catholics and Jews in North America Cardinal Cassidy of the Pontifical Commission welcomed it; but then it was shelved. Catholic participants had said that campaigns targeting Jews for conversion was no longer theologically acceptable. Avery Dulles led a fierce attack by conservatives: "*All non-Catholics must be subjected in principle to evangelization efforts.*" Cardinal Walter Kasper made no reply to Dulles even though Dulles' writings appear to challenge the validity of Israel's covenant which the Vatican and national Catholic Churches have endorsed.[41]

Antisemitism and anti-Judaism have become so rife that a number of churches have issued messages or letters of concern: The Lutheran World Federation meeting in Hungary in 2001, Canadian church leaders in 2003, the Presidents of the Council of Christians and Jews in the U.K. in 2004, the European Lutheran Commission on the Church and the Jewish People in 2004; a Presbyterian Church (USA) warning (2006) about some non-authorized materials citing Jews for Jesus' crucifixion and asserting that their covenant had been abrogated.

CONCLUDING REMARKS

Among the many theological responses to the Holocaust a few particularly stand out for their readiness to take a radically new stand.

Rudolf Pfisterer in Germany insists that Christian missionary work is "nothing more than the continuing work of the Holocaust" for it also seeks to end any *Jewish* existence.[42]

Emil Fackenheim uses the language of a new revelation when he speaks of "a commanding Voice from Auschwitz" which issued a 614th commandment to the Jewish people: "*the authentic Jew of today is forbidden to hand Hitler another, posthumous victory.*" Jews are "forbidden to despair of God . . . lest Judaism perish," and are forbidden to despair of the world "lest we help make it a meaningless place in which God is dead or irrelevant and everything is permitted."[43]

In a similar way Paul van Buren finds that the "pattern of revelation which shaped Scripture and the church's beginning has once again reasserted itself." A "revelational event" is an initiating historical happening followed by a "profound reorientation." The Holocaust is a that happening, a negative revelation of God's requirement that humans take responsibility; and the State of Israel is a positive revelation of the same requirement. When seen this way responsible Christians discover a new understanding of faith. The many church and synod statements "constitute a radical reversal of long-held teachings and present a new interpretation of the church's tradition."[44]

J. "Coos" Schoneveld insists that the resurrection was a vindication of Jesus as a Jew faithful to the Torah, as well as an affirmation of the Torah, of the Jewish people and Jewish life.[45]

Stephen Smith is prepared to go further. He suggests that much of Christian discourse about and with Judaism is really a "defense of Christian continuity rather than a challenge to it." But "the reality of the Holocaust is that you must question [all of Christian theology] and be prepared, if necessary, to let it go."[46]

Irving Greenberg has said that for people to leave everything to God is a betrayal of God; to do everything themselves is to serve God. With Roy Eckardt and Elie Wiesel, Greenberg sees the need for God to repent of the fatal burden which the covenant put on the Jewish people. After the Holocaust the covenant between the Jewish people and God is a thoroughly voluntary covenant.[47]

To enable historical events to have a genuine transforming impact on the future, they must be "assimilated by the historical consciousness of succeeding generations."[48] This is the challenge facing Christians: Can the movement of transformation that has begun be sustained?

BIBLIOGRAPHY

Bernauer, James. "The Holocaust and the Catholic Church's Search for Forgiveness." www.bc.edu/bc.org/research/cjl/articles/bernauer.htm.

Brumlik, Micha. "Post-Holocaust Theology: German Theological Responses Since 1945." *Betrayal*. Robert Ericksen and Susannah Heschel, eds. Minneapolis: Fortress Press, 1999. 169-188.

Ditmanson, Harold. *Stepping-Stones to Further Jewish-Lutheran Relationships.* Minneapolis: Augsburg Press, 1990.

Eckardt, Alice L. "Growing into a Daring and Questioning Faith," *Faith Transformed*. John C. Merkle, ed. Collegeville: The Liturgical Press, 2003. 17-36.

Eckardt, Alice L. and A. Roy Eckardt. *Long Night's Journey into Day.* Detroit: Wayne State University Press, 1982; rev. ed., 1988.

Eckardt, A. Roy. *Christianity and the Children of Israel.* New York: Kings Crown Press, 1948.

———. "Christian Responses to the *Endlösung*," *Religion in Life*, Vol. XLVII, no. 1 (1978), pp. 33-45.

Eliach, Yaffa. *There Once Was a World.* Boston: Little Brown and Co., 1998.

Ericksen, Robert P. *Theologians Under Hitler.* New Haven: Yale University Press, 1985.

———. *Complicity in the Killings*, forthcoming 2009.

Ericksen, Robert P. and Susannah Heschel, eds. *Betrayal*. Minneapolis: Fortress Press, 1999.

Fackenheim, Emil. *The Jewish Thought of Emil Fackenheim: A Reader.* Detroit: Wayne State University Press, 1987.

———. *The Jewish Return into History.* New York: Schocken Books, 1978.

Fleischner, Eva. "Can the Few Become the Many?" *Remembering for the Future*. Oxford, New York: Pergamon Press, 2001. Vol. 1, 233-47.

Gerlach, Wolfgang. *And the Witnesses Kept Silent.* Lincoln: University of Nebraska Press, 2000.

Greenberg, Gershon, "American Catholics During the Holocaust, *Simon Wiesenthal Center Annual*, Vol 4, (1987), pp. 175-201.

Greenberg, Irving. "Voluntary Covenant," *Perspectives*. New York: National Jewish Resource Center, October 1982.

————, *For the Sake of Heaven and Earth.* Philadelphia:; Jewish Publication Society, 2004.

Gutteridge, Richard. *Open Thy Mouth for the Dumb: The German Evangelical Church and the Jews 1879-1950.* Oxford: Basil Blackwell, 1976.

Krieg, Robert A. *Catholic Theologians in Nazi Germany.* New York: Continuum, 2004.

Krondorfer, Björn, Katharina von Kellenbach, Norbert Reck. *Mit Blick auf die Täter.* Gütersloh: Gütersloh Verlagshaus, 2006.

Lewy, Guenter. *The Catholic Church and Nazi Germany.* New York: McGraw-Hill. 1964.

Marrus, Michael R. "French Churches and the Persecution of Jews in France 1940-1944," *Judaism and Christianity Under the Impact of National-Socialism (1919-1945).* Jerusalem: Historical Society of Israel, 1982. 307-346.

Modras, Ronald. "The Catholic Church in Poland and Antisemitism, 1933-1939," *Remembering for the Future.* Oxford: Pergamon Press, 1989. Vol. 1, 183-196.

More Stepping Stones to Jewish-Christian Relations. New York: Stimulus/Paulist Press, 1985.

Morley, John F. *Vatican Diplomacy and the Jews During the Holocaust 1939-1943.*New York: Ktav, 1980.

Phayer, Michael. "The German Catholic Church After the Holocaust," *Holocaust and Genocide Studies* Vol. 10, no. 2 (1996), pp. 151-167.

Robertson, Edwin H., "A Study of Dietrich Bonhoeffer and the Jews, January-April 1933," *Remembering for the Future.* Oxford: Pergamon Press, 1989. Vol. 1, 121-129.

Schwöbel. Christoph. "Self-Criticism in Retrospect? Reflections in the Christian Churches on Church Attitudes During the Holocaust," *The British Journal of Holocaust Education,* Vol. 1, no. 1 (1993), 48-67.

Smith, Stephen S., "The Effect of the Holocaust on Jewish-Christian Relations," *Challenges in Jewish-Christian Relations.* New York: Paulist Press, 2006. 137-152.

Snoek, Johan M. *The Grey Book.* Assen Van Gorcum & comp. 1969.

Stepping Stones to Further Jewish-Christian Relations. Helga Croner, ed. London: Stimulus Books, 1977.

Stepping-Stones to Further Jewish-Lutheran Relationships. Harold H. Ditmanson, ed. Minneapolis: Augsburg Press, 1990.

The Theology of the Churches and the Jewish People: Statements of the World Conference of Churches and its Member Churches. Geneva: WCC Publications, 1988.

Weisberg, Richard H. "Differing Ways of Reading, Differing Views of the Law: The Catholic Church and its Treatment of the Jewish Question During Vichy," *Remembering for the Future.* Basingstoke: Palgrave, 2001. Vol. 2, 509-530.

Zahn, Gordon. "Catholic Resistance? A Yes and a No," *The German Church Struggle and the Holocaust.* Franklin H. Littell and Hubert G. Locke, eds. Detroit: Wayne State University Press, 1974. 203-237.

NOTES

1. A. Roy Eckardt, "Christian Responses to the *Endlösung*," *Religion in Life* Vol. XLVII, no. 1 (Spring 1978), pp. 34-35. The internal quote is from Gregory Baum.

2. Among the "Church Fathers" Bishop Melito of Sardis in Syria went beyond the more general contention that virtually everything Jewish was now worthless to accuse Jews of deicide – murdering God (Clark Williamson, *Has God Rejected His People?* [Nashville: Abingdon, 1982, pp. 92-93]. For more extensive consideration see

Eric Werner, "Melito of Sardes, The First Poet of Deicide," *Hebrew Union College Annual*, Vol. 37 (1966).

3. Cf. Gospel of John 8:44.

4. Augustine in the 4th century initiated the concept of the eternally "Wandering Jew," using the punishment of Cain as an allegory for Jews, and Christ for Abel. The church and Christian governments did not leave it to God's punishment but initiated their own actions with laws that increasingly restricted and excluded Jews.

5. Luther's vituperation and advice about their treatment were seized on by the Nazis and republished.

6. The United States' large German populations tended initially to be sympathetic to the Third Reich and *pro*-Nazi rallies attracted large crowds at Madison Square Garden (though equally large crowds attended anti-Nazi rallies there also). In 1938 after the *SS St. Louis* was turned away by Cuba the U.S. Government refused to allow the 911 Jewish passengers to land. They were finally admitted by Britain, France, Belgium and Holland. Britain also took in 10,000 Jewish and Christian non-Aryan children during 1938-39. .

7. Richard Gutteridge, *Open Thy Mouth for the Dumb: The German Evangelical Church and the Jews 1879-1950* (Oxford: Basil Blackwell,1976) pp. 2, 5, 8, 9, 70. One cannot exaggerate the widespread "emphasis within the churches on the curse upon Israel" (p. 71).

8. It must be noted that a number of clergy and congregations of both churches (and some smaller denominations not mentioned here) worked privately to assist Jews.

9. Gutteridge, op. cit., pp. 92-3, 275-6. As Bonhoeffer moved theologically he came to view any church which ignored those deprived of their rights, especially Jews, as no longer an obedient church. Ultimately he joined an underground resistance movement, was imprisoned and executed in 1945.

10. Snoek, op. cit., pp. 108-10.

11. Snoek, op. cit., pp. 112-13. Italics added.

12. Lecture at Muhlenberg College February 21, 2008. Compare Gutteridge: "The Church as Church did not find a decisive word from Scripture as a whole to embrace the issue as a whole . . . . Throughout the conflict nobody in a position of authority made a full and plain denunciation of antisemitism as such" (op. cit., p. 268).

13. Gordon Zahn, "Catholic Resitance? A Yes and a No," *The German Church Struggle and the Holocaust*, eds. Franklin H. Littell and Hubert G. Locke (Detroit: Wayne State University Press, 1974), p. 205.

14. Guenter Lewy, *The Catholic Church and Nazi Germany* (New York: McGraw Hill, 1964), p. 156.

15. *Approaches to Auschwitz* (Atlanta: John Knox Press, 1987), p. 343.

16. Cited by Isaac C. Rottenberg, *Christian-Jewish Dialogue* (Atlanta: Hebraic Heritage Press, 2005), pp. 210-11.

17. "The Christian Approach to the Jews," *Stepping Stones to Further Jewish-Christian Relations*, Helga Croner, compiler (New York: Stimulus Books, 1977), pp. 69ff.

18. Only in their "Message to the Christian People Abroad" did they "condemn in particular the killing of hostages and the mass murder of German and Polish Jews" (ignoring all other European Jews).

19. Gutteridge, op. cit., p. 301.

20. Micha Brumlik, "Post-Holocaust Theology: German Theolo gical Responses Since 1945," *Betrayal*, Ericksen and Heschel, pp 173-74.

21. Björn Krondorfer, Katharina von Kellenbach, Norbert Reck, *Mit Blick auf die Täter* (Gütersloh: Gütersloh Verlagshaus, 2006). See John Conway, online review, March 2007.

22. Gutteridge, op. cit., p. 303..

23. Michael Phayer,"The German Catholic Church After the Holocaust," *Holocaust and Genocide Studies,* vol. 10, no 2. (1996), p. 161.

24. This was essentially the work of Gertrud Luckner's Freiburg circle. See Phayer, op. cit., p. 154.

25. Phayer, op. cit., pp.152-53.

26. Phayer, op. cit., p. 161-62. See also James Bernauer, "The Holocaust and the Catholic Church's Search for Forgiveness," (www.bc.edu/bc_org/research/cjl/articles/bernauer.htm. p. 4).

27. Yaffa Eliach recounts her family's return to the village of Eishyshok, a Lithuanian/Polish/Russian shtetl going back to the 11th century, after its liberation by Soviet troops. Most of the returnees were cold-bloodedly murdered by the Polish Home Army (*There Once Was a World* [Boston: Little Brown and Co., 1998], pp. 7-8, 657-669).

28. President Truman's request that Britain admit 100,000 of the survivors to Palestine was refused by Prime Minister Attlee.

29. Gershon Greenberg, "American Catholics During the Holocaust," *Simon Wiesenthal Center Annual*, Vol. 4, (1987), p. 193.

30. The final vote on November 29, 1947 followed three decades of controversy over the right of Jews to a national home in Eretz Israel (Palestine).

31. Czechoslovakia surreptitiously gave aid by selling guns and ammunition, anti-aircraft guns, mortars, planes and tanks to Israeli forces.

32. Jews came from Iran, Morocco and Tunis, Algeria, Libya, and Turkey: 240,000 in 1949, 170,000 in 1950, 175,000 in 1951 (*Encyclopedia Judaica*, [1972], vol. 9, pp. 366-378).

33. In 1947 an International Conference of Christians and Jews met in Seelisberg, Switzerland to address the many troubling issues. It produced a set of guidelines for the churches' use of Scripture: "The Ten Points of Seelisberg" (*Stepping Stones to Further Jewish-Christian Relations*, pp. 32-33).

34. See *A Bibliography of the Printed works of James Parkes*, Sidney Sugarman and Diana Bailey, compilers (UK: University of Southampton, 1977).A. Roy Eckardt's initial work was *Christianity and the Children of Israel* (New York: King's Crown Press, 1948).

35. Many statements in this document seem to be contradictory. There is also criticism of Christian behavior.

36. Harold Ditmanson, *Stepping-Stones to Further Jewish-Lutheran Relationships,* pp. 19-25, 27, 28-32. Gunther Harder held out against missionary intention toward Jews; rather, Christians should urge Jews to remain Jews (p. 19).

37. Ditmanson, op. cit., pp. 64-65, 67-68, 70.

38. *Stepping Stones to Further Jewish-Christian Relations*, Helga Croner, compiler, pp. 1-2. Many following diocesan statements can be found in the same volume.

39. Ibid., pp. 48, 50, 49.

40. Some other churches have considered divestment also.

41. Edward Kessler, "A Deafening Silence," www.jcrelations.net, 2007.

42. 1975 conversation cited in Alice L. and A. Roy Eckardt, *Long Night's Journey Into Day: A Revised Retrospective on the Holocaust* (Detroit: Wayne State University Press, 1998), p. 99.

43. *The Jewish Return into History,* (New York: Schocken Books, 1978), cited in *The Jewish Thought of Emil Fackenheim: A Reader*, Michael Morgan, ed. (Detroit: Wayne State University Press, 1987), pp. 159-60. Also see *God's Presence in History* (New York University Press, 1970).

44. *Discerning the Way* (New York: Seabury Press, 1980), pp. 177, 171 182, 181,176. Dietrich Bonhoeffer also had concluded that God is forcing us to live in his world as if it were our own world, to act as if he were not there (p. 182).

45. J. Schoneveld, "The Jewish 'No' to Jesus and the Christian 'Yes" to Jews,"*Quarterly Review*, Vol 4, no. 4 (1984), p. 60.

46. Stephen D. Smith, "The Effect of the Holocausts on Jewish-Christian Relations," *Challenges in Jewish-Christian Relations,* James K. Aitken and Edward Kessler, eds. (New York: Paulist Press, 20060), p. 150.

47. Irving Greenberg, "The Voluntary Covenant," *Perspectives*, October 1982, and *For the Sake of Heaven and Earth* (Philadelphia: The Jewish Publication Society, 2004), pp. 27-29.

48. Fackenheim, *The Jewish Return into History,* op. cit., p. 210.

4

Amalek, Zionism and Belief in the Messiah: Further Reflections on Jewish Faith and Jewish Power

Arnold Eisen

Several decades ago, Yitz Greenberg forever changed my thinking about Purim. He did so in an essay that taught me to read the Book of Esther not as sacred history or holy satire – though Esther is both those things – but as Jewish political theory: one of the earliest and most sustained efforts of that sort in all of Jewish literature.[1] I first built upon Greenberg's insight in my book *Galut*, a study of ancient and modern Jewish reflection on the twin themes of homelessness/exile and homecoming/redemption.[2] In this essay I shall build further upon these foundations. I want to suggest – in what we might term (following Spinoza) a "theological-political" reflection – that the villain of the Purim story, a potent incarnation of the Jewish people's eternal enemy Amalek, spurs us to ponder the relation between the final overcoming of Amalek in the days of the Messiah and the practice of contemporary Jewish politics, particularly in the reborn Jewish State. The rabbis taught long ago, and Greenberg taught again in our generation, that Purim is actually the most serious of all Jewish holidays. It summons Jews to political work in the world that is ever fraught with paradox and danger.

1. JEWISH POLITICAL THEORY

Ruth Wisse has argued – correctly in my view – that Jews in the modern period have devoted far too little sustained thought to politics. This lacuna, she writes, is a luxury that the Jews cannot afford.[3] The enemies of the Jews are real, and they have not paused from either the theory or the practice of anti-Semitism; indeed persecution of Jews and threats against Jews are as old as the Jewish people itself. Wisse traces the few successes and the numerous failures of Jewish engagement with politics back to a rabbinic worldview that in her reading promoted the securing of vital Jewish interests in Diaspora through accommodation rather than resistance, prudence rather than power. This was most likely an astute course in many circumstances, Wisse avers, given the limits of actual Jewish power over the centuries. But its costs have been all too obvious: persecutions, expulsions, disabilities, ghettoes. Wisse is particularly critical of modern Jewish thinkers who, despite unprecedented opportunities for the accumulation and deployment of Jewish influence and even power, have in general devoted far more attention and resources to issues of meaning, culture, and religion. Precious little thought or action has been spent on political strategies aimed at Jewish survival.

There is one major exception to this rule, Wisse notes: the school of thought and activity known as political Zionism. She is correct in this claim, I think, although Diaspora leaders in the modern period, as in others, have given significant attention to the pursuit of Jewish interests. Organizations such as the Alliance Israelite Universelle played an indispensable role in developing the modes of political thought and action out of which Zionism emerged.[4] This does not change the fact that the political Zionist school of thought and action has been centrally concerned with politics to a unique degree. It took as its starting point Herzl's assertions in *Der Judenstaat* that Jews are "a nation, one nation" and that the various nations among whom Jews lived as a small minority would never leave them alone unless and until they had a state of their own, secured by force of arms and international recognition.[5]

Political Zionists have all concurred with this axiomatic claim, whether they stood on the "right" or the "left" of the Zionist spectrum. It was well and good to hold, with Ahad Ha'am's "spiritual Zionism," that the prophet Zechariah was correct: "not by might, not by power, but by My spirit [shall Israel live], says the Lord."[6] Herzl, too, recognized that the Jewish ingathering would require more than money and power-politics. Zionism had to restore Jewish souls and not just save Jewish bodies. But political Zionists from Herzl through Jabotinsky to Ben Gurion and Begin also emphasized, to a degree that other Zionists did not, that without strategic use of military and political *might*, i.e. power, Israel would not live to do right or wrong.

The dispute dividing political from spiritual Zionists is in one sense now moot. Israel's existence – and the continuing need to safeguard it against continuing threat – have together put an end to the argument between Ahad Ha'amist proponents of a "spiritual center" in Palestine and Herzlians insistent on establishing Jewish sovereignty. It seems safe to say that most Jewish political theory and practice in our day – left or right, in Israel or in Diaspora –

holds fast the twin recognitions that there can be no Judaism without Jews, and that the Jews will likely not long survive, in Israel or Diaspora, without a *raison d'etre* – cultural or religious – that motivates their survival.[7] No less important, the attainment of Jewish power and influence have engendered new interest in and respect for the nuanced picture of power that characterizes the Biblical narratives. One cannot read through the royal rises and falls chronicled in the Book of Kings without coming to the realization that power is not what it seems. It is often not so "good to be king" – and kings usually achieve something less than good. Rulers come and go. Their foibles prove the undoing of their realms. Compromises with morality are legion – and often fatal. Might and right rarely coincide.

The Biblical accounts also seem to demonstrate (with Tolstoy) that history often turns on the slightest of accidents even as it is driven by long-lasting interests and ideologies. The former are obvious in the original *Purimshpiel.* Just as Napoleon in Tolstoy's telling of history perhaps lost Moscow because of a cold, so Haman loses power in the royal court of Persia because Ahashuerus happens to be attracted to a Jewish woman, because she happens to be the cousin of Haman's mortal enemy Mordecai, because the king happens to have a sleepless night and be reminded by his courtiers in the midst of it of the favors done for him by Esther's cousin, etc. In a further series of seeming accidents, Ahashuerus agrees on a whim to accept two luncheon invitations from Esther, apparently enjoys the wine at both those meals, and, most crucially, holds out his scepter to the queen when she appears un-summoned to beg his favor. We laugh at the sexual symbolism of that gesture. We laugh, too, at Haman's final scene in the drama. He pleads for his life on the queen's couch after the king angrily storms out of the room upon learning of Haman's treachery – only to have the king find him there when he returns to the room and misinterpret Haman's position. What if any of these things had been different? History turns on thousands of "what if's." Are they signs of happenstance – or interventions in the plot from "some Other place," i.e. God?

We do not know, of course. Political activity cannot wait for us to find out. And not every Haman ends up hoisted upon his own petard: in his case the gallows on which he had intended to hang Mordecai. Greenberg sees in the Purim story a foreshadowing of the rabbinic development of the covenant saga: a newly distant God, who no longer communicates through prophets or directly pulls the strings of history, leaves much more room for error and achievement to human beings. This rabbinic turn, in Greenberg's view, offers crucial preparation and warrant for our own, more radical move after the Holocaust to a notion of "voluntary covenant." Help did not appear from some "other place" at Auschwitz, or from anywhere else, until the Allied forces arrived. Countless prayers by Jews to God, repeated invocations of the covenant, went unanswered. Many Jews praised God nonetheless, and still do — keeping *their* side of a Covenant to which God has not been faithful.[8]

Then again, as the Purim story itself reminds us, history also turns on human purpose, reasons of state, ideology, and naked self-interest. More than accident and happenstance is involved. In the midst of laughter at the dark humor of the Book of Esther, we pause – and shudder – at Haman's warning to his king that "there is a certain people, scattered and dispersed among the other peoples in all the provinces of your realm, whose laws are different from those of any other people and who do not obey the king's laws."[9] Why should they be tolerated? The same shudder overtakes us when we read the very first enunciation of anti-Semitism recorded in the Bible (coincident with the founding of the Jewish nation): Pharaoh's message to Egypt that "the Israelite people are mucgh too numerous for us. Let us deal shrewdly with them..."[10] Both warnings echo loud and clear in our own day. Jewish anxiety in the face of threat is grounded in experience and not only in texts.

Herzl expressed confidence that the Jews would have the last laugh at the anti-Semites' expense, just as they do in synagogue every year when the Book of Esther is chanted and Haman's name is ritually silenced. Hatred of Jews, Herzl believed, would lead the Jews' enemies to cooperate with the Zionists in getting the Jews out of their corners of Diaspora and home to a state of their own. This Gentile *push* – far stronger than the *pull* of Jewish longing, ideology or faith in the messiah – would prove the Jews' salvation.[11] It does not require hindsight but only history to suspect that Herzl fell victim to bravado at this point in his essay (or perhaps was overtaken by overweening confidence in his own messianic mission. I shall return to this thought). The Book of Esther gives ample ground for skepticism wherever power is concerned. Indeed, the Torah itself inculcates an attitude of suspicion toward quick fixes of every sort. The command to "remember" Amalek's perfidy, made required reading by the rabbis for the Sabbath preceding Purim, links final victory over Amelek to the coming of Messiah.

Remember what Amalek did, the Torah commands. Amalek attacked the weak and helpless – the very opposite of God-fearing behavior.[12] (It is impossible for contemporary Jews not to see the Nazis in this portrait.) "It shall be, when YHWH grants you rest from all your enemies round about, in the Land which YHWH your God is giving you as an inheritance, that you shall blot out the memory of Amalek from under the heavens. Do not forget!"[13] The text, reaching beyond all human experience thus far and so beyond language itself, falls back on an ultimate paradox. How does one remember to blot out memory, thereby apparently ensuring preservation of the very memory that one is commanded to remember to forget? One does so, I think (or, better, imagine) by so transforming the world that even the idea of doing what Amalek did is inconceivable. Only when the people Israel lives in its own land in a time of universal peace and harmony, where/when the Jews have no fear of their enemies, can they forget to remember Amalek. The memory will no longer be necessary only when it is no longer possible.

The attempt to overcome Amalek, whether in reality or in thought, is therefore a *messianic* enterprise. All Jewish politics until that point in the future – every effort to protect Jewish interests and Jewish survival, every deployment of Jewish influence and power in the service of the Good as Jews understand it – must practice the art of the possible. I have argued elsewhere that non-messianic Jewish politics is best described as a perpetual balance of *covenant* and *normalcy*.[14] It must on the one hand be responsive to the *normative demands* imposed on Jews at Sinai, according to the Torah's account, our self-understanding (Jews call these obligations *covenant*), and, on the other hand, Jewish politics must carry out the responsibility to protect Jewish lives and serve Jewish interests (Zionists termed this *normalcy*). Both are indispensable. There can be no Judaism without Jews. There is no spirit without body. And the reverse is no less true.

The demand to balance the two imperatives of normalcy and covenant, and the difficulty of doing so, are spelled out graphically in the Biblical accounts of kings versus prophets and elaborated in countless rabbinic reflections, aggadic and halakhic.[15] Modern Diaspora thinkers likewise drew on both norms, implicitly or explicitly, when they imagined the new possibility of Jewish at-homeness in places other than Zion, and pleaded with new sorts of sovereigns to aid in the fulfillment of that possibility. Such Diaspora thinkers typically played down messianic themes – except when they translated ancient religious messianism into secular humanist dreams of progress through reason. Zionist thinkers as a rule drew the balance sheet between normalcy and covenant very differently. They challenged the Diaspora contention that homecoming could be attained outside the Land of Israel. Secular political Zionists – most vociferous in the "negation of Diaspora" claims and denial of the legitimacy of Jewish life outside Zion once return to Zion had become a real possibility – boldly called the return of Jews to the Jewish homeland after two millennia "normalization." The return home, the end of wandering and statelessness, the solution to "the Jewish people," would be accomplished by human beings, using state-craft and other time-tested methods of gaining and using power. No more waiting for God and God's Messiah. Help would finally come to Jews from some "other place." The covenant binding Jews one to another would be fulfilled. The covenant with God was not relevant to this effort.

Amalek, in other words, would be fought by contemporary Jews just as the ancient Israelites had fought their enemies, including Amalek, in the Biblical account: with the sword. Zionist theory and practice have thus posed the most fundamental challenge to Diaspora Jewish political theory and practice, the most radical over-turning of the Purimshpiel and the rabbinic accounts of politics that built upon it, the most thoroughgoing attempt to take on and defeat Amalek once and for all, that Jews have ever known.

ZIONISM AND MESSIANISM

I want to look in more detail at this key element of the mainstream Zionist reading of Jewish history, unpacking the cogent articulation given that reading in the well-known essay on Jewish messianism published in the late 1950s by Gershom Scholem – not only one of the great Jewish scholars of the twentieth century but also one of the most profound advocates (and critics) of Zionism. Scholem perhaps did more than anyone to ponder the perplexing, unavoidable, and troubling relation between Zionism and messianism. The essay which Scholem himself referred to as his credo – "The Messianic Idea in Judaism" – famously links messianic hope to the "endless powerlessness of Jewish history" and calls belief in messiah, waiting for messiah, the mark of "life lived in deferment."[16] Zionism, he strongly implies, signified the end of such waiting. Scholem dramatically calls on Jews to take the stage of world history once again, to risk all, hold nothing back – and at the same time worries that Zionism, born out of Jewish messianic longing, will succumb to the powerful forces on which it feeds. Zionism might unleash messianic activity rather than restrain and sublimate messianic longing. It could channel that longing into a new burst of national creativity such as Judaism had not known since the rise of Kabbalah – but it could also cause Judaism to self-destruct because of the internal messianic forces that it could not control.

The essay abounds (and seemingly revels) in such paradox. It culminates in a final warning to the new State that is absolutely breathtaking in its daring: "Whether or not Jewish history will be able to endure this entry into the concrete realm without perishing in the crisis of the Messianic claim which has virtually been conjured up—that is the question which out of his great and dangerous past the Jew of this age poses to his present and to his future."[17]

Scholem's warning has come to seem prescient, given the rise of Gush Emunim in the wake of the 1967 war. However, the essay actually responded directly to an earlier pairing of Zionism and messianism, that linkage effected by a figure even more central to Zionism than the rabbis who provided inspiration and leadership to Gush Emunim. It was none other than David Ben Gurion, founding prime minister and principal architect of the State of Israel, who proclaimed in a series of public addresses and dialogues with intellectuals in the months and years following the Sinai campaign of 1956 that *messianism* was the central teaching of Judaism and should become the central doctrine of Israel. Indeed, as Ben Gurion told philosopher Nathan Rotenstreich that year, he no longer saw any use for Zionist or socialist teachings. The State of Israel was a fact. Immigrants were streaming to its borders. They were in many cases pushed there by hostile governments and populations, but they were also pulled by an age-old longing: messiah. Ingathering of the exiles was the prerequisite to the fulfillment of the vision of Israel's prophets. Neither Herzl nor Ahad Ha'am inspired their aliyah; Marx and Engels certainly had no role in it. Messianism was the key. Scholem was among the intellectuals who argued with Ben Gurion about his interpretation of messianism, of Judaism, and of Zionism. They repeatedly expressed concern that the prime minister was seeking to use Judaism, and messianic belief in particular, to justify government policies such as the war in Sinai and his own behavior in the Lavon affair.[18]

Their concern was well-founded. Ben Gurion, as is well-known, had no use whatever for rabbinic Judaism. He regarded it as a Diaspora product that was unsuitable for the renewed conditions of sovereignty. Joshua and the political military leaders who followed him were by contrast extremely relevant to the reborn Jewish State. So were the prophets whose ethical and universalist vision linked the return of the people Israel to its homeland with the ultimate redemption of all humanity. Ben Gurion, like the prophets, saw Jewish return to the land as prerequisite to that larger fulfillment. Zionist achievement and socialist dreams were united in the central themes of Jewish messianism. The reborn Jewish state would work in concert with forward-looking forces of all nations in pursuit of universal peace and justice.

Exile was effectively over for Jews, in Ben Gurion's view. They had re-entered history with a vengeance. Life in the Land of Israel made possible a degree of wholeness for Jews that was impossible outside the Land. The "human being" and the Jew could be one again. But sovereignty also made possible a degree of fulfillment *for Judaism* that was impossible elsewhere. Indeed, Ben Gurion proclaimed, the State of Israel declared independence not only from British rule but from two thousand years of exile. "Galut means dependence – material, political, spiritual, cultural, and intellectual dependence…Our task is to break radically with this dependence and to become masters of our own fate – in a word, to achieve independence… Independence for the Jewish people in its homeland!"[19] Messianism specified the direction of Israel's fulfillment, the ultimate meaning of its achievement, at the same time as it (and the Jewish State) left Diaspora Jewry far behind, standing by the side of the road, as it were, and gazing at the world's march toward redemption. Messianism gave larger meaning to the achievements of the Israeli state, and lent the imprimatur of holiness to the actions taken by the State in its name. Small wonder that Ben Gurion sought to make good use of messianism for his own ends

– and that intellectuals who saw themselves as guardians of Jewish tradition and keepers of the spiritual flame so opposed him.

Ben Gurion's brilliant use of messianism as the core teaching of the new civil religion drew on Biblical and rabbinic themes and imagery with consummate skill.[20] In spirited dialogue with a group of intellectuals that included Martin Buber, Jacob Talmon, and Ephraim Urbach, as well as Rotenstreich and Scholem, the prime minister deftly played the role of king to their role of exilic sages. They counseled prudence and caution. He exulted in the play of realpolitik. Rhetorically, too, his performance was inspired. Consider this high-point:

> I say, Messiah has not yet come. I do not wish that the Messiah will come. At the moment that he comes, he will cease to be Messiah. When you locate his address in the telephone book, he is no longer Messiah…But he is needed – so that he will not come. The days of Messiah are more important than Messiah, and the Jewish people lives in the days of Messiah, expects the days of the Messiah, and this is one of the main reasons for its existence.

When the intellectuals complained about his invocation of revelation at Sinai to justify the Sinai campaign of 1956, he reminded them that unlike them he received mail everyday from the mothers of soldiers, and had to take responsibility for the soldiers' welfare and achievements.[21]

Religious Zionists have had still more reason to link Israeli achievement to Messianic expectation – and possess still more powerful rhetoric to argue for that linkage. Rabbi Abraham Isaac Kook's vision of the emergent State's role in the coming of Messiah surpassed anything that could be articulated or defended on rational grounds.[22] It was later enshrined by Agnon in the prayer recited weekly by Jews inside and outside the State: Israel was "the beginning of the flowering of our redemption." From there it was an easy ideological leap to a less qualified messianic affirmation. Kook's son, Rabbi Tzvi Yehudah Kook, made it soon after the reconquest of the West Bank in 1967. The State, he declared, was not the "passageway to redemption" as his father had believed but rather the "living room" of that fulfillment. The main event had begun. Such a view of history demanded particular government policies (e.g. settling "Judea and Samaria," so as to speed the Messiah's coming) and prohibited others (e.g. returning any part of the Greater Land of Israel in return for peace, lest the Messiah's arrival be forestalled). [23]

An enormous amount has been written for, against, and in analysis of this religious-nationalist messianic ideology.[24] Much has been written, too, about the more recent development of belief among Chabad Hasidim that the late rebbe of the movement, Rabbi Menachem Schneerson, is in fact the messiah and has not really died but is awaiting return as king and savior of Israel.[25] This and other developments have speeded the unexpected merger of religious-nationalist-messianic forces with ultra-Orthodox Jews once steadfast in their opposition to both messianism and nationalism.[26] While the fervor for messiah has quieted in many religious circles in recent years, the dispute between messianists and anti-messianists simmers still, and according to some observers will burst into flame once again when the political conditions are ripe.[27]

My point is not to analyze or enter into that debate but rather to note – following Scholem – that *a significant degree of messianic belief is intrinsic to the Zionist project*. Zionism as classically conceived and recently expounded aims to return Jews from the four corners of the earth to Zion and by so doing to put an end to the "diasporic" era in Jewish history. Zionism will "normalize" Jewish history and solve the Jewish problem. It will bring the era of anti-Semitism as Jews have known it since Pharaoh and Haman to a close. In a word, it will vanquish Amalek once and for all. Zionists did not need to be "religious" in order to call on messianic hopes and vocabulary as justification for difficult personal decisions or controversial government policy. In this respect, Ben Gurion and Rav Kook spoke in one voice. Both placed messianism at the very heart of Judaism – and linked the ultimate fulfillment of prophetic visions of the end of days to the ingathering of Jews in the Land of Israel taking place in their own day.

Distinctions are important in this connection as in all others: *messianic belief and hope*, a major element of Jewish faith over the centuries of Diaspora, have translated only rarely into *messianic movements and activity*.[28] (Scholem distinguished between "passive" and "active" messianism.) Today, too, it is one thing for Jews to pray for messiah, hope for messiah, work toward messiah, and see their reborn State as "the beginning of the flowering of our redemption" – and quite another to plant settlements, brandish weapons, uproot Palestinians, defy government edicts, pursue foreign and domestic policies, or prepare for renewed worship in the rebuilt Third Temple, all in the name of the messiah's *imminent* arrival. I do not want to minimize such distinctions. That mistake is all too common among historians of Zionism, and all the moreso among observers and polemicists in contemporary Israel. One should not bandy about messianic claims lightly, whether those claims be scholarly, religious, or political.[29]

However, Ben Gurion's argument with the intellectuals demonstrates, even more than the statements of Gush Emunim ideologists, that *messianic aspiration and the dilemmas that result from it are built into the Zionist project* at its core. Messianism is *to this degree and in this sense* inherently linked to such lynchpins of Zionist ideology as the absolute centrality of the Land of Israel to Jewish history, the "negation of Diaspora," and the connection of Jewish return to Zion with the attainment of redemption by all humanity. Zionist politics, when influenced strongly by messianism, tend to push aside the *prudential* dimension of political activity and to associate that contrary impulse to Diaspora weakness; no less, Zionism tends to deny the *ephemeral* character of political achievement and the role played by accident in political success and failure. Jews learned and taught long ago that Jewish (or any other) power will endure forever only once the messiah has arrived. Yet Zionism characteristically speaks the language of eternity.

Why so? Political myth is of course essential to any state, and all the more inevitable, perhaps, when that state is bound closely to a religion in which messianism has always been a central tenet. Perhaps, too, the thought that Israel, born and defended only through immense sacrifice, alive and thriving in defiance of the Nazi death machine and Arab enemies, might be as mortal as any other state – this thought is simply unthinkable. A conclusion holds for (and holds fast) many Israeli and Diaspora Jews alike, but it is especially critical for the former, who have so much more directly at stake. The ingathering of Jews from the four corners of the earth in seeming fulfillment of Biblical prophecy, a mere handful of years after the Holocaust, must herald or at least advance redemption. Messianism of the active variety, the kind against which Scholem warned, may be theologically problematic and politically dangerous. The majority of Israelis have not embraced it. But a significant minority have done so, and the other sort of messianism, the kind about which Scholem was so obviously and profoundly ambivalent, may well be an existential necessity for Jews who have risked their own lives and the lives of their children on the viability of the Zionist project.

Diaspora Jewry, for all that it cares viscerally about Israel, has far less at stake in it directly. This difference, usually left unspoken, may lie at the heart of the growing divide between the two Jewries – another feature of Jewish politics which the Purim story as parsed by Greenberg helps to illuminate.

ISRAEL AND THE AMERICAN DIASPORA

Many observers have commented upon and sought to understand the growing gap between Israeli and American Jews in our day — the felt lack of deep connection to the other on the part of significant percentages of each community.[30] There is increasing attention to and concern about this divide, and multiple explanations for its existence. One can point, for example, to differences between Israelis and American Diaspora Jews when it comes to language and culture: few Americans are literate in Hebrew, and most do not take the trouble to follow developments in Israeli culture via sub-titled films or translated works of fiction. One can point to differences of ethos or way of life, such as the centrality of army service in Israel, for example, or the greater closeness of families. There are differences in ethnicity: Mizrachi and Ethiopian Jews are marginal to American Jewry, and the recent immigration from the FSU has a very different character from the East European immigration of a century ago. The Israeli political system is so complex that it defies comprehension and discourages Jews elsewhere from trying to comprehend it. Perhaps most alienating is the Orthodox monopoly on state-sponsored Jewish practice and life-cycle ritual. That situation leads regularly to official insult and disparagement of Diaspora Jews as well as de-legitimization of the Judaism that most of them practice. Israeli authorities frequently deny that many of those who consider themselves Jews, whether converted by non-Orthodox rabbis or the children of non-Jewish mothers, are in fact Jews. These individuals are not treated as Jews in the eyes of Israeli law. I myself have advanced such explanations at length.[31]

I have also made the case more than once – joining many others – that the divide separating Israeli from American Jews threatens the political well-being of Israel, and so of all Jews, as well as depriving Israeli Jews of the benefit of the creative forces at work in the Diaspora and vice versa. To me, the interdependence of Israeli and Diaspora Jews is so obvious as to require no further argument. My concern in this essay, following the line of reflection initiated by Greenberg about Purim and Jewish politics, is to highlight another set of factors that makes for division between Israeli and Diaspora Jews: those revolving around *the difference of basic outlook with regard to messainism*, i.e. the different means adopted by the two communities for fighting the eternal war versus Amalek. These differences, I suggest, are the most fundamental of all. They make for understandings of self and other that can be bridged only with great difficulty.

We can sum up the situation this way. American Jews are greatly concerned with the *myth* of Israel – the larger-then-life story of making deserts bloom, ingathering exile, building from the ashes of destruction; in short, the Triumph of Life over Death. They have little interest in the *reality* of Israel: messy and ambiguous like all reality, a story of achievement as well as of failure and of the two so intertwined as to be inseparable. Israeli and American Jews share the civil religion of the Jewish people worldwide, the most important tenet of which is arguably *Am Yisrael Chai*: the Jewish people lives! Despite Hitler's attempt to kill us, despite "the Arabs'" attempt to eliminate Israel, despite the seductions of assimilation: Jews are here to tell the tale. Amalek, if not defeated, has been held at bay. Israeli Jews, however, know both myth and reality. Indeed they *live* both, confront the tension between them daily – and as a result are driven to conflate the two. The more their Zionism is messianic, the greater the conflation. But even non-messianists are separated from American Jews by their variant reading of Jewish history. Each side has placed a different existential "bet" on the course of Jewish history by choosing to live *in* Zion rather than regard it from afar, whatever the host of reasons, acknowledged and unacknowledged, that motivated that decision, and regardless of whether the matter ever came to actual decision.[32]

Greater knowledge of Israeli reality might get in the way of the mythic narrative to which American Jews cleave. It might also get in the way of the other myth crucial to many Diaspora Jews: that of their own success, their exemption from the rules of Diaspora history to this point. "America is different." Zionist thinkers in America have held from the outset (viz. Louis Brandeis) that Zionist theory was inapplicable to them; if Jews were already home, they did not need to *COME* home. The purpose of Zionism was to secure freedoms and opportunities for Jews elsewhere that American Jews already enjoyed.[33] On this point, political, cultural, and religious Zionists in America have been united. Mordecai Kaplan put the matter most directly when he wrote in 1955 that the purpose of Zionism was to secure the vitality of Jewish civilization *wherever* Jews lived.[34]

Diaspora Jews like Kaplan want Israel, we might speculate, to help them feel good and find fulfillment as the Jews they are, *where* they are. Israeli Jews need Israel to prove worthy of the risk and sacrifice they bring to it – and so must endow it with ultimate significance that American Jews are free to deny or withhold. Each side fundamentally challenges the other: Diaspora Jews remind Israelis that Israel, "the beginning of the flowering of our redemption," is far from perfect and far from secure. Israelis remind American Jews that Jewish history continues to knock on the door, and that one cannot hide from that knock even in America. Mordecai's warning to Esther, they would say, still holds: "for if you remain silent now, then relief and deliverance will come to the Jews from another place, but you and your father's house will perish. Who knows if you haven't come to the kingdom for such a time as this?"[35] Each thus challenges the other at a point of greatest vulnerability and patent risk: is Israel secure? (Hardly.) Is Jewish faith in America or any other Diaspora homeland well-placed? (Perhaps not.) Each warns that the other's choice is a tragic illusion for which they will soon pay the price, or their children after them.[36] Each hears the same about its own choice. Neither can adapt the other's narrative, inhabit the other's myth, without calling into question the choice made, the bet placed, concerning where Jewish life is best lived in our day – and where that life is more secure.

CONCLUSION: BROKEN MYTHS, NORMAL COVENANTS

Greenberg, once again, has contributed significantly to this discussion, bridging the gap as best it can be bridged with the notion (borrowed from Tillich, and popular in recent discussion of theology and civil religion) of "broken myth." He calls upon each side to credit the account of the other, to hear it sympathetically, and to recognize that its own account is flawed and fissured. I echo that call, though I am not sure this recognition is possible for most Jews. Nor am I sure it is desirable. Myth is often essential for communal vitality. Israel thrives in part, if Scholem is correct, on energy stored up in two thousand years of messianic longing. It requires a myth that is far from broken. Deserts have been made to bloom. Refugees have been ingathered. Life has continued in the face of death and the threat of death. Israeli society and culture are remarkably vital. And who knows? Israel may well signify the start of a new phase in the journey toward redemption. American Jews thrive, by analogy, on the need to prove that America is different, will be different, and that Jews will help to make it so. America will not prove the end of history. It will not bring Messiah. But who knows? It might offer the best defense against Amalek that Jews have known outside of sovereignty in the Land of Israel – and prove essential to the defense of the State of Israel, as well. If so, it would justify the refusal to follow Scholem's apparent advice and put all at stake in the Land, on the Land.

Jews may well read the Purim story with new meaning, six decades into the existence of Israel as a sovereign nation and the post-war achievement of American Jewry – and read it with differing meaning, depending on where they sit in the Jewish world. Diaspora Jews have become at home in Gentile royal courts. They have attained high office and used it to protect Jews, but not only Jews. They have thrived, fostered good working relations on many levels with non-Jews, while remaining ever alert to the threats of Haman's descendants and the nuances of anti-Semitism. Israeli Jews have foregone reliance on Gentile monarchs (though not on Gentile allies). Mordecai is king and Esther queen, as it were. Jews can take up arms in their own defense without asking for Gentile permission – thereby allowing the Place (God) to offer help in ways hidden or direct. Both Israelis and American Jews must calculate the proper balance between normalcy and covenant. Greenberg has greatly assisted this accounting, I believe, by pondering these dilemmas with remarkable acuity. May Jewish thought and practice continue to prove equal to the tasks he has so resolutely identified and pursued.

NOTES

1. Irving Greenberg, *Purim Guide* (New York, 1978).
2. Arnold Eisen, *Galut: Modern Jewish Reflection on Homelessness and Homecoming* (Bloomington, 1986).

3. Ruth Wisse, *Jews and Power* (New York, 2007), Prologue & Part I. For a survey of Jewish political thought over the centuries see Michael Walzer, et al. *The Jewish Political Tradition* (New Haven, 2000).

4. For a somewhat different view of Diaspora Jewish politics, see: David Biale, *Power and Powerlessness in Jewish History* (New York, 1986). See also: Ismar Schorsch "On the History of the Political Judgment of the Jew," *The Leo Baeck Memorial Lecture*, no. 20, (New York, 1976).

5. Theodore Herzl, *A Jewish State*, Trans. Harry Zohn (New York, 1970), p. 33.

6. Zecheria 4:6.

7. See for example: Shmuel Trigano, La Nouvelle Question Juive (Paris 1979).

8. Irving Greenberg, *Voluntary Covenant* (New York, 1982). See also: Irving Greenberg, *The Jewish Way: Living the Holidays* (New York, 1988), Chapter 3.

9. Esther 3:8.

10. Exodus 1:9-10.

11. Herzl, *Jewish State*, pp. 49-51.

12. Rashi on Deuteronomy 25:18 on *v-lo yareh* .

13. Deuteronomy 25:17-19.

14. Arnold Eisen, *Taking Hold of Torah: Jewish Commitment and Community in America* (Bloomington, 1997), Chapter 4.

15. Eisen, *Galut*, Chapter 3.

16. Gershom Scholem, "Toward an Understanding of the Messianic Idea in Judaism," in *The Messianic Idea in Judaism and Other Essays on Jewish Spirituality* (New York, 1971), p. 35.

17. Scholem, *The Messianic Idea*, p. 36.

18. David Ben Gurion, "David Ben Gurion to Nathan Rotenstreich, an Inquiry Into the Matter" (Hebrew) in *Chazut* 5717 (1957), pp. 16-29.

19. David Ben Gurion, "The Imperatives of the Jewish Revolution," (1944), In Arthur Herzberg, ed., *The Zionist Idea* (New York, 1959), p. 609

20. Charles Liebman and Eliezer Don-Yehiya, *Civil Religion in Israel: Traditional Judaism and Political Culture in the Jewish State.* (Berkeley, 1983).

21. David Ohana, *Messianism and Malachtiut: Ben Gurion and the Intellectuals Between Political Vision and Political Theology* (Hebrew; Jerusalem, 2003), pp.74-80 & 157-198.

22. Abraham Isaac Kook, "The Land of Israel" (1910-1930), in Hertzberg, *Zionist Idea*, pp. 419-22

23. Eisen, *Galut*, pp. 121-31

24. See for example: Gideon Aran, "Jewish Zionist Fundamentalism: The Bloc of the Faithful in Israel (Gush Emunim)" in *Fundamentalisms Observed*, ed. Martin E Marty and R Scott Appleby (Chicago, 1991), chapter 5. See also: Yigal Elam, "Gush Emunim- A False Messianism" in *The Jerusalem Quarterly*, Vol 1, (1976) pp. 60-69. For a differing view on this topic see: Chaim Waxman, "Messianism, Zionism and the State of Israel," in *Modern Judaism* 7:2 (1987), pp. 175-187.

25. David Berger, *The Rebbe, the Messiah, and The Scandal of Orthodox Indifference* (Portland, 2001).

26. See Charles Liebman, "Jewish Fundamentalism and Israeli Polity" in *Fundamentalisms and the State*, ed. Martin E. Marty and R. Scott Appleby, (Chicago, 1993), pp. 68-77. See also: Aviezer Ravitzky, *Messianism, Zionism and Religious Radicalism*, trans. Michael Swirsky and Jonathan Chipman, (Chicago, 1996), chapters 3 & 4.

27. Gadi Taub, "The Facts on the Ground," *The New Republic,* 10 April, 2006: 28-33.

28. Scholem, *The Messianic Idea,* pp. 14-16.

29. For a survey of diverse Jewish views on Messianism over the centuries, see Zvi Baras, *Messianism and Eschatology: A Collection of Essays* (Jerusalem, 1983).

30. See for example statistics on question "How emotionally attached are you to Israel" found in Cohen and Eisen, *The Jew Within* (Bloomington, 2000), p. 218. For a summary statement of possible reasons for the divide, see Arnold Eisen, *A New Role for Israel in American Jewish Identity* (New York, 1992).

31. See for example: Arnold Eisen, "Israel at 50: An American Jewish Perspective," *American Jewish Year Book,* vol 98, 1998, pp. 47-71.

32. Ehud Luz, *Wrestling With an Angel: Power, Morality, and Jewish Identity* Trans. Michael Swirsy (New Haven, 2003).

33. Eisen, *Galut* p. 157 and sources cited there.

34. Mordecai M Kaplan, *A New Zionism* (New York, 1955), pp. 119, 130-131, 138-139.

35. Esther 4:14.

36. See for example speech made by A.B. Yehoshua at the 2006 Annual meeting of the American Jewish Committee and the subsequent uproar that ensued. Sources can be found at http://www.ajc.org/site/c.ijITI2PHKoG/b.1700373/k.8009/Reactions_to_AB_ Yehoshua_at_the_Annual_Meeting/apps/nl/newsletter2.asp Accessed October 3, 2008.

5

Colleagues and Friends: Letters between Rabbi Samuel Belkin and Rabbi William G. Braude[1]

David Ellenson

INTRODUCTION

Rabbi Irving "Yitz" Greenberg has long been one of the outstanding person-alities on the modern Jewish scene. His wisdom and humanity have graced countless settings worldwide, and his teachings and person have nurtured and inspired the lives of many. To be in his presence is to be in an embrace. Throughout the years, he has displayed an absolute fidelity to Jewish tradi-tions and texts, and his love and concern for the Jewish people can only be described as passionate and uncompromising. In a Jewish world where sec-tarianism all too frequently dominates, and divisions among Jews are all too often emphasized, his has always been a sane and sympathetic voice that has spoken out on behalf of moderation and the necessity for mutual respect among all branches of Jews.

It is in this spirit of admiration and respect for Rabbi Greenberg that I offer selected and previously unpublished 1930s correspondence between Ortho-dox Rabbi Samuel Belkin (1911-1976) of Yeshiva University and Reform Rabbi William Braude (1907-1988) of Temple Beth El in Providence, Rhode Island, as a tribute to Rabbi Greenberg. This correspondence reflects the deep personal friendship that Rabbi Belkin and Rabbi Braude had for one another. The substance of these letters also indicates that Rabbi Belkin and Rabbi Braude were both intensely interested in the subject of the dissertation on classical rabbinic attitudes and laws regarding conversion that Rabbi Braude was then preparing. The correspondence testifies to their erudition in tradi-tional Jewish sources as well as the passion they shared for classical rabbinic literature and scholarship, a passion that surely helped provide a foundation for their friendship. The relationship these men enjoyed transcended denominational lines and is a reflection of the type of Jewish values Rabbi Greenberg himself embodies – a Judaism marked by a respect for a persons and devotion to Torah.

BIOGRAPHICAL BACKGROUNDS:
THE CONTEXT OF A RELATIONSHIP

Rabbi Samuel Belkin, who served as President of Yeshiva University from 1943-1976 and was one of the foremost scholars in the world on Philo and Hellenistic Jewish literature as well as Jewish law, came to the United States in 1928, emigrating from his native Poland after being educated at the yeshivot of Slonim and Mir. While he taught for a time in Cleveland, from his first years in America he desired a secular education and wished to acquaint himself with the sources of Judaism of the Second Temple era as well as the contemporaneous sources of the ancient Hellenistic world. He therefore enrolled as a graduate student at Brown University. Working with Harry Wolfson of Harvard, Belkin received his doctorate in 1935 for a dissertation entitled, "Philo and the Oral Law: The Philonic Interpretation of Biblical Law in Relation to the Palestinian Halakhah." His student Sidney Hoenig describes the first steps of Belkin at Brown in the following words. Hoenig writes, "A description of the young man at Brown University is recorded: 'He has a woebegone look, his clothes frayed, his shoes literally down at the heel … his English was all but unintelligible …'" At the same time, Hoenig notes that although Belkin had no secondary schooling and no undergraduate degree, "the professors at Brown were greatly impressed with him and gave him graduate standing. There too he met and became a life long friend of Rabbi William G. Braude of Providence."[2]

The lifelong relationship that obtained between Belkin and Braude is further testified to by Victor B. Geller, Belkin's biographer, who observed, in his biography of Belkin, that "one of Belkin's strongest personal characteristics" was "*hakarat hatov* (appreciation of kindness)." Geller writes, "William G. Braude was a Reform rabbi in Providence, Rhode Island, who reached out to the brilliant young yeshiva bocher struggling to acclimate himself at Brown. Braude befriended Belkin and opened his home to him. When the needy young scholar became engaged, Braude gave him the money to buy an engagement ring. Their friendship continued across the ideological gap. The guest room in the Belkin home was always open to his friend from Providence. In the guest room closet hung a change of clothing ready for Braude's periodic visits to New York."[3]

Braude, also a native of eastern Europe, was born in Telz and immigrated to the United States in 1920. His father, Rabbi Yitzhak Aisik Braude, came to Dayton, Ohio, in 1922, and served there as the Orthodox rabbi of the community. Young Braude ultimately decided to follow in his father's footsteps and enter the rabbinate, though he enrolled in 1925 as an undergraduate at the University of Cincinnati as well as at the Reform Hebrew Union College.[4] Ordained in 1931 after a brilliant academic career at the College, Braude was called to the pulpit of Temple Beth-El in Providence, Rhode Island, in 1932, and served there his entire life. While in Providence, Braude attended graduate school at Brown University. There he turned his attention to Jewish law, and he, like Belkin, worked with Wolfson as well. Braude received his M.A. in 1934 and his Ph.D. in 1937. His dissertation, *Jewish Proselytizing in the First Five Centuries of the Common Era: The Age of the Tannaim and Amoraim*, was revised and published by Brown in 1940. As will be seen, the correspondence presented below between Belkin and Braude largely centers around concerns Braude had as he researched the dissertation that served as the foundation for his book.[5]

Braude taught Hebrew and Biblical Literature at Brown from 1937 to 1942, and then devoted the bulk of his time to his pulpit. However, he remained committed to academic scholarship in rabbinic literature and at the invitation of his teacher Wolfson ultimately translated the *Midrash on Psalms* in 1959 for the prestigious Yale Judaica Series. This was followed by his 1968 translation for Yale Judaica of *Pesikta Rabbati*. Later, in collaboration with Israel J. Kapstein, he translated both *Pesikta de-Rab Kahana* (1975) and *Tanna Debe Eliyahu* (1980), and his translation of *Sefer HaAggadah* appeared posthumously as *The Book of Legends* in 1992. All three of these works were published by The Jewish Publication Society. His academic fame rested on these acclaimed translations and caused numerous institutions such as Yale, the Hebrew University in Jerusalem, and the Leo Baeck College in London to invite him to serve as a visiting professor.[6]

In a necrology written as a tribute to his friend Rabbi Belkin in the *Proceedings of the American Academy for Jewish Research* in 1977, Rabbi Braude wrote of Rabbi Belkin, "Samuel Belkin had been the friend and confidant of Nobel Prize winners – Albert Einstein among them[7] —and of men in the highest echelons of government. Yet, in the eyes of his friends, he remained to the end of his days, humble and unassuming. His sole obsessions were the service of God and the love of His word."[8]

The strong bond that obtained between these two men is apparent not only in the words that Rabbi Braude uttered in his necrology for Rabbi Belkin. The correspondence contained below and published for the first time will illustrate both the personal and academic dimensions that characterized their friendship. In a contemporary Jewish world where strife among denominations is all too common, the personal respect and warmth these men had for one another as well as the devotion these men shared for modern academic scholarship and traditional Jewish learning can serve as a model for human and Jewish conduct. They indicate that whatever the genuine and principled religious differences there were that divided these men could not exceed the mutual friendship and respect they enjoyed for one another.[9]

THE LETTERS

I. Rabbi Belkin to Rabbi Braude

20 January, 1936
Dear Bill:
I just returned from Buffalo. My sister died at two o'clock Saturday morning. Words can hardly express the tragedy. My mother is completely at loss and so are my sister's children. I can hardly control myself. *Nisharti ani l'vadi* [I am left alone].

I am sorry I cannot answer your letter at length. I may write to you about it some other time. Levertoff's interpretation is wrong.[10] None of the Rabbis ever doubted that Jethro really accepted Judaism and was a *ger tzedek* and Moses himself said *al na ta'a'zov* [please do not leave].[11] The Sifre, however, interprets it that Jethro was not satisfied with his own practicing Judaism, but he wanted to return to his home and convert also his people.[12] Your interpretation is undoubtedly correct.

The language in *Sifre Zutta* means to confess their sins to a non-Jew or proselyte.[13] Your first interpretation of the passage is wrong for the last mishnah in Baba Kamma 9 interprets the Biblical passage with reference to a *ger* (see the mishnah *hagozel et ha-ger* [if one robbed a proselyte]).[14]

Bearing in mind the fact that during the time of the temple sins were confessed before a priest or at the presence of a priest you can easily understand why proselytes are also discriminated. See Ginzberg U.J.S. p. 59.[15] He makes reference to a midrash that in ancient times sins were confessed *before* a priest. See also Buchler *Sin and Atonement* pp. 417-418.[16] I have also a long note on the problem for Philo also requires public confession.
Mournfully yours
Sam

II. Rabbi Belkin to Rabbi Braude

Jan. 29, 1936
Dear Bill,
I hope you will forgive me for not having answered your letter sooner. I have not been feeling very well lately. You can imagine the circumstances. I also

regret under the confusion in the house during the week of mourning your letter was lost. I guess we will be able to analyze the subject under discussion when we meet, for I have very few books in the house to look up the matter.

I realize that you are correct in interpreting the passage about the confession 'al y'dei ger. I did not realize that it deals with a ger toshav (resident alien) The midrash I referred to appears in ... A. Epstein's Mi-Kadmoniyot XXXV – Lamah gazar ha-kadosh baruch hu lisrof par hahatat b'farhasiya hutz l'mahaneh, ela ratzah hakadosh baruch hu l'lameid shelo y'hei adam mitbayeish l'hitvadot hatato lifnei kohen sheken katuv, v'hitvadah asher hata 'aleha, sheyomar kohen gadol lo nitbayeish mi-meni ani lo etbayeish mi-menu [Why did the Holy One Blessed be He decree that the bullock for the sin offering be burned publicly outside the camp? Because the Holy One blessed be He desired to teach that a man should not be embarrassed to confess his sin before the priest, as it is written (Leviticus 5:5), "He shall confess that wherein he has sinned." Thus, the High Priest will say, "He will not be embarrassed before me nor will I be embarrassed before him"].

... Can you possibly give an explanation on the passage Yebamot 97b – haitah horatan she-lo bikedushah v'leidatan bikedushah, lo holtzin v'lo myabmin aval hayavin mishum eshet ah (If however, they [twin brothers] were not conceived in holiness, but were born in holiness, they neither participate in halitzah nor contract levirate marriage,[17] but are guilty [of a punishable offense] for marrying a brother's wife (whom even a maternal brother is forbidden to marry).

Is one born of a woman who was converted into Judaism before she begat him a Jew or a proselyte? Why are the rabbis discriminating such a man from performing the levirate marriage if they consider such a child an Israelite?

Selma sends her regards. My regards to Dorothy. I am going to be Sundays and Mondays in New York teaching in the yeshiva. In case you are coming to New York during these days leave a message ... that you are in town and we will arrange to see one another.

As ever,
Sam

III. Rabbi Belkin to Rabbi Braude

February 4, 1936
Dear Bill:
I received your letter and I am answering you immediately. I was more than happy to see how thoroughly you are acquainted with rabbinic law in the field of geirut (conversion). The purpose of my letter is to bring to your attention some sources which I believe you ought to investigate.

Your reference to Rashi is not new to me. I have the following objection to Rashi's interpretation.[18]

1. The principle of *ah min ha-av* [paternal brotherhood] with reference to levirate marriage can logically be applied only when they are brothers not of the same father, for the law of *yibum* [levirate marriage] is deeply connected with inheritance. *Yibum b'nahalah tala rachmanna* [The All Merciful has made levirate marriage dependent on inheritance -- Yebamot 17b and 24a] and since the sister of the maternal side cannot share equally in inheritance he cannot marry his brother's wife which is under ordinary circumstances prohibited. *Achavah achavah mi'bnei ya'a'kov* (Genesis 42 – see *Beit Yosef* on *Even Haezer* 172:9) is merely a midrash and has no legal value.[19] The Rabbinic principle is sound. However, when both brothers have no paternal lineage this principle can hardly be applied. In other words in the latter case they are equal brothers in every respect. There is a difference between two brothers who are not children of the same father and two brothers who have no father legally.

2. If we assume that the conversion after the conception automatically annuls the relationship between father and son, why then is she considered legally the child's mother? Why should not the child have to go through the rite of circumcision as an act of conversion. In short why is a child conceived of two pagans [to] be considered a Jew.

What I am really driving at is that *horato shelo bikedushah* [one whose conception is not in holiness] is not a Jew though he is *hayav mishum eishet ah*[20] (See *Tur, Yoreh De'ah* 269). This view I held for the last ten years. Fortunately enough I found it in Sifri Deut. On the *parashat yibum*. Since I have neither a Bible nor a Sifri in the house I cannot quote the passage literally on the verse *v'altah y'bimto ha-sha'rah* [his brother's widow shall appear before the elders in the gate – Deuteronomy 25:6] and say *he* did not want to establish a name *b'yisrael*[21] and Sifri says *b'yisrael prat l'horato shelo bikedushah v'leidtatan bikedushah.*[22] In other words the reason that *horato shelo bikedushah* is not allowed to perform the rite of *yibum* is due to the fact that he is still treated as a proselyte not as Israelite. This statement is significant. Maimonides seems to have been acquainted with the Sifri and in *perek aleph hilchot yibum* he explains that the law [is] that they are not real brothers.[23] I think that text reads *mipnei she-ein ahim gmeurim* [because they are not full brothers]. I wish you would check up carefully the source. More striking is the Ramban in *Milhamot hashem* on Yeb. 47b on *matbilin oto miyad* – [immerse him immediately] (see also the tosafot) that the circumcision of one child *horato she-lo bikedushah* is an act of conversion not a *mitzvat milah* (commandment of circumcison).[24] Thus my personal view is that a child who was conceived of pagan parents but both of them were converted before the child was born, or the mother alone, the child still needs conversion. However, here is a bit of Rabbinic jurisprudence which is very paradoxical but at the same time logical. Assuming that the child needs *geirut* (conversion) we have a unique situation now since we consider such a child a gentile when he was born of a mother who is already a full-fledged Jewess. The Rabbis therefore made the following distinction: with reference to inheritance which is a secular matter the *tomim* (twins) inherit one another's possessions, for they were both born of a Jewess. So also is he forbidden to marry his brother's wife. With reference to many laws they are Jews, but when it is a question of *l'hakim shem b'yisrael* ["to establish a name in Israel" – see Deuteronomy 25:7] we assume he is rather a *ger* [convert]. Since the law in Leviticus prohibits marrying a brother's wife, but an exceptional case is made in Deut. *Meit b'lo banim* [dies without sons] then we apply it only to a *yisrael* [Jew]. I hope you consider my suggestion carefully, for if I am correct then many difficult passages with reference to *horatan she-lo bikedushah* [those whose conception is not in holiness] may be explained.

In one of your former letters you asked me in what respect is a *ger* [convert] equal to a *goy* [gentile]. It is interesting to note that in midrash (tannaitic) literature you frequently find the expression *byisrael perat l'geirm* ['In Israel,' except for converts] and sometimes *b'yisrael p'rat l'leviyim* ['In Israel,' except for Levites]. What is the analogy? When you compare the passage in the Bible with references to the Levite and proselyte you will find a striking similarity in their status. Both of them were strangers in Palestine for both of them had no share in the land. Both of them were *geirim* [residents] in the literal sense of the word (see midrash Lekeh tov on *al na ta'azov*) where the rabbis were often ready to apply the term *yisrael* in its literal sense "Israelites." This may be a clue to your question with reference to *bikkurim* [first fruits].[25]

I am not through yet with the term *yisrael*. It is very striking that the Sifri deduces it from the term – *b'yisrael* – *v'nikra shemo b'yisrael beit halutz p'rat l'horatan v'leidtan b'ikedushah* ["'In Israel' – 'And he shall go in Israel by the name of 'the family of the unsandaled one' (Deuteronomy 25:20)' unless their conception and their birth are in holiness"]. That is that an Israelite whose father was a *ger* [convert] cannot be a judge in case of *halitzah*. According to the Sifri if one's parents were proselytes he cannot be judge because *b'yisrael* means that one's parents were *yisraelim* and [the] equivalent statement is found in Yeb. 102a. What surprises me is that with reference to levirate marriage the term *b'yisrael* is applied only to *horatan she-lo bikedushah* while with reference to judicial affairs is a *p'rat* [an exclusion] even for *horatan v'leidatan bikedushah*?[26]

Consequently I want to draw the following conclusion that even children of proselytes were not always treated as *yisraelim*. For judicial affairs and religious ceremonies such as *halitzah* which were performed with great pomp, the

Rabbis preferred to have the judicial court [composed of] real Jews – that is *b'nei yisraelim*.[27]

Finally, I want to bring to your attention another point with reference to *geirim*. In Talmudic literature we have two contradictory sources as to whether or not a proselyte can be a judge in *dinei mamanot* [financial matters]. The Talmud Sanhedrin says that he can be while in Yeb. 45b we find that only *imo meiyisrael* [one whose mother is a Jew] may be a judge but not a proselyte. Rashi in Yeb. 102 a follows the Talmudic source in Sanhedrin[28] while Tosafot accepts the statement in Yeb. 45b. The latter passage deals with an historical fact which happened in Babylonia. *U'minayei b'porasei d'bavel* [among the pursers or collectors of Babylon].[29] I want you to find out whether this would show that the Baybylonia Jews took a stricter attitude towards proselytes.[30] Furthermore, what was the nature of the *porasa* [purser or collector] in *bavel* [Babylon]?

I am under the impression that *geirm* [converts] were not appointed as mayors, life-long judges and many other positions which require appointment for life. In such cases it went under the category of *som tasim 'alehka melekh* (see Yeb. 45b)[31] but proselytes were members of courts.

Will you be kind enough to answer me as to whether or not my suggestions appeal to you. I feel convinced that the matters must be worked out by anyone who works in the field. These problems came to my mind while I was teaching in yeshiva *mitzvat halitzah*. Your reference to Blau I will love to read through more carefully.

Would you be interested to read a paper of mine on 'Repentance for Proselytes in the Halakhah and the Epistles.' I wrote it last year, only a few pages in length.

I don't remember anything about the Tarbizs. If it is so I will try to secure the copies for you. I am under the impression I returned them to you. Selma sends her regards. Regards to Dorothy.

As ever,

Sam

IV. Rabbi Braude to Rabbi Belkin

February 8, 1936

Dear Sam'l,

Thank you very much for your prompt and painstaking reply. I am most anxious to continue this correspondence not only because of your vast erudition, but because of the difference in our prejudice on proselytes: You seem determined to see their disabilities, while I am anxious to discover their complete equality to the Jew.[32] Perhaps I should also explain that I am typing the letter in order to preserve a copy so that if you refer in your cryptic manner to something to you I can tell just what it is.

In your last letter you object to Rashi's interpretation. I take it you refer to Rashi's statement on B. Yeb. 97b – *D'tzad yibum min ha-av hu, v'hani ein lahem d'zera mitzri ka-behemah*.[33] I am not quite sure that I follow your argument, particularly since one or two words in your first paragraph are not very legible. It may be well to relate it: You indicate that levirate marriage is intimately connected with the right of inheritance, *yibum b'nahalah tala rahmana* [The All Merciful has made levirate marriage dependent on inheritance] (B. Yeb. 24a), and that the principle of *ah min ha-av* [paternal brotherhood] can be invoked only where parenthood does exist but there is some question on the identity of the father. In the instance of two proselytes the principle of legal parenthood is lacking. Hence, *ah min ha-av* is irrelevant. If I understand you correctly then as I make out Rashi he says the same thing.

In your second paragraph you argue that one whose *horato she-lo bikedushah v'leidato bikedushah* [one whose conception is not in holiness, but whose birth is in holiness] is not considered a Jew by birth. You cite Sifre on Deut. Piska 289 in an effort to prove your view. Now I have read and reread Piska 289 and can't see how it sustains your contention.[34] The hermeneutics used here are a common method in the Halakhic Midrashim of limiting a particular law to Jews of Jewish blood. But I can't see how the passage proves that one whose *horato she-lo bikedushah v'leidato bikedushah* [whose conception was not in holiness, but whose birth was in holiness] is not a Jew by birth. I also consulted Maimonides (Hil. Yibbum 1,8) and he does not use the phrase *mipnei she'ein achim gmurim* [because they are considered complete gentiles]. Instead, he writes *ein lahen achavah klal* [they have no family connection whatsoever].[35] This, as I understand it, is his specific reference to *achavah* in the levirate obligation. Nahmanides' *Milhamot Adonoy* is inaccessible to me. I also consulted Tos. On B. Yeb. 47b, and if I understand that correctly the answer to the objection cited in the name of Rabba that *nochrit m'uberet she-nitgayerah b'nah eino tzarich tevilah* [If a pregnant gentile woman was converted, there is no need for her son to perform ritual immersion] (B. Yeb. 78a) is not very cogent since Rabba opines differently that the child born of a mother who underwent conversion needs no baptism. I believe another consideration might be urged against your position. If the child conceived by pagans was considered a non-Jew at the moment of his birth should not his circumcision take place immediately after his birth? Since it takes place on the eighth day, as it does with other Jewish children, it seems to indicate that he is on a par with them legally. Furthermore, the very phrase *leidato bikedushah* [one whose birth is in holiness] argues for the assumption of Jewish birth.

Frankly, I can't see why you take an either-or position. The rabbis (in B. Yeb. 97b and T. Yeb. 12.2, Zuckermanm. 250) definitely group proselytes to levirate in three divisions: *Ta shma shnei achim t'umim geirim v'chen m'shuchrarim lo holtzin v'lo m'yabmin v'ein hayavin mishum eishet ah haitah horatan she-lo bikedushah v'leidatan bikedushah, lo holtzin v'lo myabmin aval hayavin mishum eishet ah haitah horatan v'leidatan bikedushah harei hein k'yisraelim l'chol divreihen* [Come and hear: Twin brothers who were proselytes, and similarly if they were emancipated slaves, may neither participate in *halitzah* nor contract levirate marriage, nor are they guilty [of a punishable offense] for [marrying] a brother's wife. If however, they were not conceived in holiness but were born in holiness, they neither participate in *halitzah* nor contract levirate marriage but are guilty [of a punishable offense] for [marrying] a brother's wife. If they were both conceived and born in holiness, they are regarded as Israelites in all respects.]

In other words, in order that *lo yomru ba'in mikedushah hamurah likedushah kalah* [they will not say [that proselytes] have exchanged a [religion of] stricter holiness for [one of] more easy-going holiness] (B. Yeb. 22a), a reason rather well explained by Blau in his *Die alteste Eheform* (Chajes Festschrift) they [the rabbis] compromised with the principle of *ger ka'tinok she-nolad damei* [a convert is like a new-born babe]. Except for twin brothers the compromise is a neat one: Paternal ancestry may be open to doubt, but maternal ancestry is easily proved. Even the difficulty of twin brothers is circumvented by the declaration that the seed is sown by a human father whose legal status is that of an animal whereas birth is given by a mother in the state of Jewish sanctity. Hence paternal relationships remain unacknowledged while the maternal bonds are recognized.[36]

In your letter you continue with a citation from Sifre Deut. Piska 291 to the effect that a son of proselytes may not act as judge in a Halizah ceremony. May I cite the Piska? *B'yisrael ne'e'mar kan b'yisrael v'ne'e'mar l'halan b'yisrael mah b'yisrael ha'a'mur l'halan p'rat [l'geirm] af b'yisrael ha'a'mur kan p'rat l'beit din shel geirim* ["In Israel" is stated here, and "in Israel" is stated elsewhere (Deut. 25:7). Just as "in Israel" elsewhere excludes a court consisting of proselytes, so "in Israel" here excludes a court consisting of proselytes] (ed. Friedman 126). After making the analogy with Piska 289 it seems to mean that one whose *horato she-lo bikedushah v'leidato bikedushah* [whose conception is not in holiness, but whose birth is in holiness] is excluded but not one whose *horato v'leidato bikedushah* [whose conception and whose birth are in holiness]. In B. Yeb. 102a, however, Rabba definitely opines that at a Haliza the presiding judges must have Jewish fathers and Jewish mothers. This is in keeping with your suggestion that in Babylonia the rabbis were more offish toward the proselytes. You will remember that Dr. Ginzberg indicated to me sometime ago that I am to be on the lookout for this difference between Palestinian and Babylonia practice.[37]

At the present time I have no idea as to the exact meaning of the *porasei d'bavel* (Jastrow defines them as collectors, whatever that means) referred to in B. Yeb. 45b, nor can I give any opinion on the offices accessible to proselytes. I have not yet gone into the matter. Perhaps I should cite to you Bertholet's inference from the prohibition to elect an alien as king (Deut. 17.15). To him it indicates that foreigners often attained to high diplomatic positions in the royal court. Else such a prohibition were unintelligible. (Die Stellung der Israeliten und der Juden zu den Fremden, P. 40).[38] On the Talmudic development of this prohibition, I have no opinion at present, but I shall bear your suggestions in mind as I go along.

Elsewhere in your letter you point out the similarity between the status of the Levite and proselyte in the matter of landlessness. That has become evident to me as I was examining the Tannaitic midrashim. But this analogy still fails to help me get to the Peshat of SifreZ, (ed. Horovitz, p. 295) on Numbers 18:15, beginning with the words, *kol peter rehem* [the first issue of the womb].

Before closing the discussion I want to refer to your conclusion that "even children of proselytes were not always treated as Israelites." You are probably right. No doubt you are familiar with the dictum, "the daughter of a male proselyte like the daughter of a male of impaired priestly stock may not marry a Kohen." (The statement is attributed to R. Judah Hanassi in T. Kidd. 5.3, ed. Zuckerm. 341 and to R. Judah b. Illai in B. Kidd. 77a) But I believe that that is not the Halakhah. However the problem will bear more intensive investigation.

Yes, I would very much like to read your paper on Repentance for Proselytes in the Halakha and the Epistles. All that you can feed me on the subject is grist for my mill. Incidentally, I am certain you borrowed the Tarbiz (5.3, 5.4, and 6.1) issues because one of them contains an essay by G. Allon on Philo. Do look around for them. They may be lurking in one of your scatterbrained hideouts.

Excuse my delay in answering. Your thorough and suggestive letter deserved a prompt reply. But you know with all of my shirking I have a million things to attend to and my brain operates at a turtle's pace.

With love to your self and Selma, I am,

As ever,

V. Rabbi Belkin to Rabbi Braude

January 15, 1937
Friday
Dear Bill:
How are you?
I just spoke to your mother on the phone and she told me that you may be in N.Y. next week. Do come. We may go over to-gether your material. I under-

stand that your congregation gave you a sabbatical year. Why do not you come
to do your work in N.Y.

I have just noticed that for some midrashim, read for *beit din shel gerim* [a
court of converts] *beit din shel goyim* [a court of gentiles]. We shall have to
discuss it when you will be here. The Sabbath is approaching any minute. A
Shabbat shalom to you.

As ever,

VI. Rabbi Belkin to Rabbi Braude

May 6, 1938
Dear Bill,
I hope you will pardon me for not having answered your card sooner. I really
was not feeling well for the past few days.

I was delighted to hear that you have set the date for June 19. My best wishes
to you and Pearl.

I shall be glad to come to Providence and perform the ceremony. But I want
you to think the matter over carefully. If you should have first a private wedding ceremony in Providence,[39] the matter may somehow slip out to the public and the members of your congregation may feel insulted that you don't
consider the temple wedding as binding. However, this is your affair. Again, if
you do it because you want me to share in the ceremony, you don't have to do
it. You know me by now. I shall be more than delighted to be present at your
wedding without any participation.

… With best wishes for a great future and with heartiest regard to Pearl
from me and Selma

As ever,
Sam

VII. Rabbi Belkin to Rabbi Braude

June 17, 1938
Dear Bill,
I want you to know that I will certainly come to your wedding. I expect to take
a train for Providence Saturday night. I will get in touch with you as soon as I
come to Providence for I don't know how to get to Johnston. I am sorry Selma
cannot come with me on account of Linda.

Sheinkman (sic)[40] called me this week and I assured him that I would not
interfere with the ceremony. I am only interested to see that the *eirusin*
[betrothal ceremony] should be performed to satisfy your mother. If you like
I will give the *birkat eirusin* [blessing of betrothal] and if not I shall be equally
content to be only a witness to the *kiddushin* [marriage].

Mrs. Markoff wrote a very nice letter. I expect to call on her Sunday, though I would not be able to stop at her home because I expect to go immediately after the wedding to Boston.

Selma joins me in sending love and best wishes to you and Pearl.

As ever,

Sam

NOTES

1. I want to express my deepest thanks to Dr. Benjamin Braude of Boston College, son of Rabbi Braude, for sharing the correspondence contained in this article with me and for giving me permission to publish these remarkable letters. I am appreciative as well of the kindness he displayed in discussing these letters and contextualizing them for me, and the information he provided me about the life of his father. I also want to express my gratitude to Linda Rose Belkin, daughter of Rabbi Belkin, for permission to publish the letters that her father sent to Rabbi Braude. To both of them, I am most grateful. I would also note that I have elected to present the letters just as they were written and have not corrected grammar or punctuation. However, for the convenience of the reader, I have provided translations within the texts or translations and comments in footnotes of the rabbinic texts that Rabbi Belkin and Rabbi Braude cited in their correspondence.

2. Sidney B. Hoenig, *The Scholarship of Dr Sameul Belkin* (New York: Yeshiva University Press, 5737-1977), p. 21.

3. Victor B. Geller, *Orthodoxy Awakens: The Belkin Era and Yeshiva University* (Jerusalem and New York: Urim Publications, 2003), p. 185.

4. During this period large numbers of Jews from backgrounds akin to that of Braude began to attend Hebrew Union College. As Jonathan Sarna, *American Judaism* (New Haven & London: Yale University Press, 2004), pp. 196-197, observes, "A growing number of Jews from East European background were even accepted into the Reform rabbinical program at Hebrew Union College. Some 70 percent of its students from 1904-1929 were of East European descent [and] 28 percent had themselves been born in Eastern Europe."

5. In his "Acknowledgements," to his *Jewish Proselytizing in the First Five Centuries of the Common Era: The Age of the Tannaim and Amoraim* (Providence: Brown, 1940), p. 16, Braude wrote, "My teacher, Dr. J.Z. Lauterbach and my friend, Dr. Samuel Belkin read the manuscript and made many valuable corrections and suggestions. I am grateful to them ..."

6. These biographical details on Braude's life are taken from H. Blumberg, B. Braude, B.H. Mehlman, J. Gurland, and L. Gutterman, eds., "*Open Thou Mine Eyes* ...": *Essays on Aggadah and Judaica Presented to Rabbi William G. Braude on His Eightieth Birthday and Dedicated to His Memory* (Hoboken, New Jersey: Ktav Publishing House, 1992).

7. The medical school established by Belkin at Yeshiva University bears the name of Albert Einstein. In honor of the 50th anniversary of the Albert Einstein College of Medicine at Yeshiva University, YU published a letter written dated Mrach 23, 1951, to Belkin by Einstein when Einstein was at the Institute for Advanced Study at Princeton,

in which Einstein wrote to "My dear Dr. Belkin," expressing his enthusiasm for the creation of the medical school. Einstein concluded his letter by stating, "I hope that you will find full understanding and support for this worthy cause." This letter can be found on line at http://library.aecom.yu.edu/library/50thcelebration/einsteinletter.htm.

8. William G. Braude, "Necrology: Samuel Belkin (1911-1976)", *Proceedings of the American Academy for Jewish Research*, Vol. XLIV (1976), p. xx.

9. In this sense, the letters between Belkin and Braude reveal a friendship that parallels the relationship that Rabbi Jehiel Jacob Weinberg and my teacher at Hebrew Union College Professor Samuel Atlas enjoyed with one another. See Marc B. Shapiro, "Scholars and Friends: Rabbi Jehiel Jacob Weinberg and Professor Samuel Atlas," *The Torah U-Maddah Journal* 7 (1997), pp. 105-121.

10. Levertoff here refers to the Jewish apostate and scholar Paul Phillip Levertoff (1875 or 1878 – 1954), a talmudic savant born in Oshra, Belraus, who attended the Volohzin Yeshiva in his youth and who later became "a major pioneer in the Hebrew Christian movement of his time." On Levertoff, see Jorge Quinonez, "Paul Phillip Levertoff: Pioneering Hebrew-Christian Scholar and Leader," *Mishkan* 37 (2002), pp. 21-34.

11. See Numbers 10:29-31, where Moses says to Hobab son of Reuel, whom the Tradition identifies as Jethro, as the Israelites wander in the desert, "Please do not leave us."

12. See Sifre on Numbers # 78ff. In addition, there is also a tradition contained in Tanhuma, Exodus 73 that explicitly states that Jethro left Moses to spread the knowledge of the true God among his people. Braude undoubtedly based himself on midrashic passages such as these in his *Jewish Proselytizing*, p. 29, where he points out that Moses is depicted as saying to his Midianite father-in-law, "Come with us and we will deal kindly with you for God told Israel to deal kindly with proselytes."

13. See Letter II below. It seems that the passage in question here is found in Sifre Zutta, *Parashat Naso* 5:5, (Horowitz edition, pp. 229-230) on the verse found in Leviticus 5:5, that states, "When [an individual] realizes his guilt in any of these matters, *he shall confess that wherein he has sinned – v'hitvadah asher hatah 'a'le-hah*."

14. The mishnah to which Rabbi Belkin refers is found in Babba Kamma 9:11 and reads, "If one robbed a proselyte and [after he] had sworn to him [that he did not do so], the proselyte died, he would have to pay the principal and a fifth to the priests, and bring a trespass offering to the altar, as it is said (Numbers 5:8), 'If the man has no kinsmen (*goel*) to whom restitution can be made, the amount shall be go to the Lord for the priest – in addition to the ram of expiation with which expiation is made on his behalf.'"

15. The reference here is to Louis Ginzberg, *Eine Unbekannte Juedische Sekte:Erster Teil* (New York: 1922).

16. A. Buchler, *Studies in Sin and Atonement in the Rabbinic Literature of the First Century* (London: Oxford University Press, 1928).

17. The obligation of levirate marriage in Judaism arises when a woman's husband dies without male offspring. Jewish law then requires the woman to marry the brother of her husband in the hope that the union will produce a surrogate son and heir to the dead brother, so that the dead brother's name "may not be blotted out in Israel" (Deuteronomy 25:6). Should the living brother reject his deceased brother's widow and opt not to fulfill his levirate duty, he must perform the ritual of *halitzah* (unshoeing – Deu-

teronomy 25: 7-10), whereby he releases the levirate widow from her automatic marital tie to him. His sister-in-law is then free to remarry or not at will.

18. See Letter IV below, where Braude assumes that Belkin is here referring to a comment of Rashi on Yebamot 97b.

19. The principle of 'brotherhood or fraternity – *achavah*,' in regard to levirate obligation to which Belkin refers here by the citation of this Hebrew phrase concerning '*b'nei ya'a'kov* -- the sons of Jacob' is found in Yebamoth 17b, where it states, "Rabbah said, '[That legal] brothers [are only those who are descended] from the same father is deduced from a comparison of this 'brotherhood' with the 'brotherhood' of the sons of Jacob (see Genesis 42:13, where Joseph's brothers, when they first come to Egypt, say to Joseph, "Your servants are twelve brothers"). 'Brotherhood' for purposes of levirate marriage is defined as being derived from the father.

20. This quotation is taken from Yebamot 97b, where it states that if a brother "was not conceived in holiness, but was born in holiness," then he "is guilty [of a punishable offense] for marrying a brother's wife."

21. In Deuteronomy 25:7, the entire verse reads, "My husband's brother refuses to establish a name for his brother in Israel."

22. "In Israel – excluding one whose conception was not in holiness, but those whose birth was in holiness."

23. See Maimonides, *Hilchot Yibum v'Halitzah* 1:8, which states, "There is no concept of fraternity (*achavah*) among converts and freed slaves. [Thus, even two converts or two freed slaves born from the same father] are considered unrelated [with regard to the laws of levirate marriage]. Even if one of them was not conceived in holiness but was born in holiness, while the second was both conceived and born in holiness – they are not considered to have any family connection. Even if they are twins and were born in holiness – they are not considered to be brothers [for purposes of *yibum*] unless they were both conceived and born in holiness."

24. Rabbi Belkin is here stating that the circumcision of child "who was not conceived in holiness" is not an act of *mitzvat milah* (the commandment of circumcision that Jewish law requires be performed on a Jewish boy on the eighth day of his life in accord with Genesis 17:11-13), but in effect is a *milah l'shem geirut*, an "enabling" act of circumcision Jewish law requires of converts. In Letter IV below Rabbi Braude will disagree with his friend as to this conclusion.

25. See Braude, *Jewish Proselytizing*, pp. 79ff., where he deals with the issue of the rights and obligations proselytes enjoyed in respect to participation in Temple worship, and the nature of the declaration the proselyte was required to make, as opposed to the born Jew, when he presented his *bikkurim* to the priest at the Temple. On p. 83, Braude points out that in making this distinct declaration as delineated in *Maaser Sheni* 5:15 and Sotah 9:10, the analogy between the Levites and proselytes is made explicit for "levites also do not make the avowal because they had not received a share in the land."

26. In Yebamot 102a it states, "If his mother was an Israelite woman, he may sit in judgment even on an Israelite. In respect of *halitzah*, however, [no man is eligible as a judge] unless both his father and his mother were Israelites, for it is said (Deut. 25:10), 'And his name shall be called in Israel.'"

27. Ibid.

28. See Sanhedrin 36b.

29. The Talmud in Yebamot 45b states, "Raba declared R. Mari b. Rachel (whose mother was Jewish, but whose father was not) to be a legitimate Israelite and appointed him among the pursers of Babylon."

30. It is illuminating to note that Rabbi Braude had consulted the famed Talmudist at the Jewish Theological Seminary, Dr. Louis Ginzberg, on the very question Rabbi Belkin raises here regarding whether Babylonian Jews held stricter attitudes toward proselytes than Palestinian Jews did. In a note to Rabbi Braude, dated December 23, 1935, Dr. Ginzberg wrote, "Pal. & Bab. On Pros. In Palestine and because of Chr. Jews were compelled to be more lenient or else lose out to Christianity whose terms were infinitely more lenient. On the other hand in Babylon where the govt. is definitely inimical to Christ. Since it came to be identified with the Rom. Empire no concessions had to be made. Local factors complicated the situation. The Palmyrene invasions of the 4th century & the destruction of Nehardea were bittersweet for the Jews. Syncrenistic Mandaeans provoked the Jews into such utterances as those hostile to Corduenes." I am grateful to Michael Gould, grandson of Dr. Ginzberg, for permission to publish this note that Dr. Benjamin Braude shared with me.

31. This passage from Deuteronomy 17:15, "You shall be free to set a king over yourself. ... Be sure to set as a king over yourself one of your own people; you must not set a foreigner over you, one who is not of your kinsmen," is cited in Yebmaot 45b and there the Talmud comments on this verse, saying, "all appointments which you make must be made only 'from among your kinsmen', [means that] such a man (R. Mari b. Rachel – see ftn. 25), since his mother was a descendant of Israel, may well be regarded as 'one from among your kinsmen.'"

32. Interestingly, in his "Introduction" to *Jewish Proselytizing*, p. 3, Braude writes, "A personal experience led to this investigation into the rabbinic attitude toward proselytizing and the social position of the proselyte within Jewry. At the present time, the prevailing opinion, certainly among the Orthodox, is that Jews want no proselytes. This is grounded in the essentially correct feeling that in the main not religious conviction but love of a Jewish boy or girl impel converts to embrace Judaism. Consequently some Orthodox and Conservative rabbis refuse to officiate at a conversion. Reform rabbis eschew this offishness and welcome the applicant without attempting to ferret out motives ..."

33. Rashi comments here on the following passage in Yebamot 97b, "If however, they were not conceived in holiness but were born in holiness, they neither participate in *halitzah* nor contract levirate marriage," and repeats the assertion that the obligation of levirate marriage is established by paternal brotherhood alone.

34. Piska 289 to which Belkin and Braude both refer, reads, "'In Israel – and not among proselytes. Hence you learn that two proselyte brothers not conceived in holiness but born in holiness are exempt from both *halitzah* and levirate marriage ..."

35. See footnote 23 above.

36. In his *Jewish Proselytizing*, pp. 122-126, Braude presents the fruits of this discussion and writes, "Theoretically a proselyte was like a new born babe, with all of his previous family ties completely severed. He could thus marry his own sister without fear of committing incest thereby. But several considerations led to the modification of these radical theories in practice. I believe the first and the most important motive was the fear that the incoming proselyte might suppose that he had exchanged his original moral religion for a licentious one." Braude then continued on the subject of

levirate marriage by stating, "Since the proselyte has no paternal kin, levirate marriage and its alternative of *Halitzah* do not apply to him. The whole institution of levirate is intimately bound up with paternal relationships and their consequent rights of inheritance. … The general principle is laid down: 'the sons of a woman proselyte who are converted together with her neither participate in *Halitzah* nor contract levirate marriage, even if one was not conceived in holiness but was born in holiness, and the other was both conceived and born in holiness.' They are not guilty of a punishable offense for marrying a brother's wife. … Twin brothers, however, who were not conceived in holiness but were born in holiness, do not, to be sure, participate in *Halizah* nor solemnize a levirate marriage, but are liable to *Karet* or extirpation for marrying a brother's wife. For when the brothers were born their mother was already a Jewess. Hence the latter prohibition. But if two brothers were born and conceived in holiness all marriage regulations would apply to them precisely as they do to born Jews."

37. See footnote 30 above.

38. Alfred Bertholet, *Die Stellung der Israeliten und der Juden zu den Fremden* (Leipzig: 1896).

39. The wedding was held on June 19, 1938, in the home of the parents of the bride, Selma Finkelstein. There was no private ceremony. The officiants were Rabbi Belkin, Conservative Rabbi Morris Schusheim of Providence, and Rabbi Jacob Shankman of New Rochelle, classmate and close friend of Rabbi Braude ever since their student days together at HUC.

40. The reference here is to Rabbi Jacob Shankman, who co-officiated at the Braude wedding. Rabbi Belkin oversaw the halakhic parts of the ceremony – i.e., the signing of the *ketubah* and the betrothal ceremony.

6

Rabbi Shneur Zalman of Lyady as an Educator

Immanuel Etkes

To Yitz, who dedicated his life for "Clale Israel,"
A story of another great Jewish leader.

One of the prominent innovations of the Hasidic movement in its first generations was a new type of leader: the Hasidic rebbe or the "Tsadik" – as he
was called in Hasidic literature. The Tsadik was different from the traditional
rabbi with respect both to the sources of his authority and to the areas of his
activity. Although one can point to several patterns shared by all of the Hasidic leaders in the first generations, it is still possible to distinguish among
them in the light of the particular personal path in which each of them chose
to direct his Hasidim.[1] This statement is particularly apt in relation to Rabbi
Shneur Zalman of Lyadi (to whom we will now refer as RASHAZ), the leader
of Hasidim in White Russia at the end of the eighteenth and the beginning of
the nineteenth centuries, who is regarded as the founder of Habad Hasidism.
   The most appropriate label for the special path taken by RASHAZ as a Hasidic leader is "educator." His efforts to make a far-reaching change in the
consciousness and behavior of thousands of Hasidim made him an educator
in the deepest sense of the term. Indeed, the aspiration to shape the spiritual
universe and way of life of his Hasidim was central to the project of RASHAZ
and influenced all his actions.
   Who was the audience that RASHAZ addressed? What messages did he
seek to communicate to that audience? What means did he use to influence
the Hasidim? In other words: what type of Hasidism did RASHAZ wish to
spread among his followers? To appreciate the full meaning of these questions,

81

a brief discussion of the development of Hasidism as a movement in the second half of the eighteenth century is in order.

The process of turning Hasidism from an esoteric and limited circle into a broad religious movement began in the 1760s and 1770s. After the death of the BESHT in 1760, some of his companions and disciples began to promulgate the Hasidic way of serving God.[2] Along with the organized effort to spread the ways of Hasidism more widely, the Hasidic "court" was established, central to which was the figure of the Tsadik. Dov Ber of Mezirech, known as the Maggid, founded the first Hasidic court in the mid-1760s. This court served as a kind of archetype for the courts that were established in its wake. The connection between the expansion of Hasidism and the establishment of the Hasidic court was essential, because the main function of the court at that time was to convert the people who visited it into Hasidim. In other words, the people who stayed in the court for a few days and who were thereby exposed to the influence of the Hasidic leader and to the Hasidic ethos were expected to undergo a conversion process, in the course of which they adopted the Hasidic manner of worshiping God and the values underlying it. However, contrary to the prevalent view, at that stage, the Hasidic leaders did not address the popular strata of the community. Indeed, their target audience was the community of "*lomdim*," men with rabbinical education, especially young men who were studying in *Yeshivot* and *Batei Midrash*.[3]

The Maggid of Mezirech, the most prominent Hasidic leader after the death of the BESHT, died in 1772. Even during his lifetime some of his disciples began to lead groups of Hasidim. Other disciples of the Maggid, including RASHAZ, began to serve as Hasidic leaders only after his death.[4] The appearance of this generation of leaders had a decisive influence on the geographic and demographic expansion of Hasidism, because each of them chose to promulgate the way of Hasidism in the region of Eastern Europe where he had lived before attending the Maggid's court. The geographic spread of Hasidism exposed a growing community to its spiritual message. As a result, members of the popular and less educated strata of society began to be attracted to the courts of the Hasidic leaders.

This development placed a new dilemma before the Hasidic leaders: could one impart the way of Hasidism to a broad community? Was it possible to translate a spiritual and religious message, which was originally elitist and exclusive, into messages suitable to the level of education and spiritual development of the popular classes? Each of the various leaders who struggled with this dilemma resolved it in his own way. Here I will focus on the way taken by RASHAZ.

A distinction can be made between two main tendencies that characterized the ways in which the Hasidic leaders dealt with the dilemma described above.

One approach, whose most prominent representative was Rabbi Elimelech of Lyzhansk, can be called popular Hasidism. Rabbi Elimelech developed the idea of the role of the Hasidic Tsadik as a bridge and intermediary between the Hasid and God. The Hasid is commanded to cleave to the Tsadik, as expressed in recognition of his authority, in obedience to his instructions, and in following his path. For his part, the Tsadik is naturally endowed with the ability to cleave to God. Thus, by virtue of cleaving to the Tsadik, the Hasid, too, cleaves to God. Evidently this form of Devekut (mystical cleaving to God) is not the kind of mystical experience that was central to the religious ethos of early Hasidism. It is also clear that the view of the Tsadik as bridging between the ordinary Hasid and God grew up following recognition that many of the new adherents to Hasidic circles were no longer able to attain Devekut on their own.

Another idea developed by Rabbi Elimelech, and which can also be seen as a decided sign of popular Hasidism, relates to the mission that the Tsadik was supposed to accomplish in relieving the anguish of the Hasidism. According to this idea, the Hasidic Tsadik is capable and even obligated to act by means of his prayer to supply the earthly needs of his Hasidim. Among other things, he was supposed to help them in matters of health, livelihood, and fertility. The expectation that the Hasidic Tsadik would indeed act to respond to the earthly needs of his Hasidim was typical of many Hasidic courts and became a typical component of Hasidic life.[5]

RASHAZ led the second current that emerged in response to the aforementioned dilemmas.[6] Unlike Rabbi Elimelech of Lyzhansk, RASHAZ did not believe that the Tsadik was supposed to mediate between the Hasid and God. He also rejected the view that the Tsadik was expected to provide for the earthly needs of the Hasidism. In his view, the Tsadik was a guide and instructor in the worship of God. In that capacity, he was able and obliged to show the Hasidim the purposes of Hasidic worship of God and to guide them with respect to the necessary means for achieving those goals. Moreover, the guidance that the Tsadik offered in connection to worshiping God, though it contains elements that relate to the generality of Hasidism, whoever they may be, it also has a personal component addressed to each individual Hasid. Thus, while the sanctified duty of guiding the Hasidim along the right path is incumbent upon the Tsadik, the main responsibility for seeking perfection in the worship of God lies upon the shoulders of the Hasidim themselves, and, to be precise, on the shoulders of each individual Hasid.

Like other leaders, RASHAZ also viewed the visit to the court as the proper framework for the experience of conversion. However, according to his view, it was not sufficient for the visitors to the court to be exposed to the Hasidic ethos as expressed in prayer, in shared meals, and in the sermon of the Tsadik. RASHAZ believed that in order to bring a new person into the circle of

Hasidic service of God, he had to meet with him individually in an extended and deep interview. This view underlay the regulations that RASHAZ instituted in the 1790s.

These regulations, which were intended to regulate the visits of Hasidim to the court, were a unique phenomenon in the history of Hasidim. The need to impose these regulations derived from the unbearable tension between the growing number of Hasidim who reached RASHAZ' court, determined in their desire for a personal interview with him, and the deep obligation that he felt toward the masses of "new" visitors who thronged his court and wanted to be counted among his Hasidim. The dilemma that RASHAZ confronted was, therefore: whether to continue to devote most of his time and energy to the veteran Hasidim, who sought to be received for another personal interview with him, or whether it was proper to devote himself to taking in the "new" Hasidim. The regulations that RASHAZ instituted left no room for doubt that he had chosen the latter path.

The main thrust of these regulations was that an "Old Hasid," that is to say, one who had already met with him individually, even just once, was permitted to visit the court to meet with him again only once a year. Moreover, only one Sabbath per month was set aside for visits of "Old Hasidim," whereas the other three Sabbaths were intended for "New Hasidim," those with whom he had not yet met individually even once. Four times a year were set aside for the gathering of all the Hasidim, but at these gatherings RASHAZ did not receive even a single Hasid individually, whether he was "old" or "new."

Another means used by RASHAZ to influence visitors to his court was the sermon. The Tsadik's sermon during the third meal on the Sabbath was a central event in every Hasidic court at that time. However, both RASHAZ and his Hasidim gave especially great weight to this sermon, as shown by their name for it: "the words of the living God" – no less and no more! In the eyes of RASHAZ and his Hasidim, this sermon was seen not only as a means of instruction and guidance in the proper way to serve God, but also as an experiential event whose purpose was to arouse spiritual motivation in the listeners' hearts to apply that way when they returned home.

Since RASHAZ believed that the Tsadik was no more than a guide in the service of God, and that the principal responsibility was placed on the Hasid himself, he gave great importance not only to the management of his court but also to what happened on the periphery, in the Hasidic *minyanim* (prayer groups) that were dispersed throughout White Russia and beyond. Being determined in his aspiration to influence the way of life and the manner of worship of the thousands of Hasidim who were connected to him, RASHAZ developed a system of communication, supervision, and enforcement. An important function was fulfilled by the "heads of the *minyanim*," local leaders who were active within each of the Hasidic *minyanim*. The heads of the *min-yanim*, who were chosen by RASHAZ himself, were responsible, among other things, for enforcing the regulations described above.

Communication with the Hasidim who dwelt in the periphery was based on emissaries and epistles. The emissaries whom RASHAZ sent to the *minya-nim* transmitted messages orally. Sometimes these concerned matters best left in secret. Among these one may mention relations with the authorities, the struggle against the Mitnagdim, and intra-Hasidic controversies – such as that with the Hasidic leader in the Land of Israel, Rabbi Abraham of Kalisc, and controversies among the Hasidim of RASHAZ themselves. Most probably some if not most of these messages were meant for influential individuals among the Hasidim, such as the heads of the *minyanim*. Another function filled by the emissaries was the gathering of information about the conduct of the *minyanim* and reporting to RASHAZ.

RASHAZ' epistles to the Hasidim were also borne by messengers. However, unlike an emissary who came and went, the epistle remained in the hands of its addressees, and it was possible to copy it, to disseminate it publicly, and to consult it repeatedly. About 110 of the many epistles sent by RASHAZ to the Hasidim are extant. In sorting and characterizing these letters, the first dis-tinction to be made is between those that were meant for the public at large, the general audience of Hasidim wherever they were, those addressed to Ha-sidim living in a certain community, and those addressed to individuals. The subjects addressed by the epistles to the generality of Hasidim were: collecting contributions for the Hasidim who lived in the Land of Israel; collections for the needy among the Jews of Russia and to cover the expenses of the court; instructions in the worship of God; directions and criticism of the behavior of the Hasidim in certain *minyanim*; instructions regarding the mutual relations between RASHAZ and his Hasidim; ordinances governing visits to the court. As for the letters sent to individuals, some are devoted to instruction in divine worship as well as to earthly matters. Other letters are connected to the struggle against the Mitnagdim or intra-Hasidic controversies. And some of the letters are personal recommendations to provide financial support to the bearer of the epistle.

Now we will present several of RASHAZ' letters to the Hasidim. The first letter to be cited here was sent to an individual Hasid, and it has come down to us without a date or the name of the addressee. However, examination of the letter brings out several outlines of the addressee's figure. He was appar-ently a merchant who imported wine from the Austrian Empire, among other things, a man with a learned background, who devoted time to the daily study of Torah. The addressee was closely connected to RASHAZ, visited his court from time to time, and maintained correspondence with him. Most likely he was one of the more important Hasidim connected with RASHAZ, for otherwise it is doubtful whether he would have merited a personal letter of this kind. Here is the letter:

> Behold this is for you because of weakening of the hands from dealing with the Torah, since it protects and saves also when one is not dealing with it. You also must practice some self-mortification, as, God willing, I will speak with you face to face. And the main thing is to endeavor with all your strength to keep what is written, "I have set the LORD always before me" (Ps. 16:8), meaning that what stands before me to devour me is the evil impulse, and it is from God, because God ordered it to test me, to know what is in my heart whether or not I will keep His commandments. And when a person habituates himself to this thought always, that all his thoughts that the evil impulse raises up are from the God from heaven to test him. And thereby the power of the evil impulse will be weakened and it will be very easy to triumph over it, as when God willing I will speak with you face to face.
>
> And regarding bringing wine across the border clandestinely, turn away from that path and do not endanger yourself in any manner or way in the world, and it would be better for you to earn little money without any danger, because there is no incapacity of God to save in great or small things. May God send you a blessing and success in the doings of your hands...
> Shneur Zalman.[7]

The first and principal part of this letter is devoted to instruction in the service of God, and in the second part RASHAZ answers a question from the area of mundane life. Although the Hasid's question regarding the worship of God is not extant, from RASHAZ' answer it appears clearly that it concerned "distracting thoughts." This refers to mundane thoughts, and in severe cases even sinful thoughts, that break into a person's consciousness when he is praying or studying Torah and distract him. The Hasid to whom this letter is addressed therefore asked RASHAZ advice about ridding himself of distracting thoughts.

The question of distracting thoughts disturbed kabbalists and Hasidim during the generations preceding the beginnings of Hasidism and have been discussed extensively in ethical literature.[8] The BESHT was the one who paved a new way in struggling with distracting thoughts.[9] The BESHT's innovation becomes clear against the background of the attitude that was prevalent on this matter among Kabbalists and Hasidim of the generation preceding him as well as of his contemporaries. They assumed that the source of distracting thoughts lay in the powers of the *sitra aḥra* (lit. the other side), that is to say, forces of pollution of metaphysical nature. Hence anyone in whose consciousness distracting thoughts had insinuated themselves must make an effort to drive them out as quickly as possible. Moreover, the tried and tested means to prevent distracting thoughts was asceticism, because the body and its pleasures were the place gripped by the *sitra ahra*.

The new way proposed by the BESHT to rid oneself of alien thought was based on the sweeping interpretation he gave to the dictum of the Zohar: "there is no place vacant of Him." Since the divine essence filled all the worlds, the source of distracting thoughts was therefore divine. Thus, it was not proper to drive them out and repress them, but rather to raise them up and attach them to their divine source. How then was it possible to raise up an alien thought? For that purpose creative thought was necessary, which had the power to change evil into good. For example, someone who was afflicted by a sinful thought because he saw a beautiful woman could ask himself: What is the source of that woman's beauty? It is only because the Holy One blessed be He, created her and gave her comeliness. Thus reflection on the woman's beauty leads to reflection on the greatness of the Creator, and thus the alien thought rises and joins its divine source.

At the foundation of this new approach lay, as noted, a sweeping conception of divine immanence. This conception entails the view that the evil impulse does not come from an independent demonic entity but that it is an educational tool created by God. RASHAZ adopts this Hasidic view and develops it in his own way. In place of the original instruction of the BESHT to raise distracting thoughts and attach them to their divine source, a complex and dangerous practice, RASHAZ proposes that the Hasid should recognize that the distracting thoughts that torment him are nothing but a kind of moral test set for him by God. RASHAZ makes this idea depend on a homiletic interpretation of the verse, "I have set the LORD always before me" (Ps. 16:8). The word "*negdi*," translated as "before me," can mean "against me," hinting that the evil impulse that apparently acts against a person is in truth a divine emissary. This recognition, so RASHAZ believes, will help the Hasid overcome the alien thoughts. We have before us a psychological stratagem based on the Hasidic doctrine of the divinity and influenced by the BESHT's approach with respect to distracting thoughts. Nevertheless, the instruction that RASHAZ gives the Hasid exemplifies the way he adapted Hasidic practice to the spiritual level of the Hasid whom he is addressing.[10]

In addition to the instruction so far discussed, RASHAZ recommends two additional means to the Hasid so that he can overcome the distracting thoughts: to study the Torah a lot, because the Torah has the capacity to protect a person from the evil impulse, and also to "practice some self-mortification." It is not impossible that this recommendation means to reduce sexual activity, based on the assumption that increased sexual activity leads to sinful thoughts. These two measures recommended by RASHAZ sound like what the Mitnagdim advocated. The view that specifically Torah study is a tried and true method to overcome the evil impulse played a central role in the teaching of the Vilna Gaon and his followers. The recommendation of asceticism also sounds rather typical of the Vilna Gaon's teachings and contrary to the attitude of the BESHT and his disciples. Thus we find that the spiritual and religious world of Hasidism was more varied and complex than is usually acknowledged. In any event, the main instruction that RASHAZ offered to his Hasid was decidedly "Hasidic" in character.

It is noteworthy that in this short letter, RASHAZ included the phrase, "when God willing I will speak with you face to face," twice. Most likely his written message was merely a partial and temporary answer, and the Hasid was to receive the main instruction when he met with his Rebbe face to face. The present letter, like others, shows that a few of the Hasidim were not satisfied with the instruction they received from RASHAZ when they met with him individually, and they corresponded with him between one visit to the court and another.

As noted, the second part of the epistle relates to a question that the Hasid asked about mundane matters. RASHAZ justifies his recommendation not to smuggle wine by the danger to the Hasid if he were caught, and the argument that one must obey the laws of the kingdom is lacking. Evidently RASHAZ knew his flock and realized that such an argument would not be heeded, since many Jews in the Pale of Settlement were forced to violate the laws of the kingdom to support their families. In the end it should be noted that the letter under discussion represents a fact known to us from many other sources: the Hasidim who sought guidance from RASHAZ in worshiping God also wanted his advice on earthly matters.

Having discussed a letter addressed to a single Hasid, we shall now turn to letters that were sent to all the members of a Hasidic *minyan* in a certain community. We shall focus on two epistles, one sent to the members of the Hasidic *minyan* of Kapost, and the other addressed to members of the Hasidic *minyan* in Bichov. Both letters relate to the matter of prayer and in each of them RASHAZ is responding to a "rumor" that he heard, i.e. a report that he had received, regarding the behavior of the Hasidic at prayer in that *minyan*. In the first epistle RASHAZ reproaches the Hasidim, and in the second he praises them. Both letters demonstrate the supervision and instruction imparted by RASHAZ to dozens of Hasidic *minyanim* dispersed throughout White Russia. First we shall consider the reproachful epistle sent to the Hasidim of Kapost[11]

> My beloved brethren and comrades… who stand upon the Torah and upon worship in the holy community of Kapost, may God protect it, may the Lord bless you with life forever.

Behold the rumor is not good, which have I heard as the voice of them that cry for being overcome [Ex. 32:18], to answer with the stillest of still small voices [1 Kings 19:12] ... This is short prayer, and in a place where they are meant to prolong the dispositions of the heart [Prov. 16:1], let them be spoken arranged in all one's bones. And from the Lord the answer of the tongue speaks great and marvelous things, in accord with praises and songs. And it is not of you that our Sages of blessed memory said, "when the vilest men are exalted," [Ps. 12:9] these are the things that stand highest in the world, and people are contemptuous of them, and Rashi interprets that this is prayer that rises upward.

And it would not appear to be understandable how prayer that rises up is different from all Torah study and keeping of the commandments with awe and love, which rises upward. However, because without awe and fear they do not rise upward, and when prayer rises upward it raises all the Torah and commandments and their blessings and the blessings on pleasures and grace after meals that a studious person recites every day... Therefore my beloved brothers and comrades, be very very strong and courageous, according to the saying of the Sages of blessed memory, that prayer needs reinforcement, that when a person struggles with his enemy he needs to be strengthened with all courage and power and intensity, for the time of prayer is also a time of battle. And as in human wars all the people in the war must gather in one place, all of them must gather strength together, and not one here and one there, so, too, in prayer, there must be at least ten, all of them starting from "Blessed be He who said" and so on, and each person must assist his fellow and his brother and speak strongly in a strong voice to unite as one and raise a single voice.

This they must take upon themselves utterly, without an oath, and God will reward them as He promised us and receive with mercy and good will their worship and hear their prayer.

Shneur Zalman son of our teacher Rabbi Baruch of blessed memory

The admonishments in the first part of the letter are clarified in the light of the instructions that RASHAZ imparted to his Hasidim regarding the manner of holding public prayer. According to these instructions, which are alluded to in the latter part of the epistle, all the participants in a prayer quorum must gather around the prayer leader and, together with him, recite the formula of the prayer, word by word, out loud, from beginning to end.[12] This model was meant to provide an external framework for the inner experience of each of the worshipers. As we shall see below, RASHAZ attributed a decisive role to prayer in the service of God. During prayer the worshiper is expected to contemplate the greatness of the Creator. This contemplation arouses in the worshiper's soul feelings of love and awe of God, and these impel him to keep the positive commandments of the Torah and to be careful not to violate negative commandments.

The opening lines of the letter show that RASHAZ had received a report stating that the Hasidim of Kapost were not diligent in fulfilling the instructions regarding public prayer. In seeking to arouse the Hasidim to acknowledge the special virtue of prayer, RASHAZ develops an idea that he attributes to Rashi's commentary on a saying of the Sages cited in the epistle: "'when the vilest men are exalted,' [Ps. 12:9], these are the things that stand highest in the world, and people are contemptuous of them, and Rashi interprets that this is prayer that rises upward." RASHAZ challenges Rashi's statement: is it only prayer that rises upward? For all the Torah that a person studies and all the commandments that he observes – they all rise upward. And he answers: the study of Torah and the commandments that are not accompanied by proper intentions do not rise upward. Prayer, however, when it is recited with awe and love, also raises Torah study and the commandments with it, though they had not risen for lack of proper intention.

In the last part of the epistle, RASHAZ encourages the Hasidim to hold public prayer according to his instructions, and to that end he compares prayer to a battle. Just as, in time of battle, soldiers gather together and strengthen one another, so, too, in prayer. This comparison might seem surprising, because who is the enemy against whom one fights during prayer? We find that RASHAZ attributes great power to every one of the factors that impede prayer with proper intention. A person who is disturbed by mundane routine is expected to extricate himself from it and attain very powerful spiritual awakening, and he is to do so every day. To that end, RASHAZ believed that a huge spiritual effort was required, like the effort during battle. In light of this estimation, RASHAZ wished to make the *minyan* a kind of support group: when all of the worshipers stand together and recite the prayer out loud, and, of course, to a melody that expresses the heart's intentions – the combination of all these helps each individual to attain the required emotional arousal. RASHAZ concludes the letter with a request, or rather a demand, that the Hasidim of Kapost "take upon themselves utterly," that is to say, that they commit themselves to him, that henceforth they will hold public prayer in the manner of his instruction.

The second epistle, addressed to the Hasidim of Bichov, also deals, as noted, with prayer, but it is replete with words of praise. Incidentally, reading of this epistle also reveals interesting facts about the function of the emissary who bore the letter, which follows: [13]

After wishing you well in the manner of those who love His name, I will bless the good and beneficent Lord for the good rumor that that my soul heard and was revived, and who believed our rumor, which was told to me by our friend a faithful ambassador, the deliverer of this letter, about every single one, great and small, all of whom raise their souls to God, each person according to his value, and to be strengthened with full power and intensity in Torah and in worship in the heart, which is prayer, to observe all the oaths of the written covenant written in the register and the memorial book before God always, each man as he can bear it, and the weak will say I am a hero. My eyes saw and my heart was happy, and I thank God with all my heart for the past, and a request for the future, may God give you and continue to strengthen and bolster their hearts to raise up sanctity and not to bring it down, perish the thought. And each man should help his fellow and say to his brother, let us be strong and strengthen ourselves, according to the dictum of the Sages of blessed memory, that prayer needs reinforcement, to be reinforced with all strength, the way men of war reinforce themselves truly against their enemies, with whole heart and soul truly until the actual exhaustion of the soul...

And as I speak I shall remember for the good our friend the deliverer of this letter, may his candle be bright, lest he be a burden on the men of our confidence to receive his words with love and good will, even if he sometimes speaks too much to you and does not supply you with judgment sometimes, because love distorts judgment. And therefore do not remove your love from him forever. And regarding your questions, I have put words into his mouth. May God fulfill all your wishes for the best.

Shneur Zalman the son of our rabbi Baruch of blessed memory for life in the world to come

This letter also begins by relating to a report that RASHAZ had received from the emissary, but this time the report was decidedly positive. The Hasidim of Bichov endeavor and succeed in holding public prayer according to their rabbi's commandments. RASHAZ' statement that the emissary told him "about every single one, great and small" is noteworthy, for it shows that the report related not only to the *minyan* in general but also to its individual members. Consequently, RASHAZ, too, saw fit to direct his words of praise to each individual Hasid, and it is easy to imagine what educational consideration underlay this move. However, being a public leader who knows the souls of his followers, RASHAZ does not delude himself into believing that the achievements of the past are a guarantee for the future. Therefore he urges the Hasidim of Bichov to make an effort to maintain the achievement, and, if possible, to rise to a higher level. In this epistle as well RASHAZ compares prayer to battle, and here, too, he repeats the recommendation that "each man should help his fellow."

As noted, the details revealed in this epistle regarding the function of the emissary are especially interesting. In the latter part of the epistle, RASHAZ addresses the Hasidim and urges them to accept the words of the emissary "with love and good will," even if he "sometimes speaks too much to you and does not supply you with judgment." RASHAZ continues to defend the emissary with the argument that "love distorts judgment." It is not impossible that these words are a response to complaints about the emissary's coarse behavior that reached RASHAZ. In any event, the present letter clearly shows that the emissaries sent by RASHAZ to the Hasidic *minyanim* were not simply letter carriers who delivered and received messages. Rather, it appears that these emissaries played leadership roles in the name of RASHAZ and under his aegis. On further reflection, this appears to be almost self-evident, for it is difficult to imagine an emissary bearing instructions to Hasidim and answers to their questions who did not act, to one degree or another, as an independent personality while he stood alone before the Hasidim, far from RASHAZ' court. Thus we find that the emissaries and the epistles were two complementary means of supervision and instruction. The advantage of the emissaries was expressed in their ability to transmit messages best kept in secret, to negotiate with the members of the Hasidic *minyan*, and of course to report to RASHAZ about the behavior of the Hasidim in the various *minyanim*. The advantage of the epistles lay in that they remained in the hands of the Hasidim and were circulated among them in many copies. The combination of emissaries and epistles gave RASHAZ a considerable degree of control and influence over the lives of the Hasidim who were dispersed in the periphery.

As noted, another type of epistle was that addressed to all the Hasidim. One such letter was sent around 1796 and received among the Hasidim as an introduction to the Tanya. Here is the letter:[14]

> To you, men, I call, listen to me those who pursue righteousness and seek God, may God heed you, and from great to small, all our fellow HABAD Hasidim in our country and the ones neighboring it, may every person come to his place in safety and life forever...
>
> Behold this view is accepted by everyone, by all our fellow HABAD Hasidim , saying: that hearing words of ethical teachings is not the same as seeing and reading in books. For the reader reads in his own manner and according to his own understanding and the capability of his intellect, wherever he might be. And if his intellect and understanding are confused and walk in darkness in the worship of God, he can barely see the good light hidden in books, although the light is sweet to the eyes and heals the soul. Furthermore, books of ethics that are constructed according to human understanding certainly are not accessible to everyone. Because all intellects and all opinions are not equal, and one man's intellect is not impressed and aroused by what his friend's intellect is aroused... And as Nachmanides of blessed memory wrote in *Wars of God* in the commentary of the Sifri about Joshua, of whom it is said: "A man in whom the spirit is," that he can go against the spirit of every single person etc. But even in ethical books, whose foundations are in the holy mountains of Midrashim of the Sages of blessed memory, in whom the spirit of God speaks and His word is on their tongue, and the Torah and the Holy One blessed be He is all one, and all six-hundred-thousand of the people of Israel, and their individuals are attached to the Torah, and the Torah joins them to the Holy One blessed be He, as is made known in the

holy Zohar... for this is the way of inclusion to include the whole of Israel. And although the Torah was given to be interpreted in general and in minute details for each individual soul of Israel that is rooted in it, a person does not have the merit of knowing his private place in the Torah. ...

But since we are speaking of people that I know and am acquainted with, each one of them are men of our fellow HABAD Hasidim in our countries and those nearby them, and the word of affection was among us and they revealed to me all the mysteries of their heart and brain in worship of God that depends on the heart. To them my word will drip and my tongue the pen of a scribe in this book, which is called *Liqutei omrim* (collections of sayings), gathered from books and from authors of highest sanctity and their soul is in paradise, and they are famous among us. And some of them are hinted to the wise in the holy epistles from our rabbis in the Holy Land. And some of them I heard from their holy mouth when they were with us here. And all of them are answers to many questions of people asking for advice, all the men of our fellow HABAD Hasidim in our country, each according to his value to give advice in their soul in the worship of God.

Since the time does not permit anymore to reply to every single one to his question in private, and there is also forgetfulness, therefore I wrote all the answer here to all the questions to be kept as a sign to be for everyone and a memorial between his eyes. And he will no longer press to enter and speak with me alone because in them he will find solace for his soul and correct advice for every difficulty for him in the worship of God... And he whose mind is limited to understand a word of advice from these writings will lay his conversation before the great ones in his city, and they will give him understanding. And to them I asked not to put a hand before their mouth and to act in modesty and humility of a lie, perish the thought...

Shneur Zalman

RASHAZ begins this epistle by pointing out the agreement among the Hasidim, that is: it is immeasurably preferable to hear ethical teachings from a rabbi, meaning, of course, a Hasidic Tsadik, than from books. Afterward RASHAZ presents reasons in support of this opinion. A person in spiritual distress is unable to attain the benefit present in ethical books. Moreover, ethical works, which "are constructed according to human understanding," relate to readers in general and therefore they cannot influence each individual according to the leanings of his soul. The Hasidic Tsadik, by contrast, is endowed with the ability of Joshua, of whom the Midrash says: "'A man in whom the spirit is,' that he can go against the spirit of every single person." Like Joshua, the Hasidic Tsadik can direct his words to each individual according to his needs. It would appear that this ability is also found in ethical works, whose "foundations are in the holy mountains" – that is to say in kabbalistic works of moral instruction, because this literature is like the word of God, and every single Jew is connected metaphysically to the Holy One blessed be He and to his Torah. However, in order for the individual to know "his private place in the Torah," that is to say, the special message for him inherent in the Torah, he needs the instruction of the Hasidic Tsadik.

All of these arguments imply that the individual seeking instruction in worship of God needs the personal guidance of a Hasidic Tsadik. As noted, this was the goal of the personal interviews – the meetings that RASHAZ held with his Hasidism. However, RASHAZ goes on to make a surprising move: claiming that he is no longer able to devote the necessary time to personal meetings with the Hasidim, he therefore asks them to relate to the *Tanya* as a book of instruction to replace the personal interview. Most likely the consideration behind this decision was the same one that led RASHAZ when he imposed the regulations intended to limit and regulate the visits of Hasidim to his court. As noted, seeing the increase in "new" Hasidim streaming to his court, RASHAZ decided to limit the visits of veteran Hasidim. One way or another, the call to the Hasidim to relate to the instruction embedded in the *Tanya* as a substitute for the instruction given in personal interviews is surprising and, needless to say, it is in entire contradiction to what was said at the beginning of the letter.

RASHAZ was of course aware of this difficulty, and he tried to resolve it with various arguments. First, he claimed that his book was able to fulfill its task because it was intended for Hasidim whom he knew intimately, and "all the mysteries of their heart and brain in worship of God" were known to him. He also argues that his book is merely a collection of the words "gathered from books and from authors of highest sanctity," that is to say Kabbalists and books of Kabbala. Finally he also refers to "our rabbis in the Holy Land," claiming that some of the words in his book depend on their letters. This is a reference to the epistles sent by Rabbi Mena<u>h</u>em Mendel of Vitebsk and Rabbi Abraham of Kalisc from the Land of Israel to the Hasidim in White Russia.[15] However, all of these arguments cannot dull the sharpness of the change in direction that RASHAZ announces: from now on the *Tanya* will serve as a book of instruction in the worship of God, to accompany every one of the Hasidim during his daily life. This book is intended to replace, at least to a degree, personal interviews with RASHAZ.

I will now focus on the *Tanya*, or, as it is officially titled, "The Book of the *Beinonim* [Average Man]." This book, regarded as the most important work by RASHAZ, was first printed in 1797, although manuscript copies of it were circulated earlier among the Hasidim.[16] The *Tanya* is an effort to guide the reader in the path of Hasidic service of God in a systematic and comprehensive manner unparalleled in the history of Hasidism. Most of the books published in the first stages of Hasidism were books of sermons. Although they contained ideas that marked a new direction in the service of God, they were fragmentary, and the structure of the discussion was associative. Even the Hasidic books of *hanhagot* (ethical instruction), which contained practical instructions in the service of God, did not pretend to present a full system and include every possible matter. The *Tanya*, by contrast, offers an entire, comprehensive system of theoretical propositions, the actions required in the light of those propositions, and detailed instructions regarding their implementation. Moreover, the structure of the work and the many rhetorical devices invested in it indicate the huge effort made by the author to make it useful to readers. In a sense the *Tanya* can be viewed as an ethical work, because it is intended to guide the reader toward spiritual elevation and ethical self-improvement. However, the book is unique because the author filled it with kabbalistic and Hasidic elements, which he adapted and combined in a new systematic structure. The *Tanya* therefore embodies the Hasidic way of serving God as RASHAZ saw fit to present it to the reader.[17]

A thorough and comprehensive discussion of the *Tanya* is of course beyond the scope of this article. Hence I will merely present several central ideas. The educational outlook of RASHAZ is anchored in the kabbalistic doctrine of the soul, mainly as formulated in the writings of Rabbi Ḥayyim Vital. This choice reflects the assumption that understanding the structure of the soul and its activity according to this doctrine is vital for anyone who wishes to adopt the Hasidic way of serving God. The fundamental principle of the kabbalistic doctrine of the soul is that two souls dwell in the human body: a animal soul and a divine soul. The animal soul draws its vitality from the *Qelipa* (the contaminated "shells" and the *Sitra Aḥra* (lit. the "other side"), the force of evil and the source of all the evil qualities manifest in a person. The divine soul, as its name indicates, has its source in the divinity. This soul contains the powers that lead a person to serve God. Having stated this principle, RASHAZ explains that with respect to the spiritual quality of those souls, they are divided into a vast number of degrees, beginning from the highest degree of the soul of Moses down to the lowest degree of "the masses and the ignorant." However, the root of all souls, even the lowest of them, is in the divinity itself.[18] Hence, even lowly people have a chance of attaining spiritual elevation.

The question that must now be asked is: what role does the divine soul play in the service of God? This matter is made clear in the description of the various parts of the soul and the reciprocal relations among them as presented by RASHAZ. Along the way he also clarified the idea underlying the name "Habad," Hebrew initials that designate the Hasidic trend that RASHAZ headed.

He stated that the divine soul, which dwells within every Jewish person, has ten aspects, which represent the ten upper *sefirot* (aspects of the divinity), and they symbolize the divine world. Those ten aspects are divided into two groups: *ḥokhma*, *bina*, and *daʾat* (wisdom, understanding, and knowledge) correspond to the first three *sefirot*; and, similarly with respect to the seven lower *sefirot*: *ḥesed, gevura, tiferet* (mercy, power, and splendor), etc. In the opinion of RASHAZ, this division reflects the two different aspects in the human soul: the first three aspects, *ḥokhma, bina*, and *daʾat*, represent the activity of cognition and intellectual understanding, whereas the other seven *sefirot* represent *midot*, a concept which refers to emotional tendencies or psychological characteristics that motivate human action.

When a person contemplates and comes to know the greatness of God with his intellect and realizes that God "fills all the worlds," and therefore there is no reality with independent status that is not included in the divinity and nourished by it – when a person understands all of this, the emotions of fear of God and love of God are aroused in his soul. Those two emotions play a decisive role in motivating a person to serve God, because fear deters him from committing forbidden actions and love motivates him to perform positive commandments.

We find that RASHAZ distinguishes between two basic components of the soul, the intellectual-cognitive component and the emotional component. His innovation is expressed in the statement of the relation between them: intellectual contemplation of the greatness of God, which is attained by means of the three upper aspects of the soul, *ḥokhma, bina*, and *daʾat* (the initials of which form the acronym "Habad"), gives rise to the emotions that motivate a person to serve God by keeping the commandments.[19]

We shall now consider the meaning that RASHAZ attributes to keeping the commandments. According to the kabbalistic doctrine of the soul, every soul has three *levushim* (garments): thought, speech, and action. These *levushim* are outer manifestations of the soul. The concept of *levush* is ambivalent. On the one hand, it has an element of revelation, but at the same time it expresses concealment. The three divine manifestations of the soul are necessarily connected to the 613 commandments. That is to say, they are manifest solely in relation to the 613 commandments: either by *doing* the commandment or by *speech* connected to Torah study, or by *thought* that comprehends the Torah. Therefore, when a person performs the commandments, a metaphysical connection is produced between his divine soul and the commandments. What is the meaning of that connection? The answer to that question is inherent in the way in which RASHAZ interpreted the kabbalistic idea called *tsimtsum* (contraction). Basing himself on a statement in the Zohar, *oraita vekudsha brikh hu kula ḥad* (the Torah and the Holy One, blessed be He, are all one), RASHAZ explains *tsimtsum* in the following way:

> And the Holy One, blessed be He, contracted His will and His wisdom in the 613 commandments and in their laws, and in the combination of the letters of the

Bible and their interpretation in parables and homiletics of our Sages of blessed memory, so that every soul or spirit and psyche in a person's body can understand them with his mind and keep as much as it is possible to keep of them in action, speech, and thought.[20]

These words reveal the mystical meaning of the service of God. The three *levushim* of the soul, when they are connected to the Torah by observance of the commandments (action) and Torah study (speech and thought), they are in truth connected to the Holy One, blessed be He, Himself. Cleaving to God by means of keeping the commandments and Torah study is therefore the highest goal of the service of God.

We have found that keeping the commandments and Torah study are means of attachment to God. One may then ask: What then is the place and function of prayer in the teaching of RASHAZ? Early Hasidism gave prayer a senior position and relegated the study of Torah to secondary status.[21] The prayer that served as a model and source of inspiration was that of the BESHT, during which he experienced mystical ecstasy.[22] RASHAZ also gave prayer a central place. In the testimony that he gave to the Russian government authorities when he was arrested and interrogated in 1798, he claimed that prayer with intention was a central matter in Hasidism, and it was the reason for the movement's emergence.[23] The centrality of prayer was also expressed in the special instructions that RASHAZ gave to the Hasidic *minyanim* that accepted his authority. According to them, morning prayers were supposed to last a long time, and all the members of the *minyan* were to cluster around the prayer leader and pronounce the words of the prayer one by one, out loud.[24] What then was the function that RASHAZ accorded to prayer?

It may be said that in his eyes, prayer was the main motive force driving the process of the service of God, because the intellectual contemplation of the greatness of God, following which the emotions of awe and love are aroused in a person's soul, was supposed to take place during prayer. As noted, these emotions are what motivate a person to be diligent in observing the commandments. However, the emotions of awe and love have additional role. RASHAZ repeatedly calls those emotions "wings," meaning: they bear the doing of the commandments, the study of Torah, and prayer and raise them to upper realms. Moreover, these emotions are a kind of intention accompanying the totality of the service of God, and the contents of this intention is the aspiration to cling to God and merge with Him. This aspiration is directed of course by the image of God "filling all worlds."

Who, then, was the audience that RASHAZ addressed? The attempt to answer that question leads us to discuss one of the most important innovations of RASHAZ. I refer to the term *beinoni*, which is central to the *Tanya*. Indeed, let us recall that the official title of the book is, "The Book of the *beinoniim*."[25]

The definition of *beinoni* is derived from that of the Tsadik (the righteous man), on the one hand, and the Rasha' (the wicked man) on the other. The Tsadik, in the view of RASHAZ, is someone who not only fully observes all of the commandments of the Torah but also has no tendency to sin in his soul. The divine soul rules over the animal soul in such a person without any limitations, and for that reason he has no evil impulse at all. However, the high level of the Tsadik cannot be acquired. Rather it is inborn. Only someone who has been privileged to receive a gift of grace from God is a Tsadik, and the soul of the Tsadik is planted in him from birth. Hence, not surprisingly, in every generation there are very few Tsadikim. The Rasha' is someone who is not reluctant to violate the commandments of the Torah consciously. The actions and conduct of such a person are directed by the instincts and appetites that dwell in the animal soul. The way lies open before the wicked person to repent, a topic with which RASHAZ deals at length. After describing the level of the Tsadik, on the one hand, and of the Rasha, on the other, RASHAZ turns to a definition of the *beinoni*. The *beinoni* keeps all the commandments of the Torah fully. Nevertheless, unlike the Tsadik, the evil impulse still dwells within him. In other words: his animal soul continues to tempt him to violate the commandments of the Torah. As a result, the main task incumbent upon the *beinoni* is constant struggle with the evil impulse in order to suppress it. In terms of the kabbalistic doctrine of the soul, the *beinoni* is someone in whom a mighty battle is waged between the two souls. The task of the *beinoni* is to win that battle so that the divine soul will rule over the animal soul.

Hence the *beinoni* level is quite high and involves a powerful and incessant psychological struggle, so the question arises: who can be *beinoni*? The answer proposed by RASHAZ is unequivocal: any person can be *beinoni*. He repeats this claim many times. What is the source of the optimism shown by RASHAZ on this matter?

As noted, RASHAZ assumes that the intellect can arouse the desired emotions of love and awe in the soul. By virtue of these emotions, a person can vanquish his evil impulse, keep the positive commandments, and avoid stumbling in negative commandments. That is to say: RASHAZ is convinced that a person who wishes to do so can make his intellect control his emotions. In this respect the difference between RASHAZ and Rabbi Israel Salanter (1810-1883), the founder of the Musar Movement, is conspicuous. Rabbi Israel also struggled with the question of how to motivate the soul to serve God. However, unlike RASHAZ, who trusted the intellect, Rabbi Israel argued that unconscious emotional impulses control the human soul, and that they are capable of vanquishing the intellect. Moreover, he believed that emotional urges were capable of harnessing the intellect to their chariot so that it would find explanations and excuses to justify deviant behavior.[26]

Seeing the difference between these two men, one wonders what was the source of RASHAZ' optimism regarding the moral potential inherent in the intellect? Or, alternatively, what was the source of Rabbi Israel Salanter's pessimism about the intellect? The answer to these questions lies in their different attitudes toward the Kabbalistic doctrine of the soul. RASHAZ, who believed in this doctrine, had no doubt that the cognitive abilities that dwell in man's divine soul drew their vitality from the *sefirot* of Wisdom, Understanding, and Knowledge. Therefore they are capable of grappling with evil and overcoming it. By contrast, Rabbi Israel Salanter, consciously severed himself from the Kabbalistic doctrine of the soul, and in its place he adopted a view that sees the soul as a natural organism on its own. In the absence of a divine soul, it is not possible to depend on the intellect to lead men along the straight path. Therefore, Rabbi Israel Salanter was forced to rely upon fear of punishment as the spiritual force that is capable of restraining the appetites.

I will now summarize my remarks and try to answer the questions with which I began. Who was the audience that RASHAZ addressed? The central role that RASHAZ intended for the *Tanya* was to be a book of instructions for the Hasidim, and the characteristics of the book leave no room for doubt that RASHAZ envisioned an audience with considerable rabbinical education. His decision to base the book on the kabbalistic doctrine of the soul and to include in it important elements of the kabbalistic theology was not self-evident. Indeed, this decision was a subject of blunt criticism on the part of several Hasidic leaders, who disagreed with the path of RASHAZ. Those leaders, the most prominent of whom was Rabbi Abraham of Kalisc, argued that one should not reveal the secrets of the Kabbala to the general public of Hasidim, and that their spiritual instruction should be based on pure and simple faith.[27] By contrast, RASHAZ was convinced that it was impossible to lead the Hasidim to spiritual and religious elevation without exposing them to basic knowledge of Kabbala. However, that outlook assumes implicitly that the community of Hasidim was capable of digesting esoteric knowledge of that kind.

Another consideration that must be taken into account is the language and style of the *Tanya*. The book is written in *leshon hakodesh* (Hebrew with Aramaic elements), most of the discussions included in it are theoretical in nature and demand a high level of abstraction, and, in addition, there are many discussions of a scholarly nature. Indeed, RASHAZ assumed that not all the members of the community of his Hasidim could easily master the book. Therefore he created groups for guided study of the *Tanya*, both in his court and in various *minyanim*. Nevertheless, it is difficult to imagine that people belonging to the stratum of "the masses," people whose education did not go beyond elementary study in the *khayder*, were capable of taking part in those study groups.

The definition of the *beinoni* and the statement that the book was intended for the *beinonim* indicate the spiritual level of the target audience that RAS-HAZ addressed. True, RASHAZ repeatedly stated that anyone is capable of being *beinoni*. Moreover, he also distinguished among various levels of *beinonim*. Nevertheless, the spiritual and religious ideal embodied in the *beinoni* is, without doubt, extremely demanding. I do not wish to argue that RAS-HAZ turned his back on common people whose educational level was low and who did not fit the ideal of the *beinoni*. On the contrary, he certainly was interested in having a beneficial influence on such people as well. However, it seems to me that RASHAZ wanted the primary kernel of his Hasidim to be composed of men with rabbinical education. In conclusion, at a time when members of the common and uneducated classes of society began to be drawn to the circles of Hasidism, and when some Hasidic leaders were willing to adapt their messages to the level of those strata, RASHAZ continued to maintain the view that Hasidic service of God was mainly suited to the educated stratum of Jewish society.

What about the content and character of the Hasidic path that Rashaz sought to impart to his Hasidim? The outlines of that path are sharpened by comparison to the Kabbala and to early Hasidism. The mighty struggle between the powers of holiness and those of the *sitra aḥra*, which takes place on the metaphysical level according to the Kabbala of the ARI, was transferred by RASHAZ to within the Hasid's soul. Indeed, the transformation of concepts and ideas, which had metaphysical meaning in their original kabbalistic context, into psychological terms was characteristic of early Hasidism. This change implies the transfer of attention from the theosophical level to the human level. Placing man at the center and the aspiration to lead him to maximal realization of the powers inherent in him, a move that was typical of eighteenth century Enlightenment, also found expression in Hasidism. RASHAZ continued and sharpened that tendency by giving it a systematic character. In the wake of this change, the meaning of the service of God was altered. Whereas Kabbalists sought to act in the upper worlds in order to bring down *shefa* (divine abundance) or to advance the metaphysical process of *tikkun*, the main challenge placed by RASHAZ before his Hasidim was to have the divine soul within them rule over the animal soul. The practical significance of this decision was the maximal observance of the commandments of the Torah.

What about the mystical ideal of *devekut*, which was so central in early Hasidism? Was *the devekut* to which RASHAZ sought to lead the *beinoni* a mystical experience? The *beinoni* must be aware of the possibility that his worship could lead to *devekut*, and he must intend that and strive for it. However, when he succeeds, at the end of the process, in attaining *devekut* – does he have the experience of direct proximity to God? Can he even reach the experience of *bitul* (self-annihilation) and absorption into the divine?

In describing the high level of love of God, RASHAZ used the image of "flames of fire and powerful blaze rising upward, and to be separated from the wick and the wood that it grasps." Similarly he used erotic imagery such as "sick with love," and "extinction of the soul." These and similar images, which are dispersed among the chapters of the *Tanya*, show that RASHAZ did indeed aspire to lead the *beinoni* to *devekut*, and that it is a mystical experience. Nevertheless, this is the highest level of love of God, a level which is evidently attained by very few among the *beinoniim*. The mystical dimension of the experience *of devekut* is therefore possible, though it is doubtful whether it is conceived of as characteristic of the worship of a *beinoni*, and certainly it is not a necessary condition for achieving *devekut*.

The ideal of the *beinoni*, which RASHAZ presented to his Hasidim is extremely demanding. This is so not only because conduct consistent with the Halakha while repressing and restraining the evil impulse is no small matter, but also because the system of RASHAZ leaves no middle ground between commandments and prohibitions. According to the kabbalistic doctrine of the soul, a person necessarily acts either upon the inspiration of the divine soul or else he is led astray by the temptations of the animal soul. Moreover, in seeking to strengthen the influence of the divine soul and to weaken that of the animal soul, RASHAZ instructed his Hasidim to sanctify themselves with what was permitted to them, meaning that they were instructed to take upon themselves prohibitions and obligations beyond the demands of Halakhah.

In summary, in the *Tanya,* RASHAZ presented a revised and original version of Hasidism, with the intention of making it appropriate to the community of Hasidim who gathered in his court and wished to hear words of Torah from his mouth. This was no longer a kind of Hasidism appropriate for limited circles of mystics, nor was it a popular Hasidism like that of the school of Elimelech of Lyzhansk and others like him. The Hasidism shaped by RASHAZ, which came to be known as Habad, addressed men with rabbinical education and placed a demanding but not impossible spiritual and religious challenge before them.

I will conclude with a final observation: central to the activity of RASHAZ as an educator was the individual person, the Hasid capable of attaining the level of the *beinoni*. RASHAZ took upon himself the task of guiding and leading that Hasid, bringing him to know his goal and to believe in his ability to attain it. Underlying this educational process was RASHAZ' belief in the individual's moral autonomy and in his ability to chose the good and overcome evil.

NOTES

1. On the Tsadik in Hasidism, see Jacob Katz, Tradition and Crisis: Jewish society at the End of the Middle Ages; translated and with an afterword and bibliography by Bernard Dov Cooperman. New York: New York University Press, 1993, ch. 21-22. Shmuel Ettinger, "Hasidic Leadership in Formation," in *Dat vehevra betoldot Yisrael ubetoldot ha'amim*. Jerusalem: The Israel Historical Society, 1965, pp. 121-131 (Hebrew). Samuel H. Dresner, The Zaddik: The Doctrine of the Zaddik according to the Writings of Rabbi Yaakov Yosef of Polnoy (New York: Shocken Books, 1974). Ada Rapoport-Albert, "God and the Zaddik as the Two Focal Points of Hasidic Worship," *History of Religions*, 18, 4 (1979), pp. 296-325. Arthur Green, "Typologies of Leadership and the Hasidik Zaddik, in: Arthur Green (ed.), Jewish Spirituality: From the Sixteen-Century Revival to the Present, vol. 2 (New York: Crossroad, 1987) pp. 127–156.

2. See Immanuel Etkes, *The Hasidic Movement at its Inception*, Tel Aviv: 1998, pp. 57-67 (Hebrew).

3. Immanuel Etkes," The Early Hasidic Court", in: Text and Context: essays in Modern Jewish History and Historiography in Honor of Ismar Schorsch, ed. E. Lederhendler and J. Wertheimer (New York: Jewish Theological Seminary, 2005), pp. 157 - 186.

4. Ada Rapoport-Albert, Hasidism after 1772: Structural Continuity and Change, in: Ada Rapoport-Albert (ed.), Hasidism Reappraised, (The Littman Library of Jewish Civilization) London 1996, pp. 76-140; Immanuel Etkes, "Rabbi Shneur Zalman of Lyady's rise to a Position of Leadership," *Tarbiz* 54 (1985), pp. 429-439 (Hebrew).

5. On the teachings of Rabbi Elimelech of Lyzhansk, see Gedaliya Nigal (ed.), *R. Elimelech of Lyzhansk, Noam Elimelch*, Jerusalm, 1978, Introductio, pp. 10-56.

6. See Immanuel Etkes, "R. Shneur Zalman of Lyadi as a Leader of Hasidism," *Zion* (1985), pp. 321-354 (Hebrew).

7. *Igrot Kodesh, meet Kevod Kedushat ADMOR hazaken*, New York, 1980 (henceforth *Igrot Kodesh)*, epistle 91, p. 189.

8. See Mendel Piekarz, *In the Days of theEmergence of Hasidism, Tendencies and Ideas in Books of Sermons and Ethics*, Jerusalem, 1978, pp. 269-276 (Hebrew).

9. See Isaiah Tishby and Joseph Dan, "The Doctrine of Hasidism and its Literature," *Haentsiklopedia ha'ivrit* vol. 17, Jerusalem and Tel Aviv, 1965, pp. 785-786. Joseph Weiss, "The Beginning of the Growth of Hasidism," *Zion* 15 (1951), pp. 88-103 (Hebrew). Immanuel Etkes, The Besht, Magician, Mystic and Leader, (Brandeis University Press), Hanover and London 2005, pp. 144-147.

10. For words in similar spirit but formulated as a directive to all the Hasidism, see *Tanya, Sefer shel Beinonim*, ch. 27.

11. *Igrot Kodesh*, epistle 82, pp. 177-178.

12. For a detailed formulation of these directives, see *Tanya, Iggeret Hakodesh*, epistle 1.

13. *Igrot Kodesh*, epistle 83, pp. 179-180.

14. *Ibid.*, epistle 29, pp. 70-73.

15. See Yaacov Barnai (ed.), *Hasidic Letters from Eretz- Israel*, Jerusalem 1980. (Hebrew).

16. See Yehoshua Mondshine, *Liqutei omrim, which is the Book of the Tanya – its Editions, Translations, and Commentaries*, Kfar Chabad, 1984 (Hebrew).

17. For extensive discussions of RASHAZ' doctrines, including that of the *Tanya*, see Moshe Hallamish, *The Theoretical System of Rabbi Shneur Zalman of Liady (its sources in Kabbalah and Hasidism)*, Doctoral Dissertation, Hebrew University, Jerusalem, 1976 (Hebrew); Rachel Elior, The Paradoxical Ascent to God: The Kabalistic Theosophy of Habad Hasidism, (State University of New York Press), Albany 1993; Leah Orent, 'Ratso va-shov, Running and Returning', *Ethical and Mystical Perspectivesin the Teaching of R. Shneur Zalman of Liadi*, a Comperative Studi, Tel Aviv, 2007 (Hebrew).

18. *Tanya, Sefer shel Beinonim*, ch. 2.

19. This idea is first represented in the *Tanya, Sefer shel Beinonim*, ch. 3. RASHAZ repeats it in various formulations and contexts throughout the book.

20. The discussion and the citation, *Ibid.*, ch. 4

21. See Joseph Weiss, "Torah Study at the Origin of Hasidism," *Hadoar* 44 (1965), pp. 615-617.

22. See Immanuel Etkes, The Besht, above n. 9, pp. 113-151.

23. See *The Testimony Written by our Rabbi* in Yehoshua Mondshine (ed.), *Kerem Chabad 4,* (vol 1), Kfar Chabad, 1992, pp. 45-47.

24. These matters are hinted at in the Epistle of RASHAZ cited above. See also *Tanya, Iggeret Hakodesh*, epistle 1.

25. On the *beinoni* see *Tanya, Sefer shel Beinonim*, chs. 12, 13-18.

26. See Immanuel Etkes, *Rabbi Israel Salanter and the Mussar Movement*, (The Jewish Publication society), Philadelphia 1993.

27. See Raaya Haran, "R. Abraham of Kalisc and R. Shneur Zalman of Lyadi – an Interrupted Friendship," in *Kolot Rabim*, volume in memory of Rivka Schatz Upenheimer, Jerusalem, 1996, pt. 2, pp. 399-428.

7

The Jewish Outreach Enterprise: Rhetoric and Reality[1] (An essay in honor of Rabbi Irving "Yitz" Greenberg)

Sylvia Barack Fishman

INTRODUCTION: THE OUTREACH CONTROVERSY

Rabbi Irving "Yitz" Greenberg's comprehensive vision of Outreach is one of the principle aspects of his intellectual ouvre and communal influence. For decades, he has urged the creation of a whole network of bridges "for the sake of heaven and earth": from the most to the least connected Jews, and from the Jewish religion to non-Jewish religions, as well as from born Jews to the non-Jews living in Jewish households.[2] In recent years, the Jewish world, for myriad reasons, has responded to Yitz's call, giving more communal attention to the issue of Outreach. This re-focusing of priorities has brought about many new versions of Jewish identity and also has created a great deal of confusion surrounding the nature, scope and effectiveness of Outreach initiatives.

When the Boston 2005 Jewish Population Study, conducted by researchers at the Steinhardt Institute of Brandeis University, was released on November 9, 2007,[3] headlines spotlighted one finding in Jewish newspapers across America: 60 percent of Boston families with one Jewish and one non-Jewish parent (commonly known as "intermarried," "mixed married," or, in the scientific literature, "exogamous" households) reported raising their children as Jews. The national average of intermarried families reporting raising their children as Jews, in contrast, is around one-third (31 percent). If Jewish "success" in a mixed married family is measured by whether or not the children are being raised as Jews, it appeared that Boston had found a key to success.

Outreach advocates were quick to go on the offensive in editorials, Internet chat groups, and public talks, claiming Boston's "Outreach" efforts were the

reason for the high percentages of intermarried families raising Jewish chil-
dren. Within hours of the Boston study's release, Outreach advocate Edmund
Case, president of InterfaithFamily.com, and Kathy Kahn, director of the
Union for Reform Judaism's Department of Outreach, wrote an op-ed article,
"Engaging the Intermarried," declaring the Boston study proves that Outreach
transforms interfaith families into environments that raise Jewish children
(*The Forward*). They asserted:

> CJP has a dedicated line item in its budget expressly for Services to the Intermar-
> ried. CJP's funding for this area—just over $300,000 for the current year—is the
> highest in the country, yet it represents just 1 % of CJP's total allocations....If the
> Jewish community on national and local levels allocated 1 % of its funding to-
> ward outreach to interfaith families, we now know that we could see 60 % of
> them—or even more—making Jewish choices.

Case and Kahn concluded in triumph: "By spending just 1 % of its alloca-
tions" on Outreach, they asserted, "CJP has achieved dramatic results."[4]

Case and Kahn's essay used the term Outreach as it is most commonly used
in Jewish America today: the enterprise of reaching out to mixed married
families and their children, with the goal of exposing them to religious and/or
cultural Jewish experiences. Some use the Hebrew word *kiruv*, literally "to
draw one close," as a term for Outreach to the intermarried. However, it is also
common in Conservative and especially Orthodox environments, to use the
terms Outreach and *kiruv* to mean drawing born Jews, rather than intermarried couples, closer to Judaism. Thus, even in language definitions, confusion
and controversy around the subject of Outreach, along with its causes and its
effects, is widespread.

Asserting that Boston's Outreach is responsible for the higher than average
number of intermarried families raising Jewish children is one example of
Outreach rhetoric. The reality, however, is that such claims are unsupported
speculations, because accurately establishing cause and effect would require a
comparison of intermarried families who have participated in Outreach activities with those who have not. To scientifically establish what effect Outreach has, one would need the type of research conducted in Birthright Israel
(the program that offers Jews born of a Jewish parent a free ten day intensive
trip to Israel)_evaluations. Longitudinal studies comparing Birthright Israel
participants with non-participants have unequivocally demonstrated that the
program has a dramatic and lasting effect on participants, when compared
both to themselves before the program and to others in their cohort during
and for years after the program.[5] In contrast, Outreach effectiveness has to
date never been proven in a systematic study. Moreover, mixed married families say that they themselves prefer mainstream Jewish programming rather

than Outreach programs specifically designed for them.[6] Not least, the most common route to full involvement tends to be not formal Outreach programming but the mentoring rabbi, as discussed more fully later in this essay.

If Outreach programming was not the key factor in Boston's results, what was? Like Outreach advocates, those who disagreed with their interpretation of the Boston data leapt into the fray. Editorials and articles flew back and forth in newspapers and on the Internet. "Let the Outreach Debate Be Heard," declared editor Gary Rosenblatt in *The Jewish Week*, inviting Dr. Jack Wertheimer, then Provost of the Conservative movement's Jewish Theological Seminary, and Rabbi Kerry Olitzky, executive director of Jewish Outreach to the Intermarried (JOI) to exchange viewpoints. Wertheimer complained that there had been too little follow-up exploring the decline of Jewish values and norms, and accused Outreach advocates of sanitizing that decline by calling it "evolution." Olitzky insisted that Outreach aims to help raise Jewish families, making two particularly significant assertions: (1) Outreach needs more funding and attention to make a positive difference in American Jewish life; and (2) Conversion should not be considered an Outreach strategy, as it will not work.[7]

The *Jewish Week* debate was hardly the last word. In Boston, as I wrote then in a *Jerusalem Post* op-ed piece, an extraordinary broad spectrum of Jewish education programs for children and adults of all ages, on which extensive communal resources are expended, is correlated with the propensity for Boston's intermarried families to raise their children as Jews.[8] Regression analyses applied to local Jewish population surveys and to national surveys, such as the National Jewish Population Surveys in 1990 and 2000-01, establish that Jewish connections are strongly related to Jewish social networks, population density, and formal and informal Jewish education, as well as the level of Jewish activities in the home.[9] This point was emphasized by the Boston study's authors, Leonard Saxe, Charles Kadushin, and Benjamin Phillips in their own editorial written to answer Case and Kahn. Although "welcoming" intermarried families may play some role in explaining the Boston results, a more significant factor is the fact that Boston has created an elaborate network of synagogue and other Jewish education resources, as well as strong, local ties with Israel. Because of these programs, Jews of all types "are highly engaged with Jewish life," according to the authors. "Nearly half the community belongs to congregations, and nearly all Boston-area Jews participate in some way in Jewish life during the course of a year." Boston succeeds because its Jewish community is one that Jews want to be part of and feel that they are welcomed into – whether they are inmarried, intermarried, and unmarried.[10]

Other editorials posed additional objections to the Outreach rhetoric. They revealed the fact that many cities—not only Boston—differ from the national average. Demographers Steven M. Cohen, Jack Ukeles, and Ron Miller argued, "as early as the mid-1990s [city studies] reported rates [of intermarried families raising Jewish children] similar to those now reported in Boston. Among them are Cleveland (66 %), St. Louis (65 %) and Miami (56 %)." They showed that high rates are reported when studies—such as Boston, Cleveland, St. Louis and Miami—do not give respondents an opportunity to answer "Jewish and something else" as one option on how they are raising their children.[11] A later overview by Ira Sheskin and Arnold Dashefsky in the *2007 American Jewish Year Book* similarly compared city rates of intermarried families raising their children as Jews, and agreed, as Anthony Weiss noted in a subsequent issue of *The Forward* (December 12, 2007), "Boston's figure is not exceptional and may not be the result of its programming." Their conclusion was bolstered by negative as well as positive statistics, such as the fact that San Francisco only at 38 percent of San Francisco's intermarried families say they are raising Jewish children, even though that city has one of the country's longest-standing outreach programs.[12]

Tellingly, Gil Preuss, Boston CJP's Vice President for Strategy and Planning during the CJP study, noted that those intermarried families who said they were raising their children as Jews were in fact deeply enmeshed in the conventional Jewish institutional world, and looked very much like other affiliated non-Orthodox families. "They belong to congregations, they celebrate Jewish holidays, they participate in the community," Preuss said in an interview with Jewish Telegraphic Agency reporter Sue Fishkoff.[13] Despite the rhetoric praising Outreach, the reality was that the widespread educational intensity of Boston Jewish life had more impact than Outreach efforts on the Boston intermarried's high Jewish "score."

THE EMERGENCE AND ETHOS OF
THE AMERICAN JEWISH OUTREACH ENTERPRISE

The Jewish enterprise of Outreach to the intermarried emerged in response to dramatically increasing rates of intermarriage during the 1970s and 1980s. Marriage across religious and cultural lines became more common throughout the United States, as an ethos of multiculturalism had largely replaced "melting pot" expectations for ethnic assimilation. From the Christian American side multiculturalism lowered the ethnoreligious barriers. Jewish men and women were increasingly attractive to non-Jews as dating and marriage partners. From the Jewish side, the majority of marriage-age American Jews were neither immigrants nor the children of immigrants, and issues of Jewish peoplehood were less salient to them than it had been for earlier generations.

Ironically, multiculturalism also made it easier for Jews and other minorities to be overtly particularistic—hence a simultaneous growth in *kippot* (head coverings) and other distinctive ethnic garb worn in public settings among more traditional segments of the population, while intermarriage was increasing dramatically in other segments of the population.

During this time period, differences between Jews and Christians were often characterized more in terms of ethnic style than religious principles. Spirituality in the 1970s was still widely assumed to be a Christian, rather than a Jewish characteristic, in popular culture, but during the coming decades ideas of spirituality would make wide inroads throughout American culture, including the American Jewish community. Many of these spiritualist ideas were generic and not attached to any particular religious community, and at the same time highly idiosyncratic and personal—further eroding the perceived boundaries between Jews and their Christian neighbors.

Local studies of Jewish populations in various cities conducted during this time period revealed an increase of marriages between Jews and non-Jews, piquing the concern of Jewish religious and communal leaders as well as the interest of Jewish sociologists. observers of the American Jewish community became obsessed Dealing with demographic changes and intermarriage. The Reform movement deliberated on what became the Patrilineal Descent Decision of 1983, under the guidance of Rabbi Alexander Schindler, then President of the Union of American Hebrew Congregations (UAHC, now Union for Reform Judaism, URJ), declaring "that the child of one Jewish parent is under the presumption of Jewish descent" with either a Jewish father or a Jewish mother. Rabbi Schindler pressed his fellow rabbis to work not only toward conversion but also to reach out to intermarried couples regardless of whether or not conversion had taken place. Schindler eloquently pleaded for rabbis and other Jewish leaders to "take intermarriage out of the house of mourning and bring it into the house of study."[14]

Openly calling for Outreach to the intermarried was regarded by many in the Jewish community as transgressive. Outreach language in the 1970s-1980s is thus usually very carefully chosen. Nevertheless, these Outreach advocates believed strongly in their mission, and their rhetoric is colored by a conviction of prophetic insights into the future as well as pioneering courage. Extremely influential both inside and outside the Reform movement was the research of the late sociologist Egon Mayer, who began doing statistical studies and interviews with intermarried couples in the mid-1970s, and publishing articles about them by the late 1970s. His 1985 book, *Love and Tradition: Marriage Between Jews and Christians*—with ideas that were later popularized in Susan Weidman Schneider's *Intermarriage: The Challenge of Living with Differences between Christians and Jews* (1989)—changed the way many in the Jewish community regarded intermarriage.[15] The thrust of these foundational works was that intermarriage was essentially the wave of the future, and that stigmatizing Jews who chose to marry out could do no good and might do considerable harm. Instead of looking disapprovingly at intermarried couples, Outreach literature urged, the Jewish community would do well to reach out to them. [16]

In 1985, the same year that Mayer published his influential *Love and Tradition*, two other books also helped to establish Outreach as a new communal priority. David Belin's *Why Choose Judaism: New Dimensions of Jewish Outreach* recorded the development of Reform Jewish Outreach and its goals, such as Jewish communal welcoming of non-Jewish partners and the children of intermarried couples. Belin also suggested that unmarried "people not affiliated with any religion" should be given information about Judaism so that "in the event they are seeking religious identification, they consider Judaism as one of their alternatives," although he repeats several times that he is not advocating "aggressive" proselytizing. [17] Charles Silberman's *A Certain People* also incorporated ideas that supported Outreach, especially by popularizing the idea that Judaism was not declining although it was certainly changing its shape, (transformationalism), reaching a large reading audience with his upbeat message that echoed the approach of demographer Calvin Goldscheider. [18]

Belin and some other Outreach professionals began within the Reform movement, but soon moved outside of it and attached themselves to independent Outreach enterprises, as a journal for Outreach professionals recounts that history:

> In 1979 the Reform movement asked David Belin to chair a newly created Task Force to study and develop programs of outreach toward intermarried families. A prominent attorney, philanthropist, political appointee, and advocate for bringing Judaism to non-Jews, Belin led the Task Force to create programs and train staff. In 1983 the Task Force became the Commission on Outreach., for which Belin remained chairman until 1987. The following year he joined with Dr. Egon Mayer to found the Jewish Outreach Institute, in order to extend outreach across institutional and denominational lines, and through secular and cultural programming as well as religious. [19]

From the beginning, non-denominational Outreach efforts to mixed married families and their children played an important role in pushing the envelope toward greater communal attention and emphasis on their chosen cause. Unaffiliated Outreach authors eschewed judgementalism and emphasized the normalcy of intermarried families. Neither Judaism nor Christianity is the wrong choice for an intermarried family, asserted Rabbi Roy Rosenberg, Father Peter Meehan, and Reverend John Wade Payne in *Happily Intermarried: Authoritative advice for a Joyous Jewish-Christian Marriage.* [20] While the authors advocated choosing one religion—and strongly preferred a household with religion than one without it—they advised parents who hadn't yet decided when children were born to combine Christian baptism with "Jewish ceremonies of blessing and naming." Non-denominational Jewish Outreach efforts enjoyed the freedom to strategize freely, without the boundaries and limitations faced by Outreach workers within the various wings of Judaism. The rhetoric of the two types of Outreach enterprises reflects their differing realities, as well as their common concerns.

During the mid-1980s, intermarried families were just beginning to realize that they were part of a large and increasingly prominent segment of the Jewish community. They began to reflect on their situation, and to appraise the various scenarios through which they could choose to relate in some way to Jews and Judaism. For some this appraisal took the form of writing self-help books, such as Judy Petsonk and Jim Remsen's *The Intermarriage Handbook: A Guide for Jews and Christians,* (1988) and and Lee Gruzen's *Raising Your Jewish/ Christian Child: How Interfaith Parents Can Give Children the Best of Both Their Heritages,* (1987).[21] Along with similar volumes in the years that followed, these works spanned a range that reflected rather closely their own experiences and biases. A very different approach was presented, also in 1987, in Paul and Rachel Cowan's important book about the intermarriage couple's therapy groups they ran, *Mixed Blessings: Marriage Between Jews and Christians.*[22] Rachel Cowan had undergone a long and moving journey into intense Jewish life, and the couple warned against the pitfalls of intermarriage, rather than advocating a value-neutral stance.

Outreach institutions were also created in response to the perceived intermarriage crisis. Two of the most active and well-known unaffiliated outreach enterprises are the Jewish Outreach Institute (JOI), founded as an independent enterprise in 1988, and InterfaithFamily.com, Inc., created a decade later. JOI's mission statement describes it as, "a national, independent, nondenominational organization dedicated to creating a more inclusive Jewish community toward all who would join, especially intermarried families and disengaged Jews, by working to transform existing institutions and by creating new programs when necessary." JOI publishes a magazine, *The Inclusive,* as well as occasional papers and a book series, and facilitates JOPLIN: Jewish Outreach Professionals Log-In Network. In addition, JOI has initiated influential programs such as the "Mother's Circle," which reaches out to and creates programming for non-Jewish mothers with Jewish husbands and/ or children. Under the leadership of Rabbi Kerry Olitzky (after the untimely death of Egon Mayer), JOI distinguished itself by promoting to widespread communities innovative Jewish programming on neutral turf, such as Passover education in supermarket kosher food sections in the weeks before Passover.

The Outreach controversy escalated dramatically with the publication of the National Jewish Population Survey in 1990,[23] which circulated a finding that almost half of the most recent Jewish marriages were intermarriages. Interfaith-Family.com was first launched as an online magazine by Jewish Family & Life in 1998. In 1999 Edmund Case became the publisher, and in 2001 he acquired the online magazine and founded the independent non-profit InterfaithFamily.com, Inc. Publishing articles of broad interest not only to intermarried families but also to anyone interested in liberal American Judaism, its promotional literature describes it as "the online resource for interfaith families exploring Jewish life and the grassroots advocate for a welcoming Jewish community."

While they do not ordinarily work together, Case and Olitzky have become the two best-known voices in the unaffiliated Outreach world, advocating forcefully and frequently on behalf of their client population.

UNAFFILIATED OUTREACH ENTERPRISES

The word advocate used by InterfaithFamily.com in its self-description is quite accurate, and is one important difference between independent Outreach efforts and the Outreach efforts promoted with the Reform movement and other wings of Judaism, discussed later in this essay. InterfaithFamily.com and JOI frequently sound like lawyers for the defense of intermarried families against the existing religious establishment. Outreach workers within the wings of Judaism, in contrast, often sound like mediators or ombudsmen trying to find a compromise between the needs of intermarried families, on one hand, and the interests of the Jewish establishment, on the other hand.

A JOI program, for example, The Grandparents Circle, "is a comprehensive program that offers grandparents skills and techniques to nurture…their interfaith grandchildren's Jewish identities," according to *Inside: JOI: The Newsletter of the Jewish Outreach Institute*. The need for such programs is critical, as research shows, because non-Jewish grandparents are often much more assertive than Jewish grandparents in providing religious and cultural enrichment. Jewish parents tend to be much more reticent (despite stereotypical portrayals to the contrary), afraid to step on their non-Jewish in-law children's toes, and fearful of intervening by being "too Jewish."[24] As one grandmother interviewed by reporter Sue Fishkoff put it, "I didn't want to give the children the sense that there's something wrong with people who are not Jewish, but I still want to give them a sense of pride in being Jewish. It's a fine line."[25]

The language used in JOI's grandparents' circles' literature reveals the impact of advocacy attitudes expressed within non-denominational Outreach literature. The ethos of the non-denominational Outreach movement is to advocate for intermarried couples and to put the onus of responsibility on the Jewish community for a lack of Jewish engagement that those families display.

As a result of this ethos, some of the assumptions articulated as part of Outreach programs reinforce inaccurate information. For example, in their book, *Twenty Things for Grandparents of Interfaith Grandchildren to Do*,[26] Kerry Olitzky and Paul Golin assert, "interfaith marriage is more an accident of demography and not necessarily a reflection of Jewish identity." This statement is contradicted by every systematic statistical study ever undertaken on the American Jewish community on both national and local levels. The authors go on to assert, "interfaith marriage only undermines one's Jewish identity *if* the Jewish community does not allow the individual to exercise it fully."[27] The clear message is that any lack of interest in Judaism that intermarried couples display must have been caused by the Jewish community, rather than by the couple's own apathy or perhaps even hostility.

Although parents of intermarried children may find the fact painful, repeated studies reveal that the Jewish partner in intermarried households often has deeply ambivalent feelings about Jews and Judaism. Most segments of the liberal Jewish community have, in fact, worked hard in recent decades to be welcoming and to embrace interfaith couples. In most cases, weak Jewish connections precede the intermarriage—a point emphasized by Brandeis University scholars Leonard Saxe, Fern Chertok and Benjamin Philllips, "It's Not Just Who Stands Under the Chuppah: Jewish Identity and Mixed Marriage."[28] As a group (although certainly individuals differ) Jews who marry non-Jews express weaker Jewish connections than those who marry Jews, and blaming the Jewish community for not allowing "the individual to exercise" Jewishness "fully" seems to ignore at least half the story. The Jewish spouse's resistance to making or maintaining Jewish engagement—not the community's failure to allow the couple to "exercise fully" their desire for Jewishness—is often the core reason for the lack of Jewish connections.

The Jewish parent is especially likely to resist Jewish involvements in households where a Jewish male is married to a non-Jewish female. The alienation of boys and men from Jews and Judaism is a systemic problem in American Jewish societies. It affects not only religious rituals and synagogue attendance, but also attachments to Jewish peoplehood, in the form of friendship circles, marriage choices, caring about Jews in Israel and around the world. This phenomenon has been developing for many decades, but it has been virtually ignored, and today it has become sweeping and dramatic.[29]

JOI's "Mother's Circles," reaching out to non-Jewish mothers who are raising Jewish children, are effective and helpful in some ways. Because they consist of eight months of educational courses that provide the "Building Blocks" on the practicalities of creating a Jewish home, the Mother's Circles have the great educational advantage of helping to build social networks as well as Jewish cultural literacy. However, because they are aimed primarily at non-Jewish mothers and do not also deal with the ambivalence or antipathy of their Jewish husbands, Mother's Circles do not begin to touch one of the core problems within intermarried families. Intermarried men who have negative feelings about Jews and Jewishness are the "weak link" in contemporary American Jewish life. They require their own Outreach—or inreach—efforts.

American males are less attached to Jewish life not because men are innately "less religious" than women in some essential psychological way, but because American culture and society value religious activities and behaviors for women but devalue them for men.[30] Jews in Israel, or in Diaspora communities outside the United States, sometimes suspect that the impact of the Jewish mother (and the weak attachments of the Jewish father) are produced by halakhic rabbinic insistence on matrilineal descent. However, most intermarried Jews who affiliate do so in Reform temples, and matrilineal descent does not apply to American Reform congregations since the movement's 1983 Patrilineal Descent policy decision. Most Reform congregations go to great lengths to welcome the children of intermarrieds. Today, growing numbers of Reform temples employ at least one rabbi who is willing to officiate at interfaith marriages. Whatever is "turning men off" to Judaism, the attitude of the temple toward intermarried families is currently very unlikely to be the cause.

OUTREACH THAT WORKS: THE RABBI AS BROKER

Blaming the Jewish community is especially misleading because one of the most successful Outreach strategies turns out to be the rabbi as broker of Jewishness. In a broad variety of venues, rabbis reach out to intermarried individuals and families and create Jewish connections. Interviews with numerous intermarried families revealed that the most common narrative among those who had established Jewish connections was through a mentoring rabbi. Mixed married households are more likely to incorporate regular Jewish activities into their family routines when they have a connection to a Jewish leader whom they respect and feel close to.

Many couples reported meeting a rabbi, often in connection with their planning a baby naming, with whom they established an increasingly deep connection. The discovery of a personal religious mentors seems to be unrelated to who officiated at the wedding ceremony. Most couples move away from the geographical areas in which they were married. Their familial religious mentor tended to be a person they had found later through some other, post-marriage venue. A sympathetic and supportive rabbi is in a position to serve as a "broker" connecting mixed married families to both Jewish activities and Jewish social networks. Through the rabbi as conduit, the mixed married family constructs new connections.[31]

Lawrence MacDonald, writing for the *Washington Jewish Week*, told just such a story. "I knew a bit about Judaism from reading and conversations with Hannah [his Jewish wife]. But I knew nothing about Purim and was quite unprepared for the exuberant manner in which Rabbi Berkowitz, a survivor of Auschwitz, conveyed to scores of delighted children the core values of Jewish survival in the face of murderous oppression." MacDonald found himself repeatedly taking advantage of Rabbi Berkowitz's classes and Jewish events. Eventually, the rabbi sensitively and subtly made it clear, after MacDonald repeatedly questioned him, that certain activities were limited to persons who committed themselves to be part of the Jewish community. As MacDonald remembers, "I realized then, and with increasing clarity later, that the rabbi had discerned in me something that I myself had yet to recognize: an incipient desire to become a practicing Jew....I wanted to be a part of the marvelous community I had glimpsed. I wanted to be a Jew." MacDonald is convinced that "Without such programs, my interest in becoming a Jew lay dormant," but it was "awakened by the warm welcome that I received at Temple Rodef Shalom."[32]

The role of the rabbi, of course, differs depending on the wing of Judaism. Most Reform congregations go to great lengths to welcome the children of intermarriage. Strikingly, rabbis within the Reform movement often search for new strategies to ensure that intermarried families will feel welcomed and at home. For example, Rabbi Eric Bram of suburban Temple Kol Ami in Beachwood, Ohio, was one of the initiators of an innovative trend when he welcomed and honored non-Jewish members who were committed to raising a Jewish family, inviting them up to the *bima* during services and encouraging them to participate in synagogue rituals.[33] Although temples differ in whether or not they will allow non-Jews to publicly hold and make blessings over the Torah, they are united in their determination to create an inclusive and hospitable environment.

The small but important Reconstructionist movement in many ways resembles the Outreach approach of the Reform movement at its more liberal end. Maurice Harris, in an article in *Reconstructionism Today*, refers to non-Jewish partners as "fellow travelers," and argues that intermarriage may produce some benefits for the Jewish community, such as bringing fresh perspectives and new resources to the Jewish community. Harris also values highly the empathy that being involved in a mixed marriage often develops in spouses.[34] The Conservative movement has initiated its own *keruv* movement aimed at making intermarried couples and their children feel welcomed and comfortable in synagogues. More recently, under the guidance of Rabbi Jerome Epstein, some in the Conservative movement have begun using the term

edud, meaning to support and encourage with compassion." Epstein has urged
the movement to focus no only on Conversion, but also to accept and encourage the non-yet-converted intermarried families who are attracted to Conservative Judaism.[35] Unlike the Reform and Reconstructionist movements, most
Conservative synagogues actively work toward conversion into Judaism when
they work with such families, and it is typical for Conservative synagogues to
require conversion for the children of Christian mothers before being called
up to the Torah as a bar or bat mitzvah. In the Orthodox world, the terms
"Outreach" or *keruv* often refer to reaching out to unaffiliated Jews, rather
than to non-Jews. Chabad-Lubavitch has become famous for its *Keruv* efforts
of this type, and Ephraim Buchwald's National Center for Jewish Outreach is
widely admired for continuing successes in bringing alienated young Jews
closer to Judaism. Although large segments of the *haredi* (ultraorthodox)
world see intermarriage as a sin, and tantamount to the betrayal of the Jewish
people, within the Modern Orthodox world many young rabbis work quietly
with intermarried couples to help bring about conversions, if not of the non-
Jewish spouse then at least of their children. Within every wing of American
Judaism, it is fair to say, Outreach of some sort is a fact of life. And, as we have
noted, the rabbi-mentors within these wings of Judaism have become the
most effective agents of Ourtreach.

TURF-NEUTRAL OUTREACH

Jewish communities in many locations are trying to create outreach programs
in "neutral territory," places where Jews with little Jewish background or ambivalent feelings about Jewishness can explore Jewish connections without
feeling that the ambience itself ireprimands them about their weak Jewish ties.
These places and programs are also designed to be especially attractive to intermarried families. The very neutrality of the venue is thought to be a plus by
some. For example, in Cleveland, Lynda Bender, director of education and
public programs for the Maltz Museum of Jewish heritage, asserts: "We offer
a very different experience from a JCC or a temple. No rabbi is going to leap
out and say, 'Do you want to join the temple?' The experience is much less
fraught for intermarried couples who are hesitant about their situation."[36]

To avoid the "fraughtness" of anxiety about religious connotations, it has
recently become more common for cultural centers to avoid using the word
"Jewish" in their names and publicity. Thus, the Skirball Cultural Center in
Los Angeles and the New Center for Arts and Culture in Boston are projects
of the respective Jewish communities, but aim to reach out to unaffiliated and/
or intermarried Jews even with their non-sectarian names. The assumption,

explains Francine Achbar, acting executive director of the Boston Center, is that avoiding "the J-word" makes the place seem more multicultural. She says, "We want to celebrate the interconnectedness of cultures."[37]

EMERGING ADULT SPECIALIZED OUTREACH

One population for whom the neutral turf strategy is extremely important is that of Jewish "emerging adults," post-college (22-40+), often unmarried, usually unaffiliated, and frequently romantically involved with non-Jews. While an elite among Jewish emerging adults has created a thriving, cutting edge young Jewish culture that ranges from innovative religious experiences to edgy cultural expressions,[38] a much larger segment of this age group has resisted Jewish connections. In a recent study of the Riverway Project of Boston's Temple Israel, Dr. Beth Cousens found that non-Orthodox young adults with a thin Jewish educational background "have no idea what Judaism means to them," and are fearful of exploring Judaism in any setting that will make demands on them or will make them feel bad about themselves. Just as Laurence Iannacconne? found that "religious capital" is not only a consequence of "religious activity," but also "a prerequisite" for that activity,[39] Cousens found that young adults often avoid Jewish institutional settings because they anticipate those settings will cause them discomfort. They feel distressed in anticipation. Cousens explains:

> They have little knowledge of other Jews and how to blend into Jewish communities. For some of them, they still feel intimidated by some of their experiences from childhood, having felt snubbed then for not understanding the norms of the Jewish community in which they were participating....Their folk religion consist just of Jewish street knowledge and sometimes of high holiday participation, focused around the confused and somewhat empty involvement of their parents. They have little Jewish social capital: they say the wrong thing, they stand and sit at the wrong times....The Hebrew sounds muddled to them; the movement looks like acrobatics. They feel "rejected" and "lost" when they try a new Jewish community. [40]

A neutral turf setting is extremely effective with emerging Jewish adults of this type (and their non-Jewish partners) because it gives them a chance to learn about and experience Judaism without pressuring them to do anything that makes them uncomfortable. It is important to note, however, that the Riverway Project has something that many neutral turf projects lack: rather than a series of "one-off," episodic, stand alone events, the Riverway Project builds community through an ongoing program. Under the guidance of Rabbi

Jeremy Morrison, the program not only gives participants a skill set that makes them less uncomfortable in Jewish institutional settings, it also gives them a chance to develop Jewish social networks. For those who are interested, the Riverway project becomes a kind of portable Jewish village.

Another important resource on the emerging adult population, specifically dealing with the children of mixed marriage, is Pearl Beck's 2005 study, *A Flame Still Burns: The Dimensions and Determinants of Jewish Identity among Young Adult Children of the Intermarried, Findings and Policy Implications*, commissioned by JOI. Beck interviewed 90 people ages 22-30, who grew up with one Jewish and one non-Jewish parent, to determine to what extent the offspring of intermarried couples indentify as Jewish, and "what attitudes or activities connect them" to their "Jewish roots." Beck found that most of these young adult children of mixed married households said they related more strongly to cultural aspects of Jewishness than to religious aspects—but that they often defined what others might think of as religious behaviors, such as holiday celebrations, as cultural, rather than religious. Many of them perceived themselves as holding only marginal positions in the Jewish community. They felt positive about Jewish characteristics such as "being liberal and open-minded," having a strong emphasis on education, having a "Jewish" sense of humor, and Jewish cultural expressions such as films, literature, and other arts. Indeed, many said that their primary sense of Jewish history came from these cultural sources. Interestingly, grandparents were often described as having played a pivotal role in shaping their Jewish identities.[41]

WHY SOME OPPOSE OUTREACH

With such powerful testimony on behalf of Outreach, why does the enterprise have some opponents? There are at least three reasons that some Jewish leaders and thinkers oppose communal emphasis on Outreach to intermarried Jewish families. One concern is that Outreach efforts may siphon off material and intellectual energies that are needed to create a highly identified, deeply engaged Jewish generation of tomorrow. Outreach opponents argue that those intermarried couples who are most amenable to engagements will seek out Jewish connections without Outreach. It is not clear how cost effective Outreach efforts are in reaching those who are not themselves already interested in creating Jewish connections. They claim, money is limited. Communal energies are limited. And in focusing on Jews who have already made a choice that arguably takes them—and especially their children—in a mixed direction, the community may be neglecting those Jews who can make more unambiguously Jewish choices.

A second reason that some oppose Outreach is that many Outreach professionals have distanced themselves from conversion into Judaism as a primary goal of Outreach. For Jews from the more traditional wings of Judaism, the purpose of Outreach to non-Jewish spouses and children of Jews is to work toward their full entry into the Jewish religion. Conversion is the goal, and, barring that, commitment to Jewish exclusivity within the home, excluding other religious practices and avoiding religious syncretism. However, within the non-affiliated Outreach enterprise, and even for some within Reform, Outreach and conversion are consciously and conscientiously unlinked.

Rabbi Eric Yoffie, head of the Union for Reform Judaism, discovered that when he gave his sermon at the 2005 Reform Biennial in Houston. According to first-hand observers, a lot of whispering along with a scattering of half-hearted applause greeted Yoffie's assertions that conversion is a necessary form of outreach to the intermarried.[42] Yoffie charged that many Reform congregations had been so welcoming to intermarried families that they were actually discouraging conversion. In order to convey the power and lucidity of Yoffie's message here, I quote the complete section of the sermon in which he urges rabbis and congregations to be more assertive about encouraging conversion:

> Another challenge that we face is the decline in the number of non-Jewish spouses who convert to Judaism. There is much anecdotal evidence to suggest that interest in conversion has waned in our congregations. In the early years of Outreach, Alex Schindler often returned to this topic. Alex told us: "We need to ask. We must not forget to ask." And, for a while, our movement actively encouraged conversion. Many of our congregations began holding public conversion ceremonies during regular worship services. But such ceremonies are far rarer now. The reason, perhaps, is that by making non-Jews feel comfortable and accepted in our congregations, we have sent the message that we do not care if they convert. But that is not our message. Why? Because it is a mitzvah to help a potential Jew become a Jew-by-choice. Because the synagogue is not a neutral institution. It is committed to building a vibrant religious life for the Jewish people. Because we want families to function as Jewish families, and while intermarried families can surely do this, we recognize the advantages of an intermarried family becoming a fully Jewish family, with two adult Jewish partners..... The time has come to reverse direction by returning to public conversions and doing all the other things that encourage conversion in our synagogues. (My emphasis.)[43]

Whether he expected it or not, Yoffie's sermon generated resentment. Not only was it lukewarmly received at the Biennial, it was greeted with howls of outrage by Reform congregants whose children were married to non-Jews and by unaffiliated Jewish Outreach movement periodicals and Internet chat rooms.

The separation between Outreach and conversion—and the porous boundaries between Reform and unaffiliated Outreach—were most dramatically symbolized after the publication of my study, *Choosing Jewish: Conversations About Conversion* (2006), when Rabbi David Ellenson, President of the Reform movement's rabbinical seminary at Hebrew Union College: Jewish Institute of Religion, co-authored an op-ed piece in the *Forward* with Kerry Olitzky of JOI, entitled, "Conversion Is Not an Outreach Strategy."[44] For much of Jewish history, conversion into Judaism has been the *ultimate* strategy for reaching out and welcoming born non-Jews into the Jewish people as well as the Jewish religion. To many concerned observers, Ellenson's essay—echoing as it did the language of Case and Kahn a year earlier, along with the hostility that greeted Yoffie's pro-conversion talk, fueled their worst fears, and seemed a blatant contradiction of foundational Jewish attitudes.

Some Reform leaders are uncomfortable with overtly considering conversion into Judaism as the preferred outcome of Outreach. Inclusiveness, along with an emphasis on freedom of choice, is a sacred value for many leaders in the Reform religious community. This emphasis on inclusiveness and freedom of choice often contributes to an ethic and an ethos which downplay conversion as a privileged outcome. For example, Paula Brody, Director of Outreach Programs for the greater Boston metropolitan area Union of American Hebrew Congregations (UAHC), draws a "stark distinction between the Conservative Gerim Institute [which openly works toward conversion] and her Reform Introduction to Judaism class." She is, Brody says, "Not actively pushing conversion, as much as teaching Judaism and love for Judaism."[45]

Brody, who has worked for about two decades on Outreach to interfaith families, emphasizes that most of the programs she runs do not overtly gear themselves toward conversion. Many of the persons who choose to take classes do consider conversion, but the Introduction to Judaism class, for example, "is not marketed as a conversion class."

Rabbi Jonah Pesner of Reform Temple Israel consciously creates an environment in his congregation which sends "a message of inclusion," a fact that he feels is partly responsible for their very diverse congregation. The temple's policy toward intermarried families is to encourage them in their Jewish journeys, to welcome conversion, but not to make conversion a privileged conclusion to that journey. One of the factors discouraging conversion is a simple lack of time. Pesner and other busy rabbis report that they could facilitate many more conversions with more time to devote to this process.

In addition to concerns about human and financial resources, and about the retreat from emphasis on conversion as the goal of Outreach, there is yet another, complex reason that some oppose outreach. Some fear that in reaching across boundaries the Judaism out Outreach activists becomes hybridized.

Outreach opponents look at the religious and cultural syncretism as described in this essay—and at Outreach professionals who excuse this syncretism, who declare it nothing to be concerned about, and who, in some cases, condemn as narrow-minded those who describe it as problematic—and say that a meta-morphosis has already occurred. Whereas intensive Jewish societies of the past, with their rich Jewish social capital, absorbed much from surrounding cultures and made the alien elements Jewish, Outreach opponents assert that today those intermarried families who meld Judaism and Christianity—and the Outreach professionals who serve them and see the world through their eyes—work together to create a mutated new culture, a Christianized Judaism, that may have more in common with early Christianity than it does with his-torical Judaisms.

Outreach advocates see certain changes as benign developments, and po-tentially even exciting transformations, full of promise for the future. Out-reach opponents see the same changes as mutations, the triumph of flux over continuity, and a radical rupture with traditional Judaism.

This concern about the deleterious effects of cultural syncretism is sup-ported by research on ethnic cross-cultural marriages in non-Jewish as well as Jewish communities. Of particular interest is Mary Waters' *Ethnic Options: Choosing Identities in America*, which studied Roman Catholics from Irish, Italian, Polish and German backgrounds who married across ethnic lines. Waters found that having two ethnic narratives in the home usually led to the merging of the identities in some rather strange ways. For example, adults in one family insisted that corned beef and cabbage was a classic Italian dish. One ethnicity usually lost out to the other, in Waters' interviews. Waters' data shows that having a particular surname often caused people to identify one way or another way: having a German or Irish or Italian surname makes adult children more likely to identify with that ethnicity.[46] Interestingly, Beck's study of young adult children of intermarriage showed the same thing: adult chil-dren of intermarriage who had Jewish surnames were more likely to identify as Jews than those who did not.

One extreme version of disdainful attitudes toward Outreach axioms was articulated by the *haredi* Cleveland rabbi and *mohel* Daniel Schur, who com-pared the Outreach movement to a group of Chelmites trying to get them-selves out of hole by digging another hole that is even deeper:

> We realize that intermarriage is digging a pit in the heart of Jewish existence. The solution—let us accept the intermarried couple into Judaism. Is this not digging a hole larger than the first? By accepting them, there is no longer a need to con-vert....Patrilineal descent—accepting the child of a Christian mother as Jews, is another solution by the wise men of Chelm. Calling the tail of a dog a leg does not create a five legged dog![47]

Contrary to the beliefs of such Outreach opponents, both denominational and non-denominational Outreach help in different ways to forge Jewish connections for some unconnected families of Jewish background. Both types of Outreach can be useful in opening doors for weakly connected families to develope greater connections. There are individuals and families for whom the email conversations on Interfaith Family are a lifeline to Judaism. There are those for whom JOI's Mothers Circles have nurtured a spark of family Jewishness.

In far greater numbers, as we have noted, enduring connections are often forged by the personal Outreach efforts of warm rabbis within each wing of Judaism, especially but not exclusively within the Reform movement.

Nevertheless, the concerns of those who oppose Outreach are not groundless. The controversy around the interpretation of the Boston study, with which we began this essay, provides an excellent object lesson about how rhetoric—in the form of cheerleading for Outreach, and combination with an apparently willful ignoring of demonstrable facts—can do damage by misleading the Jewish community about strategies and public policies. The Outreach rhetoric that followed the Boston study urged that more money be put into Outreach. But resources are finite, some feared that this meant, by implication, fewer resources other Jewish educational venues. Reducing inreach in favor of Outreach would be an unwise choice, since in national studies Jewish educational density, along with Jewish social networks and population density, has emerged as the most important communal influence on Jewish connectedness.

CONCLUSION: IT TAKES A JEWISH VILLAGE

Examining the effectiveness of Boston in nurturing the likelihood that intermarried couples will aim to raise Jewish children is instructive, and underscores that the need for sustained communal programs over episodic Outreach efforts. Boston educational programs span a broad range, targeting under-served groups, including pre-school children and their often culturally illiterate and under-affiliated parents (Ikarim), teenagers (Prozdor), and single young adults (The Riverway Project—discussed above). Adult education is a critical part of this equation. Under the inspired leadership of CJP's Barry Shrage—who realized that most competent American Jewish adults want rigor and excellence in their programs but also don't want to be made to feel incompetent—Boston has created exciting, successful, well-attended adult educational programs. Me'ah—referring to its 100 hours of instruction—has been described by its enthusiastic Reform, Conservative, Orthodox, and Reconstructionist participants as challenging intellectually, and very compelling. Indeed, many participants opt to continue with yet another course of rigorous study—the Ve'od Me'ah (another hundred hours) program. Each of the programs produces as a very important side effect social networks, as participants bond over books and discussions.

Moreover, Boston has brought education to the people by supporting programs both inside and outside of synagogue settings. Rather than seeing synagogues as their competitors and enemies, as unfortunately happens in many communities, CJP has supported innovative synagogue programs as natural gateways to much of the Jewish community. Even Outreach activists Case and Kahn, as noted early in this essay, pointed out in advocating Outreach, "CJP directly supports the outreach programming of the religious movements."[48] Again, synagogue placement is important because of the ease of maintaining social networks in ongoing synagogue programs.

A second reason for the Boston difference is its Israel connection. Boston leadership has made constant engagement with Israel—in particular Haifa, Boston's sister city—a critical part of the city's synagogue, communal, and educational Jewish culture. Frequent Israel trips, and ongoing interactions between individual families, schools, and other institutions have contributed to the peoplehood profile of Boston Jewry. As Israeli sociologist David Mittelberg asserts, both Israeli and American Jewish identity are enhanced by reciprocal relationships between the two societies.[49]

Not least, Boston study data underscore the critical importance of gender: within intermarried families raising their children as Jews, the majority had a Jewish mother. As numerous studies show, Jewish mothers are the group most likely to insist on raising Jewish children, to provide them with Jewish education, to encourage Jewish friendship circles for themselves and their children, and to create Jewish rituals and Jewish memories in the home. One of the differences between the roles of Jewish men and Jewish women in a family setting is that the women are far more likely to create the social networks for the whole family, whereas men tend to create only their own personal social networks. Jewish women—including affiliated intermarried women—create largely Jewish social networks. Intermarried Jewish men, in contrast, have far fewer Jewish friends with whom to celebrate Jewish holidays and life cycle events.[50]

The research in Boston, in other city studies, and in the national data is clear: Programs that intensify the Jewish connections of born Jews and Jews by choice are also most effective for mixed married households. Outreach can perform very useful functions, including serving as a gateway to Jewish connections. However, claiming that Outreach is more critical than and can replace educational activities is harmful because it can lead communities to make unproductive Jewish strategic and policy decisions.

If either inreach or Outreach for some incomprehensible reason needed to be abandoned, it would be better to abandon Outreach than inreach. We don't have to chose, but if we did, inreach trumps Outreach. Fortunately, having to chose is nothing more than a "straw man." Except for the most insulated segments of the Orthodox community, very few knowledgeable American Jews advocate abandoning Outreach efforts.

The American Jewish community needs Outreach within each wing of Judaism, as well as non-denominational Outreach. Most American Jews realize how necessary Outreach is. However, Outreach is not and should never be presented as a panacea or a substitute for lifelong Jewish education and the inreaching forging of Jewish connections. Nevertheless, it is critically important to honestly confront the limits of Outreach, and the far greater efficacy of mainstream formal and informal educational programming.

For intermarried as well as inmarried families, providing a rich educational and experiential environment gives individuals the Jewish social capital to nurture Jewish connections, and makes all the difference. In a very real and practical sense, *Talmud torah k'neged kulam*, Judaic formal and informal education facilitates the rest of Jewish life. Jewish educational experiences are effective because they provide Jews and their non-Jewish spouses with a Jewish literacy level and skills set that

(1) enable them to function as "insiders" rather than "outsiders" in Jewish settings;
(2) de-mystify Jewish settings and activities; and
(3) provide meaning for Jewish activities.

All three of these factors are critical to Jewish engagement.

Discovering Jewish meaning is especially salient for younger than older American Jews, because many of them are unpersuaded by—and even disdainful of—the civic religion of Jewish survival that was so meaningful to older American Jews. For younger American Jews, including many intermarried Jews, Jewish cultural survival is only compelling if they can find meaningful substance in it, not for its own sake.

Episodic Outreach events on neutral turf can pique the Jewish interest of unengaged individual Jews as well as intermarried families. Jewish films, Jewish rock concerts, Jewish events in supermarkets can and do play a role in raising Jewish awareness. However, research on young/ emerging Jewish adults shows that social connections support Jewish connections. Without becoming involved in social networks—whether they are Jewish friendship circles, or Jewish associational groups, or formal Jewish affiliations—Jews drift out of Jewish engagements just as they drift in. Just as it "takes a village" to raise Jewish children, it takes a village to sustain adult Jewish connections as well. Despite much-vaunted American individualism, the inner Jew needs the nurture of other Jews, and the rabbinic principle of *al tifrosh min ha-tzi-bur*—not separating oneself from the community—takes on fresh meaning in today's society. Outreach is most effective if it succeeds in leading to full identification with and membership in the Jewish people.

Finally, it is critical that Outreach never degenerate into religious relativism that looses a sense of the uniqueness of Judaism—and forgets why it matters that Jewish culture be transmitted to the next generation. As "Yitz" Greenberg so brilliantly ascertained, the backdrop for intermarriage is the fluidity between Jews and non-Jews in liberal Western countries today, an encounter "unprecedented in human history." For the first time, Jews and non-Jews encounter each other in "a highly open and sympathetic environment between religions, identities and cultures." This unprecedented encounter has created "a kind of crisis and an opportunity." The opportunity, as Greenberg defines it, is the chance to appreciate realistically the positive qualities of other religions. This appreciation can, under the best of circumstances, foster true dialogue and friendship across religious lines, and often, paradoxically, a more realistic appreciation of the particularism of one's own religious philosophy and community. However, Greenberg notes, too often the dialogue leads people to fall into a "relativist position that "religion is a source of conflict," and to reject religion altogether. This relativist rejection of religion is tragic, Greenberg argues, because religions encourage people to ask hard questions about individual and government decisions, and to seek for meaning in daily life. Without religion—and religious differences—cultures become "homogenized," and people make "a global religion of materialism and consumerism." Greenberg challenges Jews to create the kind of pluralism that enables the cherishing of one's own religion—the ability to be nurtured by Judaism's "source of life and goodness," while affirming "diversity, which reflects God's love for humans and human diversity."[51]

NOTES

1. (*To distinguish the Outreach enterprise from the various other meanings of that word, in this essay Outreach is capitalized.)

2. Irving Greenberg, *For the Sake of Heaven and Earth: The New Encounter between Judaism and Christianity* (Philadelphia: Jewish Publication Society, 2004).

3. Leonard Saxe, *et. al.*, *Jewish Population Study of Greater Boston* (Waltham, MA.: Brandeis University Cohen Center for Modern Jewish Studies, and the Boston Combined Jewish Philanthropies, 2005).

4. Edmund Case and Kathy Kahn, "Engaging the Intermarried," *Forward*, November 17, 2006.

5. Leonard Saxe and Barry Chazen, *Ten Days of Birthright Israel: A Journey in Young Adult Jewish Identity* (Dartmouth, MA.: Brandeis University Press/ University Press of New England, 2008).

6. Fern Chertok, Mark Rosen, Amy Sales, and Leonard Saxe, *Outreach Families in the Sacred Common: Congregational Responses to Interfaith Issues* (Waltham, MA.: Cohen Center for Modern Jewish Studies at Brandeis University, sponsored by UAHC-CCAR Commission on Reform Jewish Outreach, 2001), p. 16.

7. Gary Rosenblatt, "Let the Outreach Debate Be Heard," with Jack Wertheimer and Kerry Olitzky, *The Jewish Week,* November 11, 2005.

8. Sylvia Barack Fishman, "Education is Destiny," in *The Jerusalem Post,* December 5, 2006.

9. Quantitative data is drawn from the 2000-01 National Jewish Population Survey conducted by the United Jewish Communities, and distributed through the North American Jewish Data Bank, unless otherwise cited.

10. Leonard Saxe, Charles Kadushin, and Benjamin Phillips, "Boston's Good News on Intermarriage," in *The Jewish Week,* November 21, 2006.

11. Steven M. Cohen, Jack Ukeles, and Ron Miller, "Read Boston Study on Intermarriage with Caution," in *The Forward,* December 8, 2006.

12. Anthony Weiss, "Intermarriage Study Muddies Waters," *Forward,* Wednesday, December 12, 2007.

13. Sue Fishkoff, "Intermarriage: Is it a big problem? *Jewish Telegraphic Agency (JTA) News Service,* December 23, 2007.

14. Janet Marder, "New Perspectives on Reform Jewish Outreach," in Avis Miller, Janet Marder, and Steven Bayme, *Approaches to Intermarriage: Areas of Consensus* (New York: American Jewish Committee, 1993), p. 5.

15. Egon Mayer, *Love and Tradition: Marriage between Jews and Christians* (New York: Schocken, 1985); Susan Weidman Schneider, *Intermarriage: The Challenge of Living with Differences between Christians and Jews* (New York: Free Press, 1989).

16. The discussion on pages 7-15 benefitted greatly from the information gathering, bibliographical, and analytical assistance of two graduate researchers affiliated with the Hadassah-Brandeis Institute in 2007: Jill Michelle Smith, Ph.D. candidate in Sociology at Brandeis University, and Rachel Gross, Ph.D. candidate in American Religion at Princeton University.

17. David Belin, *Why Choose Judaism: New Dimensions of Jewish Outreach* (New York: Union of American Hebrew Congregations, 1985), pp. 21-25.

18. Charles Silberman, *A Certain People: American Jews and their Lives Today* (New York: Summit Books, 1985). While Silberman popularized the concept of transformationalism, the idea was originally applied to the Jewish community in Calvin Goldscheider, *Jewish Continuity and Change: Emerging Patterns in America* (Bloomington: Indiana University Press, 1986).

19. "The Outreach Hall of Fame Inaugural Class," in *Joplin: Jewish Outreach Professionals Log-In Network* (http://joplin.joi.org/index.php?page).

20. Roy A. Rosenberg, Peter Meehan, and John Wade Payne, *Happily Intermarried: Authoritative Advice for a Joyous Jewish-Christian Marriage* (New York: Macmillan Publishing Company, 1988).

21. Judy Petsonk and Jim Remsen, *The Intermarriage Handbook: A Guide for Jews and Christians* (New York: William Morrow, 1988); Lee F. Gruzen, *Raising Your Jewish/ Christian Child: How Interfaith Parents Can Give Children the Best of Both Their Heritages* (New York: Newmarket Press, 1987).

22. Paul and Rachel Cowan, *Mixed Blessings: Marriage Between Jews and Christians,* (New York: Doubleday, 1987).

23. NJPS, see note # 4.

24. Sylvia Barack Fishman and Daniel Parmer, *Matrilineal Ascent/ Patrilineal Descent: The Gender Imbalance in American Jewish Life* (Waltham, MA.: Cohen Center for Modern Jewish Studies at Brandeis University and Hadassah-Brandeis Institute, 2008).

25. Sue Fishkoff, "Program helps grandparents nurture Jewishness of interfaith grandkids," *Jewish Telegraphic Agency,* January 8, 2008; reprinted in *Inside JOI,* May/June 2008.

26. Kerry M. Olitzky and Paul Golin, *Twenty Things for Grandparents of Interfaith Grandchildren to Do* (Torah Aura Productions, 2007).

27. "What is Grandparents Circle?" in *Inside JOI: Newsletter of the Jewish Outreach Institute,* May-June 2008, p. 2.

28. Leonard Saxe, Fern Chertok, and Benjamin Phillips, *It's Not Just Who Stands Under the Chuppah: Jewish Identity and Mixed Marriage* (Waltham, MA.: Brandeis University's Steinhardt Social Research Institute, 2007).

29. Fishman and Parmer, *Gender Imbalance in American Jewish Life,* pp. 59-60.

30. For a thorough discussion of religiosity and gender, see D. Paul Sullins, "Gender and Religion: Deconstructing Universality, Constructing Complexity," in *American Journal of Sociology*112, No. 3 (November 2006), pp. 838-880.

31. These data are drawn from the 254 interviews conducted for Sylvia Barack Fishman, *Double or Nothing? Jewish Families and Mixed Marriage* (Hanover, N.H.: Brandeis University Press/ University Press of New England, 2004), pp. 70-73.

32. Lawrence MacDonald, "Welcoming Synagogue Led Me to Judaism," in *Washington Jewish Week,* reprinted in InterfaithFamily.com, August 1, 2008.

33. Arlene Fine, "Outreach Expert Speaks About the Urgency of Inclusion," in *The Cleveland Jewish News,* January 3, 2007.

34. Maurice Harris, "Jews and Fellow Travelers: Appreciating the Gifts of Non-Jewish Partners," in *Reconstructionism Today* 12, No. 13 (Spring 2005).

35. Jerome M. Epstein, "Edud: A New Approach to Interfaith Outreach," *United Synagogue Review,* Spring 2006.

36. Cara Sissman, "Neutral Territory? Jewish Museums and Cultural Centers Reach Out to Interfaith Families," in www.interfaithfamily.com/news_and_opinion/outreach.

37. Sissman, *op. cit.*

38. For a very useful round-up of information on these innovative Jewish enterprises, see Steven M. Cohen, J. Shawn Landres, Elie Kaunfer and Michelle Shain, *Emergent Jewish Communities and their Participants: Preliminary Fidnings from the 2007 National Spiritual Communities Study* (Los Angeles and New York: Synagogue 3000, 2007).

39. Laurence Iannacconne, "Religious Practice: A Human Capital Approach," *Journal for the Scientific Study of Religion* 29, No. 3 (Sept. 1990): 297-314.

40. Beth Cousens, *Shifting Social Networks: Studying the Jewish Growth of Adults in their Twenties and Thirties* (Unpublished doctoral dissertation: Brandeis University Near Eastern and Judaic Studies, August 2008), pp. 33, 451.

41. Pearl Beck, *A Flame Still Burns: The Dimensions and Determinants of Jewish Identity Among Young Adult Children of the Intermarried: Fidnings and Policy*

Implications, JOI, June 2005 (www.joi.bloglinks/Children%20of%20Intermarriage%20 Identity%20Study.doc).

42. Sue Fishkoff, "At Reform Conference, Movement Calls for a Push Toward Conversion," InterfaithFamily.com, 5/28/07.

43. Eric Yoffie, "Sermon by Rabbi Eric Yoffie at the Houston Biennial," Union for Reform Judaism, November 19, 2005 (urj.org/yoffie/biennialsermon05/).

44. David Ellenson and Kerry Olitzky, "Conversion is Not an Outreach Strategy," in the *Forward,* May 12, 2006.

45. Personal interview with Paula Brody, conducted for Sylvia Barack Fishman, *Choosing Jewish: Conversations About Conversion* (New York: American Jewish Committee, 2006).

46. Mary C. Waters, *Ethnic Options: Choosing Identities in America* (Berkeley: University of California Press, 1990).

47. Rabbi Daniel Schur, "Intermarriage vs. Preserving the Jewish Way of Life," http://www.mnemotrix.com/heights/schur16.html.

48. Case and Kahn, "Engaging the Intermarried."

49. David Mittelberg, *The Israel Connection and American Jews* (Westport, Connecticut: Praeger Publishers, 1999).

50. Fishman and Parmer, *Gender Imbalance in American Jewish Life,* pp. 59-60.

51. Alice Chasan, "Disagreeing in the Service of God: An Interview with Rabbi Irving Greenberg," *Beliefnet* (http://www.beliefnet.com/story/187/story), Copyright 2008 Beliefnet, Inc.

8

The Kippah Comes to America

Lawrence Grossman

MAKING A SPLASH ON BROADWAY

The musical Silk Stockings, starring Don Ameche and Hildegard Neff, opened at the Imperial Theater on Broadway on February 24, 1955. It would run for 478 performances, closing April 14, 1956. A film version was released in 1957.[1] Whatever its place in the annals of American theater, Silk Stockings stands as a landmark in the history of American Jews: it was the site of Irving ("Yitz") Greenberg and Blu Genauer's first date.

All did not go well. Years later Blu vividly remembered "the great discomfort" she felt at the fact that Yitz kept his kippah on throughout the show, unlike all of her previous dates—Orthodox young men, some of them rabbinical students—who would bare their heads in a public space. "Even though it was he and not I" who wore the skull cap, she noted, "I was extremely self-conscious, and while I knew it wasn't right to ask him to 'hide his religion' … I sure as anything wished he would remove it so I could relax and enjoy myself."[2] Her discomfort did not fade quickly. On a subsequent date at the opera, she recalled, "I didn't hear a word, while I sat thinking the whole time, 'Why can't he be more sensible, less conspicuous?'"[3]

Such courtship reminiscences would be incomprehensible to young Orthodox couples of the early-twenty-first century. Not only is it almost unthinkable now for a first—or any—date to take place at a Broadway musical, but today's young woman would be appalled if her date took her anywhere *without* a kippah. (To complicate matters further, on second thought, *wearing* a kippah on a date would automatically doom the relationship in those ever-widening circles where the woman fully expects to see a black hat!)

In fact, Yitz Greenberg's kippah at the theater that night exemplified a momentous turning-point for American Orthodox Judaism. It was at that time, the mid-1950s, that Modern Orthodoxy was taking shape, and the public appearance of the kippah was one of its primary symbols. Greenberg was riding the wave of the future.

EVOLUTION OF A CUSTOM

The history of men's head covering in Jewish law is both obscure and complex.[4] There are several references in the Babylonian Talmud to keeping one's head covered at all times as a sign of exceptional piety, *midat hasidut*, but little evidence that it was a widespread practice. It plays an even smaller role in the Palestinian Talmud, where covering the head is mentioned only in connection with the recitation of the Grace After Meals. Medieval sources give a varied picture, some stressing the importance of head covering and others indicating that it was not practiced, even during prayer.[5]

Rabbi Joseph Karo's authoritative sixteenth-century Jewish law code *Shulhan Arukh* rules that a man may not walk more than four cubits *be-gilui rosh,* with head uncovered (*Orah Haim* 2:6). Rabbi Moses Isserles, who presents the Ashkenazi alternative to the Sephardi *Shulhan Arukh,* apparently maintains that head covering is only required for prayer and reading the Torah (*Darkei Moshe* to *Tur Orah Haim,* 2:2; *Shulhan Arukh Orah Haim,* 282:3). Another outstanding sixteenth-century Polish rabbi, Shlomo Luria (known as the Maharshal), denied any validity to the custom even during prayer—except for the exceptionally pious—and bemoaned the fact that many ordinary Jewish men who meticulously covered their heads showed shocking laxity about religious practices that were far more important.

The highly influential seventeenth-century Polish commentator Rabbi David Halevi (known as the Taz, the acronym for his work *Turei Zahav* on the *Shulhan Arukh*) significantly strengthened the obligatory nature of male head covering by stressing an additional rationale. Not only was it a custom demonstrating exceptional piety, it also signified separation from Gentile practice. Since Christians bared their heads as a sign of respect, for Jews to do so would constitute a violation of *hukkot hagoyim,* going in the ways of the Gentiles, a prohibition considered to be of biblical origin. (*Orah Haim* 8:3). This view triumphed in Eastern Europe, and not even the opposition of Elijah, the Gaon of Vilna, in the eighteenth century, who ignored the view of the Taz and considered head covering to be just a matter of etiquette, or limited to people of great holiness (*Shulhan Arukh Orah Haim* 8:2), could shake it.[6]

The onset of modernity drew a geographical dividing line within European Jewry on the subject of men's headgear. In Western and Central Europe the promise of emancipation and equality provided a powerful inducement to adopt the mores of the Christian majority: respectable men wore hats while walking down the street, but indoors baring the head was a sign of culture and good breeding. As the nascent Reform movement debated whether to adopt bareheadedness even in prayer, for Orthodox men, covering the head indoors came to be restricted to religious activities.[7] The leading historian of German Orthodoxy notes that "uncovering one's head in a roofed enclosure had become the rule on occasions when keeping one's head covered could be regarded as unmannerly or disrespectful." At the Jewish school founded by Orthodox leader Rabbi Samson Raphael Hirsch in Frankfort in the mid-nineteenth century, male students covered their heads only during Jewish studies classes and removed them for secular studies. In a famous incident, Rabbi Hirsch berated a young rabbinical scholar from Hungary for appearing at the school for a job interview with his head covered, charging that this sign of disrespect towards him could undermine discipline in the school, especially if witnessed by the non-Jewish teachers of secular subjects.[8]

In striking contrast, Eastern European rabbis considered the ideals of emancipation and enlightenment threats to Jewish survival, and so traditional practices that maintained boundaries between Jew and Gentile, such as male head covering—as emphasized by the ruling of the Taz noted above—became more important than ever. Indeed, one of the reforms promulgated by Czarist Russia in the 1840s and 1850s to "modernize" Jewish life was banning covering of the head outside of religious services. Such edicts, unenforceable as they were, impelled faithful Jews to cling to the practice even more, and interpret it more stringently. At the same time, the growth and influence of Hasidism gave prominence to mystical interpretations of male head covering.[9]

One of the most authoritative rabbinical scholars of the time, Rabbi Shlomo Kluger of the Ukrainian city of Brody, issued a landmark ruling on the subject that added a further stringency and had a profound impact on popular practice. He claimed that all the earlier sources seeming to indicate permission for *gilui rosh* did not literally mean bareheadedness, but rather that a skullcap was sufficient in those situations, and it was not necessary to place a hat *on top of* the skull cap. Out of doors, he wrote, one could not walk more than four cubits without a hat that covered the entire head.[10]

Evidence for the central role that the originally peripheral practice of male head covering came to play in the East European Jewish consciousness is the classic Yiddish story by Y.L. Peretz, *Drei Matonos* (Three Gifts), in which it is elevated to a valid cause for *kiddush hashem,* martyrdom. In the story a simple Jew dies, and the heavenly judgment reveals that his good and bad deeds are exactly balanced. In order to tilt the scales in his favor, the soul is instructed to descend to earth and brings back three "gifts" for the saints in paradise. The first gift is earth from the land of Israel that a Jew died defending from robbers, even as he allowed them to take his valuables. The second is a pin that a Jewish girl used to fasten her clothing, so as to maintain her modesty while being dragged through the streets to her death for allegedly desecrating the Christian host. The third and final gift is a skullcap. It falls from the head of its owner, a Jew being forced to walk the gauntlet between two rows of soldiers who are whipping him. "He stopped short, he hesitated, he reflected a moment, he made up his mind, and he turned around: he would not go with his head uncovered. He retraced his steps to the spot where the cap had fallen. He bent down and picked it up. Then he continued on calmly, gushing blood but with the Jewish cap on his head. He walked erect until he collapsed…. The third gift was also accepted." It is the gift of the skull cap—actually the self-sacrifice of the Jew who insists on picking it up and putting it back on despite the added lashings he would have to endure—that enables the soul to enter paradise.[11]

THE AMERICAN SCENE

For American Jews up until the late nineteenth century there could be no such attribution of religious significance to male head covering. Neither the Western Sephardim, who arrived in colonial times, nor the Ashkenazim of Central Europe, who became the majority of the American Jewish community by the mid-eighteenth century, came from cultures that stressed head covering outside the synagogue.[12] Only a new wave of immigrants from Eastern Europe, starting in the 1880s, would bring large numbers of Jews to American shores who shared the tradition of male head covering.

To be sure, that head covering was just one detail of the East European Jewish immigrant's much more extensive set of exotic characteristics—including old-world garb, beards and sometimes side curls, and Yiddish speech—that drew the attention of the American public and generated some degree of embarrassment from the already Americanized Jewish community. Even so, the hats and skullcaps of so many of the newcomers contrasted especially sharply with the bareheadedness of the preexisting Jewish male population (even that portion of it that identified as Orthodox), and both sides noticed. The cultural clash was played out in what might be called a battle of the encyclopedias.

The 12-volume *Jewish Encyclopedia,* published between 1901 and 1906 was edited by leading Jewish authorities, both Reform and traditional. Its entry on "Bareheadedness" was authored by two well-known Reform scholars, Gotthard Deutsch, professor of Jewish history at Hebrew Union College (HUC), and Kaufmann Kohler, then serving as a rabbi in New York but soon to be appointed HUC president. After delineating the historical development of the practice they identified three contemporary schools of thought. American Reform, they noted, had largely discarded the requirement of head covering during services—some congregations barring it entirely. As for those outside Reform, they wrote, "the conservative Jews in civilized countries insist on the covering of the head merely during the performance of religious acts, while the rigid adherents of the ancient custom keep their heads constantly covered, and therefore wear a skull-cap." The paragraph on the non-Reform practices is given the sub-head title "Concessions of Modern Orthodoxy."[13]

The Orthodox journalist and activist Judah David Eisenstein, who contributed more than 150 articles to the *Encyclopedia,* was nevertheless dissatisfied with the work, believing that it gave Orthodoxy short shrift. Eisenstein proceeded to edit a ten-volume encyclopedia of his own, in Hebrew, *Otzar Yisrael,* which was published between 1906 and 1913. Curiously, he commissioned two separate articles about male *"Gilui Rosh"* (Bareheadedness), showing his awareness of the split in the non-Reform community over the issue. The first was penned by Rev. Dr. Nehemiah Mosessohn, rabbi of a traditional congregation in Portland, Oregon, and editor of that city's *Jewish Tribune.* Mossesohn's piece briefly reviews the sources, concludes that male head covering is nothing more than a pious custom, and ends with a citation of the Vilna Gaon's opinion to that effect.[14]

The other article on the subject in the *Otzar* was by Rabbi Zalman Yaakov Friederman of Agudat ha-Kehilot in Boston. A product of Lithuanian yeshivot and the son-in-law of the private secretary of the renowned Rabbi Isaac Elhanan of Kovno, he had arrived in the U.S. in 1893 and quickly gained a reputation for hard-line opposition to any deviation from the strictest Orthodoxy.[15] Predictably, his contribution echoed both Rabbi Kluger's position that bareheadedness is never sanctioned and the view of the Taz that uncovering the head amounted to *hukat hagoyim,* and was therefore absolutely prohibited. Friederman even cited sources supporting male head covering during sleep and at the bathhouse. He found room for leniency only in a case where one must swear before a Gentile court of law, and the judges required bareheadedness.[16]

A historian of Boston's Orthodox community notes that Friederman "rejected Americanism and sought to reduce its attractive power over American Jews."[17] The new immigrants, however, and even more so their American-born children, wanted to be absorbed into the culture of their new land, an impossible goal if they did not look like other Americans. The Friederman approach did not stand a chance. For the vast majority of Jews who entered the U.S. during the great wave of East European immigration that lasted until World War I, and for the smaller numbers who came in the 1920s and early 1930s, Americanization trumped any religious obligation—Shabbat, a kosher diet, Jewish education—let alone regulations about clothing. This immigration was, after all, selective: most of the rabbinical elite and others intensely committed to Jewish practice would not leave Eastern Europe until forced to by Communist and Nazi policies in the late 1930s, 1940s, and thereafter—if indeed they could get out at all. The earlier immigrants tended to be those least rooted in the traditional way of life, and who were therefore willing to pull up stakes and cross the ocean in search of new opportunity in defiance of rabbinic strictures against placing one's family's Jewish identity at risk in the *trefene medinah* (unkosher land).

FITTING IN

To be sure, covering one's head while walking down the street did not make one stand out. The American style in the first half of the twentieth century, as in Europe, remained to wear hats out of doors, and "it was seen as improper for a man to leave the house without a hat." This was "a time when gentlemen tipped their hats to strangers, tossed them in celebration, or waved them as ships left the docks…." And so the Orthodox could "pass" as true red-blooded Americans while unobtrusively fulfilling a Jewish custom. "Abroad they wore hats," recalled Ruth Gay about her father and his friends, "modern American hats, and most favored was the snap-brim fedora."[18]

But indoors, especially in public spaces, etiquette demanded bare heads. Blu Greenberg recalled her father taking her to visit a marine base. He removed his hat "without replacing it, as he always did, with his black rayon, slightly bepurpled yarmulke. I had never before seen him bareheaded," she explained, "and it startled me."[19] This pattern held not only for individuals but also for Orthodox institutions and their leaders. The board of directors of The Jewish Center in New York was photographed sitting in the boardroom of the synagogue building with heads uncovered in 1942. Yeshiva University publicity shots four years later showed board members and top administrators bareheaded; only the president, Rabbi Dr. Samuel Belkin, wore a skull cap. As late as 1954 Yeshiva was still using two-year-old photographs of five students, heads uncovered, who had won National Science Foundation fellowships, meeting with Albert Einstein.[20]

Young American boys and teenagers did not wear hats out of doors, and tensions triggered by the head-covering custom were especially intense for Jewish children and adolescents, who found it more problematic than just about any other religious restriction. While eating kosher could be done unobtrusively, and keeping Shabbat entailed one day of rest, the skull cap on the head made one a perpetually marked man on city streets, subject to ridicule and even physical violence for this deviation from the American norm. No wonder so many boys removed it immediately upon leaving synagogue on Shabbat, or when departing yeshiva or after-school Hebrew lessons.[21] Complicating the psychic trauma, that removal could bring negative consequences of its own. Literary critic Morris Dickstein, who attended yeshiva in the late 1940s and early 1950s, recalled: "On the East Side I was always looking over my shoulder, since some of the teachers were fond of spying on their charges in off hours, pouncing on them if their heads were uncovered, or G-d forbid, they were caught violating the Sabbath."[22]

In more modern Orthodox circles, where rabbinical authorities asserted not only the possibility of melding Jewish tradition with Americanism but actually advocated that path, any gratuitous public display of Jewish identity was shunned. "There was no such thing as wearing a kippah in the street" when he was growing up in Manhattan during the 1930s and 1940s, recalled Rabbi Haskell Lookstein. Ramaz, the Orthodox day school his father, Rabbi Joseph H. Lookstein, founded, operated on the principle that the skull cap was an "indoor garment."[23] The caps that boys from such schools were expected to don outside marked them off as different from their public school peers who did not wear them, and so bareheadedness on the street was often the result, however unintended, of the Ramaz policy.

Even young men from the most committed Orthodox families did not feel comfortable manifesting their observance publicly during those years. Israel Friedman, a son of the Boyaner Rebbe, admitted that he and his friends

> were not too sure of their pride in being Orthodox Jews.... Nobody thought of wearing a yarmulke outside the home. Certainly no one who went to City College ever thought of wearing a yarmulke while being in school. I frankly was ashamed. I never would have done it. Neither I nor anybody else. When I had to eat I snuck myself away to the Great Hall in some corner and put on my yarmulke and ate there in the corner so that no one would notice me.[24]

In his autobiographical novel *Inside Outside*, Herman Wouk evoked the full significance of male Jewish head covering both as stigma and symbolic barrier between parochial Orthodoxy and the inviting American world outside its precincts. Wouk's alter ego, I. David Goodkind, raised in an Orthodox family, attends Talmudical Academy, Yeshiva University's high school in the

Washington Heights section of Manhattan, in the mid-1930s. His fondest wish is to gain entry into American society and high culture, in pursuit of which he applies to Columbia College. Goodkind takes the subway from the academy to Morningside Heights for his Columbia interview:

> I passed from the crowded bet midrash full of Talmud chant to the campus of a great American university; to green playing fields, broad lawns, and stately red and gray buildings. The domed library atop a sweep of stone staircases was itself much bigger than Yeshiva University. The students strolling the brick walks looked to me like extras in a college movie: the boys all spiffy and gentile, the girls all elegant and gentile, their clothes all collegiate and gentile. Not a yarmulka in sight!

Weeks later, notified of his acceptance to Columbia, Goodkind "walked out into the sunshine, into the American open air; strode a few blocks away from the yeshiva to a little park, took off my yarmulka, and threw myself on the grass, in happy shock."[25]

VARIETIES OF ORTHODOXY

In marked contrast, the Orthodox Jewish immigrants who fled or survived the Holocaust did not come to America of their own free will and, in most cases, would have preferred to live out their lives steeped in the thickly Jewish culture of Eastern Europe, had not Hitler intervened. Far from longing to Americanize, they wanted to replicate Jewishly, in whatever measure possible, the communities from which they had been uprooted. Those coming from mitnagdic (anti-Hasidic) backgrounds revivified existing American yeshivas and created their own, placing the study of Talmud at the center of the (male) Jewish experience and devaluing other pursuits. The Hasidim who arrived—some with their prewar rebbes, others, whose rebbes had been killed, attaching themselves to new ones—constituted visible enclaves, mostly in New York neighborhoods with preexisting Jewish communities.[26]

Members of both Jewish immigrant groups valued dressing the way they had in Europe, but since it was the Hasidim who had put up the greatest resistance to modern clothing styles in the old country, they were the ones who attracted notice in their new surroundings. Invariably, their breaking of the social taboo against public wearing of the skull cap drew special attention. The final impression left on one Jewish visitor to Williamsburg in the mid-1950s was "little boys in skull caps" streaming out of yeshiva at lunchtime. A few years later two other visitors to that neighborhood reported that there were men with uncovered heads sitting on benches, but they were all "in their fifties, or older," and that, obviously for commercial reasons, "almost all the storekeepers, even those without the *peyes* [Hasidic ear locks] wear skullcaps."[27]

The trend unleashed by the newcomers began to spill over and affect the children of earlier Orthodox migrations. In their eyes, the Hasidim and yeshiva students were more authentically Orthodox, having recently arrived from the Eastern European homeland, and they evoked in the "Americans" a mixture of admiration and resentment as well as a dose of guilt. Thus an Orthodox resident of Boro Park who, growing up there between the wars, covered his head only at home, told sociologist Egon Mayer, with some amazement: "My own boys think nothing of wearing a *yarmulke* on the subway or in college," and attributed the shift to "the Jews who came in the '40s and the '50s" who "brought in, shall I say, the need of identifying ourselves as Jews." Similarly, Israel Friedman recalled that "to put on a yarmulke in the street, to even think of wearing a yarmulke when studying and going to school and college, or working with a computer or as a scientist at IBM or for a fancy law firm" was only conceivable "after World War II, when the influx of immigrants came...."[28]

It would be profoundly misleading, however, to attribute the vogue of head covering solely to the new immigrants. In the decade and a half after the end of World War II a new generation of native-born Orthodox Jews came to maturity that differed both from the newcomers and from their own immigrant parents in feeling utterly at home in America. Never having suffered serious anti-Semitism or the trauma of being uprooted from their homeland, these young men and women did not sense any compulsion to reject or hide their Orthodox practices in order to Americanize. And what is more, the formative Jewish experience for them was the saga of the creation of the State of Israel out of the ashes of the Holocaust, a historic accomplishment that instilled immense Jewish pride, rather than the sense of marginality from which so many of the immigrant generation suffered.

By the late 1940s and 1950s they were attending college and graduate school in large numbers, and, thanks to the postwar easing of Jewish admissions quotas, were taking their places even at Ivy League institutions. As early as 1947 a group of graduate students formed the Association of Orthodox Jewish Scientists; during the 1950s an Orthodox synagogue body, the National Council of Young Israel, began to set up kosher kitchens on several campuses; and 1960 saw the establishment of Yavneh, a national organization to meet the social and intellectual needs of Orthodox college students.

Yitz Greenberg and Blu Genauer were of this generation. And although Blu was unaware of it on their first date, Yitz's distracting kippah in the theater resulted from a decision he had made only recently. In 1953 Greenberg began graduate studies in American history at Harvard because it was "*the* American school, the acme of the American experience." He "just knew that you could not wear a *kippah*" there. In the traditional Orthodox effort at camouflage, Greenberg wore a hat on campus, "took it off when I went into class," and re-placed it when leaving the classroom. He recalled, "It was awkward, it was uncomfortable, but what could I do?" At student-faculty cocktail parties he would "hold a drink in my hand all the time because I would not drink it without covering my head and making a *bracha*." After about two years—not long before the fateful *Silk Stockings* date—Greenberg, telling himself, "Look, I have a right to do it," started wearing a *kippah* at all times. "That coming-out was a key transition for me," he noted many years later.[29]

That same decision, to wear a skull cap in public, would mark the Jewish coming-out of many others. As in Greenberg's case, these were men very much at home both within Orthodox Judaism and the most "American" pre-cincts of American life. For many of them the decision was not primarily a matter of religious punctiliousness: Greenberg and others were undoubtedly aware of the shaky Halakhic basis for the practice. Rather, it was a statement of Orthodox Jewish identity and pride, an overt if silent expression of the conviction that the ancient tradition could persist, indeed thrive, within American modernity.[30]

THE KIPPAH SUPPLANTS THE HAT

It was at this time, too, that men's clothing styles changed and it became ac-ceptable for adult males to be seen hatless in public (the same process affected women's wearing of hats as well). Poet Billy Collins (born 1941, U.S. poet lau-reate 2001–03), movingly portrays the shift as a marker between generations in "The Death of the Hat." "Once every man wore a hat," the poem opens, "in ashen newsreels," on streets, in ballparks: "Hats were the law." His father "wore one to work every day." But now "we go bareheaded into the winter streets,/ stand hatless on frozen platforms." The final stanza reads: "And now my father, after a life of work,/wears a hat of earth,/and on top of that,/a lighter one of cloud and sky—a hat of wind."[31]

Although the common belief that President John F. Kennedy personally launched the new look by appearing at his inauguration on January 20, 1961, bareheaded is not, strictly speaking, accurate, his penchant for the hatless look, combined with his youthful and vigorous appearance, accelerated a trend that had been gradually building.[32] In "How JFK Killed My Father," an-other contemporary poet (and psychiatrist), Richard Berlin, whose father re-turned from World War II and went into the manufacture of the sweat bands that were placed inside men's hats, addressed the onset of the hatless era and its fatal impact on his father's business and health from a Jewish perspective.

Berlin presents a cavalcade of recent political figures: "Truman in a Scala wool Hamburg/Ike's bald head steamed in fur felt,/Stevenson's ideals lost in the glory/of a two-inch brimmed Stetson." But "thick-haired Kennedy/rode top down and bare-headed," and so "men all over America took off their hats" and "flung them in the street forever." The result: "Hat factories closed quiet as prayer books," and his ruined father would never be the same. "Years later," Berlin continues, "yarmulke on my head,/they asked me to view him in his coffin," and he had to laugh "that they dressed him up for eternity/without a hat." The son could "still hear/the old men murmur in the graveyard,/*Kennedy did it to him,*/fedoras held close to their leathered hearts."[33]

Whatever its unsettling impact, the new style reinforced the example presented by the yarmulke-clad new refugees and helped liberate Orthodox baby boomers. Up-to-date Orthodox young men increasingly walked the streets of America wearing skull caps, no longer camouflaging their religious identity behind hats or caps, and the free market began producing kippot far more interesting and varied than the old standard silk version, which, clumsy and usually too big, had made wearers feel awkward and self-conscious. The new variety was smaller, providing a much neater look, and some had colorful designs. A true art form was the knitted skullcap, *kippah srugah,* often with the Hebrew name of the bearer, which evoked the ethos of the new State of Israel, bore the personal identity of the wearer, and could be produced by a young lady for her boyfriend. Indeed, one could often determine the particular religious, political, and social leanings of a young man by the type of *kippah* he wore.[34]

Orthodox male head covering, previously dismissed by most as an Old World relic, and, if practiced, done surreptitiously, had become, at least in some neighborhoods, ubiquitous. This naturally aroused great interest in the community, and Jewish journals that had never previously mentioned the practice now gave it attention. Within the span of ten months, spanning 1953–54, three influential organs of American Jewish opinion ran articles about it, each targeting a different audience and transmitting a different message about its religious and cultural significance.[35]

Jewish Life was the monthly publication of the Union of Orthodox Jewish Congregations, the major body of Orthodox synagogues, founded in 1898. The great bulk of its constituent congregations and their members were Americanized Modern Orthodox. In this era many of the synagogues had men and women sitting together, and driving to services was common—albeit the drivers were careful to park around the block, out of respect. Male members, generally speaking, did not cover their heads outside the synagogue, and *Jewish Life* had never discussed it.

In the March 1953 issue, however, appeared an article entitled "Why Wear a Yarmulka?" Rabbi Joseph Weiss, its author, was instructor of Talmud and "research specialist in Talmud and Halachah" at Yeshiva University, as well as secretary of the Commission on Halachah of the Rabbinical Council of America, the organization of Modern Orthodox rabbis. Weiss's aim was to advocate head covering, and he laid down the gauntlet in his very first sentence: "One of the most respected and best loved Jewish traditions is to cover our heads at all times, in all places, and on every occasion." Ignoring the actual dubious and checkered history of male head covering in Jewish law, Weiss declared that "deviation from the practice... was always considered as an assault on Jewish tradition and as a step toward breaking with Divine religion." Non-Orthodox streams of Judaism, he charged, uncovered their heads as a sign of "removal of traditional Torah and the adoption of secular doctrines." After citing both of the traditional reasons for head covering—the Talmudic view that it creates an aura of fear of God, and the Taz's position that it differentiates Jews from bareheaded non-Jews—Weiss added that "bareheadedness symbolizes unguided freethinking.... We cover our heads to show that there is yet something higher than our own limited intelligence...."[36]

The *National Jewish Monthly* was published by B'nai B'rith, the largest and most influential Jewish fraternal organization in America. Very few of its members were Orthodox Jews. Nevertheless, it published an article on "Why Cover the Head?" by Rabbi Leon Stitskin, a Modern Orthodox rabbi then serving a Philadelphia congregation, who was a member of the Rabbinical Council of America executive board. Stitskin began by explaining that he wrote this essay to satisfy popular curiosity: the practice of male head covering "has recently assumed particular importance among Orthodox religious circles in America.... Especially... in New York City, where one can find young and old wearing skull caps in stores, on the street, and even in the playground for school children." In stark contrast to Weiss, his review of the sources led to the conclusion that there was no legal prohibition on bareheadedness, but that the practice of head covering was a venerable custom that denoted piety.[37]

Commentary, the intellectual monthly published by the American Jewish Committee, also ran an article on "Why Jews Cover the Head." The author, R. Brasch, an Australian Reform rabbi, pointed to the paradox that the "very Orthodox" viewed constant male head covering as crucial to "the very foundations of their faith," even though, Brasch assured the reader, the practice "is neither Biblical nor Jewish," and "is of relatively recent origin among the Jews." He claimed it was picked up by Babylonian Jews "from their heathen environment," from there transferred to Spanish Jewry, and on to Ashkenazi centers after the Spanish expulsion of 1492. In later centuries this "meaningless physical act was justified by symbolic interpretation." Brasch listed commonly cited explanations, grouping them under the categories of "Hygiene,"

"Manners," "A Sign of Identity," "Symbols of Independence," and "Symbols of a Priestly Nation."[38]

P'SAK IN MULTICULTURAL AMERICA

The trend of young adult Orthodox men whose fathers wore hats to don kippot out of doors triggered the first *teshuvot* (rabbinic responsa) on the subject by Rabbi Moshe Feinstein, the leading American *posek* of the era. Not only do his rulings indicate an acute understanding of social reality, but they (and the queries that they address) suggest the swift evolution of the American skull cap. In 1956, when the phenomenon was still relatively new, a questioner asked Feinstein if the current practice even of "many who fear God" of wearing a kippah on the street was sufficient. After all, Rabbi Shlomo Kluger had ruled that the whole head should be covered, and that could only be accomplished by a hat. Feinstein responded by rejecting Kluger's view as a minority opinion. Although one who wishes to be extra stringent could certainly follow Kluger, it was not mandatory, and so a simple skull cap was sufficient.[39]

By 1960 the skullcap had become such an identification badge of Orthodoxy that the audacious statement Yitz Greenberg made five years earlier by wearing one to *Silk Stockings* was being made by others as well in similar venues (and hence was no longer so audacious). That year someone asked Rabbi Feinstein if a man who enters "a theater or museum" should remove his head covering. The rabbi's decision—absolutely not—supported Greenberg's practice, although his reasoning was probably quite distant from Greenberg's outlook. Attending such a place was itself prohibited, Feinstein argued, and baring the head would only add a second sin. He rejected the argument that removing the head covering could be justified to avoid the *hilul hashem* (desecration of God's name) of an Orthodox Jew being seen in an improper place; Feinstein believed that the very act of entering a theater or museum clearly indicated a lack of concern about *hilul hashem*.[40]

Two years later Feinstein was asked a similar question about attending places of "licentiousness," where young men and women who otherwise abided by Jewish law danced together. Should the men be told to remove their *kippot* when entering, since if they did not bystanders might come to believe that mixed dancing was sanctioned by Orthodox Judaism? On the contrary, the rabbi replied, violation of one mitzvah should not be addressed by instructing the guilty party to violate another. The correct strategy, he concluded, was to educate the community to observe both.[41]

Rabbi Feinstein also received queries about covering one's head in the workplace. Was it permissible to remove the kippah for a job interview, or on the job itself, if not doing so would endanger the prospects of obtaining or keeping employment? The rabbi replied that *parnassah,* the necessity of making a living, could override the practice of male head covering. He based this view on the fact that non-Jewish men no longer wore hats out of doors, and thus their bareheadedness indoors was no longer *hukkot hagoyim* but simply a matter of convenience. Since, then, the view of the Taz on the need to cover the head to differentiate Jewish from non-Jewish males no longer applied, Jewish head covering was only on the level of venerated custom, which did not require the sacrifice of one's livelihood. [42]

Beginning in the late 1960s, the revolution in clothing styles that began with discarding the hat proceeded to decimate suits and ties as well. The influence of the counter-culture, the civil rights movement, and multiculturalism meant, sartorially, that "anything goes" in many spheres of American life. The skullcap, it turned out, could seem quite staid compared to what other people were wearing, even to work. One Orthodox psychiatrist told sociologist George Kranzler:

> I have never taken off my *yarmulke,* not at medical school, nor in the hospitals where in which I worked, and not on the job as administrator of a hospital unit. They consider me just as another of those crazy guys around here. My colleagues wear jeans and T-shirts, just like their patients. To tell the truth, I am still one of the best-dressed doctors around here.[43]

The triumph of Orthodox male head covering in the 1960s was not without its strains. Within the Orthodox community itself the practice triggered a degree of generational tension, as middle-age men who had grown up bareheaded in public suddenly found that their children deemed this insufficiently Orthodox. As early as 1963 the issue created a stir at Yeshiva University. That May, the school appeared on the popular Sunday quiz show "GE College Bowl," its team attracting enormous publicity by winning twice before losing its third match. The three young men on the team wore kippot. The professor serving as faculty adviser, however, appeared onscreen bareheaded. This would have raised no eyebrows a decade earlier, as the studio was an indoor public space where one would not, in those days, cover the head. But now it provoked a storm of controversy on the Yeshiva campus. As the professor's critics and supporters clashed over proper interpretation of the traditional sources about male head covering, a clear sociological consensus emerged: the kippah had become a hallmark of American Orthodoxy, and therefore a professor representing an Orthodox institution should have worn it.[44]

Male head covering also aroused discomfort among some older non-Orthodox Jews, for whom it seemed an un-American atavism that bespoke the immigrant past. Such resentment was especially sharp among Jews who had grown up Orthodox, like Professor Harry Steinhauer, who was both learned enough to know just how recent the practice was (constituting, he wrote, "nothing more than a mark of identity, like a sheriff's badge or an 'I like Ike' button"[45]) and outspoken enough to vent his resentment. So upset was he, during the 1960s, when a kippah-clad University of Michigan student turned up when he was interviewing applicants for Woodrow Wilson Fellowships that he asked the young man "if he considered covering the head a central principle of Judaism." Receiving a hesitant, negative reply, Steinhauer told the applicant, "I *could* ask you: if so, why are you wearing this unusual piece of headgear on this occasion, but I shall forbear to ask that question."[46] Steinhauer urged all Jews to adopt the Gentile custom of demonstrating reverence by uncovering the head, and warned of dire anti-Semitic consequences if the Orthodox persisted with their nonconformist skull caps.

The kippah also became a symbolic flashpoint in the 1960s for simmering ethnic tensions. On December 26, 1968, in the midst of the conflict between black community groups and the mostly Jewish teachers union over control of the schools in the Ocean Hill-Brownsville section of Brooklyn, Julius Lester, hosting a radio program on listener-supported WBAI-FM, allowed a black teacher to read a poem on the air written by a 14-year-old black girl. The teacher said the title was "Anti-Semitism" and that it was dedicated to Albert Shanker, the Jewish head of the teachers union. It began, "Hey, Jew boy, with that yarmulke on your head/You pale-faced Jew boy—I wish you were dead."[47] The outrage generated by this broadcast marked the end of any lingering hopes of resuscitating a black-Jewish civil-rights coalition.

While some were discomfited and others angered by the increasingly ubiquitous kippah, the ease with which it found acceptance into the mainstream of American life during the 1960s and beyond spoke volumes about the openness of the society to minority religious practices. Even today, other Western countries—not to speak of the non-Western world—have difficulty coping with multiculturalism and accommodating the unconventional. In this regard, at least, America remains a beacon for the world. Arguing recently for an end to the ban on women's head scarves in Turkish universities that had been instituted to protect the secular character of the country's institutions, Ankara law professor Ergun Ozbudun said: "It's an issue of human rights, not secularism. In the U.S., I had Jewish students wearing yarmulkes and nobody cared."[48]

A GOVERNMENT SEAL OF APPROVAL

Nowhere was the meteoric rise of the skullcap into a religious "requirement" for Orthodox Jewish men more evident than in American law. Unlike the old days, when Orthodox boys would sit in their public school classes bareheaded, their families now filed lawsuits against school districts that did not allow the children to wear skullcaps in class. The Jewish defense agencies—American Jewish Committee, American Jewish Congress, Anti-Defamation League, and local Jewish community relations councils—intervened in these cases with briefs arguing that deprivation of the right was a violation of religious freedom. Already in the 1960s, courts and local authorities in two states with large Orthodox populations, New York and New Jersey, acquiesced.[49]

Two decades later the right to wear a skull cap was publicly and officially endorsed by the U.S. government, and with it the underlying idea that Orthodox Judaism required males to cover their heads at all times. In 1981, Simcha Goldman, an Orthodox psychologist serving in the Air Force, was told not to wear his skull cap while on duty, and filed suit charging a violation of his First Amendment rights. The district court found for Goldman, the Court of Appeals for the District of Columbia reversed, and, on appeal, the U.S. Supreme Court ruled against Goldman by 5-4 in March 1986. The legal point at issue was whether the constitutional guarantee of free exercise of religion could override the military's considered judgment that uniformity in appearance was necessary for discipline and esprit de corps. Congress then overrode the Supreme Court decision by passing legislation in 1987 allowing members of the Armed Forces to wear religious apparel on duty so long as it was "neat and conservative" and did "not interfere with the performance" of military duties.[50]

The question of whether Orthodox Judaism required male head covering—a matter, as we have seen, not easily resolved—was not directly at issue since earlier precedents had established that neither the courts nor Congress had the competence or the authority to determine religious law, and thus Goldman's sincerely held religious convictions had to be accepted. Nevertheless, Jewish teachings lurked as a subtext at every stage of the case, suggesting that both sides felt that the degree of importance male head covering enjoyed in Jewish law and tradition might sway the judges.

In the original suit in district court, the Air Force referred to a recent popular digest of Jewish law that cited Rabbi Moshe Feinstein's view (noted above) that a Jew might uncover his head if required by his employer, and Goldman himself let slip that "some Orthodox Jews who consider themselves devout do not feel obliged to cover their heads at all times."[51] In Goldman's appeal to the Supreme Court his lawyers claimed that Jewish law required their client to keep his head covered, and the government once again pointed to Feinstein's ruling. Goldman's lawyers also brought up a new, sociological argument. Since the skullcap was now "commonly seen and accepted" on, for example "university campuses, city streets, and other public places," it constituted no more than "slightly idiosyncratic apparel," and therefore was not likely to stand out and interfere with military uniformity. The government countered that what might not seem odd in civilian life could still be highly obtrusive in a military setting.[52]

In oral argument before the U.S. Supreme Court in January 1986, Goldman's lawyer, Nathan Lewin, sought immediately to establish the skullcap's centrality to Judaism. In his opening statement, before the usual interruptions from the justices, Lewin described Goldman as "an individual who was raised as an Orthodox Jew and has during his entire adult life followed the religious obligation incumbent on Jewish males of keeping his head covered at all times during waking hours." As for the Feinstein responsum suggesting that it was not so "incumbent," Lewin declared that the government "acknowledged in response to our requests for admissions… 'that it is a well established religious tradition and a practice among adherents to Orthodox Judaism that males keep their heads covered at all times.'"[53]

Obviously puzzled, one justice asked Lewin for clarification "as to whether the wearing of the yarmulke is required by Jewish law." Lewin replied that it was not found in biblical law but was required by rabbinic law, and that Rabbi Feinstein's position allowing bareheadedness if one's livelihood was at stake "was not the view of the rabbis he [Goldman] followed and from whom he requested opinions…." The government's lawyer, Kathryn Oberly, was also asked about this, and responded that head covering was "a strong, well-established practice and tradition," but not a "requirement." She acknowledged that Goldman's "sincere religious belief" had legal status even it was not religiously mandatory under Jewish law.[54]

None of the five opinions rendered in the Court's 5-4 decision in favor of the government cast doubt on the significance of male head covering for Orthodox Judaism, and two of them explicitly pointed out that significance. Justice Stevens's concurring opinion (joined by Justices White and Powell) did allow the military dress code to override it, but acknowledged that "the yarmulke is a familiar and accepted sight. In addition to its religious significance for the wearer, the yarmulke may evoke the deepest respect and admiration—the symbol of a distinguished tradition and an eloquent rebuke to the ugliness of anti-Semitism." The dissent of Justice Brennan (joined by Justice Marshall) castigated the majority for not letting Goldman "fulfill one of the traditional religious obligations of a male Orthodox Jew—to cover his head before an omnipresent God," setting up "an almost absolute bar to the fulfillment of a religious duty."[55]

In 1987, offering an amendment to the Defense Department Appropriations bill that would override the Supreme Court ruling and allow members of the armed forces to wear "neat and conservative" religious apparel while in uniform, Representative Steven Solarz, a Brooklyn Democrat, appeared to rule on a question that had perplexed rabbis for centuries. He explained, "Orthodox Jews, by the dictates of their religion, are required to cover their heads at all times." Solarz opined—more than thirty years after Yitz Greenberg embarrassed Blu Genauer by wearing a kippah to a Broadway show—"A yarmulke is a symbol of religious conviction. It is not extreme, is not unusual, and is certainly not a fad."[56] The amendment was approved and the bill passed.

The young Greenberg, it turned out, had helped pioneer the creation of a new Jewish "tradition," the first of many innovative, even revolutionary, accomplishments that would mark his career.

NOTES

1. International Broadway Database, http://www.ibdb.com/production. asp?ID=2504; "Silk Stockings," http://en.wikipedia.org/wiki/Silk_Stockings.

2. Blu Greenberg, *How to Run a Traditional Jewish Household* (New York: Simon and Schuster, 1983), p. 194.

3. Blu Greenberg, *On Women and Judaism: A View from Tradition* (Philadelphia: Jewish Publication Society, 1981), p. 24. She eventually overcame her discomfort; they married on June 23, 1957. *Who's Who in World Jewry: A Biographical Dictionary of Outstanding Jews* (New York: Pitman Publishing Corp., 1972), p. 351.

4. The following paragraphs rely largely on Yitzhak (Eric) Zimmer's outstanding study "Kisui Ho-Rosh Li-Gevarim," in his *Olam Ke-Minhago Noheg* (Jerusalem: Zalman Shazar Center, 2006), pp. 17–42.

5. Ibid, pp. 24–26.

6. Ibid, pp. 26–28. This application of *hukkot hagoyim* had already been suggested by Rabbi Israel Bruna in the fifteenth century, but the Taz made it normative. Zimmer suggests that Jewish-Christian tensions in mid-seventeenth-century Poland, leading to pogroms in which two sons of the Taz were killed, played a role in the latter's strong views on the subject.

7. Samson Raphael Hirsch, *Horeb*, trans. I. Grunfeld (London: Soncino Press, 1962), II, pp. 334, 335.

8. Mordechai Breuer, *Modernity Within Tradition: The Social History of Orthodox Jewry in Imperial Germany* (New York: Columbia University Press, 1992), pp. 235–36, 9. That young man was David Zvi Hoffmann, who would become the leading rabbinic scholar in Germany in the next generation. His description of the episode is quoted in Zimmer, *Olam Ke-Minhago Noheg*, p. 32. A reproduction of a lithograph showing Hirsch himself, as a young rabbi, bareheaded, is in Alfred Rubens, *A History of Jewish Costume* (New York: Funk & Wagnalls, 1967), p. 185.

9. Zimmer, *Olam Ke-Minhago Noheg*, pp. 32, 34. Dan Rabinowitz, in "Yarmulke: A Historic Cover-up?" (*Hakirah* 4, Winter 2007), pp. 221–38, shows that once male head covering achieved a central role in East European Orthodoxy, certain older texts and pictures that suggested a different perspective were censored.

10. Shlomo Kluger, *Ha-Elef Lekha Shlomo*, I (reprint ed.; Jerusalem: H. Wagschal, 1989), p. 9 (item 3).

11. Sol Liptzin, trans. and ed., *Peretz* (New York: YIVO, 1947), pp. 182–99. This edition provides the original Yiddish and English translation on facing pages. The quotation is from p. 198.

12. American Reform Jews, like their counterparts in Europe, largely eliminated the requirement of head covering during the prayer service, and a good number banned it entirely. See Jacob Z. Lauterbach, "Should One Cover the Head When Participating in Divine Worship?" *Central Conference of American Rabbis Yearbook* 38 (1928), pp. 589–603.

13. "Bareheadedness," *Jewish Encyclopedia* vol. II (New York and London: Funk and Wagnalls, 1903), p. 533. Jonathan Sarna, in his *American Judaism: A History,* (New Haven and London: Yale University Press, 2004), p. 190, reproduces a photograph from just a few years later showing four scholars, two of them Reform—Kohler and Emil G. Hirsch—and two associated with the traditionalist Jewish Theological Seminary—Solomon Schechter and Louis Ginzberg—"on a country outing." All of them served on one or another editorial board of the *Encyclopedia.* Sarna notes, "all of them went bareheaded in the countryside." Actually, they are holding their straw hats in their hands. Following Western custom, they wore hats out of doors, and took them off for the photographer.

14. "*Gilui Rosh,*" *Otzar Yisrael* vol. III (reprint ed.; New York: Pardes Publishing House, 1951), p. 290. For information about Mosessohn see Steven Lowenstein, *The Jews of Oregon, 1850–1950* (Portland, Oreg: Jewish Historical Society of Oregon, 1987), pp. 123–24. On p. 123 there is a picture of Mosessohn bareheaded.

15. Moshe D. Sherman, *Orthodox Judaism in America: A Biographical Dictionary and Sourcebook* (Westport, Conn.: Greenwood Press, 1996), pp. 70–72.

16. *Otzar Yisrael* vol. III, pp. 290–291. Editor Eisenstein, in his later work *Otzar Dinim U-Minhagim* [Digest of Laws and Customs] (New York: Hebrew Publishing Co., 1938), p. 75, takes a position more sympathetic to Friederman than to Mosesson, though without reference to sleep time or the bath house.

17. Seth Farber, *An American Orthodox Dreamer: Rabbi Joseph B. Soloveitchik and Boston's Maimonides School* (Hanover, N.H.: University Press of New England, 2004), p. 4.

18. Alexia Webster, "The Hatters," *New York Times,* March 2, 2008, City Section, p. 4; Ruth Gay, *Unfinished People: Eastern European Jews Encounter America* (New York: W.W. Norton, 1996), p. 108.

19. Greenberg, *How to Run a Traditional Jewish Household,* p. 193.

20. The Jewish Center photo is reproduced in Jenna Weissman Joselit, *New York's Jewish Jews: The Orthodox Community in the Interwar Years* (Bloomington: Indiana University Press, 1990), p. 90; the YU pictures are in *Jewish Forum,* May 1946, pp. 114–16, and April 1954, back cover.

21. For a humorous account of what could happen, in the late 1940s, to a young man who forgot to remove his skull cap upon leaving Shabbat services in an Irish neighborhood, see Hillel Halkin, "Rooting for the Indians—A Memoir," *Commentary* 124, October 2007, p. 45.

22. Morris Dickstein, "The Law of Return," *Culturefront* 5–6 (Winter 1997), p. 46.

23. Cited in Joselit, *New York's Jewish Jews,* p. 21.

24. Friedman quoted in Jerome R. Mintz, *Hasidic People: A Place in the New World* (Cambridge: Harvard University Press, 1992), p. 19. Covering the head for meals was necessary because of the blessings recited over the food. Also see Egon Mayer, *From Suburb to Shtetl: The Jews of Boro Park* (Phladelphi: Temple University Press, 1979), p. 29, and Julian Ungar-Sargon, "The Agony of the Yarmulka—A Confession," *Judaism,* Summer 1987, p. 320.

25. Herman Wouk, *Inside Outside: A Novel* (Boston: Little Brown and Co., 1985), pp. 251, 254–55.

26. On the American "yeshiva world" created after World War II see William B. Helmreich, *The World of the Yeshiva: An Intimate Portrait of Orthodox Jewry* (augmented ed.; Hoboken, N.J.: Ktav, 2000). For studies of the postwar Hasidic influence see Mayer, *From Suburb to Shtetl;* Mintz, *Hasidic People;* George Kranzler, *Hasidic Williamsburg: A Contemporary American Hasidic Community* (Northvale, N.J.: Jason Aronson, 1995); and Israel Rubin, *Satmar: Two Generations of an Urban Island* (2d ed.; New York: Peter Lang, 1997).

27. Walter Goodman, "The Hasidim Come to Williamsburg," *Commentary* 19, March 1955, p. 274; Harry Gersh and Sam Miller, "Satmar in Brooklyn: A Zealot Community," ibid 25, November 1959, p. 391.

28. Mayer, *From Suburb to Shtetl,* p. 29; Mintz, *Hasidic People,* p. 373, n. 15.

29. Irving Greenberg and Shalom Freedman, *Living in the Image of God: Jewish Teachings to Perfect the World* (Northvale, N.J.: Jason Aronson, 1998), pp. 6–7.

30. One of the first to notice the Orthodox resurgence was Milton Himmelfarb, See his "An Unknown Jewish Sect," *Commentary,* January 1962, pp. 66–68, especially the reference to skullcaps on p. 66.

31. http://www.whysanity.net/creative/collins.html/#hat.

32. Neil Steinberg, *Hatless Jack: The President, the Fedora, and the Death of the Hat* (New York: Granta, 2005). The American hat industry has never recovered.

33. Richard M. Berlin, "How JFK Killed My Father," *Psychosomatic Medicine* 62, March/April 2000, p. 219. The poem won the Pearl Poetry Prize for 2002.

34. My first was knitted for me in the summer of 1961. Subsequent developments in kippah design and some problems they posed can be followed in "The Yarmulke Is Now a Fashion Item," *New York Times,* September 23, 1990, p. 54, and Sarah Kershaw, "A Sign of Judaism Gets a Swoosh: Commercial or Trendy Skullcaps Alarm Some Jews," ibid, April 19, 2000, p. B1.

35. Yet a fourth brief article appeared in 1955 whose theme was linguistic rather than substantive: W. Gunther Plaut, "The Origin of the Word 'Yarmulke,'" *Hebrew Union College Annual* 26, 1955, pp. 567–70.

36. Joseph Weiss, "Why Wear a Yarmulka?" *Jewish Life,* March 1953, pp. 20–26.

37. Leon Stitskin, "Why Cover the Head?" *National Jewish Monthly,* November 1953, pp. 8, 13–14, 26–27.

38. A. Brasch, "Why Jews Cover the Head: A Case Study in Tradition," *Commentary,* January 1954, pp. 37–40. Brasch later incorporated this material into his book, *The Judaic Heritage: Its Teachings, Philosophy, and Symbols* (New York: David McKay Co., 1969), pp. 249–56.

39. Rabbi Moshe Feinstein, *Igros Moshe, Orah Haim* 1: 1 (New York, 1959), pp. 5–7. A careful review of the writings of Rabbi Eliyahu Henkin, the leading U.S. *posek* over the previous quarter-century, yielded no rulings on male head covering. Feinstein's may have been the first written responsum on the subject ever produced in America.

40. Feinstein, *Igros Moshe, Orah Haim* 3: 95 (1963), pp. 288–89.

41. Ibid, *Yoreh De'ah,* 2:33 (1973), p. 45. One wonders if he would have reacted with similar equanimity to the act of a Yeshiva University student a few years later who wore his *kippah* to a Christmas Eve performance of Handel's *Messiah,* but, on the advice of a rabbi, remained seated for the "Hallelujah Chorus." "This is New York," the

young man explained to a friend, "you can hear the *Messiah* with a yarmulke." Ari L. Goldman, *The Search for God at Harvard* (New York: Random House, 1991), p. 140.

42. He ruled this way in 1962 and again in 1974. See *Igros Moshe, Hoshen Mishpat,* 1:93 (1963), pp. 158–59, and *Orah Haim* 4:2 (1982), pp. 1–2.

43. Kranzler, *Hasidic Williamsburg,* p. 32.

44. After congratulating the team, an editorial in the student newspaper satirically added, "Hats off also to Dr. Linn for his great work in coaching the team and helping to spread Yeshiva's image." "College Bowl," *The Commentator,* May 27, 1963, p. 2. For YU's bareheaded image in the 1950s see the citation in footnote 20 above.

45. Harry Steinhauer, "Holy Headgear," *The Antioch Review* 48, Winter 1990, p. 18.

46. Ibid, p. 17.

47. Julius Lester, *Lovesong: Becoming a Jew* (New York: Henry Holt & Co., 1988), p. 51. As the subtitle indicates, Lester subsequently converted to Judaism. The back of the book jacket shows him wearing not only a kippah but also a tallit, and apparently praying from a siddur.

48. Sabrina Tavernise, "For Many Turks, Head Scarf's Return Aids Religion and Democracy," *New York Times,* January 30, 2008, http://www.nytimes.com/2008/01/30/world/europe/30turkey.html.

49. "Yarmulkas in Public Schools," *Jewish Observer,* April 1966, pp. 27–28; Leo Pfeffer, "In Support of a Ruling Permitting Pupils to Keep Their Heads Covered in Class if Their Religion So Requires," petition and statement to State of New Jersey Department of Education, September 29, 1967.

50. Earl Raab, "Intergroup Relations," *American Jewish Year Book 1989* (New York: American Jewish Committee, 1989), p. 176.

51. S. Simcha Goldman. Plaintiff-Appellee, v. Secretary of Defense, et al., Defendants-Appellants, No. 82-1723. U.S. Court of Appeals, District of Columbia Circuit, http://bulk.resource.org/courts.gov/c/F2/734/734.F2d.1531.82-1723.html, p. 4.

52. S. Simcha Goldman, Petitioner, v. Caspar W. Weinberger, Secretary of Defense, et al., No. 84-1097. In the Supreme Court of the United States October Term, 1985, http://www.usdoj.gov/osg/briefs/1985/sg850109.txt, pp. 2, 5, 16–17.

53. "Oyez: Goldman v. Weinberger, 475 U.S. 503 (1986), http://www.oyez.org/cases/1980-1989/1985/1985_84_1097/argument/, p. 2.

54. Ibid, pp. 9–10.

55. U.S, Supreme Court: Goldman v. Weinberger, 475 U.S. 503 (1986), http://caseelaw.lp.findlaw.com/scripts.printer_friendly.pl?page=us/475/503.html, pp. 5, 7.

56. Hon. Steven J. Solarz, "The Religious Apparel Amendment," May 11, 1987, *Congressional Record,* vol. 133, no. 75, http://www.resnicoff.net/amendment.html.

9

Jewish Religious Thought and Practice during the Holocaust

David Hartman

It is a pleasure to contribute this chapter to the special Festschrift in honor of Yitz Greenberg in his 75th Birthday year. Yitz, in my mind, represents the spirit of Maimonides in the modern world. I have never seen him shy away from the confrontation of Halakha with modern thought. He is a paradigm of intellectual openness and belief in Judaism's ability to live creatively in the modern world. This article on Maimonides reflects deeply the intellectual and religious spirit of Yitz Greenberg.

A central theme of my book *Maimonides: Torah and Philosophical Quest* was my disagreement with the dualistic approach to Maimonides by scholars such as Isaac Husik and Leo Strauss.[1] These scholars suggested that there were, in fact, two Maimonides: Maimonides the halakhist, the responsible judge who served his community in accordance with their temporal and spiritual needs, and Maimonides the philosopher, who served God through knowledge of the structure of nature within the privacy of his esoteric Aristotelian universe. This dichotomy is reflected in Maimonides' two major works: *The Guide of the Perplexed*, which was addressed to the singular individual capable of emulating Maimonides' philosophic quest, and the *Mishneh Torah* which was addressed to the general public who required a clear and comprehensive normative framework to live by.

In *Torah and Philosophical Quest* I argued that this binary understanding of Maimonides and of his works, the *Guide* and the *Mishneh Torah*, was fundamentally mistaken. I proposed "the way of integration" as my interpretive model and tried to show that Maimonides the philosopher and Maimonides the halakhist were one and the same. I argued that the author of the *Guide* and

Mishneh Torah held a unified worldview in which the God of Abraham, Isaac, and Jacob and the God of the Philosophers were integrated harmoniously into a full and rich religious life.

A key text that I used to corroborate this thesis was the following section from the end of the *Guide* (III, 51).

> From here on I will begin to give you guidance with regard to the form of this training so that you should achieve this great end. The first thing that you should cause your soul to hold fast onto is that, while reciting the *Shema*, you should empty your mind of everything and pray thus. You should not content yourself with "being intent" while "reciting the first verse of *Shema*" and saying "the first benediction" [of the *Amidah*]. When this has been carried out correctly and has been practiced consistently for years, cause your soul, whenever you read or listen to the Torah, to be constantly directed—the whole of you and your thought— toward reflection on what you are listening to or reading. When this too has been practiced consistently for a certain time, cause your soul to be in such a way that your thought is always quite free of distraction and gives heed to all that you are reading of the other discourses of the Prophets and even when you read all the benedictions, so that you aim at meditating on what you are uttering and at considering its meaning. If, however, while performing these acts of worship you are free from distraction and not engaged in thinking upon any of the things pertaining to this world, cause your soul—after this has been achieved—to occupy your thought with things necessary for you or superfluous in your life, and in general with "worldly things," while you eat or drink or bathe or talk with your wife and your small children or while you talk with the common run of people. Thus I have provided you with many and long stretches of time in which you can think all that needs thinking regarding property, the governance of the household, and the welfare of the body. On the other hand, while performing the actions imposed by the Law, you should occupy your thought only with what you are doing, just as we have explained.[2]

I interpreted this description of the philosophic Jew's new appreciation of Halakhah as follows:

> Although the Halakhah, as stated in the Mishneh Torah, only requires that one have *kavvanah* (intent) during the first verse of the *Shema* and the first benediction of the *Amidah*, the philosophic Jew of the *Guide* is not satisfied with this minimal standard.[3]

Now, however, I feel compelled to revise the position I put forward in *Torah and Philosophical Quest*. There, I understood Maimonides' recommendation about extending *kavvanah* beyond the minimal halakhic requirement to mean that after achieving knowledge and love of God the philosophic Jew would adopt a more stringent and demanding attitude to Halakhah. My mistake was in claiming that the change vis-à-vis Halakhah entailed a more rigorous observance of Halakhah and that the *kavvanah* (intent) mentioned by Maimonides was essentially halakhic in nature, i.e., that it led the philosophic Jew to adopt a stricter, more demanding standard of legal obligation. In contrast to this position, I now contend that the object of the *kavvanah* Maimonides describes is not legal authority and obligation but rather it is the content of the ritual acts and/or the ultimate object of religious worship, God. *Kavvanah* in this context is less a legal, halakhic category – like *kavvanah la'tseit*, the intention to fulfill one's legal obligation – than a cognitive state of reflection on the content of the action.

Maimonides recommends to the student of the *Guide* practical "worldly things" ("Thus I have provided you with many and long stretches of time in which you can think all that needs thinking regarding property, the governance of the household, and the welfare of the body") and advice on religious meditation in keeping with the student's new spiritual aspirations. Although the student continues to perform the rituals prescribed by Halakhah, in doing these actions he consciously trains himself to concentrate fully on what he is doing and to exclude all distractions. "While performing the actions imposed by the Law," writes Maimonides, "you should occupy your thought only with what you are doing, just as we have explained." By so doing the student begins to appreciate the meaning of meditative worship.

In reciting the *shema* ("Hear, Oh Israel"), says Maimonides, you should focus fully on this act to the exclusion of all else. In addition to the significance of the *shema* itself (traditionally, the acceptance of the kingdom of heaven), Maimonides introduces the value of total and undivided concentration on all three chapters of the *shema*. This perspective is applied to other halakhic performances as well, such as listening to the Torah reading or reciting blessings. Any religious act not related to practical human needs, i.e., any purely expressive, symbolic act, becomes an occasion for training the philosophic individual in meditative worship. The student's attitude to halakhic ritual that Maimonides provides to the student emphasizes and cultivates single-mindedness rather than submissive obedience to the authority of Halakhah. The Halakhah to which the student of the *Guide* returns is not the same as before he embarked on the philosophic path.

In *Torah and Philosophic Quest* I claimed that "[b]y emphasizing that the observance of and perspective on Halakhah changes for the philosophic Jew, Maimonides clearly indicates that he does not adopt the way of dualism regarding tradition" (p. 195). This conclusion as it was formulated was mistaken because it minimized the essential differences between the philosophic and halakhic spiritual orientations. Halakhah and philosophy are distinct, albeit significant, parts of Maimonides' religious philosophy.

The spiritual life of Maimonides' philosophic Jew involves meditative worship of God both within and outside the framework of Halakhah. Maimonides believed that Halakhah served an indispensable role in the development of human beings and in the establishment of an ordered society. Nonetheless, the purpose and ultimate goal of this framework was the knowledge and love of God as described at the end of the *Guide*. This religious ideal cannot be realized in a relationship to God based on the paradigm of petitional prayer, where a person turns to God for help in coping with his human condition. In contrast to this paradigm, the philosophic individual turns to God because of his attraction to the ultimate reality whose perfection is revealed in the existence and structure of the world. The philosopher's spiritual orientation is free of utilitarian self-interest. The individual self with its particular needs and concerns recedes from the worshipper's consciousness when entering into the theocentric context of philosophic love of God.

The ideal of knowledge and love of God appears not only in the *Guide* but also in the *Mishneh Torah*, the code of Jewish law. Maimonides openly acknowledges and discusses a hierarchy of worship. I shall now analyze three texts from the *Mishneh Torah* where Maimonides discusses the relationship between Halakhic and philosophic religious sensibilities. I shall also show how his commentary offers an alternative to the traditional belief in halakhic exclusivity, which denies the legitimacy of spiritual commitments outside of Halakhah.

In the *Mishneh Torah* Maimonides publicly states that the philosophical quest for God through the study of physics and metaphysics is superior to the legal discussions of halakhic jurisprudence.

13. The topics connected with these five precepts, treated in the above four chapters, are what our wise men called *Pardes*, (Paradise), as in the passage "Four went into *Pardes* (Hagiga 14). And although those four were great men of Israel and great sages, they did not all possess the capacity to know and grasp these subjects clearly. Therefore, I say that it is not proper to dally in *Pardes* until one has first filled oneself with bread and meat; by which I mean knowledge of what is permitted and what forbidden, and similar distinctions in other classes of precepts. Although these last subjects were called by the sages "a small thing" (when they say "A great thing, *Maaseh Mercabah* [the story of the chariot (see Ezekiel 10, Isaiah 6)]; a small thing, the discussion of Abayye and Rava"), still they should have the precedence. For the knowledge of these things gives primarily composure to the mind. They are the precious boon bestowed by God, to promote social well-being on earth, and enable men to obtain bliss in the life hereafter. Moreover, the knowledge of them is within the reach of all, young and old, men and women; those gifted with great intellectual capacity as well as those whose intelligence is limited.[4]

The distinction and relationship between these two frameworks, Halakhah and philosophic love of God, is best explained in Maimonides' treatment of messianism. The messianic idea refers to a historical period when the majority of human beings will be sufficiently free of economic, social and political concerns to be able to devote themselves to reflection and the acquisition of knowledge. Under such historical conditions, the majority of people will have the opportunity to develop morally and intellectually to the level of love of God. Pure love of God —the goal and fulfillment of human nature—is ultimately an individual achievement, which Maimonides identifies with the meaning of *olam haba,* the world-to-come. *Olam haba,* the ahistorical, immaterial world of pure intellects, represents human fulfillment in its most perfect form.

According to Maimonides messianic hope should focus on the political conditions that facilitate the pursuit of knowledge leading to love of God by individuals who, in a pre-messianic world, would be totally occupied with their more basic human needs. Given this perspective, we can say that the *Guide* was written for those singular individuals capable of achieving the goal of *olam haba,* intellectual love of God, in a pre-messianic society. For the vast majority of people, messianism is a necessary condition for pursuing and realizing this goal.

> Hence, all Israelites, their prophets and sages, longed for the advent of Messianic times, that they might have relief from the wicked tyranny that does not permit them properly to occupy themselves with the study of the Torah and the observance of the commandments; that they might have ease, devote themselves to getting wisdom, and thus attain to life in the world to come (*olam haba*).[5]

The functional relationship between *olam haba* and messianism is analogous to the distinction between the "great thing," philosophic knowledge that leads to love of God and the "small thing," knowledge of what is permitted and forbidden.

The second text in the *Mishneh Torah* which I have chosen is Maimonides' description of how a Jew ideally should organize his day.

> For example, if one is an artisan who works at his trade three hours daily and devotes nine hours to the study of the Torah, he should spend three of these nine hours in the study of the Written Law, three in the study of the Oral Law, and the remaining three in reflecting on how to deduce one rule from another. The words of the Prophets are comprised in the Written Law, while their exposition falls within the category of the Oral Law. The subjects styled *Pardes* [Esoteric Studies] are included in *Talmud.* This plan applies to the period when one begins learning. But after one has become proficient and no longer needs to learn the Written Law, or continually be occupied with the Oral Law, he should, at fixed

times, read the Written Law and the traditional dicta, so as not to forget any of
the rules of the Torah, and should devote all his days exclusively to the study of
Talmud, according to his breadth of mind and maturity of intellect.

("The Laws Concerning the Study of the Torah," 1:12)

It is important to notice that Maimonides places the study of philosophy
under the rubric of "Talmud." The significance of this becomes apparent when
considering the subsequent statement "after one has become proficient and no
longer needs to learn the Written Law, or continually be occupied with the
Oral Law... [one] should devote all his days exclusively to the study of Talmud..." In other words, after a person is confident in his knowledge of
"Halakhah," he should devote the majority of his time to the study of philosophy. Again we see the hierarchical, functional relationship between "Halakhah"
– the normative rules of conduct and social organization – and "Talmud" –
the study of nature and of God as manifest in nature leading to love of God.

It is interesting that Maimonides uses the expression "according to his
breadth of mind and maturity of intellect" with respect to the study of "Talmud" but not with respect to the study of Halakhah. Halakhah is a legal system and therefore must be comprehensible and achievable by the vast majority of the public. By contrast, philosophic love of God is conditional on the
study and mastery of philosophy. Its realization is dependent not only on will
and determination but also on a person's intellectual capacities and powers of
concentration.

The third text which demonstrates the religious significance of philosophic
spirituality is Maimonides' dramatic demystification of divine worship in the
cultic practices of the Temple.

12 Why did the tribe of Levi not acquire a share in the Land of Israel and in its
spoils together with their brothers? Because this tribe was set apart to serve God
and to minister to Him, to teach His straight ways and righteous ordinances to
the multitudes, as is written: "They shall teach Jacob Your ordinances and Israel
Your law" (Deut. 33:10). Therefore, they were set apart from the ways of the
world; they do not wage war like the rest of Israel, nor do they inherit land or
acquire anything for themselves by their physical prowess. They are rather the
army of God, as is written: "Bless, Lord, his substance" (ibid. 33:11). He, blessed
be He, acquires (goods) for them, as is written: "I am your portion and your inheritance" (Num. 18:20).

13 Not only the tribe of Levi but every single individual from among the
world's inhabitants whose spirit moved him and whose intelligence gave him the
understanding to withdraw from the world in order to stand before God to serve
and minister to Him, to know God, and he walked upright in the manner in
which God made him, shaking off from his neck the yoke of the manifold con-
trivances which men seek—behold, this person has been totally consecrated and

God will be his portion and inheritance forever and ever. God will acquire for him sufficient goods in this world just as he did for the priests and Levites. Behold, David, may he rest in peace, says: "Lord, the portion of my inheritance and of my cup, You maintain my lot" (Ps. 16:5).[6]

The tribe of Levi is freed from ordinary worldly activities in order to be engaged fully in the worship of God. The cultic role assigned to them by Jewish law is not based on individual merit or achievement (e.g., the "breadth of mind and maturity of intellect" noted above with regard to the mastery of "Talmud"). The qualifications of the priests and Levites derive from their birth. The child of a priest is priest. The child of a Levite is a Levite. Their special status and prerogatives are defined by halakhic norms. Service of God in the Temple cult has nothing in common with the knowledge and love of God that Maimonides describes in the *Guide* and the *Mishneh Torah*.

Nevertheless, after describing the unique role of the Levites, who are "set apart from the ways of the world" to serve God and to teach Torah, Maimonides states: "Not only the tribe of Levi but every single individual from among the world's inhabitants…" can also become God's portion and inheritance. The spiritual vocation of the tribe of Levi is not the exclusive prerogative of that tribe alone. Any individual who is sufficiently motivated and capable of devoting his life to God can reach the spiritual level represented by the tribe of Levi regardless of lineage, social class or even of membership in the Jewish people.

It is as if Maimonides were telling the reader not to be misled by the particular ritualistic categories by which the Halakhah organizes communal life. The tribe of Levi is an organizing category of halakhic society. In the end, Levites and *Kohanim* (Priests) represent the ideal of consecrating one's life to God. This ideal is independent of the particular structural forms of this or any other tradition. Any individual, Jew or non-Jew, anywhere in the world can achieve what the Priests and Levites represent.

Maimonides counters a possible exclusivist interpretation of halakhic worship by declaring that the ideal of passionate love of God which he described in the *Guide* (III: 51) and in the "The Laws Concerning the Study of the Torah" (1:12) has autonomous significance independent of any particular tradition or revelatory system. This kind of internal commentary on the law is not uncommon in the *Mishneh Torah*. In these descriptive digressions from the otherwise prescriptive content of his code of Jewish law Maimonides provides what he believes is the proper context in which to understand the law or laws in question. Though these comments are non-binding in the strict legal sense, they reveal the dialectical relationship between Maimonides the philosopher and Maimonides the jurist.

The conclusion I draw from the above three texts is that while believing in the value and importance of both Halakhah and philosophic love of God, Maimonides placed the latter above the former in the hierarchy of human activities. As mentioned previously, Maimonides' conceptions of messianism and *olam haba* express his multidimensional worldview. By freeing people from the debilitating demands of physical and social survival, messianism makes contemplation of God in nature into a realistic goal for the community at large.

This functional relationship between Halakhah and philosophy is not adequately described by the "the way of integration" I argued for in *Torah and Philosophical Quest*. I reject this formulation because I now believe that "integration" is not the only way of appreciating and embracing two different traditions. Maimonides was a complex religious personality who felt the claims of two passions: his passion for the Halakhic tradition and his passion for philosophical spirituality. Both lived side by side within him. Both influenced his creativity and activities as an individual and as a leader.

The individual infused by the theocentric passion described at the end of the *Guide* is not necessarily a person interested in the synthesis of philosophic contemplation and halakhic jurisprudence. Such a person is primarily interested in enabling the two frameworks to live together without excluding one another. Consequently, one of Maimonides' tasks in the *Mishneh Torah* was to circumscribe the traditionalists' belief in the all-inclusive, self-sufficient nature of Halakhah. According to this not uncommon approach, Halakhah claims the totality of one's life while absolutely precluding allegiance to any other spiritual framework.

It is not surprising that the first rabbinic text Maimonides deals with in the introduction to his *Commentary* on the *Mishnah* is "From the day that the Temple was destroyed, the Holy One, blessed is He, dwells only in ['has nothing in His world except for'] the four cubits of Halakhah" (T.B., Berakhot 8a). Maimonides couldn't accept this statement at face value because, as he argued, this would exclude our acknowledging that the generations of Noah and of Abraham *who lived before Sinai* served God. Maimonides therefore felt compelled to interpret this statement so as to neutralize its implications regarding the exclusivity of Halakhah in defining what constitutes authentic Judaism.

Maimonides' efforts at countering halakhic exclusivity took two basic forms. First, he repeatedly informed his readers about the ideal of love of God mediated by philosophic knowledge. As shown above, there are several places in the *Mishneh Torah* where Maimonides openly declares the supremacy of the philosophic spiritual ideal.

Second, as a halakhic commentator and codifier, Maimonides shunned strict formalism when dealing with morally problematic rulings choosing instead to acknowledge the legitimacy of "extra-legal" moral arguments. By allowing what I call "self-corrective mechanisms" into halakhic discussions in the *Mishneh Torah* he challenged the doctrine regarding Halakhah's completeness and self-sufficiency. Maimonides' comments on halakhic legislation in the *Mishneh Torah* include moral and theological arguments that, from a purely formal legal point of view, have no relevance. Although these "extra-legal" considerations have no immediate impact on halakhic legislation, the very fact that they were included shows that Maimonides wanted them to be part of the broader context in which the Jew viewed Halakhah. The acknowledgment of "self-corrective mechanisms" in Halakhah weakens the claim to exclusivity by empowering Jews to critically evaluate halakhic legislation on the basis of values and ideals not derived exclusively from formal halakhic hermeneutics.

For example, Halakhah makes a distinction between Jewish and non-Jewish slaves with respect to the prohibition of working a slave with rigor [*befarech*] (Leviticus 25:43).

> It is permitted to work a heathen slave with rigor. Though such is the rule, it is the quality of piety and the way of wisdom that a man be merciful and pursue justice and not make his yoke heavy upon the slave or distress him, but give him to eat and to drink of all foods and drinks.
>
> The sages of old were wont to let the slave partake of every dish that they themselves ate of and to give the meal of the cattle and of the slaves precedence over their own. Is it not said: "As the eyes of slaves to the hand of their master, as the eyes of a female servant to the hand of her mistress" (Ps. 123:2)?
>
> Thus also the master should not disgrace them by hand or by word, because Scriptural law has delivered them only to slavery and not to disgrace. Nor should he heap upon the slave oral abuse and anger, but should rather speak to him softly and listen to his claims. So it is also explained in the good paths of Job, in which he prided himself:
> "If I did despise the cause of my manservant,
> Or of my maidservant, when they contended with me . . .
> Did not He that made me in the womb make him?
> And did not One fashion us in the womb?" (Job 31:13, 15)
> Cruelty and effrontery are not frequent except with heathen who worship idols. The children of our father Abraham, however, i.e., the Israelites, upon whom the Holy One, blessed be He, bestowed the favor of the Law and laid upon them statutes and judgments, are merciful people who have mercy upon all.
>
> Thus also it is declared by the attributes of the Holy One, blessed be He, which we are enjoined to imitate: "And His mercies are over all His works" (Ps. 145:9).
>
> Furthermore, whoever has compassion will receive compassion, as it is said: "And He will show you mercy, and have compassion upon you, and multiply you" (Deut. 13:18).[7]

Biblical legislation against treating a slave with rigor [*befarech*], which was interpreted in the tradition to refer to dehumanizing work (tasks with no useful purpose or end ("do this until I return")), was limited to the Hebrew slave. From a strict Halakhic point of view a Jew may treat a non-Jewish slave harshly. Nonetheless, writes Maimonides, there are compelling reasons to ignore this distinction and to adopt a higher standard of behavior. First, the "quality of piety and the way of wisdom" preclude treating any slave, Jew or heathen, harshly. The Jewish tradition commends the "sages of old" for their merciful treatment of heathen slaves.

Maimonides also offers a legalistic halakhic argument to the effect that the power given to the master over the slave does not override the latter's right to human dignity. Enslavement does not entail degradation. Furthermore, the teleology of this system develops compassion towards others and as a consequence cruelty is infrequent among Jews who "are merciful people who have mercy upon all."

Another argument invokes theological motifs by setting the Divine Legislator against His alter ego, the Divine Creator. Drawing on a Midrashic source, Maimonides quotes Job's use of the egalitarian implications of Creation ("Did not He that made me in the womb make him?") to argue against the discriminatory treatment of non-Jewish slaves which the Halakhah based on revelation permits.

Indeed, the yearning for and knowledge of God in nature provides a person with a theological *and moral* outlook independent of revelation.

On the basis of the multiple arguments Maimonides presents, one can conclude that his religious universe can be represented by two theological models: 1) the God of revelation, the source of law and legal authority, and 2) God as He is unto Himself, the ultimate source of all contingent existents. Torah and Halakhah mediate the will and authority of the personal God of history; nature mediates the divine presence by enabling us to discover and imitate the "moral" qualities of the Creator manifest in the world.[8]

This two-fold theological perspective of creation and revelation has implications for the way in which the philosophic Jew relates to the tradition. In terms of Halakhah, this means that the revelatory framework does not exhaust the sources of spiritual meaning and moral inspiration in Jewish life. The currently codified law may permit treating pagan slaves in ways that conflict with the goodness we associate with the God of creation. The divine "actions" we strive to imitate may not coincide with the principles embodied in current halakhic practice. This is the meaning of living with two frameworks and accepting their differences. The "way of integration" oversimplifies the complexity of living in multiple religious frameworks.

Maimonides codifies legislation and at the same time presents forceful moral arguments against this legislation, an indication that he rejects halakhic exclusivity. The halakhic system does not exhaust the divine word. While the word of God is expressed in mitzvah, it is not expressed only in mitzvah. Love of God and imitation of God is not dependent on revelation but can be achieved by any human being. This awareness, this knowledge that "His mercies are over all His works," can act as a corrective to an overly obedient and submissive attitude to halakhic legislation.

Although Maimonides advises his readers to view halakhic practice as an opportunity to engage in concentrated moments of worship, this approach does not fully capture Maimonides' understanding of the relationship of philosophy to the normative practice of Judaism. The key text describing this relationship is in the *Mishneh Torah*, "The Laws of Repentance," chapter 10.

1 Let not a man say, "I will observe the precepts of the Torah and occupy myself with its wisdom in order that I may obtain all the blessings written in the Torah, or to attain life in the world to come; I will abstain from transgressions against which the Torah warns, so that I may be saved from the curses written in the Torah, or that I may not be cut off from life in the world to come." It is not right to serve God after this fashion for whoever does so, serves Him out of fear. This is not the standard set by the prophets and sages. Those who may serve God in this way are illiterate, women, or children whom one trains to serve out of fear, until their knowledge shall have increased when they will serve out of love.

2 Whoever serves God out of love, occupies himself with the study of the Law and the fulfillment of commandments and walks in the paths of wisdom, impelled by no external motive whatsoever, moved neither by fear of calamity nor by the desire to obtain material benefits—such a man does what is truly right because it is truly right, and ultimately, happiness comes to him as a result of his conduct. This standard is indeed a very high one; not every sage attained it. It was the standard of the patriarch Abraham whom God called His lover, because he served only out of love. It is the standard which God, through Moses, bids us achieve, as it is said, "And you shall love the Lord your God" (Deut. 6:5). When one loves God with the right love, he will straightway observe all the commandments out of love.

3 What is the love of God that is befitting? It is to love the Eternal with a great and exceeding love, so strong that one's soul shall be knit up with the love of God, and one should be continually enraptured by it, like a love-sick individual, whose mind is at no time free from his passion for a particular woman, the thought of her filling his heart at all times, when sitting down or rising up, when he is eating or drinking. Even intenser should be the love of God in the hearts of those who love Him. And this love should continually possess them, even as He commanded us in the phrase, "with all your heart and with all your soul" (Deut. 6:5). This, Solomon expressed allegorically in the sentence, "for I am sick with love" (Song of Songs 2:5). The entire Song of Songs is indeed an allegory descriptive of this love.

6 … One only loves God with the knowledge with which one knows Him. According to the knowledge will be the love. If the former be little or much, so will the latter be little or much. A person ought therefore to devote himself to the understanding and comprehension of those sciences and studies which will inform him concerning his Master, as far as it lies in human faculties to understand and comprehend—as indeed we have explained in the "Laws of the Basic Principles of the Torah."[9]

The relationship of philosophy to mitzvah described here differs from the functional description in the *Guide.* "When one loves God with the right love," writes Maimonides (10:2), "he will straightway observe all the commandments out of love." The term Maimonides uses is *miyyad*, immediately, straightway. When a person becomes a philosophical lover of God he immediately begins to perform the commandments out of love.

I understand this to mean that the relationship to God that grows out of philosophical knowledge is essentially a yearning to be in the presence of God. The human effect of this type of love is total and all-consuming. Individual self-interest, symbolized by the biblical concern with reward and punishment, is replaced by an overwhelming longing for the beloved. Philosophic knowledge of God engenders a kind of infatuation, a love-sickness, to be in God's presence.

The study of philosophy is not only an intellectual pursuit but also a process that shapes human character. Philosophy involves the transformation of a person's character as well as the acquisition of knowledge. The relationship to God that results from philosophic knowledge is not grounded in self-interest but in the joy of discerning the presence of God in nature. This change in one's basic character also affects one's relationship to Halakhah. This is the meaning of *miyyad*, immediately.

Advocating passionate love of God without allowing for the slow but necessary change in one's character is dangerous and irresponsible. Presenting the idea of disinterested worship to people in need of the reassurance and motivational incentives of the providential biblical framework of reward and punishment can be disastrous. For this reason Maimonides describes the method of nurturing service of God out of love as a gradual process beginning with serving God "out of fear" (for the sake of reward) and proceeding incrementally to service out of love ("we reveal to them this secret truth little by little, and train them by easy stages until they have grasped and comprehended it, and serve God out of love" (10:5)).

It is noteworthy that one of the paradigms of love of God Maimonides cites is Abraham ("It was the standard of the patriarch Abraham whom God called His lover, because he served only out of love" (10:2)). As I explained in *Torah and Philosophical Quest*, for Maimonides Abraham is the archetypal lover of God independent of Halakhah who established a religious community based on knowledge of God. Moses is the figure who establishes Halakhah and legal authority as a result of the historical realization that Abraham's community of knowledge was insufficiently strong to withstand the pagan influences of Egyptian culture. It was this contingent fact of history that made it necessary to transform the Abrahamic community into a legal community.[10]

The relationship between Abraham and Moses as archetypal figures mirrors the relationship between the God of nature and the God of revelation. Moses is the source of legal authority; he is the prophet of the revelatory God who legislates and demands compliance with Torah as a way of life. Yet the models of Abraham and of the God of nature continue to serve as ideals and to exert corrective influences on the possible distortions of the Halakhic framework, specifically the belief in its self-sufficiency. The Abraham-Creator God motif acts as a corrective to using the Sinai-revelation motif to exclude spiritual and moral influences outside of Halakhah and mitzvah. Sinai, on the other hand, acts as a corrective to believing that human beings can establish a community solely on the basis of disinterested contemplative love. Legal authority, discipline and structure are necessary for maintaining a communal framework in which the human potential to transcend self-interestedness can be nurtured.

Two biblical figures, two images of God: the God of Abraham and the God of Moses, the God of nature and the God of revelation. The God of the cosmos inspires the yearning to understand and be passionately related to the source of existence. Passionate love of God, however, is not the only ideal of Judaism. The other ideal is to establish a covenantal community that can survive in history. Halakhah and its theological counterpart, the God of history, are necessary to create a community that can persist in an unredeemed world replete with pagan allurements.

As I explained at the beginning of this essay, in *Torah and Philosophic Quest* I argued extensively against the polarized view of Maimonides that both Isaac Husik and Leo Strauss advocated. Although I am now more sympathetic to the dualistic approach, I still disagree strongly with Leo Strauss' failure to appreciate the central role of Halakhah in Maimonides' philosophic worldview. Nonetheless, I now realize that my main disagreement is with Yeshayahu Leibowitz' approach to Maimonides and to Halakhah.[11] The key to Leibowitz' understanding of Maimonides is his interpretation of the following passage in the *Guide* (III, 51).

> Know that all the practices of the worship, such as reading the *Torah*, prayer and the performance of the other *commandments*, have only the end of training you to occupy yourself with His commandments, may He be exalted, rather than with matters pertaining to this world; You should act as if you were occupied with Him, may He be exalted, and not with that which is other than He.

The crucial sentence for Leibowitz is: "You should act as if you were occupied with Him... and not with that which is other than He," which he interprets to mean that worship of God can only be realized through the observance of Halakhah. According to Leibowitz, Maimonides believed that there could be no genuine worship outside of the normative tradition of Judaism. Furthermore, he defines worship of God in terms of the duty to perform *mitzvoth*, commandments. "Love of God" is equated with a person's unconditional acceptance and disinterested observance of Halakhah. You love God by observing Halakhah because you are obligated to do so. Love of God and worship of God are fully exhausted by halakhic observance. Outside of this framework they have no meaning.

This approach to Halakhah and to Maimonides is diametrically opposed my own. As I argued previously, Maimonides countered the claim of Halakhic exclusivity in two ways. First, he challenged the spiritual hegemony of the halakhic legislation by emphasizing the value of philosophy and contemplative love of God grounded in philosophic knowledge. Second, he challenged the claim of normative completeness and self-sufficiency by allowing for the presence of self-corrective mechanisms within the tradition.

While I agree with Leibowitz' approach to Maimonides in terms of his appreciation of the importance of Halakhah and his emphasis on the existential posture of disinterested love independent of its metaphysical content, in contrast to Leibowitz, I ascribe great importance to the non-Halakhic, cosmic motif in Maimonides' religious worldview.

The passionate yearning for God and love-sickness experienced by the lover of God when meditating on the cosmos are integral parts of Maimonides' religious worldview. Although Maimonides developed his "negative theology" because of his belief that knowledge of God in terms of essential attributes was impossible, nonetheless he maintained in the *Mishneh Torah* and throughout all his works that love of God is proportionate to knowledge. While both Leibowitz and I accept Maimonides' avowed skepticism with regard to knowledge of God's essence, I maintain that for Maimonides the knowledge of and interest in nature provide a person with a theological framework that nurtures a religious personality grounded in passionate love of God.

I accept Maimonides' emphasis on the centrality of philosophy and nature in terms of the existential goal of love of God. Leibowitz, however, rejects the religious significance of the philosophical quest altogether. For him the one and only framework for worship of God is the practice of Halakhah. He, therefore, places Maimonides' concept of love of God exclusively within Halakhah. Disinterested love of God means doing *mitzvot* because one is commanded to and not for any self-serving reason. It is with Leibowitz' pan-Halakhism—of confining a Jew's religious life to the "four cubits of Halakhah"—that I strongly disagree.

1. This God, honored and revered, it is our duty to love and fear; as it is said "You shall love the Lord your God" (Deut. 6:5), and it is further said "You shall fear the Lord your God" (ibid. 6:15).

2. And what is the way that will lead to the love of Him and the fear of Him? When a person contemplates His great and wondrous works and creatures and from them obtains a glimpse of His wisdom which is incomparable and infinite, he will straightway love Him, praise Him, glorify Him, and long with an exceeding longing to know His great Name; even as David said, "My soul thirsts for God, for the living God" (Ps. 42:3). And when he ponders these matters, he will recoil frightened, and realize that he is a small creature, lowly and obscure, endowed with slight and slender intelligence, standing in the presence of Him who is perfect in knowledge. And so David said "When I consider Your heavens, the work of Your fingers—what is man that You are mindful of him?" (Ps. 8:4-5). In harmony with these sentiments, I shall explain some large, general aspects of he works of the Sovereign of the Universe, that they may serve the intelligent individual as a door to the love of God, even as our sages have remarked in connection with the theme of the love of God, "Observe the Universe and hence, you will realize Him who spoke and the world was."[12]

In this description of the meaning of love and fear of God at the beginning of the *Mishneh Torah*, Maimonides clearly describes the connection between these religious attitudes and philosophic knowledge. "When a person contemplates His great and wondrous works and creatures… he will straightway love Him." For Leibowitz the philosophic quest is bereft of spiritual meaning. Love of God is related exclusively to the individual's decision to submit to the authority of the Halakhah and the commandments. I, however, maintain that Maimonides wanted to check the exclusivity of Halakhah by making philosophy and the study of nature constitutive elements of his religious philosophy of Judaism.

I would summarize my position in terms of Maimonides' parable of the palace of the King (*Guide*, III, 51), which he uses to describe the proximity of human beings to God. Those Jews who believe that God can only be served from within the confines of traditional halakhic authority and legislative practice "have come up to the [King's] habitation and walk around it." They do not enter the antechambers, which are accessible only to those who "have plunged into speculation concerning the fundamental principles of religion." Among the latter, differences in philosophic knowledge and love of God make for differences in closeness to the ruler.[13]

Unlike the "jurists," the halakhists who reject the legitimacy of religious worship not grounded exclusively in Halakhah, these philosophic individuals study "the natural things" and gain understanding in "divine science" and thus "come to be with the ruler in the inner part of the habitation." Given their knowledge of God as revealed in nature, they then "set their thought to work on God alone."

As we have suggested in our analysis of the religious significance of philosophy for Maimonides, knowledge of God in nature engenders a distinct religious passion.

> This is the worship peculiar to those who have apprehended the true realities; the more they think of Him and of being with Him, the more their worship increases.[14]

Knowledge of God in nature gives the individual a perspective on God independent of tradition and revelation. The goal of their religious practice (as indicated in our earlier analysis of Maimonides' instruction to the student of the *Guide* regarding halakhic ritual) is to "engage in totally devoting yourself to Him." Unlike religious practice based on submission to legal authority, the goal of this kind of worship is to "endeavor to come closer to Him, and strengthen the bond between you and Him—that is, the intellect."

For Maimonides, Halakhah and philosophy constitute two valid and vital religious perspectives. This is the complex world of a medieval Jew committed to Jewish history and Halakhah, as well as to the reigning science of his day, the Aristotelian conception of the "natural" and "divine sciences." This is Maimonides' legacy to Jews in any age seeking a way—or ways—to express their commitment to and love for Jewish history and its tradition, as well as their yearning for God who "is good to all; and his tender mercies are over all His works" (Ps. 145:9).

NOTES

1. David Hartman, *Maimonides: Torah and Philosophic Quest* (Philadelphia: Jewish Publication Society, 1976), pp. 20-27

2. Moses Maimonides, *The Guide of the Perplexed* , trans. Shlomo Pines vol. II (Chicago: University of Chicago, 1963), pp.622-623

3. David Hartman, *Maimonides: Torah and Philosophic Quest*, p.194

4. Moses Maimonides, *Mishneh Torah, Sefer ha-Maddah*, 4:13

5. *Mishneh Torah, Hilkhot Teshuva*, 9:2

6. *Mishneh Torah, Hilkhot Shemitah ve-Yovel*, 13:12-13

7. *Mishneh Torah, Hilkhot Avadim*, 9:8

8. Moses Maimonides, *The Guide of the Perplexed* , vol.1, pp. 82-85

9. *Mishneh Torah, Hilkhot Teshuva*, 10:1-6,

10. David Hartman, *Maimonides: Torah and Philosophic Quest*, pp.57-61

11. Yeshayahu Leibowitz, *Judaism, Human Values, and the State of Israel*, trans. and ed. Eliezer Goldman (Cambridge, Mass.: Harvard University Press, 1992), p.38

12. *Mishneh Torah, Hilkhot Yesodei ha-Torah*, 2:1-2

13. Moses Maimonides, *The Guide of the Perplexed* , trans. Shlomo Pines vol. II, pp. 618-619

14. Ibid., p.620

10

The Murder of Jewish Children during the Holocaust

Steven T. Katz

I

It is a great pleasure to contribute to this *Festschrift* in honor of Dr. Irving (Yitz) Greenberg. A friend of thirty-five years, Dr. Greenberg has been one of a small group of Jewish thinkers who have truly attempted to respond to the situation the Jewish People found themselves in after the Holocaust and the creation of the State of Israel. By "truly" I mean not just in terms of his thinking but also in terms of trying to understand the practical, actionable, implications of these events, especially for the American Jewish community of which he has been a leader for the past three decades. Even when one disagrees with him on specific matters one cannot doubt the profound existential commitment that he has to the Jewish People and to the State of Israel. Everyone who shares these commitments owes him a debt for what he has accomplished in, and on behalf of, these two entities.

In a paper that Dr. Greenberg delivered at a major conference on Jewish-Christians relations in light of the Holocaust, held in New York City in June, 1973, he cited the following testimony given at the Nuremberg trials:

WITNESS: . . . . When the extermination of the Jews in the gas chambers was at its height, orders were issued that children were to be thrown straight into the crematorium furnaces, or into a pit near the crematorium, without being gassed first.

SMIRNOV (Russian prosecutor): How am I to understand this? Did they throw them into the fire alive, or did they kill them first?

WITNESS: They threw them in alive. Their screams could be heard at the camp. It is difficult to say how many children were destroyed in this way.

SMIRNOV: Why did they do this?

WITNESS: It's very difficult to say. We don't know whether they wanted to economize on gas, or if it was because there was not enough room in the gas chambers.[1]

Dr. Greenberg's paper then worked out that the gas saved in killing Jewish children in this manner was "forty-five hundredth's of a cent per person," and he went on to point out that: "In the summer of 1944, a Jewish child's life was not worth the two-fifths of a cent it would have cost to put it to death rather than burn it alive."[2]

In the present essay I would like to take up this topic of the murder of Jewish children by the Nazi state and attempt to provide a fuller, though still not complete,[3] accounting of what this entailed and what this meant. My interest in doing so arises from two different concerns. First, despite the enormous literature on the Holocaust – and the fact that it is commonplace when discussing the murder of European Jewry to refer to the fact that up to 1,500,000 Jewish children were killed by the Nazis – the details of these children's deaths are rarely presented in one coherent narrative focusing solely on this issue.[4] I have therefore, tried to organize this essay to be such a presentation. Second, I have been drawn to this subject by my long standing interest regarding the issue of the Holocaust's uniqueness as an historical phenomenon.[5] In pursuing this topic it has become clear to me that the genocidal Nazi assault on Jewish children was not only a distinctive feature of the *Shoah* but also represented a singular historical event. Put simply, I believe that the obsession with the murder of Jewish children by the Third Reich represents an historical *novum*.

II

Jewish children were the threat that the Nazis feared most. Such children represented the future and directly challenged the dystopian ambition that the Nazi *Weltanschauung* aspired to – a future that would be *Judenrein*. Reichsführer Heinrich Himmler was very clear on this point. Speaking to a select group of SS and *Wehrmacht* officers he openly told them of his operating principle with regard to the murder of Jewish women and children:

When I was forced somewhere in some village to act against partisans and Jewish commissars…then as a principle I gave the order to kill the women and children of those partisans and commissars too. … Believe you me, that order was not so easy to give or so simple to carry out as it was logically thought out and can be stated in this hall. But we must constantly recognize what kind of primitive, primordial, natural race struggle [*Rassenkampf*] we are involved in.[6]

Children, usually spared by the victors in war and by masters in slave societies, were, in the *Shoah*, considered the ultimate racial enemy. Insofar as the Aryan people were engaged in an uncompromising life and death struggle with the Jewish People, Jewish children had to be killed in order to end this world-historical racial conflict once and for all.

In the life of the ghettos of Nazi Europe this annihilatory racial dogma was made a ruling axiom. It was first institutionalized in 1941, in the reorganization of the ghetto economy by Max Bischof, head of the Third Reich's transfer agency, whose plans intentionally entailed that large numbers of Jewish children would starve to death. The reason for this outcome was that the envisioned reorganization involved the implementation of the principle that: "Conditions of undernourishment could be allowed to develop without regard for the consequences,"[7] meaning that the new economic model that was now to be utilized to govern the ghettos consciously mandated starvation for a segment of the incarcerated Jewish ghetto population. And, as a result, deaths from starvation escalated in all the ghettos in the second half of 1941 and onwards. Furthermore, the new economic strategy sharply, if only temporarily, divided "productive" from "unproductive" ghetto residents. It made this distinction absolute by instituting a new food policy that called for feeding workers soup in the workshops twice a day and supplementing this soup with bread rations, as opposed to the earlier method of food distribution that allowed workers to share their rations at home with their wives and children. In this way, "unproductive" individuals, not employed in one of the ghetto's workshops, were, in effect, given a death sentence. The rate of deaths by starvation now rose to about, "11 percent of the entire ghetto population when projected over a twelve month period."[8]

As a result of this change in the food policy, Jewish children in all of the ghettos had been sentenced to death by starvation, if not killed by other means. What this meant in quantitative terms can be readily appreciated by recalling the number of Jewish children living in the ghettos. The census done in the Warsaw Ghetto in late October 1939, soon after its creation, indicated that there were 91,611 children under 15 years old out of a total population of 359,827 Jews. Measured as a percentage of the ghetto population, children represented 25.4 percent of the entire Warsaw Ghetto community. In Łódź, a census taken in 1940, soon after the enclosing of the ghetto, indicated there were 36,188 children under age 14 out of a total population of 157,955. In percentage terms children represented 22.9 percent of the ghetto population.[9] In Riga, on November 1941, the German census reported that there were 5,652 children under 14 in the ghetto population of 29,602.[10] Children, therefore, represented 19 percent of the Riga ghetto community. Given these figures we can reasonably project that, except where the Jewish population had first been reduced by the action of the *Einsatzgruppen* before ghettoization occurred, most if not all the ghettos had populations in which children under fifteen represented a sizeable segment of the community.

Keeping this in mind one also remembers that, in addition to the ghettos already mentioned, the Bialystock Ghetto had 60,000 inhabitants, the Minsk Ghetto 80,000 to 90,000 inhabitants, the Lvov Ghetto approximately 160,000 inhabitants, the Chernowitz Ghetto 62,000 inhabitants, the Kishinev Ghetto 80,000 inhabitants, and the Vilna Ghetto 60,000 to 70,000 in 1939. Together these larger ghettos had a cumulate initial population of approximately 500,000 souls, about 100,000 (or more) of whom were children. And the smaller ghettos, for example, those in Chelm (population of 14,000 in 1939), Grodno (population 22,000), Dinaburg (population 15,000 to 18,000), Radom (population of 25,000 in 1939), Drohobycz and Borashaw (which taken together had a population of 27,000), Zhitomir (population 35,000), Berdichev (population 35,000), and Kelice (population 21,000), all had substantial numbers of Jewish children who must be accounted for.[11]

And when we do account for all of these children, from both the large and small ghettos, we learn that, given Nazi policy, almost none of these hundreds of thousands of children survived the war. So, for example, in Warsaw, consistent with the ruling food policy, the death of children through starvation was a daily occurrence. And those who did not die from hunger were routinely rounded up and deported to be gassed as part of the more general destruction of the ghetto population that began on July 22, 1942, the eve of *Tisha B'Av*, the Jewish day of mourning for the destruction of the First and Second Temples. Between July 22 and September 12, 1942, 265,000 Jews were deported from the Warsaw Ghetto to Treblinka. This included nearly all of the 126,300 plus children aged 19 or younger – less those who had already died -- in the ghetto. Before the deportations began there were 25,759 boys in the ghetto aged nine and under and 25,699 girls aged nine and under. After the deportations there were only 255 boys and 243 girls under age nine left in the ghetto. Ninety-nine percent of the young boys in the ghetto and 99.1 percent of the young girls in the ghetto had been deported and killed. For children between 10 and 19 years of age, the rate of loss was also staggeringly high. Of 35,238 boys, only 2,183, 6.2 percent, remained. Of the 39,700 girls in this age group, only 2,263, 5.7 percent, were still alive.[12] Thus, when this *Aktion* was completed almost all the ghetto children had been murdered. Those few older Jewish children who remained alive in Warsaw after September 12 had been exempted from death temporarily because they were needed for work in the ghetto workshops and industries.[13] The younger children had no such utilitarian value and therefore there was no reason to keep them alive.

No Jewish child, given the racial threat it represented, could be permitted to escape the *Führer's* demand that s/he must die. So, for example, though deemed utterly worthless while, from a racial perspective, judged to be terribly dangerous, the 192 young charges in Janus Korzak's [14] Warsaw Ghetto orphanage had to be sent to be gassed in Treblinka. "Useless eaters" – as well as future "racial criminals" – they could not be allowed to live. Wherever a Jewish child was found it had to be murdered. Mira Pizyc, in her memoir on the reduction of the Warsaw Ghetto, remembers the following incident:

> … Another sight that freezes the blood in your veins; Behind me marches a young woman. She has a pack on her back. The German smiles a satanic grin, walks up to her, raises a whip, and lands a blow to the pack. A terrible scream erupts from the concealed child. The German grabs the pack and, together with its living contents, smashes it up against the wall. The stricken mother wants to go after her child; the executioner explodes with laughter – the scene amuses him. With a blow of the [whip's] handle, he pushes the woman, blue with agony, back into line.[15]

I repeat: no Jewish child from the Warsaw Ghetto could—should—be left among the living.[16]

In Lódź the pattern was similar. From the middle of January 1942, to May 15, 1942, the first round of deportations from the ghetto took place. The first train left for Chelmno on January 16, 1942. The initial group of deportees included 780 men, 853 women, and 154 children.[17] Then every day thereafter until April 2, 1942, a period of 76 consecutive days, a transport of Jews that included Jewish children left the ghetto for the Chelmno death camp to be gassed.

Between January 16th and May 15th, 1942 54,990 people, including thousands of children, were sent from the Lódź Ghetto to Chelmno. To keep the remaining Jews alive Rumkowski, the Elder of the ghetto, sought to turn the ghetto into the most productive workshop in the Reich. "Work for Life" became the ruling motto governing all activities. But this adopted system also entailed that "unproductive" elements within the population, such as children, had to be sacrificed. Accordingly, on September 1st, in conformity with this ruling agenda, those in ghetto hospitals were rounded up. This included 320 children who were sent to Treblinka on September 2nd. But this was just the opening gambit. The Nazi authorities next demanded that 20,000 Jews be handed over for deportation, including all children under 10 and those over 65.[18] When these two groups were tallied they numbered 13,000, including 850 orphans from the Marysin orphanage.[19] After these September deportations the ghetto held 89,446 Jews, very few of whom were children. By July 1944, this population was reduced to 68, 516 at which point, in August 1944, the ghetto was ordered closed by Himmler and the remaining 67,000 Jews (approximately),[20] including Rumkowski and his family, were sent to

Auschwitz. By the end of 1944 almost no Jewish children of the 36,188 children who had been alive in Lódź in 1940 remained among the living.

In Vilna, home to between 60,000 and 70,000 Jews on the eve of World War II, the mass killings, undertaken by *Einsatzgruppe* A, began in July 1941 when 5,000 Jewish men were murdered at the pits in nearby Ponary. During August the murder of Jewish men continued. Then women and children began to be included among the victims. On September 2, 1941 when 3,700 Jews were murdered, 2,019 of them were women and 817 of them were children. At the same time, the building of a ghetto for the surviving Jews of Vilna began and by September 7th the creation of the ghetto had been completed. It was built in two parts. In Ghetto 1 there were, after the first round of shootings, approximately 30,000 Jews, and in Ghetto 2 approximately 10,000 Jews. Another 6,000 were penned up in nearby Lukiozki. On September 10th and 11th the deportations and mass murders in the nearby woods of Ponary resumed. In their summary report of December 1st, 1941, *Einsatzkommando* 3 reported: "On 12 September, 993 males, 1,670 Jewish women, and 771 children, a total of 3,334, were liquidated in Vilna."[21] On September 17th this same *Einsatzkommando* reported killing 1,271 Jews, 687 of whom were female, and 247 of whom were children.[22] On *Yom Kippur*, October 1, 1942, a large *Aktion* killed approximately 2,000 additional Jews, the majority of whom were women and children. On October 15th and 16th, the last two days of the festival of *Succot*, another *Aktion* in Ghetto 2 claimed 1,146 Jewish lives, of whom 507 were women and 257 were children.[23] On October 21, Ghetto 2 was subject to its final liquidation. About 2,500 Jews were taken to Ponary and shot. Of these, 1,036 were females and 586 were children.[24]

In the larger of the two Vilna ghettos, Ghetto I, deportation and mass killing began after the final liquidation of Ghetto 2. The first mass *Aktion* took place on October 24 and 25, 1941. The *Einsatzkommando* reported that on the 25th 2,578 Jews were shot at Ponary of whom 1,766 were women and 812 were children. This was followed by an *Aktion* on October 29th in which 1,533 Jews were taken to Ponary and murdered. Of these, 789 were women and 362 were children. On November 6th the act was repeated: 1,341 Jews were killed at Ponary and, again, women and children made up a majority of those killed. The *Einsatzgruppe* commander, reporting on the successful completion of these massacres, told this to superiors in Berlin: "The goal of the systematic cleansing operation in the Ostland was a complete purge of the Jews, in accordance with the basic Order."[25] (This excluded 15,000 Jews who were kept alive as slave laborers until late September 1943, when the Vilna Ghetto was completely liquidated. At the time of the final closing of the ghetto, 6,000 women and children were separated from the men. Of these, 1,400 to 1,700 women were sent to work as slave laborers in Estonia; the other 4,300 to 4,600 women and children were shipped to Majdanek where they were gassed. With this final *Aktion* almost no Jewish children from the famous, historic, Jewish community of Vilna remained alive).[26]

In Kovno, one of the first acts after the establishment of the ghetto[27] was the murder of 3,000 women and 5,400 children by *Einsatzkommandos* 3 and 11. Again in October 1941, 581 children were murdered in Kovno as part of a larger *Aktion* in which 1,608 Jews were murdered. A few days later, in connection with still another round up, 818 children were murdered (out of 1,845 Jews). On October 29th, 9,200 Jews were killed at the Ninth Fort. Of these 2,920 were women and almost half, 4,273, were children.[28] On November 25, 1941, 175 Jewish children were executed by *Einsatzkommandos* led by Karl Jäger at the Ninth Fort in Kovno. This was repeated on November 29, 1941 when these same killers murdered another 152 Jewish children (and 1155 Jewish women) at the same location.[29]

The Lithuanian Jewish community numbered approximately 240,000 persons before the war. I have been unable to arrive at an exact statistical count relative to the number of Jewish children in Lithuania in 1939 on the eve of the Nazi invasion. One reasonable estimate puts the number at approximately 71,000[30] and I will adopt this number in the present context as a roughly correct tally. Based on this estimate I would suggest, given the decimation of this community that included the special targeting of Jewish children, that fewer than two percent of these youngsters survived the war.

In Riga (Latvia), thousands of Jewish children were also murdered by the conquering Nazis. In the first days of the occupation, according to an eyewitness:

> . . . . . . sadistic tortures continued unabated. On Gertrude Street a group of storm troopers went up to the roof of a six-story building and from there threw Jewish children to the ground. Some official was about to order them to stop these executions. From the roof they answered him:
>
> "We are conducting scientific work here. We are testing the accuracy of the law of universal gravity."
>
> "Donnerwetter! Well said! Continue, gentleman. Science requires sacrifices."[31]
>
> Killing Jewish children was a joke, a source of cruel humor. For these *Einsatzkommandos*, this murder of Jewish children provided a light moment of recreation, of "sportmachen."

This barbaric incident was followed by the shooting of a number of Jewish children in Riga on November 8, 1941. Then on November 30 and December 1, 1941 a major *Aktion* took place in the ghetto. A report detailing the event tells us:

> Toward six o'clock in the evening [on November 30] the women, children, and

old men were forced out of their apartments. The police tore through the quarter in the Moscow Vorstadt. They finished off the sick on the spot. Mothers burdened with large families were left with no more than two children; the rest were shot right there........ Groups of women and children driven from their homes were standing in the streets. They were forced to wait there until the next morning. Numb and shivering from the cold, they watched the bloodbath in horror. Toward morning the Germans began forming columns of two to three hundred people; under the armed guard of an equal number of policemen, they were sent eastward............

No one cleared away the bodies inside the ghetto; but once the column had passed barbed wire, carts and wheelbarrows immediately joined up with it. Without giving it a second thought, the guards shot crying children and people who lagged behind; their bodies were tossed onto a cart or wheelbarrow.

A survivor of the massacre adds:

By evening the shooting subsided.......I decided to crawl out from under the pile of shoes........ I heard the faint voice of a weeping child coming from the pit, where the ones who had been murdered were lying: 'Mama, I'm cold......Why are you just lying there, Mama?' Well, I thought, what will be will be. I'll try to save the child. But the Germans beat me to it. They went up to the pit, poked around for the little boy with their bayonets, and stabbed him. One of the Germans said, 'No one gets away from us alive.' [32]

To make sure that this pronouncement would not be proven false, the *Einsatzkommando* conducted another, and final, round of murdering Jewish children in Riga on December 8th, 1942.

So it went, ghetto by ghetto. In the Kolomyja Ghetto, in December 1941, a large number of Jewish children were selected for deportation. On one day, almost 1,000 were shipped out in cattle cars. And those few who remained were deported in the early fall of 1942. In the Sialui Ghetto the same pattern was repeated with children (and women) disproportionately targeted for murder in the woods of Bubjai. And those not murdered in the Lithuanian forest outside the ghetto were sent to Auschwitz to be killed. In a document left by a Jewish *Sonderkommando*, that was buried at Auschwitz and found after the war, the following report is included.

It was winter, the end of 1944. A contingent of children were brought in. They were from Shavel, Lithuania, where German patrol cars had picked them up from their homes. In broad daylight six hundred Jewish boys, aged twelve to eighteen, were brought in wearing flimsy striped pajamas all in tatters and wearing down-at-heel shoes or wooden clogs. The children looked so handsome, so radiant, so well-built that they shone through their rags. It was the end of October 1944. They arrived in twenty-five trucks guarded by heavily armed SS men. They got out in the yard of the crematorium area. The *Kommando* leader gave an order: 'Take your clothes off in the yard!' The children saw the smoke from the chimney and instantly realized that they were being led to their death. Crazed with fright, they started running around the yard, back and forth, clutching their heads. Many of them broke into frightful crying. Their wailing was terrible to hear. The *Kommando* leader and his aide hit out ferociously at the children. He whacked so hard that his wooden club broke in his hand. He got himself another club and flailed at the children's heads. Brute strength prevailed. The children, panic-stricken though they were, with death staring them in the face, undressed. Stark naked, they pressed against each other to shield themselves from the cold, but they would not go downstairs [into the gas chamber]. A bold little boy went up and begged the *Kommando* leader to spare him. He would do any kind of work, no matter how hard. The answer was a tremendous whack on the head with the club. Many of the boys darted off frantically to the Jews of the *Sonderkommando*, threw their arms around their necks, imploring: 'Save me!' Others raced about the yard, naked, running from death. The *Kommando* leader called in the SS *Unterscharführer* with his rubber baton to help.

The boys' high-pitched voices grew louder and louder in a bitter lament. Their wailing carried a great distance. One was completely deafened and overcome by this desperate weeping. With satisfied smirks, without a trace of compassion, the SS men triumphantly hailed savage blows on the children and drove them into the gas chamber. On the stairs stood the *Unterscharführer*, still wielding his club and giving a murderous crack at each child. A few lone children were, all the same, still running back and forth in search of a way out. The SS men chased after them, lashing out at them and forcing them at last into the chamber. The glee of the SS men was indescribable.[33]

In Lublin, the final roundup of Jews in the city took place on March 13-14, 1943 and included the murder of hundreds of children. In the Bialystok region, almost all the children in the smaller ghettos were sent to die in Treblinka in October and November 1942. What this meant in late 1942 and early 1943 when the liquidation of the Polish ghettos was reaching its apogee was that not all the children could be gassed on arrival. Instead, as Jankel Wiernik, an eyewitness to what went on at Treblinka in this period, tells us:

All through that winter small children, stark naked and barefooted, had to stand out in the open for hours on end, awaiting their turn in the increasingly busy gas chambers. The soles of their feet froze and stuck to the icy ground. They stood and cried; some of them froze to death. In the meantime, Germans and Ukrainians walked up and down the ranks, beating and kicking the victims.

One of the Germans, a man named Sepp, was a vile and savage beast, who took special delight in torturing children. When he pushed women around and they begged him to stop because they had children with them, he would frequently snatch a child from the woman's arms and either tear the child in half or grab it by the legs, smash its head against a wall and throw the body away. Such incidents were by no means isolated. Tragic scenes of this kind occurred all the time.[34]

Jewish children were worthless, even less than worthless, and the cruel manner of their death reflected this valuation.

In the large Bialystock Ghetto where 60,000 Jews were incarcerated, violence against Jewish children began almost immediately after the arrival of the Nazis. On June 27, 1941 1,000 men and boys were locked in the main Synagogue of the city and burnt alive.[35] Those Jewish children who remained alive in the ghetto, despite the deprivations of ghetto life, were—except for 1,260 of them—sent to their death in Treblinka on August 21, 1943. The 1,260 children of Bialystock not deported to Treblinka were shipped instead to Theresienstadt. They had been saved in connection with a Nazi plan to exchange Jews for German prisoners of war in Allied hands. As part of the negotiations then in progress, Britain had agreed to take 5,000 Jews, 85 percent of whom should be Jewish children from Eastern Europe. In the end, however, the bureaucrats at *Auswärtiges Amt* decided not to finalize the deal and the 1, 260 Jewish children from Bialystock were sent to be murdered in Auschwitz instead.[36]

In Galicia, by mid- 1942, all the Jews had been marked for death. Though 20,000 Jewish women had previously been given work passes, the time for Jewish women to be preserved for their labor was coming to an end. Likewise, in March, 1942, as part of "March Operation," a large number of ghetto children were deported to Belzec. By mid June, SS Police Leader Fredrich Krüger had negotiated an expansion of Jewish murder in the region. Nearly all Jewish women and children were now to be sent to Belzec to be gassed. All mediating arguments about economic concerns, that might be invoked to keep Jewish women and children alive, no longer had any significant weight. When the *Kreishauptmann* of Stryj remarked on the unfortunate economic effects of these *Judenaktionen* the local SS and Police Leader Fritz Katzmann brushed these reservations aside and replied that: it was imperative, "to get this [Jewish] pestilence under control in a very short time."[37] This "Jewish Pestilence," included over 30,000 Jewish children nearly all of whom were killed either in the nearby forest of Lesienice—the so called "Valley of Death" in the hills northwest of Lvov—or the extremely brutal Janowska Road camp. In the final liquidation of the large Lvov ghetto, that at its peak housed 160,000 persons, it is reported that, "the Germans murdered the children, often in the most cruel manner: they threw them alive into the fires or dashed the heads of babies against the walls and street lights." In addition, the Hitler *Jugend* (Nazi Youth) participated in this massacre "and held shooting practice, using Jewish children, as live targets."[38] The small number of Jewish children who survived the forced move out of the ghetto, then became part of the *Sportmachen* organized at the Janowska Road camp where the SS competed to see who could, most efficiently, tear children in two or dash their brains out.[39] When the war ended, of the approximately 32,000 to 35,000 Jewish children in Lvov at the start of the war, 85 were alive.[40]

The answer to the question of whether Jewish children had to die was, ultimately, always yes. This rule was confirmed in a telling encounter that occurred in early August 1941 in Byelaya Tserkov, a small Ukrainian village 70 kilometers from Kiev, where *Sonderkommando* 4A murdered all the Jewish adults and many of the Jewish children. But, inexplicably, 90 Jewish children under the age of five were allowed to remain alive. When they were discovered by the Catholic military chaplain Ernst Tewers and the Protestant chaplain Gehard Wilczek, the two men tried to save the children's lives by appealing to the *Generalstafofficer* Lieutenant-Colonel Helmut Groscurth. Groscurth was unsure what to do and, over the protests of *Oberscharführer* Jäger, the commander of the *Einsatzgruppe* A that had murdered the town's Jewish adults and who now wanted to execute these remaining youngsters, referred the case up the chain of command to Field Marshall von Reichenau, commander of the Sixth Army, and *Standartenführer* Paul Blobel. After consideration, "Blobel ordered the children executed." SS Colonel Riedl, in explaining the decision to Groscurth, told the latter that, "the elimination of the Jewish women and children was a matter of urgent necessity, whatever form it took." SS *Oberstrumführer* August Häfner, who carried out this sentence, recalls what happened next:

> I went out to the woods alone. The Wehrmacht had already dug a grave. The children were brought along in a tractor. I had nothing to do with this technical procedure. The Ukrainians were standing round trembling. The children were taken down from the tractor. They were lined up along the top of the grave and shot so that they fell into it. The Ukrainians did not aim at any particular part of the body. They fell into the grave. The wailing was indescribable. … I particularly remember a small fair-haired girl who took me by the hand. She too was shot later…The grave was near some woods. It was not near the rifle-range. The execution must have taken place in the afternoon at about 3:30 or 4:00. It took place the day after the discussions at the *Feldkommandanten*…. Many children were hit four or five times before they died.[41]

Blobel and Riedl knew where their duty to the Fatherland lay. And so did Häfner. Jewish children were a threat that had to be expunged "by whatever form it took."[42] The duty of German soldiers to kill Jewish children was widely obeyed. SS man Ernst Gobel reported this *Aktion* in the area of Scholochowo, in the Ukraine.

> The victims were shot by the firing-squad with carbines, mostly by shots in the back of the head, from a distance of one metre on my command. Before every salvo Täubner gave me the order – 'Get set, fire!' I just relayed Täubner's command. The way this happened was that I gave the command 'Aim! Fire!' to the

members of the firing-squad, and then there was a crack of gunfire. Meanwhile *Rottenführer* Abraham shot the children with a pistol. There were about five of them. These were children whom I would think were aged between two and six years. The way Abraham killed the children was brutal. He got hold of some of the children by the hair, lifted them up from the ground, shot them through the back of their heads and then threw them into the grave.[43]

Five young Jewish children ages six and younger were perceived as a mortal threat to the mighty Third Reich that had to be extinguished. And so Abraham the faithful Nazi soldier, unlike the Abraham of the *Akedah*, the binding of Isaac,[44] killed these five children.

Throughout the Ukraine similar massacres occurred on both large and small scales. Whereas in Belaya Tserkov the number of Jewish women and children was relatively small, in Kamenets-Podolsky *Einsatzgruppe* C murdered 23,600 Jewish men, women, and children between August 27 and August 30, and, then in late September, 33,000 Jewish men, women, and children in Babi Yar on the edge of the large city of Kiev. By mid-October, 1941, *Einsatzgruppe* C reported killing more than 100,000 Jewish men, women, and children. At the end of the war there were almost no Jewish children left alive from families that had resided either in Kamenets-Podolsky or Kiev. And further south, *Einsatzgruppe* D, led by Otto Ohlendorf, began the genocidal elimination of the Jews in their region of operation with the murder of all the Jewish men, women and children in Nikolayen in mid-September 1941. The murder of Jewish children had by now become routine. The 454th Security Division reported: "in some places providing for Jewish children and infants who lost their parents presented some difficulties; but also in that respect a remedy has been found by the SD." As Field Marshal von Reichenau described it, these measures were the "harsh but just punishment of Jewish subhumanity"— *judischen Untermenschentum*.[45]

The murder of the Jewish women and children of Serbia also indicate the absolute worthlessness assigned to these two groups. After nearly all the Jewish men in Serbia had been killed a concentration camp was created, primarily for Jewish women and children, in Sajmiste. At the end of 1941 it was ready to be occupied. In early 1942 approximately 7,000 women and children and 500 surviving Jewish men, along with a group of elderly Jewish men, together with 292 Gypsy women and children, were transferred to this ghetto. But their stay was very short-lived. Starting in March, 1942, after liberating the Gypsy women and children, the Jewish women and children began to be gassed in gas vans sent to the camp from Berlin for this purpose. By the end of May, 7,500 Jews, including almost all the women and children, had been murdered.[46]

In Slovakia when Eichmann began to deport the country's Jews on March

12, 1942, the first deportation, at the request of the Slovakian regime, was comprised of women and children.[47] (This mirrored the first deportation from Vienna also organized by Eichmann that consisted of sixty percent women and girls.)[48] Likewise, out of 15,000 Czech Jewish children deported to various camps only 28 survived.[49]

The abundance of evidence that testifies to the murder of Jewish children throughout Eastern Europe is overwhelming. In no specific order, I cite some of this further data. In Minsk thousands of Jewish children were murdered by *Einsatzgruppe* A in early November 1941. Defending this, and related *Aktions*, at the war's end, General Friedrich Jeckeln who headed SS units in Minsk testified that he had received an order from Himmler that stated: "all the Jews in the Ostland down to the last man [woman and child] must be exterminated."[50] In Slonim, 12,000 Jews living in the local ghetto – mostly women and children – were shot. In explaining this Aktion the district commissioner referred to these women and children as *Unnütze Fresser*, "useless gobblers." And promised that: "Early next year [the Jews] will be rigorously checked and sorted for further reduction."[51] In the Plazów labor camp, manned by Jewish workers from Krakow, the 300 children who still remained alive in 1943 were rounded up and deported to their death. The *Aktion* occurred to the singing of 'Mammi, Rauf mir ein pferdchen" that was broadcast over loudspeakers the Nazis had set up for the occasion.[52] In one of the villages near Slonim "they chased children, women, and the elderly into a barn and set it alight."[53] In the Commissariat of Zhitomir all of the Jewish children were killed between September 1941 and January 1942. In eastern Belorussia almost every Jewish child (and woman) was murdered by the end of 1942.[54] Walter Mattner who participated in the mass-murder of Jewish women and children in Mogilev, Belorussia in early October 1941, wrote home to his wife about his activities in this massacre.

> When the first truckload [of victims] arrived my hand was slightly trembling when shooting, but one gets used to this. When the tenth load arrived I was already aiming more calmly and shot securely at the many women, children, and infants.[55]

In the small village of Krynichno, 16 kilometers to the north of Mir, the policeman Willy Schultz, head of the squad sent to do the killing of the Jews, gathered all the Jews together in one house. He listed their names and counted them: 21 Jews. Then he "counted those under 16….. and wrote in his notebook: 'acht Stück bis sechzehn Jahre' – 'eight items up to age sixteen'.[56] Jewish children, like black slave children, were things, items, to list. But in the case of slave children they were listed as assets that enriched their owners. In the case of the children of Krynichno they were listed so that they could be targeted to be shot. And all of these eight children were soon corpses. Again, policeman Schultz reported that 850 Jews, mostly women and children, tried to hide in the Mir Ghetto, but were captured and shot on October 2, 1942. In this orgy of violence against children with Jewish blood even half-Jewish children were rounded up and murdered. So, for example, in Izraylovka (Ukraine) the police collected 20 children of mixed parentage and murdered them in a mass grave in Ustenovka.[57]

In Western Europe, too, Jewish children (and their mothers) were targeted for deportation to the death camps. The story of Anne Frank, who was arrested in August 1944, after years of hiding in the attic of 263 Prinsengrachtstelt in Amsterdam, and who then was deported to, and died of disease in, Bergen Belsen should be taken as paradigmatic of Dutch Jewish children.[58] Of 140,000 Jews in Holland in 1944, approximately 112,000, some 80 percent, were killed during the war. 46.455 Jews, men, women and children, were deported from the Westerbork concentration camp in Holland between July 1942 and February 1943. Of these 3,500 men were sent to work as slave laborers in the Bleckhammer Camp, and then later to the industrial camp at Auschwitz III – Monowitz and GrossRosen. Of this group 181 men survived the war. Of the remaining 42,915, 85 survived the war. Included among those Dutch Jews killed in Auschwitz were thousands of Jewish children.[59] From the first 42 transports sent to Auschwitz between July 15, 1942 and December 12, 1942 it is difficult to ascertain if any of the thousands of children deported on these trains survived. For the last 29 transports sent between August 28, 1942 to December 12, 1942 "every single one of the women and children…….was exterminated." From the first five transports sent between January 11 and February 23, 1943 carrying 3,600 persons including 800 children under sixteen, perhaps 1 or 2 of the children survived. From the nine transports sent during this six week period in total, carrying 7,900 Jews, only seven women, and a few children survived. Of the thousands of Jews deported between August 24 and November 16, 1943, which included 8970 children, almost none of the children survived. In all, the Nazis deported 107,000 Dutch Jews to the East, of whom only 5,450 returned.[60]

In France,[61] deportations of foreign Jews to Auschwitz began in March 1942. The deportation of French Jews began in June 1942 – by the end of 1942, 42,500 Jews had been shipped out to Auschwitz – and continued uninterrupted until the end of 1943. Then further trainloads of Jews were deported, mostly to Auschwitz, through the first half on 1944, the last shipments leaving France in July 1944. In total, 100 convoys were sent, mainly from the Drancy concentration camp outside of Paris, to Auschwitz, with a small additional number of transports to Sobibor and Majdanek and the Natzweiler-Struthof Camp near Strasbourg. These journeys involved up to 75,000 Jews.[62] Almost no one returned. In this cohort there were over 6,000 Jewish children aged below thirteen, and of these 2,000 were under the age of six. The total of French children and adolescents who arrived in Auschwitz came to 9,800.

And, depending on the mix of local conditions and the degree of Nazi pressure to deport the Jews in the different countries of Western Europe, the Jewish population, and the number of Jewish children, was reduced in all the countries under German control, with the exception of Finland, which was technically an ally of Germany. In the west, as in the east, Jewish children were seen as future enemies by virtue of their race and, as such, had to be exterminated.

By the end of the war, in all of occupied Europe, the Nazis had killed up to 1,500,000 Jewish children under the age of 16.

ON THE KILLING OF JEWISH CHILDREN AT AUSCHWITZ

To end this brief review on the fate of Jewish children under the Third Reich I would remind readers of the information and statistics we possess on the extermination of Jewish children at Auschwitz.

SS physician Johann Paul Kremer, during his interrogation after the war, reported on August 19, 1947:

As soon as a transport of people assigned to the gas chambers arrived at the railroad ramp, SS officers selected from among the new arrivals the persons who were fit for work, both men and women. The rest, including old people, all children, women with children in their arms and other persons unfit for work, were loaded onto trucks and taken to the gas chambers. I would drive all the way to the bunker with such a transport.[63]

And Rudolf Höss, commandant at Auschwitz noted in his Nuremberg testimony that "children of tender years were invariably exterminated since by reason of their youth they were unable to work." [64] Accordingly, when transports began to arrive at Auschwitz in the spring of 1942 Jewish children began to be murdered. Between April 17 and July 17, 1942, 656 older children arrived as part of a transport of 9,749 Jewish men and boys from Slovakia. By mid-1942 "the majority had died." At the same time younger Jewish children from Slovakia, both boys and girls, who arrived in Auschwitz between April and the end of October 1942 were gassed on arrival. A transmission of November 1942 to the Polish Government in Exile in London regarding Auschwitz reported that: "there is a huge percentage of women's and children's clothing among the garments of those who are liquidated. In the last Jewish transport from Slovakia (200 people) there were about 80 children…They were poisoned in Birkenau." In the 1942 transports from Slovakia, Bratislava, Novaky, Sered and Zilina to the camp "about one-fourth of such transports on the average, and more than one-third in particular cases" were made up of

Jewish children. Altogether, it is estimated that 9,000 of the 27,000 Slovakian Jews sent to Auschwitz and gassed there were children.

Between March 27, 1942 and August 11, 1944, 71 transports carried 69,000 Jews from France to Auschwitz. The number of children and adolescents included in these transports, as noted above, totaled 9,800 – 14 percent of the aggregate. Of these 7,400 were below the age of 14. Almost every one of these children was murdered. From Holland, via Westerbork concentration camp, Jews began being deported to Auschwitz in July, 1942. In total 60,000 Dutch Jews were sent to the camp in 68 transports. An exact statistical analysis of 38 of these transports that together carried 31,661 Jews revealed that among these deportees there were 3,832 children up to age 15, and another 969 adolescents aged 16 and 17. Thus 15.5 percent of the Dutch deportees on these transports were children. Among the entire population of 69,000 Dutch Jews sent to Auschwitz, the number of children and adolescents exceeds 8,000. Very few of these children lived until the end of the war.

Between 1942 and 1944, as the "Final Solution" gained momentum, Jewish children from all over Europe were systematically isolated and shipped by cattle car to Auschwitz. From Belgium 24,906 Jews were deported, in 27 transports, to Auschwitz. Of these 4,654, or 19 percent, of those sent to die were children aged 16 or younger. From Poland it is estimated that 300,000 Jews were shipped to Auschwitz of whom 66,000, 22 percent, were children 17 or younger. As late as May 14, 1944, 300 to 400 Jewish children, the remnant of the Krakow Ghetto, arrived in Auschwitz from Plaszów. By the war's end only a few hundred, primarily older children, of this cohort of 66,000 Polish Jewish youngsters were still among the living. (More generally, from a Polish Jewish community of 3,300,000, at least 20 percent of the community, some 660,000 individuals, were children. Of these 660,000 souls only 5,000 survived the war).[65] From Yugoslavia, 10,000 Jews were sent to Auschwitz, of whom about 1,500 were children. From Germany 2,621 of the deported 20,405 Jews were children. From Norway, 84 children and adolescents were sent to Auschwitz. Few returned. From Austria, 200 Jews, including 15 children, were sent to Auschwitz from Vienna in eight transports between March 1943 and September 1944. Additional numbers of Jews from Austria and elsewhere also came to Auschwitz via Theresienstadt beginning in October 1942. Almost all of the children in these transports were directed on arrival to the gas chambers. The data available on the transports from Theresienstadt to Auschwitz indicates that between 1942 and 1944, 46,212 Jews made this fateful journey. Of these, 3,807 were children aged 14 or younger. Almost none of them survived the camp.

In March 1943, Greek Jews began arriving at the camp. Most of these came from the great Jewish community of Salonika. But there were also deportations from the Greek islands of Korfu and Rhodes. In total, 48,633 Greek Jews were shipped to Auschwitz, including 12,000 children. All the children were gassed on arrival. In the further 1944 deportations of 3,500 Jews from Athens and Korfu and 2,500 Jews from Rhodes there were approximately 1,000 Jewish children all of whom were gassed on arrival. Italian Jews began to arrive in Auschwitz on October 23, 1943. (This followed the overthrow of Mussolini on July 25, 1943, the surrender of the successor government led by Marshall Badoglio to the Allies, and the Nazi takeover of Italy in late July and August 1943.) Altogether 7,400 Italian Jews were deported to Auschwitz, about a quarter of whom (approximately) are estimated to have been children. And from the liquidated Lithuanian and Estonian labor camps Jews were transported to Auschwitz in the summer of 1944. In the transport of June 26, 1944 there were 1,423 people—899 children and 524 women. On August 1, 1944 a transport from Kovno also arrived comprised solely of 120 Jewish boys aged 8 to 14. And still another transport that arrived on September 12, 1944 was made up entirely of 300 boys who were liquidated on arrival.

In the final, desperate act of the *Shoah*, 437,402 Jews were deported from Hungary when the new government of Prime Minister Döme Sztójay, working directly under German control, took office on March 22, 1944. The first deportations to Auschwitz began in mid-May 1944. It is estimated that of these deportees, approximately 90,000 were children, very few of whom survived.

By war's end a total of 216,300 Jewish children and adolescents had been sent to Auschwitz. (This represented 93.4 percent of all children sent to the camp.) Of these 216,300 children, 212 adolescents and 239 children were still alive when the camp was liberated by the Russians in late January 1945.[66]

The planned, systematic, murder of all Jewish children was the most radical, distinctive, feature of the *Shoah*.[67] More than any other act of the Third Reich, it reveals the absolute, dogmatic, racial-manichean principles at the very core of the Hitler state. As a result, the phenomenological character of the Holocaust is different from all other instances of mass murder that are known to me.

NOTES

1. Eva Fleischner (ed.), *Auschwitz; Beginning of a New Era? Reflections on the Holocaust* (New York: Ktav Publishers, 1977), pp. 9-10.

2. Ibid., p. 11.

3. This essay concentrates mainly on the murder of Jewish children in, or in connection with, the ghettos established in Eastern Europe. A relatively brief comment is also included on the extermination of Dutch and French Jewish children in order to indicate the breadth of the Nazi policy. The final section, mainly for emphasis, records details on the killing of Jewish children at Auschwitz. I do not, however, review in detail the events at the other Death Camps, though I mention some of these in passing,

nor do I discuss at length the vast killing operations of the *Einsatzgruppen*. This essay, therefore, is meant only as an introduction to a very large subject.

4. There are a few discussions of this issue but none are comprehensive. See, for example, Deborah Dwork, *Children With a Star: Jewish Youth in Nazi Europe* (New Haven: Yale University Press, 1991) and her bibliography of works on this topic.

5. For more on this concern see volume 1 of Steven T. Katz, *The Holocaust in Historical Context* (New York: Oxford University Press, 1994). Volume 2 will soon go to the publisher, Oxford University Press. In this second volume I pursue the analysis of the murder of Jewish children more fully than I can in this essay.

6. Cited from Carol Rittner and John Roth (eds.), *Different Voices: Women and the Holocaust* (New York: Paragon House Publishers, 1993), p. 392. The original can be found in Bradley F. Smith and Agnes F. Peterson (eds.), *Heinrich Himmler: Geheimreden 1933 bis 1945* (Frankfurt: Propyläen Verlag, 1974), p 201.

7. Götz Aly and Susan Heim, *Architects of Annihilation: Auschwitz and the Logic of Destruction* (Princeton: Princeton University Press, 2002), p 203.

8. Ibid., pp. 204-205.

9. For more on the fate of Jewish children in the Lodz Ghetto see: Alan Adelson (ed.), *The Diary of Dawid Sierakowiak* (New York: Oxford University Press, 1996); Lucjan Dobroszycki, *Chronicle of the Lódź Ghetto* (New Haven: Yale University Press, 1987); Alan Adelson and Robert Lapides, *Lódź Ghetto: Inside a Community Under Siege* (New York: Viking, 1989), and Isaiah Trunk, *Lódź Ghetto: A History*, (New York, 1942; in Yiddish), translated and edited by Robert Moses Shapiro, introduction by Israel Gutman (Bloomington: Indiana University Press, 2006).

10. The figures on the Warsaw Ghetto are drawn from Joseph Kermish, *To Live with Honor and Die With Honor: Selected Documents on the Warsaw Ghetto* (Jerusalem: Holocaust Publications Inc., 1986), p 137. Those on the Riga Ghetto are cited from Bernhard Press, *Judenmord in Lettland* (Berlin: Metropol-Verlag, 1992), p 65.

11. I cite these statistics from Philip Friedman, "The Jewish Ghettos of the Nazi Era," in his *Roads to Extinction: Essays on the Holocaust* (Philadelphia: Jewish Publication Society, 1980), pp. 75 and 76. This list is not exhaustive. There are many ghettos that I have not mentioned and whose populations would need to be included in a full account of the number of Jewish children in the ghettos.

12. Israel Gutman, *The Jews of Warsaw, 1939-1943: Ghetto Underground Revolt* (Bloomington: Indiana University Press, 1982), Table 6, p 271. The quote from Gutman is cited from *ibid.*, p 270.

13. This data is cited from Gustavo Corni, *Hitler's Ghettos: Voices from a Beleaguered Society, 1939-1944* (London: A Hodder Arnold Publication, 2002), pp 265-275.

14. For more on this remarkable man see Janusz Korczak, *Ghetto Diary* (New Haven: Yale University Press, 1978); and Betty Lifton, *The King of Children: The Life and Death of Janusz Korczak* (New York: American Academy of Pediatrics, 1988).

15. Cited from I. Gutman, *The Jews of Warsaw*, p. 217.

16. For more on the fate of children in the Warsaw Ghetto see Raul Hilberg, et al. (eds.), *The Warsaw Diary of Adeam Czerniakow* (New York: Ivan R. Dee, 1979), Abraham L. Katsh (ed.), *Scroll of Agony: The Warsaw Diary of Chaim A. Kaplan* (Bloomington: Indiana University Press, 1999), Emanuel Ringelblum, *Notes from the Warsaw Ghetto*, edited by Jacob Sloan (New York: Schocken, 1974), and Mary Berg, *Warsaw Ghetto: A Diary*, edited by S. L. Shnayderman (New York: L.B. Fischer, 1945).

17. Figure cited from I. Trunk, *Lódź Ghetto*, p. 23.

18. Ibid., pp. 241-244.

19. Ibid., p. 242 and p. 244.

20. Ibid., p. 300.

21. Cited from Yitzchak Arad, *Ghetto in Flames: The Struggle and Destruction of the Jews in Vilna in the Holocaust* (Jerusalem: Yad Vashem, 1980), p 116.

22. Ibid., p. 134.

23. On the Yom Kippur *Aktion*, Ibid., pp 136-138; on the Succoth *Aktion*, p 141.

24. Ibid., pp. 141-142.

25. The data on the *Aktionen* in Ghetto I are drawn from ibid., pp 143-163. The citation from the *Einsatzkommando* report is cited from ibid., p 170.

26. Ibid., p 431-432. For more on the Vilna Ghetto see Y. Arad, *Ghetto in Flames*; Herman Kruk, *The Last Days of the Jerusalem of Lithuana: Chronicles from the Vilna Ghetto and the Camps 1939-1944*, ed. by Benjamin Harshav, transl. by Barbara Harshav (New Haven: Yale University Press, 2002); and Yitschok Rudashevski, *The Diary of the Vilna Ghetto: June 1941-April 1943* (Tel Aviv: Ghetto Fighters House, 1973).

27. Ibid., p. 288.

28. Wolfgang Benz, Konrad Kwiet, and Juergen Mattheus (eds.), *Einsatz in 'Reich-Kommissariai Ostland'. Documente Zum Volkemord im Baltikum und in Weissrussland 1941-1944* (Berlin: 1998), Table, p 190.

29. I draw this information from Karl Jäger's report of December 1, 1941 covering the activities of *Einsatzkommando* 3 of *Einsatzgruppe* A. This report can be found in Ernst Klee, Willi Dressen and Volker Reiss (eds.), *"The Good Old Days:" The Holocaust as Seen by its Perpetrators and Bystanders* (New York: William S. Konecky, 1988), pp., 46-54.

30. Jacob Lestshinsky, "Balance Sheet of Extermination," *Jewish Affairs*, vol. 1, no. 1 (February 1: American Jewish Congress, 1946), p. 13.

31. Ilya Ehrenburg and Vasily Grossman (eds.), *The Complete Black Book of Russian Jewry*, translated and edited by David Patterson (New Brunswick: Transaction Publishers, 2001), p. 383.

32. Ibid., pp. 387, 388 and 393. I note parenthetically that this *Aktion* was also the one in which the great Jewish historian, Simon Dubnow, was murdered. This is described in the same source I am quoting from, pp. 387-388.

33. Reprinted in *Aleph-Tav: Tel Aviv Review* (Spring: Ah'Shav (Now) Pubishers, 1975). I cite it from Azriel Eisenberg (ed.), *The Lost Generation* (New York: Pilgrim, 1982), pp. 141-142..

34. Yankiel Wiernik, "A Year in Treblinka," in Alexander Donat (ed.), *The Death Camp Treblinka* (New York: Schocken Books, 1979), p. 163.

35. P. Friedman, "The Extermination of the Polish Jews," in *Road to Extinction*, p. 222.

36. See for further details of this exchange plan H. G. Adler, *Theresienstadt (1941-1945)* (Tübingen: J.C.B. Mohr, 1960), p. 154.

37. Cited from Thomas Sandkühler, "Anti-Jewish Policy and the Murder of the Jews in the District of Galicia, 1941/42," in Ulrich Herbert (ed.), *National Socialist Extermination Policies* (New York: Berghahn Books, 2000), p 121.

38. P. Friedman, "The Destruction of the Jews of Lwów," in *Road to Extinction*, p. 298.

39. Ibid., p. 311.

40. Ibid., p. 317.

41. Quote is taken from Ernst Klee, Willi Dressen and Volker Reiss (eds.), *The Good Old Days:" The Holocaust as seen by its Perpetrators and Bystanders*, trans. by Deborah Burnstone (New York: William S. Konecky Associates, 1988), p. 154.

42. Here I would remind readers of Otto Ohlendorf's testimony at Nuremberg. Ohlendorf was the Commander of *Einsatzgruppe* D which killed 90,000 Jewish men, women and children. When the prosecutor asked him why he had killed Jewish children Ohlendorf replied as follows: "I believe that it is very simple to explain [such killing of children] if one starts from the fact that this order did not only try to achieve a [temporary] security but also a permanent security because for that reason the children were people who would grow up and surely being the children of parents who had been killed they would constitute a danger no smaller than that of their parents." *Proceedings of the Trials of Major War Criminals*, (Nuremberg: Hamso 1947), vol. 9, p. 147.

43. Wendy, Lower, *Nazi Empire Building in the Ukraine* (Chapel Hill: University of North Carolina Press), p. 218.

44. See the full biblical tale as narrated in *Genesis* 22.

45. Christopher Browning, *The Origins of the Final Solution: The Evolution of Nazi Jewish Policy* (Lincoln, Nebraska: University of Nebraska Press, 2004), pp. 291-293. See also Randolph Braham, "The Kamenets, Podolsk and Delvidek Massacres," *Yad Vashem Studies*, vol. 9 (1973), pp. 133-156; Dieter Pohl, "Schauplatz Ukraine: Der Massenmord an den Juden im Militärverwaltungsgebiet und im Reichskommissariat 1941-1943," in Norbert Frei, Sybille Steinbacher and Bernd C. Wagner (eds.), *Ausbeutung, Vernichtung, Öffentlichkeit:neue Studien zur nationalsozialistischen Lagerpolitik/ herausgegeben im Auftrag des Instituts für Zeitgeschichte* (Munich: K.G. Saur, 2000), pp. 135-173.

46. Walter Manoschek, "The Extermination of the Jews of Serbia," in U. Herbert (ed.), *National Socialist Extermination Policies*, pp 178-181.

47. Yehuda Bauer, "The Problem of Gender," in his *Rethinking the Holocaust* (New Haven: Yale University Press, 2001), p 177.

48. Götz Aly, *Final Solution: Nazi Population Policy and the European Jews* (London: A Hodder Arnold Publication, 1999), p 168.

49. This statistic was provided by the head of the child care department of the Central Committee of Polish Jews in 1945. See *Zydowska Agencja Prasowa Bulletin*, no. 12 (Nov. 1945). I cite it from Kiryl Sosnowski, *The Tragedy of Children under Nazi Rule* (Warsaw: Howard Fertig, 1962), p. 73.

50. Cited from C. Browning, *The Origins of the Final Solution*, p. 305.

51. Quoted from the situation report of *Gebeitskommissar Gehard Erren*, January 25, 1942 and reprinted in E. Klee, et al. (eds.), *The Good Old Days*, p. 179.

52. George Eisen, *Children and Play in the Holocaust: Games Among the Shadows* (Amherst: University of Massachusetts Press, 1988), p. 17.

53. Martin Dean, *Collaboration in the Holocaust: Crimes of the Local Police in Belorussia and the Ukraine* (New York: Palgrave Macmillian, 2000), p. 116.

54. Christian Gerlach, "German Economic Interests, Occupation Policy, and the Murder of the Jews in Belorussia, 1941/43," in U. Herbert (ed.), *National Socialist Extermination Policies*, p 223 and p 224.

55. I cite this from C. Browning, *The Origins of the Final Solution*, p. 298. It was earlier published in German by Christian Gerlach, *Kalkulierte Morde: Die deutsche*

Wirtschafts und Vernichtungspolitik in Weissrussland, 1941 bis 1944 (Hamburg: Aufl edition, 2001), pp. 588-589.

56. I cite this testimony from M. Dean, *Collaboration in the Holocaust*, p. 80.

57. Ibid., p. 84. The killing in Mir that I have just cited is reported in ibid., p. 92.

58. Anne Frank, *The Diary of a Young Girl: The Definitive Edition*, edited by Otto Frank and Miryam Pressler (New York: Doubleday, 1995). The literature on Anne Frank and her diary is enormous. For an introduction to it see: Alex Grobman, *Anne Frank in Historical Perspective* (Los Angeles: Martyrs Memorial and Museum of the Holocaust of the Jewish Federation Council of Greater Los Angeles and Alvin Rosenfeld, "Popularization and Memory: The Case of Anne Frank," in *Lessons and Legacies,* vol. 1, edited by Peter Hayes (Evanston: Northwestern University Press, 1991), pp. 243-278. I cite the statistics from Jacob Presser, *Ashes in the Wind: The Destruction of Dutch Jewry,* translated by Arnold Pomerans (Detroit: Wayne State University Press, 1988), pp. 482-483.

59. The full tragedy of Dutch Jewry is described by Louis Jong, *The Netherlands and Nazi Germany* (Cambridge, Ma.: Harvard University Press, 1990); idem, "The Netherlands and Auschwitz," in *Yad Vashem Studies,* vol. 7 (1968), pp. 39-55; Jacob Presser, *Ashes*; Bob Moore, *Victims and Survivors: The Nazi Persecution of the Jews of the Netherlands, 1940-1945* (London 1997); Gerhard Hirschfeld, *Nazi Rule and Dutch Collaboration: The Netherlands under Nazi Occupation, 1940-1945* (Oxford: Berg Publishers, 1988); and briefly by Saul Friedlander, *Nazi Germany and the Jews 1939-1945*, pp. 406-413. I cite the statistics on deportations from Westerbork to Auschwitz from Friedlander, p. 413.

60. The figure cited is drawn from the article on the "Netherlands" written by Werner Warmbrunn in *The Holocaust Encyclopedia* (New Haven: Yale University Press, 2001), p. 442.

61. The story of French Jewry has been retold by Michael R. Marrus and Robert O. Paxton, *Vichy France and the Jews* (New York: Columbia University Press, 1981); and Renée Poznanski, *Jews in France During World War II* (Waltham, Ma.: Brandeis, 2001).

62. There is some dispute over the numbers of French Jews sent to Auschwitz. In putting this total at approximately 75,000 I follow the research of M. R. Marrus and R. O. Paxton, *Vichy France and the Jews*, p. 343.

63. I cite this from C. Browning, *The Origins of the Final Solution*, p. 298. It was earlier published in German by C. Gerlach, *Kalkulierte Morde*, pp. 588-589.

64. R. Höss, *Proceedings of the Trial of Major War Criminals* (Nuremberg: HMSO, 1947), vol. 11, p. 417.

65. This statistic was provided by the head of the child care department of the Central Committee of Polish Jews in 1945. See *Zydowska Agencja Prasowa Bulletin,* no. 12 (Nov. 1945). I cite it from Kiryl Sosnowski, *The Tragedy of Children under Nazi Rule,* p. 73.

66. Helena Kubica, "Children and Adolescents in Auschwitz," in Tadeusz Iwasko, Helena Kubica, Franciszek Piper, et al., *Auschwitz 1940-1945: Central Issues in the History of the Camp,* vol. 2, (Oświecim: Auschwitz-Birkenau State Museum, 2000), Table 4, p. 290.

67. In light of this assault on Jewish children one can understand post-Holocaust thinkers such as Emil Fackenheim and Jonathan Sachs who have made having Jewish

children after the *Shoah* a crucial *theological* issue. This is not the place to evaluate these proposals but, given the data presented in this paper, it is relevant to make note of them. For more on this matter see Emil Fackenheim, *The Jewish Return into History: Reflections in the Age of Auschwitz and a New Jerusalem* (New York: Schocken Books, 1978), p. 48; and Jonathan Sachs, *Crisis and Covenant: Jewish Thought after the Holocaust* (Manchester: Manchester University Press, 1992), pp. 44-48.

11

Mah Tovu as a Psychological Introduction to Prayer

Reuven Kimelman

It is a privilege to join in celebrating the achievements of my long term colleague and mentor Yitz Greenberg. I have already expressed my regard for his achievements on the American Jewish scene in a review of his book *For the Sake of Heaven and Earth* in *Modern Judaism* 27 (2007). Here, I am glad to dedicate this study which seeks to renew the meaning of Mah Tovu as a unified whole to one who has tirelessly worked for Jewish renewal as a unified whole for over a half century.

The more I realize that the problems of prayer are as much psychological as theological, the more the question "does God answer prayer" is superseded by the question "can I pray." The problem lies in the sequence of the words "can I pray." The "I" keeps sneaking in before the word "pray;" indeed, hovers over it even while praying.[1] The pervasive ego so hampers prayer that we should not be surprised to find a liturgical unit struggling with it. The unit that does is called Mah Tovu, after its initial words. It serves strategically as the opening prayer of most traditional rites as well as of most modern denominations.[2]

Mah Tovu goes as follows:

1. How lovely are your tents, 0 Jacob, your dwelling places, 0 Israel (Num. 24:5).

2. As or me,[3] out of Your abundant graciousness,[4] I enter Your house.

2a. I shall bow towards Your holy ark in awe of You / with Your awe (Ps. 5:8).

3. Adonai, I love Your house;

3a. The place where Your glory dwells (Ps. 26:8).[5]

4. I shall bow, kneel, and prostrate myself before Adonai, my Maker (see Ps. 95:6).

5. As for me, may my prayer be to You Adonai at a favorable time.

5a. O God, by Your abundant graciousness, answer me with Your unfailing help (Ps. 69:14).[6]

In our exploration of ways of construing Mah Tovu, we focus on its location and function in the liturgy as well as where and how it is said.

Mah Tovu is both a prelude to prayer itself and an entrance prayer to the synagogue. In antiquity, entrance to a temple was accompanied by feelings of awe and trepidation. *Targum Jonathan* rendered Lev. 19:30 as "and to My temple you shall go with awe." In some places, cultic etiquette required special entrance preparations such as ritual cleansing, reciting of pledges, or physical examinations for defects. In general, access to sacred space was qualified by ritual or moral requirements.[7] Only the pure could enter. Whereas some limited this to the ritually pure, the psalmist expanded it to the morally pure.[8] He asks:

> Who may ascend the mountain of Adonai?
> And who may stand in His holy place?

and answers:

> He that has clean hands and a pure heart,
> Who does not long after what is worthless,
> And has not taken an oath in deceit (Psalm 24:4).

Or:

> Who may abide in Your tent?
> Who may dwell on Your holy mount?
> He who lives without blame, Who does what is right,
> And in his heart acknowledges the truth,
> Whose tongue is not given to evil;
> Who has never done harm to his fellow,
> Or borne reproach for [his acts toward] his neighbor (Psalm 15:2-3).

The goal of this give and take is to impress upon the worshiper the moral prerequisites and goals of service to God. Access to the holy is through the portals of the good.

The synagogue, however, is not technically sacred space, but rather prayer space.[9] The concern of its entrance prayer, Mah Tovu, with inclusion counters any exclusionary considerations, whether ethical or ritual, for entering sacred space.[10] Mah Tovu serves as a threshold prayer seeking to help the would-be worshiper overcome his/her reluctance and uneasiness of entering the Lord's house. It hence does not open as invitingly as the Kabbalat Shabbat service with a psalm such as Psalm 95:

> Come, let us sing joyously to Adonai.
> Raise a shout for our rock and deliverer;

Let us come into His presence with praise;
Let us raise a shout for Him in song.

or as exuberantly as Psalm 100:4:

Enter His gates with praise,
His courts with acclamation.
Praise Him!
Bless His name!

Instead, Mah Tovu opens with a verse from Numbers followed by verses, with some alterations, from Psalms.[11] None of the verses are juxtaposed in their biblical context. The arrangement creates a new liturgical piece. As the rearrangement of musical notes produces a new melody so the rearrangement of verses creates a new prayer. Since it will no longer suffice to discern their biblical meaning, we have to ask what was the liturgist's aim in recontextualizing these verses to orchestrate a new prayer for crossing the threshold of the synagogue.[12] As a poem, we need to explore also the relationship between its form and its content. By tracing the flow of the feelings and ideas line-by-line we should be in a position to present a reading of the material which deals with the whole rearrangement.

The first thing that strikes us is that the opening verse derives not from Psalms, but from none other than the infamous soothsayer Balaam. Balaam had been hired by king Balak of Moab to curse Israel. One late sixteenth century authority found it so offensive to begin the synagogue liturgy with this scoundrel's words that he omitted it.[13] Why did our liturgist include it?

From the Torah, all we know is that Balaam, swept away in rapt admiration of the Israelite encampment in the wilderness of Sinai, had his curse transformed into a blessing. The Midrash ascribes the source of his astonishment to the layout of the encamped tents. To assure the privacy of each family unit, each tent was pitched to minimize peeking. Struck by the concern for propriety of a camp on the move, Balaam exclaims: "How *good* are your tents O Jacob."[14] Since the theme of modesty, however, has little to do with the whole Mah Tovu, commentators have been drawn to the alternative midrashic-talmudic understanding of the tents as academies and the dwelling places as synagogues.[15] This midrashic overhauling of the verse has synagogues and academies crop up so large on the horizon that they block from view the ancient desert tents. Updated, the verse now introduces the worshiper to the two loci of prayer — the academy and the synagogue. By disengaging verses from their original context, they assume new midrashic meanings. When these midrashic meanings displace the original ones, as often occurs in the liturgy, biblical *midrash* becomes liturgical *pshat*.

Still the question remains: Why begin with Balaam when others began with such exquisite openers from the Psalms such as "I rejoiced when they said to me we are going to the house of the Lord" (Ps. 122:1),[16] or "Into the house of the Lord we shall go with trepidation" (Ps. 55:15b).[17]

The genius of the selection will become evident upon understanding the function of the whole prayer. To achieve such an understanding, we need to continue our analysis with the next verse. In contrast to Balaam, who kept his distance looking down at Israel, the would-be worshiper is about to make his way into the synagogue, saying: "As for me, out of Your abundant graciousness, I enter Your house." In contrast to the focus on the synagogue of the opening verse, this one zooms in on the self, as if to say, "It is all very well that the synagogue is so lovely, but what am I doing here? How do I fit in?" It is not easy to extricate oneself from quotidian reality and cross over to the spiritual. Even greater is the difficulty of letting go of the preoccupation with the self and centering on the Divine. Still, by virtue of God's unconditional graciousness, responds the verse, one ventures haltingly across the threshold aware that by making one's way into the synagogue one is coming into "Your house."[18]

But if it is not my house, who am I to enter? It is as if I were knocking on someone's door only to find a party in progress. Such excruciating self-consciousness! Out of the blue, the host bolts out and ushers me in warmly, saying "Had I known you were in town, I would have personally invited you." Here God graciously whispers to me, the would-be worshiper, "It's My home, come in." That's why I can say, "As for me, out of Your abundant graciousness, I enter Your house."[19] Relieved, overcoming my reluctance if not outright feelings of estrangement,[20] I bow in the direction of the holy ark,[21] saying, "I shall bow to Your sanctuary in awe of You" (or: "with Your awe" [2a]).[22] In the Bible, God's house and sanctuary refer to the ancient Temple; in the Siddur, they refer to the synagogue and ark.[23] Having dithered at the entrance of the synagogue, I now venture forward, bowing towards the holy ark across from the entrance.[24]

Bowing before the ark, my feelings are buoyed by an enveloping sense of God's awe reminiscent of Jacob's blurting out, "How awesome is this place" (Gen. 26: 17).[25] Such stirrings of awe prove how inadequate my previous gesture was. Redoubling my efforts, I add kneeling and prostration like King Solomon in the Temple.[26] Since the first of these synonyms, אשתחוה, obviously retraces the previous bowing, why add another two? Such compounding of synonyms is more than a juggling of semantic equivalents, it reflects a staged intensification. I am not only bent, but on my knees, flat on my face.[27] Suddenly, I no longer feel that I am bowing *towards Your holy ark,* but rather *before Adonai, my Maker.* The difference between these expressions, each comprising three Hebrew words, is telling. "Towards" has become "before" and "Your holy ark" has become "Adonai my Maker."[28] Distance has been replaced by intimacy, and God's elusiveness by His presence. Prior to feeling God's awe, my gesture, a symbolic bow, in the direction of the holy ark sufficed. Prostrating myself totally before God, however, has transformed the opaque symbol of the ark into the transparent presence of God. As the Talmud says: "You should not stand in awe of the sanctuary, but in awe of He who commanded with regard to the sanctuary."[29] Thus while in the sanctuary, one's awe should be directed to God, not to the sanctuary.[30]

So why am I not praying now? Why the wavering? Wracked by my insecurities, I am unsure whether this is the right time. Who am I to be importuning God now? Are there not set times for prayer? Does not the Midrash cite this verse, "And as for me, may my prayer to You Adonai be at a favorable time," as evidence that "the gates of prayer are sometimes open and sometimes closed," and claim that even King David so fretted over the issue of time that he entreated: "Master of the world, when I pray to You may it be a favorable time," as it is written, "And as for me, may my prayer to You Adonai be at a favorable time."[31] Just as my anxiety about being in the right place was allayed by assurance of "Your abundant graciousness," so my nervousness about the right time is resolved here by assurance of "Your abundant graciousness,"[32] "For what great nation is there that has a God so close at hand as is Adonai our God whenever we call upon Him" (Deut. 4:7).[33] Once getting through, there is no being put on hold. Having gotten over my doubts about place and time, my diffidence crumbles in the face of my resurging confidence and I, by the grace of God, no longer falter at the prospect of addressing God.[34] So, I plead, "Answer me with Your unfailing help" (5b).[35] After all, did not Isaiah cite God as saying "At a favorable time I answer you, and on a day of salvation I help you" (49:8). In the end, awareness of God's presence intensifies the desire for Divine closeness. When such feelings of intimacy lead me to believe that my needs are God's concerns, I venture to pray.

Of the whole Mah Tovu, only the last three Hebrew words constitute a prayer of petition. The rest consists of prayer-therapy. It outlines a strategy for working through one's hang-ups with regard to prayer. Since it is an intensely personal activity, Mah Tovu is ill-served by underscoring its public function. Those who see in line 2 only ten words for ascertaining the presence of a quorum,[36] or who see in the three-fold genuflection only an allusion to thrice-daily prayer,[37] or who deem "favorable time" only a reference to the hour of public prayer,[38] miss the point.

The point in selecting the verses from Psalms was their beginning with I/me. So overriding was this consideration that line 4 not only has its biblical plural form of Ps. 95:6 transmuted into the singular,[39] but its own beginning "Come" is lopped off in favor of "I."[40] Indeed, the Hebrew word for "I" is the leitmotif of the whole composition.[41] No wonder that the first liturgical attestation of the beginnings of Mah Tovu is included under "private prayers."[42]

For Mah Tovu, the problem of prayer is the overweening sense of self. Haunting the very words of prayer, the "I" reverberates incessantly. How much of our prattle is nothing but configurations of the word I? Still, Mah Tovu does not seek that self-transcendence of total disregard of the self about which Heschel wrote: "Prayer comes to pass ... (in) the momentary disregard of our personal concerns, the absence of self-centered thoughts... (when) we forget ourselves and become aware of God."[43] Rather in struggling with the problems of the ever-intrusive self, Mah Tovu seeks to contain the ego's stranglehold on consciousness allowing for the divine to come into view.[44] It accomplishes this by decentering the ego through centering on the Divine. There is nothing like prayer to ventilate a suffocating ego through the glimmerings of the divine: just like there is nothing like kneeling before God to bring about self-abnegation. The I, however, is never eliminated, it crops up even in the last verse. The difference is that by the last verse the explicit mentions of God outnumber those of the self by two to one. The transition from self-centered consciousness to divine-centered consciousness is made through the two-fold reference to "bowing" and to "Your abundant graciousness." Both serve as up and down pulleys lowering self-centeredness and raising God-centeredness. For Mah Tovu, release from the clutches of the self paves the way for attentiveness to the Divine. Through Mah Tovu, the self discovers itself in relation to the Divine.

This discovery is choreographed in a series of steps in which outward movements are correlated with inward transformations. The movements advance from approaching the entrance of the synagogue, standing on the threshold, entering, bowing to the ark, bowing again to God to making supplication. The transformations involve movement from self-consciousness, trepidation, assurance, relief, gratitude, reverence, and seeking to pray to praying. Working through the movements of Mah Tovu generates a correspondence between motion and emotion, action and reaction.

To return to the question of Balaam: Why does his encomium open the composition? It is, of course, one thing were we to promote ourselves, but quite another were the knave Balaam, a Gentile prophet no less, to do so.[45] Mah Tovu presents a way of wrestling with our insecurities and dealing with our skittishness at crossing the threshold of a synagogue. What better example than one coming from afar to curse, who but surveying Israel's places and modes of worship ends up blessing.

ABBREVIATIONS AND CITED WORKS

ARN   *Avot de-Rabbi Natan*, ed. S. Schechter, New York: The Jewish Theological Seminary of America, 1997. Version A, Version B

B.   Babylonian Talmud

f.   immediately following

Gen. Rab   *Genesis Rabbah*, ed. J. Theodor and Ḥ. Albeck, 3 vols. Jerusalem 1965

Kasher TS   Kasher, Menaḥem. *Torah Sheleimah*, 42 vols., Jerusalem: Beth Torah Sheleimah, 1949-1991.

Lieberman, TK   Lieberman, Saul. *Tosefta Ki-fshutah*, 10 vols., New York: The Jewish Theological Seminary of America, 1955-1988.

MHG   *Midrash Ha-Gadol*, Genesis-Deuteronomy, 5 vols. Jerusalem: Mosad Harav Kook, 1967-1975.

OH   *Oraḥ Ḥayyim* (first of four volumes of Joseph Qaro, *Shulkhan Arukh*)

PRK   *Pesikta De-Rav Kahana* , ed. B. Mandelbaum, 2 vols., New York: The Jewish Theological Seminary of America, 1962

Rab.   *Rabbah*

Tanh.   *Tanḥuma*

YS   *Yalqut Shimoni: Genesis--Former Prophets*, 10 vols., ed. Heyman-Shiloni, Jerusalem: Mosad Harav Kook, 1973-1999.

Aaron of Lunel. *Sefer Orḥot Ḥayyim*, Jerusalem, 1996. (late 13th-early 14th cent., Narbonne, Provence)

Eleazar b. Judah (of Worms). *Peirushei Siddur Ha-Tefillah La-Roqeaḥ*, ed. M. Hershler and Y. Hershler, 2 vols., Jerusalem: Machon Harav Hershler, 1992 (1160-1238, Mainz, Germany).

Fishbane, Michael. *The Exegetical Imagination: On Jewish Thought and Theology*, Cambridge, MA: Harvard University Press, 1998.

Gold, Avie. *The Complete ArtScroll Selichos (Sefarad)*, Brooklyn: Mersorah Publications, 1993.

Goldschmidt, E. D. *Maḥzor Le-Yamim Ha-Nora'im*, 2 vols., Jerusalem: Koren, 1970.

Goldschmidt, E. D. *Maḥzor Sukkot, Shemini Aṣeret, Ve-Simḥat Torah*, Jerusalem: Koren Publishers, 1981.

Goldschmidt, E. D. *On Jewish Liturgy* [Hebrew], Jerusalem: Magnes, 1980.

Ḥakham, Amos, *Sefer Tehillim*, 2 vols., Jerusalem: Mossad Harav Kook, 1984.

Heschel, Abraham J. *Man's Quest for God: Studies in Prayer and Symbolism*, New York: Charles Scribner's Sons, 1954.

Hilvitz, A. "Amirat Pesuqei 'Mah Tovu' Lifnei Ha-Tefillah," *Sinai* 78 (5736): 263-278.

Kimelman, Reuven, "Identifying Jews and Christians in Roman Syria-Palestine," ed. Eric M. Meyers, *Galilee through the Centuries: Confluence of Cultures*, Duke Judaic Studies Series, I , (Winona Lake, Indiana: Eisenbrauns, 1999): 301-331.

Kimelman, Reuven. "Rabbinic Prayer in Late Antiquity," ed. Steven Katz, *The Cambridge History of Judaism*, Volume 4: *The Late Roman-Rabbinic Period* (Cambridge: Cambridge University Press): 573-611.

Lawat, Abraham David ben Judah Leib, *Shaar Ha-Kolel*, Brooklyn: Kehot Publication Society, 2005.

Maḥzor Vitry. R. Simḥah Me-Vitry, ed. A. Goldschmidt, 2 vols. Jerusalem: Oṣar Ha-Posqim, 5764 (d. 1105, Vitry, France).

MaHaRSHaL (Rabbi Solomon Luria 1510–1573), *Responsa*, Jerusalem 1969.

Maimonides, *Liturgy*. see Goldschmidt, *On Jewish Liturgy* (twelfth cent. Egypt).

Makhir, Moses. *Seder Ha-Yom*, Jerusalem 1978 (late 16th cent. early 17th cent. Safed).

Margulies, Mordecai. *Hilkhot Ereṣ Yisrael Min Ha-Genizah*, Jerusalem: Mossad Harav Kook, 1973.

Moshe [ben Abraham] of Przemysl. *Matteh Mosheh*, ed. M. Knoblowicz, Jerusalem: Oṣar Haposqim, 1978. (1540-1606, Przemysl, Poland)

Qopel, Jacob (Lifschuetz). *Siddur Qol Ya'qov*, New York 1961 (d. 1740)

Qordovero, Moses. *Siddur Tefillah Le-Moshe*, 2 vols., Premislau: Zupnik, 1892 (1522-1570, Safed, Israel).

Qordovero, Moses. *Tomer Devorah*, cited according to the annotated translation of Louis Jacobs, *The Palm Tree of Deborah*, New York: Sepher-Hermon Press, 1974.

Sarfatti, Gad. "Ohel = Beit Ha-Midrash," *Tarbiz* 38 (1969): 87-89.

Sarna, Nahum. *Songs of the Heart: An Introduction to the Book of Psalms*, New York: Schocken Books, 1993.

Siddur Ha-Meyuḥas La-RABaN (1090-1170), *Genuzot* 3, ed. M. Hershler (Jerusalem: Shalem, 1991): 1-128.

Siddur of Shabbatai Sofer. ed. Y. Sats, 4 vols., Baltimore: Ner Israel Rabbinical College, 1987-2002 (The fourth volume is not designated vol. 4. It consists of a preface and addenda.) (c. 1565 - c. 1635, Przemysl, Poland)

Siddur Rabbenu Hazaqen, Brooklyn: Kehot Publication Society, 2004 (1745-1813, Russia)

Siddur Rabbenu Shelomoh b. R. Natan (Hasigilmasi), ed. Sh. Ḥaggai, Jerusalem, 1995. (12 cent., Morocco)

Siddur Rashi, ed. Buber-Freimann, New York, 1959. (12th cent. France).

Sperber, Daniel. *Minhagei Yisrael: Meqorot Ve-Toledot*, 8 vols., Jerusalem: Mossad Harav Kook, 1989-2007.

Ta-shma, Israel. *The Early Ashkenazic Prayer: Literary and Historical Aspects* [Hebrew], Jerusalem: Magnes Press, 2007.

Tigay, Jeffrey. *Deuteronomy, The JPS Torah Commentary*, Philadelphia: The Jewish Publication Society, 1996.

Yehudah b. Barzillai of Barcelona. *Sefer Ha-Ittim*, ed. Jacob Schorr, Berlin 1903. (early 12th cent., Barcelona, Spain)

Verdiger, Abraham. *Siddur Ṣelutah De-Avraham, Shabbat Qodesh*, 3 vols., Jerusalem, 1991-1993.

Vidas, Elijah. *Reishit Ḥokhmah Ha-Shalem*, ed. H. Waldman, 3 vols., Jerusalem: Or Mussar, 5744 (3:297-400 = *Toṣe'ot Ḥayyim*). (16th cent., Safed)

Vital, Ḥayim. *Prie Eṣ Ḥayyim*, Jerusalem: Or Bahir, 5780. (1543-1620, Safed)

Wieder, Naftali. *The Formation of Jewish Liturgy in the East and the West: A Collection of Essays* [Hebrew], 2 vols., Jerusalem: Ben-Zvi Institute, 1998.

NOTES

1. Compare the order of the common prayer expression מודה אני ("grateful am I") where the I succeeds the verb. Two instances are prominent in morning prayers. One summarizes the idea of morning prayer (see *Gen. Rab.* 68, 9, p. 779, and parallels), and the other is in the middle of the once wake-up prayer *Elohai, neshamah* (*B. Ber.* 60b), from which was reworked the more recent wake-up prayer which instructively also begins מודה אני (see Makhir, *Seder Ha-Yom*, p. 3). Even though the order reflects common Hebrew syntax, there is a difference in ego-awareness in waking up and saying "grateful am I" versus "I am grateful."

2. For *Mah Tovu* in the various traditional rites, see Hilvitz, "Amirat Pesuqei 'Mah Tovu' Lifnei Ha-Tefillah," pp. 263-78; and Sperber, *Minhagei Yisrael* 7:41-64. For the exceptions, see Sperber, ibid., p. 62f.

3. ואני, taking the *vav* as conversive as in Jon. 2:10, Hab. 3:18, Ps. 13:6.

4. חסד. In the Bible it has a range of meanings from love, grace, and kindness to faithfulness, fidelity, and commitment denoting repayment of kindnesses or keeping faith with; see Tigay, *Deuteronomy*, p. 67, n. 10.

5. The verse is missing in the London MS of *Maḥzor Vitry* (1:79) and in *Siddur Rabbenu Hazaqen*, p. 90.

6. Some English translations of the Siddur follow the King James Version and translate "answer me with your saving truth." This is philologically and theologically unsound. Philologically, באמת modifies ישעך meaning בישעך שהיא אמת אמת שהיא (*Sefer Kolbo* 40, p. 152a). Theologically, the idea of "saving truth" is closer to Christianity's "believe and thou shalt be saved" than to the Jewish idea that the truth of one's life saves more than the truth of one's beliefs; see Kimelman, "Identifying Jews and Christians in Roman Syria-Palestine," p. 322.

7. On liturgies of entrance, see Sarna, *Songs of the Heart*, pp. 98-103 with notes.

8. For the foundational story of the ethicization of the cult in Rabbinic Judaism, see R. Yoḥanan b. Zakkai's use of Hos. 6:6 ("For I desire goodness, not sacrifice...") in *ARNA* 4, p. 23, and *ARNB* 5, p. 23. This process is already apparent in Jeremiah's (9:6) reworking of Hos. 6:6 together with his response to Isa. 1:11. Ironically, in the lectionary calendar when the elimination of the sacrificial cult and the destruction of the Temple are commemorated, Jer. 9:6 ("For in these [justice and equity] *I* [God] *delight*") follows Isa. 1:11 ("burnt offerings of rams, and suet of fatlings, and blood of bulls *I* [God] *have no delight*"). The latter is in the Sabbath haftarah before the ninth of Av, and the former is in the morning haftarah of the ninth of Av. About midway between Jeremiah and Yohanan b. Zakkai, *Ben Sira* (ca. 180 BCE) emphasized the atoning power of kindness and charity; see *Ben Sira* 1:14, 30; 29:12; 35:3.

9. See Kimelman, "Rabbinic Prayer in Late Antiquity," pp. 573-79.

10. Despite the fact that the biblical context of the second verse (Ps. 5:8) does underscore the ethical qualities that qualify one to plead "Hear Adonai my voice at daybreak" (ibid. 5:4).

11. *Seder Rav Amram Gaon*, p. 182, already mentions the recitation of the opening verse Num. 24:5 followed by Ps. 8:5. According to *Maḥzor Vitry*, 1:99, and *Siddur Rashi*, 417, p. 208, ten verses are recited while entering the synagogue in the morning beginning with Ps. 5:8, whereas in the afternoon Ps. 5:8 alone is recited (ibid, 1:145). The first five of these verses correspond to our version following the order of 2,5,1,3, and then Ps. 122:1 without any mention of our 4. A medieval *Seliḥah* (for the fifth day of repentance) plays on the first two of these by associating Ps. 5:8 and 69:14; see Gold, *The Complete Art Scroll Selichos*, p. 632. The Tosafist R. Eleazar b. Natan (1090-1170) mentions all five verses; see *Siddur Ha-Meyuḥas La-RABaN*, p. 12. A century later, R. Aaron of Lunel notes (*Sefer Orḥot Ḥayyim*, p. 90, *Hilkhot Berakhot* 66) both practices; one beginning with Num. 24:5 and the other with Ps. 5:8. By the time of R. Jacob Molin (1365-1427), it was common to say *Mah Tovu* and several other verses upon entering the synagogue (*Responsa of HaMaHaRIL*, 150, 9, p. 249). Ashkenazic authorities of the sixteenth and seventeenth centuries maintained the practice of beginning with Num. 24:5, which has since been the norm of ashkenazic siddurs, whereas their qabbalistic contemporaries, such as Qordovero (*Tomer Devorah* 10, p. 124, see idem, *Siddur Tefillah Le-Moshe* 1:1) and Makhir (*Seder Ha-Yom*, p. 11), held, following the *Zohar* (1:11a), that Ps. 5:8 be recited before entering the synagogue and the Mah Tovu verse upon entering the synagogue.

12. According to *Seder Rav Amram Gaon*, p. 182, and others (see Sperber, *Minhagei Yisrael* 7:45, and 63, n. 77), Ps. 5:8 is to be recited upon entering the synagogue and Ps. 5:9 upon departing. This may be taking its cue from the talmudic practice (*B. Ber.* 28b) of reciting a prayer upon entering and leaving the academy.

13. MaHaRSHaL, *Responsa* 64, p. 53c; see *Siddur of Shabbatai Sofer* 1:63. Some "Sefardic" or Eastern rites still omit Num. 24:5; see Sperber, *Minhagei Yisrael* 7:62f. Balaam's expression in Num. 23:19 also influenced one of the opening strophes of *Barukh She'amar*.

14. See *B. Bab. B.* 60a; *YS* 1:771 (ed. Heyman-Shiloni, *Num.*, p. 498 with n. 17); *Midr. Leqaḥ Tov, Balaq,* 2:256; *Midr. Aggadah, Balaq,* 2:142. Alternatively, Balaam was condemned for his hypocrisy; see *Deut. Rab.*, ed. Lieberman, p. 90, with Sperber, *Minhagei Yisrael* 7:44, n. 8. In any event, like the word "fair," טוב has both ethical and aesthetic vectors. Here מה טובו is understood ethically ("how good"), not aesthetically ("how lovely").The expression has also an ethical sense in Ps. 133:1, and in Mic. 6:8 -- a verse that (coincidentally?) appears in the haftarah for the *parshah* (Balaq) that contains the Mah Tovu verse. In The Song of Songs 4:10 its meaning borders on the sensual.

15. *Midr. Leqaḥ Tov, Balaq,* 2:257. *B. San.* 105b applied "tents" to both. Biblically, אוהל is frequently a poetic term for sanctuary or Temple; see Isa. 16:15, 33:20, 54:2; Jer. 10:20; Ps. 27:5-6; Lam. 2:4. Indeed, another midrash understood "tent" as the tent of meeting, and "dwelling places" as the Temple; see *MHG Num.*, p. 427, l. 3f., with n. 3. On the equation of tent and academy, see Ṣarfatti, "Ohel = Beit Ha-Midrash," pp. 87-89.

16. *Maḥzor Vitry* 1:99 lists this as the fifth verse following Num. 24:5. Verdiger (*Ṣluta De-Avraham* 1:42 -- Corrigenda), recommended reciting this opening verse of Psalm122 upon leaving the house for the synagogue or upon entering the synagogue.

R. Jacob Qopel (*Siddur Qol Ya'aqov*, p. 23b) recommended saying Ps. 119:N59 and all of Psalm 22 on the way out of one's house to the synagogue. *Siddur U-Maḥzor Kol- Bo*, p. 4, includes all of Psalm 122 to be recited upon entering the synagogue.

17. As the verse was understood; see Vital, *Prie Eṣ Ḥayyim, Sha'ar Olam Ha-Asiah*, 1, p. 112a. Since this verse underscores the fear of God upon entering the house of God it should be said prior to entering. Qabbalistic authorities accepted this logic except for R. Shneur Zalman who initially recommended (*Shulkhan Arukh, OH* 46, 11, p. 171) reciting Ps. 5:8 before entering the synagogue but then reverted in his Siddur to the Ashkenazic norm of first reciting *Mah Tovu* because of changing practices; see Lawat, *Sha'ar Ha-Kollel*, 3, p. 10; and Sperber, *Minhagei Yisrael* 7:50f. The original position held that it made sense to mention the fear of God upon entering the synagogue since one had already donned *tallit* and *tefillin* at home, but not now when the practice is to don them after entering. This idea that *tallit* and *tefillin* are part of an awe-engendering pre-prayer rite takes its cue from the Zohar: "When daylight comes, one dons the *tefillin* with the holy impress on his head and his arm, and enrobes himself with the *tallit*. As he issues from the door of his house he passes the *mezuzzah* containing the imprint of the holy Name on his doorpost, then four holy angels join him and exit with him from the door of his house and accompany him to the synagogue and proclaim before him: Give honor to the image of the Holy King, give honor to the son of the King, to the precious countenance of the King" (3:265a). Donned in *tefillin*, wrapped in *tallit*, accompanied by angels, one entered the synagogue enveloped in awe.

18. This explains the practice of starting with Ps. 5:8 followed by Ps. 55:156 which R. Ḥayyim Azulai deems a mistake to delay its recitation until after entering the synagogue; see Azulai, *Siddur Ha-Ḥidah*, p. 30; and Hilvitz, "Amirat Pesuqei 'Mah Tovu' Lifnei Ha-Tefillah," p. 264. One should enter the synagogue as reverently as one once entered the Temple, about which it says: "Revere my sanctuaries" (Lev. 19:30). This verse had once been used to sanction the washing of hands and feet prior to entering the synagogue; see Margulies, *Hilkhot Ereṣ Yisrael Min Ha-Genizah*, p. 132, ll. 1-3, with Kimelman, "Rabbinic Prayer in Late Antiquity," p. 575.

19. According to R. Ḥayyim Vital, the reference is "to God's supernal love upon which we are constantly dependent particularly to enter the sanctuary of the King so that He fulfill one's requests with the power of that love" (*Prie Eṣ Ḥayyim, Sha'ar Olam Ha-Asiah*, 1, p. 112a).

20. R. Elijas Vidas feels the worshiper is struggling here with his sense of unworthiness and by saying

> "As for me, out of Your great graciousness, I enter Your house," means You did me a great kindness that I am among those who enter Your house ... and "I shall bow down" means since I got to be among those who see the face of the King by virtue of Your graciousness though I am unworthy ... that when I bow down to Your sanctuary, which is the holiest place, the place where the King actually is, and I bow there to pray before You, it is necessary that it be done out of reverence for You (*Reishit Ḥokhmah Ha-Shalem, Toṣe'ot Ḥayyim* 3:369).

21. *Maḥzor Ma'aglei Ṣedeq* (1557-1560) states: "when one enters the synagogue one should bow towards the ark and recite Ps. 8:5 (cited by Sperber, *Minhagei Yisrael* 7:49, n. 32). After entering with trepidation and reciting Ps. 8:5, Vital (*Prie Eṣ Ḥayyim, Sha'ar Olam Ha-Asiah*, 1, p. 112b) suggests citing Psalm 67 because of kabbalistic calculations of its seven verses.

22. See *Zohar* 1:11a with Sperber, *Minhagei Yisrael* 7: 56; and Makhir, *Seder Ha-Yom*, p. 11.

23. On the templization of the synagogue, see Ta-shma, *The Early Ashkenazic Prayer*, pp. 199-213; and Kimelman, "Rabbinic Prayer in Late Antiquity," pp. 573-80.

24. On the location of the ark across from the entrance, see Kasher, *TS* 19:310.

25. The *Zohar* (1:11a; see 3:8b) finds in this verse (Ps. 5:8) allusions to the three patriarchs. According to one approach, חסד stands for Abraham, קודש stands for Isaac, and יראה stands for Jacob. This identification goes hand in hand with the correlation of their respective sefirah: *ḥesed* (Abraham), *gevurah* (Isaac), and *tiferet* (Jacob). The theme is developed in different ways by qabbalistic authorities; see Sperber, *Minhagei Yisrael* 7:56f. Some deem the point to be to pray with the merit of the patriarchs, others to mention the three who are accredited with instituting the various daily services. For R. Moses Qordovero (*Tomer Devorah* 10), thinking about the patriarchs while reciting this verse and entering the synagogue bowing towards the ark brings about an integration of thought, word, and deed making for the quintessential religious act.

26. 1Kgs. 8:54, 2 Chron. 6:3. For present purposes, line 3 is excluded from the analysis. The formal reason is because of its exclusion in some rites (see *Maḥzor Vitry* 1:99, variants, n. 1; and Zalmen, *Siddur Rabbeinu HaZaken*, p. 94). The informal reason is that its mention of love, albeit of God's house, seems too facile at this juncture. Its inclusion points to the theological tendency of underscoring the compatibility of fear and love -- a combination deemed unique to the divine human relationship; see *Sifre Deut.* 32. Another example of adding love to fear/reverence is the second blessing of the morning Shema liturgy which alludes to Ps. 86: 11 by saying, "Unite our heart to revere and love Your name," even though the verse itself only says, "Unite my heart to revere Your name." Fear/reverence is also added to love in the request that God "open up our hearts to love and to revere your name" based on the verse "Then the Lord your God will open up your heart and the hearts of your offspring to love the Lord you God with all your heart and soul, in order that you may live" (Deut. 30:6); see Goldschmidt, *Maḥzor Le-Yamim Ha-Nora'im* 2:289, l. 12. A fascinating example of coupling love and fear is the *Uva Le-Ṣion* prayer that asks God to open "our heart to (or: by means of -- *Seder Rav Amram Gaon*, p. 39, l. 55; *Maḥzor Vitry* 1:129) His Torah and place in our heart X to do His will and to worship Him with a complete heart." For X, *Seder Rav Amram Gaon*, p. 39, l. 55, reads: יראתו (the fear of Him); *Maḥzor Vitry*, 1:129, reads: אהבתו (the love of Him); while Maimonides, *Liturgy*, p. 205, l. 10, and *Siddur Rabbenu Shelomoh b. R. Natan Hasigilmasi*, combine both: אהבתו ויראתו. On this combination, see Maimonides, *Mishneh Torah*, "Laws of the Fundamentals of the Torah" 2:1f.

27. As understood by midrash (*Pitron Torah*, p. 239), as stated by piyyut (ואשתחוה ואכרע ואקד לך אפים -- Goldschmidt, *Maḥzor Sukkot*, p. 32, l. 11), and as advocated by geonic authorities (see *Pitron Torah*, p. 239, n. 48). For a biblical example, see 2 Chron. 7:3. For the Second Temple period, see Johnson, *Prayer in the Apocrypha and Pseudepigrapha*, p. 57.

For the issues of bowing in prayer, see Weider, *Formation* 2:701-14.

28. אל היכל קדשך

לפני ה' עושי

29. B. Yev. 6b, *MGH Lev.*, p. 564, 1. 15 and parallels. Otherwise it is problematic to bow down to an ark, see Kasher, *TS* 19:310f.; and Sperber, *Minhagei Yisrael* 3:99, n. 76.

30. See Commentary of RABaD *Sifra*, *Qedoshim* 7, ed.Weiss, 90d.

31. *PRK* 24, 2, p. 349f. with parallels, and so understood by Eleazar b. Judah, *Peirushei Siddur Ha-Tefillah La-Roqeaḥ* 2:581.

32. See *PRK* 24, 2:350, variants.

33. Eleazar b. Judah, *Peirushei Siddur Ha-Tefillah La-Roqeaḥ* 2:580f., correlates the twelve Hebrew words of Ps. 69:12 with the twelve hours of day and twelve hours of night to show that He answers us every moment that we pray by citing this verse from Deuteronomy 4:7.

34. See Ibn Ezra to Ps. 66:20.

35. See *Midr. Ps.* 65, 4, p. 314.

36. See Yehudah b. Barzillai, *Sefer Ha-Ittim*, p. 253f., who attributes it to Rav Hai Gaon; see Hilvitz, "Amirat Pesuqei 'Mah Tovu' Lifnei Ha-Tefillah," pp. 265-67.

37. Following *Tanh., Kie Tavo* 1.

38. Following *B. Ber.* 8a.

39. On the propriety of plural-singular reversals, see Abudarham, *Tehillah Le-Dovid*, p. 223; Lieberman, *TK* 5:1222f.; Hilvits, "Amirat Pesuqei 'Mah Tovu' Lifnei Ha-Tefillah," p. 278; and Goldschmidt, *Maḥzor Le-Yamim Ha-Nora'im* 1:88, l. 9.

40. As late as the end of the sixteenth century, Makhir, *Seder Ha-Yom*, p. 11, and Moses of Przemysl, *Matteh Mosheh*, p. 52a-b, are still retaining the original verse among a host of other verses, two of which, according to *Matteh Mosheh* are "I" verses.

41. See Hilvitz, "Amirat P'suqei 'Mah Tovu' Lifnei Ha-Tefillah," p. 263.

42. *Seder Rav Amram Gaon,* p. 182. The prayer was probably originally recited whenever entering a synagogue; see Judah b. Barzillai, *Sefer Ha-Ittim*, p. 253.

43. Abraham Joshua Heschel, *Man's Quest for God*, p. 15.

44. In tune with the purpose of Mah Tovu, commentators reflected on how to enter a synagogue to enhance the experience of prayer. One early source states: "My son, when you enter before your Creator enter in awe and fear and when you pray know before whom you stand" (Abrahams, *Hebrew Ethical Wills* 1:39 [my translation] = Oṣar Midrashim, p. 29b, #18). According to a qabbalistic source of the late fourteenth century, the Mah Tovu verse was to be recited upon entering the synagogue followed by Ps. 5:8 and a moment of silence "until you can concentrate on before whom you stand and He who hears your words. When you are clothed in awe and fear, open your mouth and say your prayers" (*Sefer Ha-Peliah* 1:31b). This tradition of mental preparation was extended by subsequent commentators. R. Meir Poppers of Cracow (d. 1662, Jerusalem) states with regard to the first two verses of Mah Tovu

Before one enters a synagogue, one should get rid of any negative thoughts that distract him from the meanings of prayer. One should not enter hurriedly without the proper presence of mind as if he were entering his own home or that of a friend. Instead he should stand a little at the entrance and instill in his heart the fear of God whose holiness resides in the synagogue, as Jacob said: "how awesome is this place ...." And let him first mention the merits of the patriarchs before God, for in their merit will their (sic., his?) prayers be accepted. He should then enter submissively, reverentially, and fearfully bowing toward the ark in surrender of the heart and then pray with heartfelt devotion (*Or Ha-Yashar*, Introduction to Qordovero, *Siddur Tefillah Le-Moshe*, Chap. 9, p. 7b).

In a similar vein, R. Jacob Qopel Lifschuetz (d. 1740) writes:

When one enters the courtyard (of the synagogue) one should take care to properly arrange his clothes, as it says: "Prepare to greet your God" (Amos 4:12). He should take a moment to instill the fear (of God) in his heart, for he is entering the house of the King of kings. He should remove all worry and anxiety, for the Shekhinah does not reside where there is sadness. Accordingly, it says, "Worship God in fear and rejoice in trembling" (Ps. 1:11). And as our rabbis of blessed memory said: "Where there is rejoicing, there should be trembling" (*B. Ber.* 30b), that is, instead of unnecessarily fretting about one's sins or any other worry, one should trust in God" (*Siddur Qol Ya'aqov*, p. 24a, sources added).

45. See *Song Rab.* 6, 9, 4; *Deut. Rab.* 1, 4.

12

"Interpreting Rabbinic Religion through the Lens of the Three Eras"

David Kraemer

It was roughly twenty-five years ago that I first sat down to study with Yitz, I one of the first three "Rabbinic Fellows" ever to work at CLAL (then still called The National Jewish Resource Center). Yitz began immediately to lay out the contours of what was already—and continues to be—his Torah, dividing Jewish history, from its beginnings to the present, into three eras. During all of these eras, he explained, the Jewish people were identified by their covenantal relationship with God. But the nature of that relationship changed from era to era.[1]

The first era, the Biblical era, was characterized by a covenant in which God was the senior partner in the contracted relationship. God commanded, Israel did or did not obey. If they obeyed, they were rewarded, if not, they were punished. But the terms were all set by God, and it was God who controlled the outcome. The second era, the rabbinic era beginning after the destruction of the Jerusalem Temple by the Romans, saw a significant shift in the covenantal relationship. As the events under the domination of Rome proved, God would no longer necessarily take the initiative to protect or to save Israel, so Israel would have to initiate far more. In other words, at this stage of the covenantal relationship, God no longer took so senior a role in the partnership. Israel and God were on far more equal terms.

And the third era, the era that commenced with the Holocaust, was the era of Voluntary Covenant (Yitz's term).[2] In the Holocaust, God had broken the historical covenant with Israel by utterly failing to uphold God's covenantal commitments. Since God had broken the covenant, Israel was no longer bound by it. But the secular in Israel swore "never again!," and therefore committed themselves to building, in the State of Israel and in the diaspora, an infrastructure that would allow Jew to protect Jew. By volunteering into the covenant though they were technically released from its conditions and strictures, Israel made a demand of God: we insist, they said (according to Yitz's interpretation, of course), that you God, too, remain a partner in this covenant. But it all begins with us, the Jewish people.

When I studied with Yitz those many years ago, I was in my last pre-Ph.D. year. My field was Talmud and Rabbinics, my training was at The Jewish Theological Seminary, and my dissertation was largely complete. Like many graduate students at that stage, I had great confidence and little humility, so I did not hesitate to express my critiques of what I saw as Yitz's oversimplifications, particularly of the period I knew best, the early rabbinic era. Many of the shifts he tied to the destruction of the Temple had in fact begun earlier, as early as the conquest of the Near East by the Greeks. For example, Jewish autonomy had not come to an end with the destruction (as "Hatikvah" falsely suggests); before the Hasmoneans, and then again after them, Jews in their own land were subject to foreign powers. In this respect, the destruction had changed nothing. Oversimplifications of this sort left me in a bind: I was attracted to the theological beauty of the scheme that Yitz proposed, but my immature critical self did not allow me to accept it genuinely.

In the twenty-five years since those study-sessions, I have had many opportunities to teach the history of the centuries Jews commonly refer to as "the Second Temple period" and "the Rabbinic period," both in academic and popular settings. And I have had many opportunities to study and write about the meaning of the shift from pre-rabbinic to rabbinic Judaism. As I have studied these matters in greater depth and detail, what I have discovered is that, despite its "oversimplifications," Yitz's interpretation of the First and the Second Era does a better job making sense of the transition to rabbinic religion than any alternative interpretation I have seen. In the pages that follow, I would like to share some of what I have discovered, applying Yitz's interpretive scheme, again and again, to make sense of features of rabbinic religion that were unprecedented in the Jewish systems that preceded it.

I begin with the Sabbath. As is well known, the Torah has relatively little to say about Sabbath practice. "Work" (*melakhah*) is forbidden (Ex 20, 31, and elsewhere), but the Torah never elaborates on the meaning of this term. The only act that is prohibited explicitly is the lighting of fire (Ex 35:3), and narrative portions suggest that both the gathering of wood and the preparation of food (Exodus 16) are also forbidden. But however inclusive one wants to be, one will still have a hard time constructing a recognizable Sabbath on the basis of the information given in the Torah.

Subsequent biblical materials, along with documents written by Jews during the Second Temple period, fill in many of the gaps. Of biblical texts, Isaiah

58:13 emphasizes the need to refrain from engaging in one's business, while encouraging Jews to rejoice on the Sabbath. Nehemiah 13:14-22 carries the message against work (as in "going to work") further, condemning those who tread on winepresses, bring in sheaves of grain, and transport and sell their goods on the Sabbath. To assure that the Sabbath in Jerusalem will not be profaned through such activities, Nehemiah commands that the gates of the city be closed from the beginning of the Sabbath until its end, guaranteeing that nothing may be carried into or out of the city on the sacred day.

This latter narrative is evidently understood to be precedent-setting, for the translation of the prohibition of "doing business" or "trading" into a prohibition of carrying in and out is supported by all later elaborations of Sabbath practice in different Jewish communities. For example, in the most detailed quantification of Sabbath prohibitions yet offered, the Book of Jubilees (c. 100 BCE) goes into great detail in delineating the "carrying" prohibition:

> Keep it holy and do not do any work on it, and don't defile it, for it is holier than all other days... It is not lawful to do any work that is unseemly or do business on it, or draw water, or carry any heavy load through their gates on it, either in or out, and that they should not prepare on it anything to eat or drink... and they shall not bring in or take out anything from one house to another on that day... (2:27-30).

The so-called Damascus Covenant of the Dead Sea Scrolls, while adding prohibitions that are likewise unprecedented (many of which foreshadow the Sabbath law of the rabbis), is also very specific in articulating its prohibition of carrying (CD XI, 7-11).

Before interpreting the emphasis of Second Temple sources on the carrying prohibition, it is essential to draw attention to another one of the laws in this scroll, one that stands in opposition to everything that is commonly known about Jewish Sabbath tradition. I am referring to its direction that "any person who falls into source of water [a well] or a gathering [of water; a mikveh?], a man should not raise him out with a ladder or rope or [other (?)] vessel" (ll. 16-7)." What is shocking about this law is that it contradicts a principle that Jews who know anything about Sabbath law take for granted, that is, that saving a life pushes aside Sabbath restrictions. In fact, the shock of what the scroll says—clearly and unmistakably—has led some scholars to translate it as saying just the opposite, proposing that its present formulation is the product of a scribal error.[3]

But considered from the position of an outsider to Jewish law, there is nothing at all shocking about what the law requires. What it says is simply this: if saving a life requires profaning the Sabbath—through, for example, using a tool—then the sanctity of God's Sabbath takes precedence. After all, which is more important, God's prohibition or an individual human life? The evidence of history suggests that many religious souls, including the author of this rule, have judged that the individual life is insignificant relative to the divine institution.

What this law says is that the Sabbath is far more about God than it is about humans, about Israel. On the face of it, this shouldn't be surprising. The Sabbath begins, in the Torah itself (Gen 2:1-3), as God's creation day, a day sacred to God, with nary a mention of humans as part of what makes the Sabbath the Sabbath. And even when human observance seems to become central to the definition of the day, as in the Ten Commandments (Ex 20:8-11), God emphasizes that the seventh day is a "Sabbath to the Lord" (vs. 10); therefore, humans must refrain from profaning it through their actions. So if the Sabbath is God's sacred day, then it makes sense that humans must "set themselves down" (*shavat*), must restrict themselves, in space and in action, to assure that that sanctity is protected. God's Sabbath commands subservience, Israel responds with meek submission. This is the relationship that this first Sabbath, biblical and Second Temple, defines.

In this context, the ancient traditional emphasis on the carrying prohibition will be seen in a new light. Carrying is about intercourse, social and commercial. If the gates of the city are shut tight, then the exchange and hubbub that is an expression of commerce will be impossible. But to accomplish this, everyone must, relatively speaking, stay in place. (If one finds oneself on the road when the Sabbath is about to begin, one's restriction and isolation in space will be extreme.) And when carrying is rendered symbolic and forbidden in and of itself, then even carrying a baby will be prohibited, and the natural social exchange of families in a community will be greatly curtailed. The carrying prohibition leads to passivity and relative isolation. It makes the buzz of human social exchange more difficult. It privileges greatly God's concerns over those of humans, who are social creatures by their nature. But if this is what is necessary to protect the sanctity of God's Sabbath, then so be it. There are six other days when human society can be human.

Against this background, rabbinic Sabbath law takes on a radically new meaning. Let us begin with what may no longer be taken for granted: the rabbinic judgment that saving a life pushes aside Sabbath restrictions. The gemara in which this principle is discussed (Yoma 85a-b) suggests an interesting "history" for this law. Chronologically speaking, the rule is first articulated in the Mishnah on which the gemara comments (8:6-7). The gemara's discussion begins by citing a baraita in which six separate tannaim offer proofs from scripture for the Mishnah's rule. Immediately following the tannaitic proofs, the amora, R. Judah, quotes Samuel as saying "had I been there, I would have said 'mine [=my proof from scripture] is better than theirs,'" following which he offers his proof. In response Rava adds "all of them have a refutation except for that of Samuel, which has no refutation." He then goes on to refute all of the suggested tannaitic proofs.

Now, the Mishnah which states the law of saving life typically offers no history and no proof for its ruling. The gemara—baraita and amoraic comments—fills this in. But considered as a whole, this discussion makes it clear that the law privileging life developed before there was a good (= accepted scriptural) reason for it. To begin with, if there are six proffered scriptural sources for this law, clearly no one of them has the status of authoritative foundation. If one did, there would be no need for five others. But, accepting the gemara at its own word, we may go even further: in fact, the Mishnah which offered this ruling had no good source because no good source was available until after the Mishnah was completed! In other words, the rabbis originally insisted that saving life should take priority despite the fact that they had no good source for this opinion. Their only source was their own clear conviction. Nothing else seems to have mattered.

I review all of this because it makes one thing clear: even the rabbis recognized that their ruling in favor of saving life was "radical"—an act of sheer *chutzpah*. As we learn from the contrasting historical precedent we saw earlier, this conclusion was not necessary or obvious; it would make just as much sense religiously to give the sanctity of God's Sabbath priority. By ruling for individual humans, the rabbis were, in effect, enacting a new relationship with God. More will be said on this below.

The other outstanding innovation in rabbinic Sabbath law is in precisely the area where earlier records spend so much time: the carrying prohibition. As we have seen, the carrying prohibition was already central to Sabbath practice six centuries before the rabbis emerged as aspiring leaders of the community (that is, at least by the time of Nehemiah). But every mention of the prohibition before the rabbis represents it as unyielding; each new detail in the law (see, in particular, the Damascus Covenant) seems to restrict mobility more and more. By contrast, the rabbis add many details the consequence of which is the great loosening of the law. By inventing a system of demanding definitions, the rabbis opened up the Sabbath map as it had not been opened in centuries.

What is unprecedented in rabbinic Sabbath law is the four Sabbath domains (public domain, private domain, neutral area, and *carmelit*) and their definitions. The most important of their innovations pertains to the definition of the public domain. To be a public domain, a settlement (city) must have a main thoroughfare leading directly (=straight) from the open gate on one of its sides to the open gate on the opposite side. This thoroughfare must be at least 15 cubits wide and must itself be eligible to be a "public domain;" it may not, therefore, be covered over at any point along its length. There are also some who add that 600,000 people must pass through the thoroughfare in the course of the day.

This is an "all or nothing" proposition. That is to say, if any of the necessary criteria is missing—even if all of the others are present—then the area is not a public domain. Needless to say, it will be very difficult to find an area that meets all of these criteria—so difficult, in fact, that in the opinion of both Talmuds, "there is no public domain in this world."[4] And if there is no public domain, there can be no prohibition of carrying a distance of four cubits in the public domain, or of carrying from a private to the public domain or vice versa.

Unless, of course, the rabbis say there should be a prohibition. In fact, what they do is this: after defining a public domain *de'oraita* ("from the Torah") out of existence, they extend the prohibition to a *carmelit* (an area that looks like a public domain but for technical reasons is not) *and then provide the means to get around their own prohibition by means of an* eruv. Simply put, they take control of the entire system, offering their own prohibition and then their own way to circumvent the prohibition. The practical consequence of these manipulations is to make carrying on the Sabbath permissible for virtually anyone who lives in a rabbinically-observant Jewish community. This means, of course, that the things made difficult by the prohibition are rendered once again easy. The baby may once again be carried so the natural social exchange of families in a community will be facilitated. Not "settled" in one place, the passivity and relative isolation created by the carrying prohibition will yield to the buzz of human social exchange. Being more social, the system is by definition more human, and the unyielding sanctity of *God's* Sabbath yields, therefore, to new definitions of the sanctity of the Sabbath.

Also more human is the way this condition was created. As indicated earlier, this new freedom was achieved by the rabbis taking control of the system. Not because the scriptural tradition actually said so did the system of the four domains develop, but because the rabbis derived it, teased it out, and invented it. They took control of the system, prohibited what they said was permitted (carrying in or into a *carmelit*) but then permitted what they said was forbidden (= the same). It was humans—the rabbis—who defined this Sabbath, not God.

So both in substance and in process, the rabbinic Sabbath is one in which the relationship between God and Israel has been renegotiated. Precisely as Yitz's scheme would predict, the Sabbath in which God is the senior partner—the biblical and Second Temple Sabbath—has been replaced by a Sabbath where the human partner to the covenant has a far more prominent role. The Second Era Sabbath is one in which the human partner and his or her needs matter much. Hence, it is a Sabbath of light and joy, of appetites and of social intercourse. Of course, God is also centrally and crucially present on this Sabbath, but the configuration of relationship has clearly shifted.

A second area in which the history of religious development will be explained by Yitz's system is Jewish eating practices, what we call kashrut. As I have elaborated at length in my recent book, *Jewish Eating and Identity Through the Ages* (Routledge, 2007), Jewish eating practices both remained static and developed significantly during the Second Temple era. Permit me to explain.

In significant respects, biblical eating laws continued to be in force, during this entire period, according to their simple meaning and without significant elaboration. The reviews of these laws offered both by the Letter of Aristeas, on the earlier side, and Philo, on the later, make this clear. Both comment in detail on the meaning of the Torah's laws, but neither suggests that the laws had been significantly changed or supplemented. As late as the first century CE, the Torah was understood to mean what it said.

But there was a problem: the Torah's eating regulations, including the long lists of permitted and prohibited animals, the blood prohibition and the suet prohibition, all share one common quality—they all pertain to creatures that were once living (animals, birds, fish, bugs). Outside of certain limitations relating to first fruits, gleanings, and the like ("priestly" concerns and concerns relating to the poor), no vegetable substance is, categorically speaking, subject to prohibitions. In a world where most people (excepting the wealthy and priests) ate vegetarian diets on an everyday basis—chicken and fish would have been restricted to recurrent "special" occasions like the Sabbath and the meat of larger animals would have been consumed at special celebratory or commemorative events—the Torah's focus would have been utterly ineffective at separating Israelites from their neighbors.[5]

Yet, the Torah is explicit in declaring that the purpose of its eating regulations is to make Israel, like God, holy (Lev 11:43-7), and holiness is inevitably expressed in restriction and separation. So after the return from the Babylonian exile, Jewish pietists sought to do for the Torah what it failed to do successfully for itself, that is, to use eating restrictions to separate Jews from gentiles. To do so, they effectively prohibited *all* foods prepared by gentiles. Only unprocessed foods—foods untouched by gentile culture—were considered acceptable. Cold vegetables were fine, wine or bread or cooked dishes—no good.

What we see in the late Second Temple period, then, is this: on the one hand, biblical laws continued to be in force, according to their simple meaning. On the other hand, a high, vast fence was erected by pietists, the purpose of which was to assure separation from the nations. This latter development is in the spirit of the Torah's law, though it is not necessitated by its letter.

As we anticipate rabbinic developments in Jewish eating practices, both of these late pre-destruction realities are important, but particularly the former.

It is fair to say that the most significant area of rabbinic eating law that finds no obvious precedent in pre-rabbinic materials is the prohibition of mixing meat and dairy. Philo's testimony in this connection is significant. Commenting upon the Torah's command that we not cook a young animal in the milk of its mother, Philo suggests that the Torah's concern is symbolic; the milk represents the mother's sustenance of life, the slaughtered offspring represents death. Life and death should not be mixed. He then goes on to emphasize the immense perversity and cruelty of spirit such an act would express:

> There are innumerable herds of cattle in every direction, and some are everyday milked by the cowherds, or goatherds, or shepherds… So, that, as there is a great abundance of lambs, and kids, and all other kinds of animals, the man who seethes the flesh of any one of them in the milk of its own mother is exhibiting a terrible perversity of disposition. ("On the Virtues," 143-4)

There are so many animals around producing so much milk that a person would actually have to go out of his way to cook a kid in the milk of his own mother. This would be nothing less than perverse.

"The man" of whom Philo is speaking is the Jewish man (or woman; a non-Jew is obviously not bound by the Torah's restriction). So what Philo is saying is quite clear: there would be no problem for a Jew to prepare the meat of a kosher animal in milk—let alone to mix meat and dairy—provided that the milk was not taken from its own mother. Simply put, neither Philo nor any other pre-rabbinic author has heard of the meat-dairy mixing prohibition. The law remains as the Torah had enunciated it ("don't cook a calf…"). The evidence is powerful: the rabbis, in whose Mishnah mention of the prohibition first appears, invented the prohibition.

The rabbis' dairy-meat mixture prohibition constitutes an elaborate system (one that becomes increasingly more elaborate as the centuries progress). As spelled out in the eighth chapter of Mishnah Hullin, cheese and meat may not come into direct contact, nor may they be placed on the same table. They may not be cooked together, eaten together, or sold after having been cooked together. The gemara adds a variety of details, including the requirements of washing one's hands and mouth between eating them, and possibly of waiting "until the next meal" after eating meat before allowing oneself again to eat dairy. Cooking pots, too, should not be used for both, at least not on the same day, and the same would apply to bowls.[6]

By the rabbis own admission, some of this system "derives" from the Torah and some is their own invention. In the rabbis' understanding, the Torah prohibits eating or otherwise deriving benefit from these foods only when they have first been cooked together. They derive the three categories of prohibition (cooking, eating, and deriving benefit) from the three-fold repetition of the "don't cook a calf..." verse in the Torah. From the fact that the verse explicitly says "cook" they derive the notion that the prohibitions apply—according to the Torah—only when there is actually cooking. In their reading of the Torah, cold Swiss cheese on cold kosher salami would be perfectly acceptable.

This means that everything else here is a rabbinic addition. Complete separation of meat and dairy is itself a rabbinic extension because if there is no cooking there is no Torah prohibition. Waiting between one category of food and the other is utterly unnecessary according to the Torah because if they are eaten sequentially they cannot be cooked. The requirement to wait, however conceived, is rabbinic. So are steps to keep cold meat and cold cheese separate on the hands or on the table. The list could go on and on.[7]

But it would be wrong to imagine that the rabbinic intervention in the system inclines only toward increasing stringencies (in which case this could all be viewed as a huge "fence" around the Torah). In fact, as the rabbis take control of and generate elements of this system, they also introduce principles the result of which is significant leniencies. Two of these are most significant. The first is the notion that the introduction of a bad taste does not have halakhic consequences; for example, the taste of meat introduced into a dairy dish is a problem, the taste of putrid meat is not. Add to this the fact that, in the rabbis' opinion, any taste that has remained in a pot or vessel for a day is *by definition* rendered a negative taste and you will see the leniency that results: meat cooked in a pot that was used for dairy a day earlier is not rendered unkosher.[8]

The second significant principle with lenient consequences is this: the secondary transmission of the taste of a permissible substance has no halakhic affect. So, for example, if the taste of meat has been absorbed into a pot, and water is subsequently boiled in that pot, the water is not considered to be (what we would call) "fleishig" (at least it wasn't so considered by the Talmud or by most rabbinic codifiers for many centuries following). The consequences of this principle are, to the modern observant Jew, at least, startling. For example, according to the opinion of R. Moses Isserles, if boiling water is poured upon dirty dairy and meat dishes which have been mixed together, they are all, nevertheless, permitted![9] And Isserles' position is the more stringent one recorded in that context! Needless to say, the prerogatives that this principle, along with the one described just above, afford the rabbi who masters this system are extraordinary.

Given just these details—and it would be possible to add many more—it is fair to say that what characterizes the eating laws of the rabbis is their utter taking control of the system. They at the same time (1) extend the Torah's foundation significantly through their aggressive interpretation, (2) expand the law considerably through their own legislated additions, and (3) take control of the system by introducing principles that allow them to significantly direct its outcomes (to the latter I would add all of their laws pertaining to mixtures).[10] The system they elaborate requires masters, and the rabbis as masters master the system. There is relatively little mere submission to inherited prohibitions here. If anything, it is the system that submits to the rabbis.

So if we were to characterize the condition of Jewish eating laws in the Second Temple period, we would use terms like "submissive" and "protective," while for the rabbinic condition a term like "mastering" would be far more accurate. Of course, these are relative terms, and they should not be understood to imply that Second Temple authorities were only submissive (protection can be aggressive) or that the rabbis were only aggressive masters (they surely inherited much). But as relative descriptions they are accurate. And they are also, given what Yitz's schematization anticipates, fully to be expected.

Once again, we see First Era Judaism (pre-destruction) to be a Judaism in which God and God's commandments stand as fearsome masters and Israel restrains itself in submission. By contrast, in Second Era Judaism—rabbinic Judaism—Israel emerges as a forceful and often initiating partner. Do you want to know what God wants of you? Ask the rabbis. But it is not just God who makes demands of you; it is the rabbis as well. Their voice joins God's voice in a far more equal partnership, and Israel enjoys the fruits (both stringent and lenient) of this realignment.

The third area we will consider in our exploration of Yitz's interpretive scheme is the writing of sacred texts. The ancient world—both the Second Temple period and the rabbinic age—was a world of enormous Jewish literary productivity. The earlier of these periods saw the writing of the latest of the biblical books, the Apocrypha (Judith, Maccabees, ben Sira, etc.), many pseudepigraphic works (Jubilees, Enoch, etc.), and many otherwise unattested Dead Sea scrolls. The rabbinic period produced the many classical rabbinic works, from the Mishnah and the halakhic midrashim to the Talmuds and monumental aggadic midrashim. In terms of productivity, these two ages were quite similar. When we consider the nature of what was produced in each, though, we discover profound and stunning dissimilarities.

Let us first consider representative examples of the literary production of Jews in the latter part (= post-biblical) of the Second Temple period.

The book of Jubilees, composed in Hebrew in c. 100 BCE, was a popular work among at least some groups of the Jews in the pre-destruction period.[11] It claims to be a revelation given to Moses at Mt. Sinai at the same time he received the tablets of the law. In fact, much of Jubilees is a direct "quotation" or relatively close restatement of the biblical text. But it also embodies notable divergences from or supplements to our received text. For example, it organizes biblical history from the creation to the exodus according to a carefully structured time-scheme that does not appear in our Torah. It adds to the biblical narrative in ways that render that narrative clearer or more logical. It is peppered with imaginative fancy, but fancy that has a purpose.

The following is a good example of Jubilees and its method. The text recounts that "in the seventh week, in the first year of it, in the first month of the jubilee, on the twelfth of this month, it was said in heaven about Abraham, that he had been faithful in doing everything the Lord has told him to do..."

> And the prince Mastema [=Satan] came and said in God's presence, Behold, Abraham loves his son Isaac dearly and dotes on him more than on anything else: tell him to offer him as a whole-offering on the altar, and see if he will carry out this order; and then you will know if he is really faithful in every test you subject him to. (Jubilees 17:15-6)

The text continues that the Lord knew that Abraham was faithful for he had passed a number of prior texts. So He had no hesitation taking Mastema's challenge. Thus,

> God said to him, Abraham, Abraham; and he said, Behold, here I am. And he said, Take Isaac your beloved son, whom you love... (18:1-2)

And so forth. Obviously, Jubilees has appropriated the text of Genesis, expanded and reworked it. Its reasons for doing so are also obvious: How, it wonders, could God have commanded that Abraham offer his son on the altar? What kind of test is this and who is the God who would subject His beloved subject to such a test?

The answer of the work's author is familiar. He appropriates the introductory narrative of the book of Job to make sense of Genesis 22. In this version, God does not "test" Abraham out of cruelty or caprice, nor does God do so because He doesn't know whether Abraham will prove to be true (in a section of the text not quoted here [17:17-8], Jubilees has God emphasizing His confidence in the outcome by reference to the many prior tests that Abraham has withstood). God simply accepts Satan's challenge—knowing full well the outcome—to show Satan the righteousness and deep commitment of His covenantal choice.

What is crucial to this discussion is our recognition that virtually this entire analysis of Jubilees' motivations would be impossible if we didn't know the Torah-text to which it was responding. Yet, we must admit, there is nothing in Jubilees that requires us to know the Torah-text that lurks in the background. Jubilees here (as elsewhere) is entirely self-sufficient, offering quotations from the Torah—which are, however, *not recognizable as quotations*—and its own additions in the same language without any mark to distinguish one from the other. In other words, Jubilees presents itself as scripture, even as Torah. It does not represent itself as derivative from or as commenting upon something else (as much as we might recognize this to be the case). As far as its author is concerned, it is new scripture, simple and unadorned.

The same can be said about another work from this period that, on the surface, seems to have little in common with Jubilees. I am referring to I Maccabees, a work similarly produced in c. 100 BCE. I Maccabees was originally written in Hebrew—biblical Hebrew. Though its narrative describes "contemporary history," its structuring of that history makes its theory of that history abundantly clear: Maccabean history is biblical history, the Maccabees are the next Judges. This is made evident not only through repeated Judges-like formulae that punctuate the text (e.g., "Then the sword ceased from Israel...," 9:73; "The land had rest all the days of Simon...," 14:4) but also from the Deuteronomic structuring of its events (sin leads to punishment, which might then be followed by repentance and recovery).

Consider just the earliest part of the book, where this scheme is, if anything, less evident: Just after introducing us to Antiochus in the first chapter of the book, the author tells us that "in those days certain renegades came out from Israel and misled many, saying, 'Let us go and make a covenant with the Gentiles around us...'" (vs. 11). This, of course, is the sin of (part of) Israel. Shortly after this, "Antiochus returned... He went up against Israel and came to Jerusalem with a strong force..." (vs. 20). So sin is followed by punishment. Later in the chapter, many Jews follow the king's directive to give up their own laws and follow the customs of the Gentiles (see vss. 41-3 and 52). This leads again to punishment, now the desecration of the altar (vss. 54-61) at the hands of the Greeks. But, even still, many Jews remain steadfast (vss. 62-3), and as a consequence (the cause and effect is suggested by juxtaposition), the Maccabees arise to lead to the delivery of Israel (beginning of ch. 2).

Once again, the evidence of what he wrote shows that this author understood himself to be writing new scripture. Unlike the author of Jubilees, he did not intend to write another Torah. But Judges is sacred history nonetheless. Neither of these authors has heard that the sacred writings of Israel have been canonized. On the contrary, they, like others around them (the authors of Judith, Tobit, Enoch, The Temple Scroll, The Dead Sea Psalms, etc., etc.), think that new scripture can still be written, and that they are still living in the biblical age. Evidently, in this age the only voice of legitimate authority is the voice of scripture, so those who want to claim such authority (for their ideas, if not for themselves) must do it in that voice. To be sure, there were some Jews during this period who composed different sorts of works,[12] but the surviving evidence is overwhelmingly of the sort we have identified. If what survived did so primarily because it was accepted as authoritative by some community, this is testimony to the fact that authority could only reside in the voice of scripture, that is, in words understood to be, in one way or another, words inspired by God.

Consider, by contrast, the writings of the classical rabbis in their three major genres: Mishnah, midrash and Talmud. It is safe to say that all are anything but scriptural.

The Mishnah claims authority in its own voice, a distinctly non-biblical and possibly vernacular Hebrew that is clearly the language of the sage.[13] Accordingly, the authorities who speak in the Mishnah are the sages, either named (R. Judah, R. Meir, etc.) or unnamed (= the anonymous voice of the Mishnah). Unlike earlier texts, words are not put into the mouths of biblical characters and scripture is deployed relatively infrequently.[14] When it is deployed, it is quoted—clearly and explicitly. But the crucial point is that scripture is not necessary, not by any means.

In fact, the Mishnah's relationship with scripture is quite complex. In brief, the Mishnah might rely heavily on scripture by restating or slightly elaborating its laws. It might begin with scripture but then go in entirely unexpected directions. It might ignore scripture, clearing new paths of Jewish law and practice that are entirely its own. And it might even contradict scripture. Whichever it does in any given case, what is clear is that scripture is not necessary.[15]

What does all of this add up to? The simplest explanation is that, as far as the framers of the Mishnah are concerned, the authority of the rabbis is quite sufficient. To be sure, they often—though not always—enter into a kind of dialogue with scripture, but scripture does not control the direction of that dialogue; if anything, they do. In a piece of Jewish literature, this is virtually unprecedented. This is the first time after the bible that we witness a Jewish composition, speaking essentially to all of Israel, claiming to speak in an authoritative voice, that does not hide behind the claim to be scripture. Against the historical background, this is quite startling.

What of the midrash, a genre of texts that are obviously in profound relationship with scripture? The first thing to notice, in light of what we saw in Second Temple texts, is their clear quotation/referencing of scripture. There is no confusing the "base text" = the scriptural quotation from its elaboration/ commentary. Second, no reader of midrash can miss the extent to which the rabbis who compose the midrash take command of scripture, either by shaping it through the eyes of their own methods and assumptions or by "writing" new text with it—taking scripture from here and from their, refracting it through their own lens, with their own voice, and creating an entirely new fabric.[16] Finally, the lesson of midrash is always the rabbis' lesson, even if the scripture that serves as purported focus would agree. In other words, again it is the voice and authority of the rabbis that is evident in these compositions. Scripture forms part of the rhetoric, but, if anything, the power in the relationship between God's voice and the human (= rabbinic) voice inclines, in this genre, toward the human.

How much more is this the case when we turn to Talmud, and particularly to the Bavli? We may, of course, consider the Bavli as a whole: the governing voice of the Bavli is the unattributed Aramaic voice of the *"stam ha-talmud,"* a voice that, employing the common language of the day, controls—in the name of the Talmud—the entire deliberation. Cited regularly are rabbinic teachings, their masters identified by name, and authority resides in these teachings according to their periods: the Amoraic and, before it, the Tannaitic above all. Scripture may be cited, but not programmatically (= it is not the Bavli's programmatic task to identify scriptural sources for the teachings it includes), and it is never cited unmediated as an authoritative source to support this or that ruling. In other words, scripture never stands alone in the Bavli; its authority is only via its rabbinic interpretation.

The outstanding phenomenon that illustrates, in the Bavli's clear opinion, the relationship between rabbinic teachings and scripture, is identified with the term אי בעית אימא—"if you wish, I will say...." This Talmudic method, purportedly identifying possible sources for particular teachings, always offers a source in both scripture and human reason, with reason usually offered first ("if you wish, I will say that it is reason, if you wish, I will say that it is scripture"). When this convention is employed, a source in both reason and scripture is always offered for each of two opposing rabbinic opinions and a conclusion is never reached. What this convention claims, therefore, is that neither reason nor scripture is a sure source for determining conclusions because *reason can always be used to argue for different conclusions* and, likewise, *scripture can always be interpreted to argue for different conclusions.* In other words, scripture is in no way superior to reason as an authoritative source for arriving at conclusions because *there is no such thing as scripture that does not demand the mediation of reason = interpretation.* The highest authority is human reason because there is no alternative, at least no so far as the writers of the Bavli are concerned.[17]

If we step back and consider classical rabbinic writings as a whole, we will notice one overarching quality: all put the human = rabbinic voice front and center. Unlike earlier Jewish writings that claimed sacred authority, they do not write themselves as scripture, nor do they obviously claim inspiration or prophecy.[18] The rabbi, human through and through, speaks, and his speech carries sufficient weight that it must be heard, if not always obeyed. Furthermore, in the most "extreme" expression of developing early rabbinic writings (in the Bavli), the human voice, representing human reason, emerges supreme, for it is only though the human that we have access to the divine at all.

Once again, Yitz's theologizing scheme of Jewish history serves best to explain what we have seen. Jewish writing during the Second Temple Period—still the First Era—is dominated by the notion that only God can speak with full authority. Thus, works that assert religious authority claim to be scripture (some actually become scripture)—recording God's word, as conveyed or transmuted by an angel, through a prophet, or via inspiration. Admittedly, the apparently human voice is more central to what we call wisdom literature, but even this genre is buttressed by the claim of inspiration, at least on the part of the believing community.

By contrast, surviving Jewish writings from the Second Era, the rabbinic period, are characterized by a prominent human voice, a voice that is always powerful and sometimes dominant. These writings clearly declare that the God-human relationship has changed: God is, in significant respects, no longer the "senior partner" in this relationship. In fact, the divine partner has come so much to rely on the human partner that is fair to say that the mantel of authority is now being passed to this once junior partner.

All of the instances examined above (Shabbat, Kashrut, Jewish writing) lead to the same conclusion, a conclusion of which Yitz's interpretive scheme makes clear sense. In their own land, worshipping in their own Temple, Jews remained submissive servants to a powerful God who both protected and punished. When that Temple was destroyed and Judea utterly defeated, at least rabbinic Jews came to understand that something profound had changed. It is perhaps the famous midrash that captures this understanding best: God would not save Israel from Egypt until Nachshon ben Aminadav plunged himself into the sea up to his nose. If the human partner in the historical drama wasn't going to step into the water to split the sea, redemption wasn't going to come. The evidence of rabbinic religion—Second Era religion—makes it clear: it begins with us, with Israel, and we hope that God will heed our decisive call.

NOTES

1. See Yitz Greenberg, "Voluntary Covenant," in *Persepectives* (New York: CLAL, 1987), pp. 27-44.

2. Ibid., particularly pp. 33-40.

3. See Theodore H. Gaster, *The Dead Sea Scriptures* (Garden City: Anchor Books, 1956), p. 84, and p. 111, n. 54.

4. I have quoted the formulation of the Yerushalmi, Eruvin 8:8. In the Bavli, Eruvin 22a, R. Yohanan declares, "we are not liable for the public domain in the Land of Israel [= it doesn't exist]." Admittedly, the Bavli's precise formulation does not exclude the possibility of a public domain somewhere. But for R. Yohanan, of Tiberius, the

Land of Israel is all that really matters. With respect to the rest of the world, I would interpret this teaching as effectively "agnostic."

5. For a fuller discussion, see *Jewish Eating and Identity Through the Ages* (New York and London: Routledge, 2007), pp. 15-9.

6. For a fuller discussion, see *Jewish Eating and Identity Through the Ages*, pp. 99-101.

7. See *Jewish Eating and Identity Through the Ages*, pp. 41-6 and 99-101.

8. *Jewish Eating and Identity Through the Ages*, pp. 99-107.

9. Shuchan Arukh, Y.D. 95:3

10. *Jewish Eating and Identity Through the Ages*, pp. 55-66.

11. Fragments from ten different manuscripts of Jubilees were found in four different caves. The work is referred to explicitly by the so-called "Damascus Covenent" (or "Zadokite Document").

12. I have in mind particularly the writings of Philo and Josephus. The "pesher" materials of the Dead Sea Scrolls write in a different voice, unmistakably quoting scripture and not pretending to be scripture. But those materials seek one-to-one correspondences between biblical prophecies and contemporary events (often somewhat masked in the scrolls' descriptions). In their way too, therefore, the pesher compositions grant utmost authority to scripture.

13. See E.Y. Kutscher, *A History of the Hebrew Language* (Jerusalem and Leiden: Magnes Press and E.J. Brill, 1982), pp. 115-20. But see my discussion in "The Mishnah," in Steven T. Katz, ed., *The Cambridge History of Judaism*, v. IV, *The Late Roman-Rabbinic Period* (Cambridge: Cambridge University Press, 2006), p. 304, n. 3

14. I count a total of approximately 265 quotations of scripture in the Mishnah (excluding references to liturgical recitations of scripture and excluding tractate Avot, which is arguably post-Mishnaic). There are 517 chapters in the entire Mishnah (again, excluding Avot), meaning that scripture is quoted only slightly more than once every two chapters. Given that there are certain chapters that are unusual for the quantity of scripture they do quote, this means that in the bulk of the Mishnah quotation of scripture is relatively rare.

15. See m. Hagigah 1:8 and my discussion in "The Mishnah," pp. 306-8.

16. What I have in mind here is articulated in the title of Jacob Neusner's book, *Writing with Scripture* (Minneapolis: Fortress Press, 1989), and in his introduction, pp. 1-4.

17. For a fuller discussion of this and related phenomena, see my *The Mind of the Talmud* (New York and Oxford: Oxford University Press, 1990), pp. 146-56.

18. The sages, beginning with Avot, do claim that their teachings have the status of "Torah." But, with the exception of one extreme claim (the Yerushalmi's version, at Peah 2:4, is this—"scripture, Mishnah, Talmud and aggadah, even that which an experienced student would in the future teach before his master was spoken to Moses at Sinai;" the Bavli has a different and somewhat more modest version of this teaching), they do not claim that the sum total of their teachings has the status of revelation, nor do they claim that their many individual and often innovative teachings are inspired. Notably, if the student studying these texts, page after page, does not know where to find these exceptional status claims, nothing in the common rhetoric of the documents will lead to the same conclusion. For a more detailed discussion of the maximalist claim, see Kraemer, "Concerning the Theological Assumptions of the Yerushalmi," in Peter Schäfer, ed., *The Talmud Yerushalmi and Graeco-Roman Culture* III (Tübingen: Mohr Siebeck, 2002), p. 367 and n. 15 there.

13

Yavneh and Irving Greenberg: Envisioning a Jewish Educational Revolution[1]

Benny Kraut

YAVNEH: ORIGINS AND MISSION[2]

During a conclave over the Shabbat weekend of February 5-7, 1960, at the Mayflower Hotel in Lakewood, NJ, eighty students representing thirteen college campuses—Barnard, Brown, City College of New York, Columbia, Cornell, Harvard, NYU, University of Pennsylvania, Princeton, Queens College, Rutgers, Stern College, and Yale—founded a remarkable new national organization, Yavneh: National Jewish Students Religious Association. It was an independent Orthodox, student-run national collegiate organization serving primarily undergraduates in the United States, although graduate students from time to time served as national officers and joined the organization as members.[3]

The organization was led by a National Executive Board (NEB) of student officers elected at annual four day Labor Day weekend national conventions from a slate of nominees assembled by the outgoing national board. Charged with running the national organization and its national office headquartered in New York, the NEB guided its constituent Yavneh campus chapters around the country, offering them programmatic assistance and advice, keeping them informed about Yavneh activities everywhere, and engaging them in nationally sponsored programs and projects. In its heyday during the 1960s, Yavneh counted thirty-five to forty-five affiliated chapters at universities in the Northeast, Midwest, and Western United States and in several Canadian cities; annual membership in these years hovered between twelve hundred to fourteen hundred, a figure that does not include the untold numbers of additional students who participated in individual programs at any given time.

219

Yavneh quite rightly advertised itself as the only national student organization independent from adult supervision; policies, directions, and activities were approved and implemented essentially by the students.[4] Over the years, its student leaders successfully resisted all attempts to have it controlled by an adult parent body and insisted on organizational autonomy.[5] Nevertheless, even the first NEB realized that the organization needed guidance, financial support, and an image of responsibility and heft, all of which could be furnished only by adults of acknowledged reputable status. Within a year after its establishment, therefore, a National Advisory Board (NAB) of prominent rabbis and laymen was established. The first three chairs of the NAB were Rabbis Irving Greenberg (1960-66), Norman Lamm (1966-69), and Aharon Lichtenstein (1969-71).[6] From the members of the NAB and especially from its respective chairs, the Yavneh national leadership received advice, the patina of organizational continuity, and entrée into the adult world for moral and financial assistance.

Although it was to exist for only two decades—the organization gradually dwindled by the end of the 1970s and dissolved during 1980-81—Yavneh was lavishly praised in the 1960s for its revolutionary impact on Orthodox Jewish life. Rabbis, communal leaders, academics, and Israelis touted its historic significance.[7] Perhaps most representative of these feelings is the declaration in 1968 by Rabbi Norman E. Frimer, Director of Brooklyn College Hillel, that "Yavneh, without exaggeration, is one of the most dramatic manifestations of the power and vitality of *Yisrael Saba* [the Jewish people] on the American scene; Yavneh contributed a revolutionary reaction to the preachments of despair and prediction of demise both within and without the Orthodox community."[8] Orthodox demographic, religious, and institutional rejuvenation in the sixties was proving the 1950s predictions of its doom by pundits and academics premature.[9] For Frimer, as well as for some other modern Orthodox pulpit rabbis and communal leaders, Yavneh was seen as one of the most concrete instantiations of the confident, enthusiastic modern Orthodox promise of that day.[10]

Modern Orthodox spokesmen, moreover, praised Yavneh's dynamism, creativity, and multi-faceted educational innovations. But it is only with historical hindsight that one can appreciate fully the organization's genuine accomplishments and even marvel at those attempted initiatives that did not fully succeed or those ideas conceptualized on paper but never quite realized. Indeed, Yavneh's manifold educational projects—publications, summer institutes, Labor Day weekend national conventions, and Israel study programs—foreshadowed the current (ArtScroll) revolution in publishing traditional texts and commentaries in English; the one-year post-yeshiva high school study-in-Israel programs; the dissemination of weekly *parsha* analyses by many yeshivot and synagogues; summer institutes for study of Torah, Jewish

philosophy, and other texts, such as offered by Drisha; and, intellectual Orthodox periodicals such as *The Torah u-Madda Journal* and the former *Edah
Journal* (now *Meorot: A Forum of Modern Orthodox Discourse*). In its animat-
ing philosophy and concrete undertakings, Yavneh was to some degree the
intellectual progenitor and spiritual forebear of Saul Berman's now defunct
Edah, albeit not in any causal sense.[11]

What accounts for the historical appearance of Yavneh at this time? A confluence of social and cultural forces came into play, as did the particular environment of the college campus during the 1950s and early 1960s. The postwar
boom of the 1950s led to a momentous expansion of universities and colleges
nationally, which opened doors to unprecedented numbers of qualified students, Jews included. Simultaneously, a new Orthodox Jewish student constituency had emerged on the post-war scene, young men and women graduates of Orthodox Jewish high schools, multiplying who were ready to take
advantage of the new educational possibilities. Hence, the 1950s witnessed the
first numerically significant generation of Orthodox high school graduates,
primarily though not exclusively in the Northeast, to attend institutions of
higher learning. It was from this cohort of students that the leaders and members of Yavneh would emerge.

Arriving on campus, these day school graduates confronted daunting practical, religious, and intellectual problems. A good number, feeling intense intellectual and social discomfort as a tiny minority within an almost normative
assimilative campus culture, weaned themselves from Orthodox ritual obser-
vances and religious pieties. Other students experienced a kind of liberation
by the campus intellectual environment, and also gradually shed or reconfig-
ured their Jewish attachments. Still others, however, opted not to follow this
acculturating route but rather to maintain their Orthodox identification in
beliefs and practices. But they too confronted feelings of social isolation. As
well, they found that their prior inadequate Jewish education had left them
utterly unprepared to contend intellectually with the philosophic and human-
istic ideas and scientific perspectives they were being taught in their courses,
which often conflicted in fundamental ways with their Orthodox religious
premises and convictions. These students also faced difficult pragmatic problems in day-to-day life on campus: exams on the Sabbath and holidays, for
which there were often no exemptions; unavailability of kosher food, and, in
dormitory schools that demanded both mandatory residence and board plans,
the unfair requirement of having to pay for food that they could not eat. College administrators, moreover, were often entirely unsympathetic to Orthodox student needs and complaints; in such instances the message that Orthodox students, with their particularistic religious needs, were really not all that
welcome on the campus was received loud and clear.

Finally, Orthodox students discovered that, with notable exceptions, the official spokesmen for Jews and Judaism on campus, Hillel directors or appointed Jewish chaplains, were often singularly unhelpful if not downright antagonistic to their concerns. The vast majority came from Reform or Conservative backgrounds, and their open disdain for Orthodox Judaism and dismissive attitude to its student adherents was palpable. Not surprisingly, these folks were perceived by Yavneh students to be self-hating Jews, whose perspective on Jewish life on campus simply echoed that of the majority of Jewish students and the American Jewish establishment, to wit: Jews had finally gained access in significant numbers to non-denominational and non-sectarian institutions of higher education. They, therefore, ought to be sincerely grateful, not make any special Jewish ethnic and religious demands, and melt into the cultural mainstream.

It was in response to these social, religious, and intellectual challenges that a small cluster of students spontaneously banded together as independent groups on several campuses: Yeshurun, at Columbia in 1957; Taryag, at Harvard in 1958; and Ari, at Barnard in 1959. Their initial goals were modest yet focused: to create a daily *minyan* and to gain access to kosher food and relief from Sabbath exams. And it was from these groups that Yavneh eventually emerged. In several conversations during the summer of 1959, the two student heads of Yeshurun and Ari, Joel Levine and Rivkah Teitz (Blau) respectively, decided that the time was ripe to convene a meeting of traditional students from other campuses to share feelings and to explore the feasibility and merit of a unified national campus organization of religious Jewish students to address the practical and intellectual issues confronting them on campus. Columbia students Zvi Gitelman and Michael (Mickey) Hochstein joined them in the deliberations and helped plan and organize the February 1960 inaugural convention that launched the new student association.[12]

Yavneh's initial national constitution listed five essential goals to which the national organization and its constituent chapters were committed:

- *Jewish education*—chapters were expected to arrange weekly *shiurim* in Bible and Talmud, periodic lectures, and, within a designated multi-chapter region, regional *shabbatonim* and other centralized activities linking individual chapters together.
- *Jewish observance*—chapters were encouraged to organize daily *minyanim* and, where needed, Shabbat prayer services. They were also supposed to ameliorate the major bane of Orthodox student life on campus in the fifties and early sixties: exams on Shabbat and holidays, the lack of kosher food on campus, and, in some dormitory schools, the requirement to pay for mandatory board plans without being able to eat the food.[13]

- *Communication*—chapters were expected to advance the intellectual dialogue between Judaism and Western culture, and to integrate the insights of college study with the values and thinking of Judaism, and thus solve some of the intellectual challenges facing its members. In the process, they would show that the Orthodox Jew has a legitimate mutually-enriching place in the world of secular learning, and that one could be an Orthodox Jew and attend an Ivy League school.
- *Jewish unity*—chapters were expected to cultivate an awareness of traditional students on campus about each other, which, it was felt, would both ease the possible alienation experienced by traditional Jews on campus and encourage full pride and dignity in an individual's personal religious observance. In this sense, by serving as a kind of social *miklat*, a social shelter, for its members, Yavneh would also strengthen their religious identity.
- *Community*—Yavneh sought to instill in its members a sense of leadership and responsibility for the Jewish community at large and the need to disseminate traditional Judaism widely, thus demonstrating the reality of their status as forerunners of a new kind of traditional Jew.

How these goals were actually translated into reality and the degree to which the attempts were successful is a larger story that cannot be told here.[14] However, it is imperative to underscore the two critical ideas undergirding Yavneh's self-understanding and educational philosophy. First, Yavneh leadership jealously guarded its vaunted self-conception that it was preeminently an intellectual organization and not a mere social enterprise. By official national policy, all Yavneh programming at all levels, local, regional and national, had to have a central educational component. Indeed, the NEB censured any Yavneh chapter that scheduled strictly social events, as, for example, Saturday night *Melaveh Malkahs* that had no speakers. In this respect, its leaders pointedly contrasted themselves with the Young Israel Intercollegiates of the modern Orthodox Young Israel movement, whose primary programming consisted of adult-chaperoned social weekends. In distinction to them, Yavneh stood for a compelling religious and intellectual agenda. Not unexpectedly, those who did not share Yavneh's goals perceived it to be an elitist organization.

Second, in terms of educational philosophy, there was one overarching approach upon which all Yavneh student leaders in the 1960s agreed: the study of Judaism, its texts and ideas, must be engaged in with the same intellectual seriousness, analytic rigor, and conceptual depth that one pursued secular studies. Only in this way would the conflict experienced on campus between secular studies and Jewish thought be meaningfully confronted and ultimately reconciled. On the manner of pursuing that engagement, however, two broadly framed orientations surfaced that signified for the most part preferred intellectual tendencies or nuances in student outlook and organizational emphasis. One avowed the need for intellectual encounter with Judaism and its integration with the secular thought of Western civilization; the other called for an intensification of Jewish religious study focusing primarily on Jewish texts. These distinctive educational inclinations existed side by side in creative tension with each other. Both objectives were urged as essential and were regarded as complementary; they were not perceived as standing in binary opposition. Functionally, to be sure, Yavneh's educational programming quite clearly reflected both perspectives, and the national organization and its chapters planned both kinds of educational opportunities.

YAVNEH AND IRVING GREENBERG

The central adult figure during Yavneh's first six years was Rabbi Irving (Yitz) Greenberg, who had been invited to speak at the organization's founding convention in February, 1960. He electrified much of his audience and was, in turn, utterly stirred by them. An instructor of American history at Yeshiva University and an ordained rabbi holding a Ph.D. from Harvard, he proved the perfect role model for Orthodox students on campus. As chair of Yavneh's National Advisory Board from 1960-66, he invited eminent colleagues to join the Board and help bolster the student organization; he was a frequent and much sought-after speaker at local, regional, and national Yavneh functions; and he raised vital funds for Yavneh from among his lay contacts and congregants. In addition, some of Yavneh's most innovative ideas during the sixties emerged from Greenberg's fecund mind, including the Merkaz HaRav Kook study-in-Israel program, the Yonah project, and the agreement between national Yavneh and national Hillel, and he worked tirelessly to see them realized. He also represented Yavneh to adult leaders of communal agencies and advocated on its behalf among his rabbinic peers, as well as to the Union of Orthodox Jewish Congregations of America, the Rabbinical Council of America, B'nai B'rith Hillel Foundation, and the Torah Education and Culture Department of the Jewish Agency.

This match between Greenberg and Yavneh was fortuitous for both parties. While pursuing *semikhah* at Beth Joseph Seminary, a small mussar yeshiva in Brooklyn, Greenberg in the early fifties simultaneously attended Brooklyn College, gaining ordination and a B.A. in 1953. Taking an expansive liberal arts degree and exposed to psychology and sociology, he experienced religious doubts and tensions similar to those of the next generation of Orthodox Jewish students in the late fifties and sixties. Already in the 1950s, he tried to work out the terms by which Orthodox Judaism and the best of Western culture could be made to address each other—in effect, attempting to provide a guidepost for modern Orthodox Judaism. As a graduate student in American history at Harvard in the mid-fifties, he wore a fedora on campus, which he took off only in the classroom, thus anticipating in his own way the later Columbia University Yavneh beret. While in Boston, Greenberg was hired for a year in 1957 as Hillel director at Brandeis University, whose University institutional kitchen Greenberg was wont to describe as "glatt treif," not atypical among other Hillels around the country. Brandeis University president Abraham Sachar, moreover, requested that Greenberg not publicly wear his yarmulke on campus. Greenberg did not comply, and he came to be quite cognizant of the assimilative culture pervading Hillel organizations at that time, as Yavneh students also discovered in subsequent years.[15]

Given this background, when Yavneh was established it became Greenberg's ideal group—intellectually alive college students, committed traditional Jews who were seeking serious religious answers to serious questions. This was precisely his lonely predicament just a few years before. Hence, there was a profound meeting of the soul between Greenberg and many Yavneh students over a decade or more, and many became ardent devotees of his intellectual and religious positions. To be fair, it must be noted that he had his critics within Yavneh—some rather harsh—both among students and his colleagues: some perceived his educational emphasis on the value of a genuine synthesis of Judaism and the best of modernity to be excessive, some found his insistence on the importance of religious questioning even if it disturbed one's faith dangerous, and still others rejected as unfair his periodic and pungent public criticism of the intellectual failure of the *roshei yeshiva* and the intellectual timidity of their students. As one Yavneh founder put it, with an admitted tinge of religious regret given her perception of Greenberg's unacceptable contemporary religious views, "Yavneh made Greenberg." This may or may not be true, but however one feels about this issue, the opposite claim made by another founder of Yavneh in large measure is equally true: "Greenberg made Yavneh," certainly for the better part of the 1960s.

Without question, in his capacity as Chair of the NAB, Greenberg infused Yavneh students with his visionary ideals for a reconstructed Orthodox Judaism and helped steer them along to realize some truly path-breaking educational ventures. The speech he delivered to the third annual national Yavneh convention September 2, 1962, "Yavneh: Looking Ahead, Values and Goals," with idealistic passion outlined a blueprint for future Yavneh activities. It also foreshadowed Greenberg's own future Torah-centered but pluralist agenda, which he later took with him to CLAL and other institutional settings. Post-Emancipation and post-Holocaust Jews, he declared, live in revolutionary times, which called for nothing less than a fully revolutionized Jewish life with an intense devotion to God, Jews, and Jewish intellection on the one hand and an understanding of Jewish history that would propel Jewish destiny on the other. This goal would be fulfilled, he asserted, by Jews steeping themselves thoroughly in Jewish learning: Tanakh and Talmud, but also midrash, Jewish philosophy, literature, and history. Although Western Civilization was morally bankrupt, secular liberalism desiccated, and scientism in its death throes, Greenberg nevertheless insisted that Jews should take the best of Western Civilization and suffuse it with Torah, while illuminating Torah with the insights and achievements of Western culture. And because Jews live in a post-Holocaust era, religious Jews who seek to improve themselves educationally and spiritually ought to incorporate all Jews, even secularists, into their community of concern, and embrace all Jews, even the non-religious and those affiliated with other religious movements, and bring them closer to Torah. In the early 1960s, Yavneh students represented to Greenberg the vanguard of a revolutionary movement, espousing a compelling religious world view, a fresh educational approach, and a sound intellectual and philosophical Weltanschauung that could translate his imposing vision into reality. It is no wonder, therefore, that in 1964, he depicted the students of Yavneh as the "the first Jewish university generation that produced an intellectually revolutionary atmosphere and reorientation of Jewish attitudes and reevaluation of Jewish ideals and values."[16]

AN EDUCATIONAL REVOLUTION: YAVNEH'S ISRAEL INSTITUTE AT THE MERKAZ HARAV KOOK YESHIVA

Yavneh was an extraordinary educational pioneer during the 1960s. It sought to have Orthodox college students become Jewishly literate and transformed intellectually into sophisticated and religiously thoughtful, and hence elevated, Jews. But how was this to be accomplished? The organization's constitution mandated that each chapter was to conduct at least one weekly text shiur, one lecture per month, and one large function—for example, a day-long seminar or a weekend shabbaton dedicated to the study of a particular theme—each semester. Depending on the students' religious and educational backgrounds, the chapter's membership size, and access to rabbinical advisors in the city or region, different chapters in different geographic locations fulfilled these obligations to varying degrees. Additionally, the geographic regions (New York, Midwest, Atlantic, West, Canada) held programs uniting several chapters at least once a year for such regional events as weekend retreats or individual lectures by renowned Orthodox thinkers.

Without question, however, the organization's most striking and path-breaking educational innovations were its annual Labor Day National Conventions, Institutes for Summer Study, and Israel Institute, as well as its various publication projects. Highlighting the real originality of these undertakings, one can better appreciate what was missing from the Orthodox religious and cultural landscape of that time. Examined below is one such initiative.

In 1963, Yavneh inaugurated at the Merkaz Harav Kook Yeshiva in Jerusalem the first ever yeshiva study program in Israel specifically designed for American collegiates. It was hailed by Shaul Hochstein, former national treasurer of Yavneh and chair of its Israel Institute Committee in 1963-64, as "Yavneh's proudest achievement."[17] Both Mickey Hochstein (second Yavneh national president) and Jacques Gorlin (fifth Yavneh national president and a member of the first Merkaz Harav Yavneh class) credit Irving Greenberg's bold vision and guiding impetus for this novel undertaking, although strong general student interest in such a venture had also been voiced.[18] While finishing up his Fulbright year in Israel (1961-62), Greenberg received Gitelman's June 14 letter requesting that he investigate the possibility of a full-year Yavneh study-in-Israel initiative. Specifically, Gitelman wanted him to determine which yeshivot might be appropriate as a home base; how supplemental programs of study, of Tanakh and Jewish history for example, could be insinuated into a yeshiva curriculum; how the *roshei yeshiva* might react to the latter idea; who in Israel could emerge as a partner for Yavneh in this project; and what tuition costs for such an enterprise would be. Gitelman also proposed to work through the Jewish Agency to obtain potential subsidies for partiticipating Yavneh students. Greenberg took up the challenge with alacrity. By the time he headed home to the United States, he had already made key Israeli contacts with Dr. Chaim Chamiel of the Department for Torah Education and Culture of the Jewish Agency in Jerusalem and with Rabbi Chaim Druckman of the Merkaz Harav Kook Yeshiva.[19] And he had concretized some ideas as to how to proceed.

Greenberg returned from his sabbatical year impassioned by the vibrancy of Israel, deeply impressed by the intellectually sophisticated religious scholars/teachers of Tanakh whom he encountered there, particularly Nehama Leibowitz and Yehoshua Bachrach, and convinced that the Jewish future can be saved only by serious Torah study, pedagogically overhauled. As he proclaimed in September, 1962,

> Torah is still too much taught on the child's level of simple translation. This is inexcusable when in our classical commentators and in modern pedagogy in Israel, the profundity, relevance and excitement of Scripture have been brought out and taught. We know that in most places Talmud still gets the lion's share of the time students spend in Yeshiva at all levels. Yet, little has been done to make

vivid the religious implications, to eliminate the playing with texts in favor of a solid derech in learning, or to restore the wholeness of Talmud by proper attention to Agada. Little has been done with Jewish philosophy, history, literature. We feel these weaknesses sharply, when in college we are faced with the challenge of well formulated challenging philosophies.[20]

For Greenberg, this heartfelt analysis was not mere rhetoric, and he inspired some Yavneh students to share his passion. He preached the vital necessity of Yavneh students to engage in a full year of Torah study in an Israeli yeshiva environment, but with an expanded conception of what modern Torah study ought to include. In the third and final iteration of the Yavneh booklet advertising the Israel Institute, which clearly tried to enthuse its members, he grounded that conviction in the psycho-religious self-fulfillment rhetoric of Rabbi Yisrael Salanter, whom he quoted as saying: "You work at many jobs to make a living but you actually only live when you work at the job of making yourself a mensch." True, Greenberg observed, "We spend four years—and more—in college to train ourselves for a career," and that is as it should be; yet we need to develop our inner selves as well, and "in self-respect and conscience, we must spend at least one year working full-time at becoming a mensch."[21] And how is that to be done? In language reminiscent of any Orthodox advocacy of the primacy of Torah study especially in Israel, Greenberg proclaimed:

> For us, authentic existence is impossible without a deep understanding and experience of Torah. Yet despite Yavneh's efforts and Yavneh classes on campus, we know that our Jewishness is frankly secondary during the college years. Only a year of full time study of Torah, deepened by encounter with the holiness and pulsating life of Jerusalem and Israel, can begin to give the inspiration and knowledge of authentic Jewish living to illuminate a lifetime.

He then concluded, "so great is our need for such an experience, that if there were no Israel Institute, we would have to invent one. This is just what Yavneh has done."[22]

And so was born the Yavneh Israel Institute, which sponsored one full year of study in a specialized Yavneh program at Merkaz Harav Kook Yeshiva for men and at the Machon Gold Teacher Training Institute for women. Both were supposed to begin in Fall 1963, but only the men's program actually opened then; it was held in three successive years.[23] Administrative and financial factors initially dampened interest in the women's program, which was cancelled for 1963-64 and 1964-65. But after two years of negotiations among Yavneh, Machon Gold, and the Jewish Agency, Yavneh's women's program finally took place for one year, in 1965-66, corresponding to the final year of the men's program.[24] Although labeled a Yavneh program, in reality the young women were merely integrated into the regular Machon educational framework. Because there were fewer than fifteen students, Machon Gold and the Jewish Agency (which was footing most of the bill for foreign students and the extra personnel it would have to supply for additional separate Yavneh classes) would not permit a separate Yavneh curriculum with added teachers; nor did they assign to the girls a personal *madrichah* to attend to their specific needs, as the boys enjoyed in their Yavneh Merkaz Harav Kook program.

Until 1963, men from North America and Europe seeking yeshiva study in Israel generally ventured on their own to one of the two religious Zionist yeshivot, Kerem B'Yavneh and Merkaz Harav. Typically in these pre-1967 years, those participating came from especially strong Zionist homes and had been affiliated with religious Zionist youth groups such as Bnai Akiva. Yavneh's second national president, Mickey Hochstein, for example, studied at Kerem B'Yavneh in 1957-58, as did his two younger brothers, Shaul and Ben Zion. National president Martin Ritholtz (1967-68) studied there during 1963-64. Danny Tropper, eventual co-founder of Gesher, the Israeli organization which tries to build bridges between secular and religious Israelis, was one of the isolated Americans who studied at Merkaz Harav in the early 1960s.[25] In the course of that decade, however, the numbers of individuals joining both yeshivot gradually increased: Kerem B'Yavneh had 24 boys in 1964 and 40 in 1965; Merkaz Harav had less than a handful in the early 1960s and 10 in 1965.[26] As for women, some in this period who sought Jewish teacher training found their way to Machon Gold, although those enrolled in an educational degree program at Yeshiva University's Teachers Institute for Women often went there in larger group numbers for one half-year of study during the sixties.[27] One feature, however, was constant in all frameworks: learning in these yeshivot entailed totally integrating oneself into the existing institutional curriculum and daily routine.

For the men, Yavneh proposed an alternative, revolutionary program of study: a half-day of immersion in intensive Talmud learning, supplemented by a very un-yeshiva-like afternoon curriculum of assorted *shiurim* on Tanakh, midrash and aggadah, *mahshevet Yisrael* (Jewish thought), Jewish philosophy, and the history of halakhah, all to be located and incorporated within the institutional framework of Merkaz Harav Kook Yeshiva. Had the women's program succeeded in attracting sufficient numbers of students, its self-contained Yavneh program headquartered at Machon Gold would have offered a similar curriculum, supplementing courses in Tanakh and Hebrew language and literature with courses in *mahshevet Yisrael*, mishnah and midrash, but without study of Talmud.[28]

In the course of Fall 1962 and Spring 1963, a stream of ongoing communications and delicate negotiations took place between Irving Greenberg and

Rabbi Chaim Druckman of Merkaz Harav and between him and Dr. Chaim
Chamiel of the Jewish Agency's Torah Education Department in Jerusalem to
thrash out the precise details of a Yavneh Israel Institute. This Yavneh plan was
slated to be a three-way partnership and all three agents had to agree to its
terms. The issues concerned administrative logistics, yeshiva curriculum,
identity of teachers, costs and cost sharing,[29] and temporary living accommodations, since the yeshiva dormitory had not yet been finished. Beyond his
institutional interest, Druckman had a distinct personal stake in all the issues
as well, since he was scheduled to be the Yavneh *madrich* and main Talmud
teacher to its students.[30] (Appointed *rosh yeshiva* of Ohr Etzion in August
1963, just prior to the arrival of the first Yavneh contingent, Rabbi Druckman
was replaced by Rabbi Zephaniah Drori, "among the best and most established" students in Merkaz Harav. Today, Rabbi Drori is City Rav of Kiryat
Shmoneh and of its *hesder* yeshiva).[31]

Merkaz Harav was selected as the home for the men's Yavneh Israel Institute
because of its philosophy of Ahavat Yisrael, its location in Jerusalem, and its
willingness to work with the Torah Education Department of the Jewish
Agency, which offered great financial assistance both to the Yavneh applicants
and to the yeshiva itself. Cost for full tuition, board, tours, and airfare for the
first program year was $650; it was raised marginally to $695 in the second
year and to $750 in the third. Machon Gold, which charged several hundred
dollars more,[32] was chosen because at the time it was the only non-haredi religious institution offering post-high school learning for Orthodox women. Its
famed faculty, including Nehama Leibowitz, Yehoshua Bacharach, and Yonah
ben Sasson, was another critical reason for its appeal.

The unique feature of Yavneh's Israel Institute at Merkaz Harav was its
structural relationship to the yeshiva and its curriculum. Conceptually, the
proposed model was a special intellectual Jewish studies program of college
students integrated into the yeshiva, utilizing its faculty, staff, and facilities,
but one also set apart because of its distinctive classes and broader specialized
educational offerings. Both the structure and the curriculum were drastically
new ideas to a yeshiva, and ultimately proved not as workable in practice as
conceived in theory.

The actual logistics of enrollment and publicity for the Israel Institute were
handled by Yavneh students who had direct communications with the Jewish
Agency and Merkaz Harav staff. These students also had enormous responsibility for and bureaucratic oversight of the program, and served, with the advisory assistance of Irving Greenberg, as middle-men when problems arose.
Co-chairs of the Israel Institute in its first planning year of 1962-63 were
Ralph Dessau and, until her resignation after a few months, Lila Gelbart; chair
during the program's first year of operation was Shaul Hochstein (1963-64),

while Samuel Pilzer, alumnus of the first Institute program in 1963-64, chaired the Institute Committee during its final two years, 1964-66.

The Yavneh Israel Institute curriculum was essentially molded by Greenberg in consultation with Yavneh students. In the initial publicity brochure advertising the Institute, the curriculum called for three hours of intensive Talmudic study in the mornings led by Merkaz Harav faculty, paralleling the main yeshiva schedule. In the afternoons, however, a series of "Jewish Studies" *shiurim* was to be offered for the Yavneh group alone for two to four hours per topic per week.[33] Subjects included: Humash, stressing the analytic methodology of *parshanut* (commentary and interpretation) and comparison of medieval to modern commentators; *Nakh*, emphasizing the midrashic and philosophic points of view of the prophets, designed to crystallize their message; Oral law, seeking to understand its authority, transmission, and methodology; literature of the *Rishonim* and *Aharonim*, as a study for the sources of halakhah in each generation; *Dinim*, focusing intensively on laws in selected topics; Jewish philosophy and thought, concentrating on the great thinkers of the medieval age, such as Halevi, Rambam, Bahya and Chasdai Crescas, as well as modern thinkers—Samson Raphael Hirsch, Martin Buber, and Franz Rosenzweig—and the writings of Rav Kook. It was also expected that the young men would write an original research thesis in Jewish Studies by the end of the year. (Not one student in any of the three years attempted that kind of project.) In addition, the brochure promised an ongoing colloquium of guest speakers—prominent personalities and scholars on "topics related to Jewish Studies and the contemporary Israeli scene." The formal curriculum was to be supplemented with special Shabbat programs for the Yavneh boys, as well as various touring opportunities throughout Israel.[34]

Radical in conception, this projected curriculum reflected Greenberg's vision of a reconstructed Jewish education rooted in classic texts and sources as studied in a standard yeshiva on the one hand, but plumbing the depths of *mahshevet Yisrael*, Jewish philosophy, and the historical evolution of ideas and practices, both ancient and modern, on the other. Properly pursued, it was intended to relate classical texts to modern sensibilities, not the type of concerns ordinarily addressed in traditional yeshiva study. Equally important, Greenberg wanted the tradition to be studied deeply, but also to have its values and concept-world crystallized and mined with academic rigor. But the questioning was not to reflect merely dispassionate scholarly investigation for the sake of neutral scholarship—an intellectual orientation often advocated by academic Jewish scholars—but rather an investigation rooted in personal religious commitment. It was to be existentially transformative, revealing an implicit spiritual quest in the modern scholarly study of classical Jewish texts and world of thought. One can even speculate that perhaps what Greenberg conceptualized was a program that Yeshiva University should have been offering, but was not. At any rate, he was fully aware of the ground-breaking features of his model; as he noted with great understatement, "this program bids fair to be unique."[35] And indeed, the breathtaking conceptual sweep of this paradigm presaged an array of subsequent Israeli programs at all levels with similar intellectual ambitions, from university and post-university-oriented programs such as those at Midreshet Lindenbaum and the Pardes Institute to scholarly think tanks such as the Shalom Hartman Institute.

So much for the Yavneh Israel Institute in concept. What actually transpired in reality? The first thing to note is the program rigor's the young men had ample opportunity to be truly absorbed in a traditional style of learning, and those who were diligent made progress in their studies. In a letter to the national office on October 23, 1963, and published by *The Jewish Collegiate Observer* in its November 1963 issue, Jay Iskowitz of the first year group furnished the daily schedule of study in which the boys were immersed:

Daily *minyan*:	7:00am	
	(Shabbat, 7:30)	
First Talmud preparation seder:	8:30-11:30	
Talmud *shiur*:	11:30-12:30	Rabbi Zephaniah Drori

(9:30- 11:30: boys with limited Talmud skills were taught separately by Rabbi Drori's father)

Lunch:	12:30-1:00pm	
Minhah:	1:00	

(2:15-3:30pm: boys with weak Hebrew language skills received special and intensive language instruction in the Machon Gold premises, taught by one of its teachers)

Dinim:	3:00-4:15pm	Rabbi Chaim Steiner
Talmud review:	4:15-5:30pm	

Then other classes begin:

Navi: Sundays	5:30-7:00pm	Rabbi Yehoshua Bach-rach
Mahshevet Yisrael: Mon/Wed	5:30-7:30pm	Rabbi Zephania Drori
Torah She'bealpeh: Thursday	5:30-7:00pm	Rabbi Eliezer Eliner
Supper:	7:00-7:30pm	

Maariv:	7:30pm	
Free Time:	7:30-8:30pm	
Humash: two to four times/	8:30-9:45pm	Dr. Nehama Leibowitz
week		
Bedtime:	10:00pm	

Tuesdays after minhah and Fridays after 11:30am were free time, and the boys used these slots to write letters, travel, or study on their own or, when possible, with an Israeli *hevruta* (study partner). Some were intent on finishing all of Tanakh or all of the mishnah in their private study sessions.

As full as the educational program was, the ambitious intellectual scope and objective of Greenberg's vision was not fulfilled by Yavneh's program at Merkaz Harav; the Institute, so remarkable on paper, enjoyed only mixed success. Considerable structural, intellectual, and pragmatic variables worked against it. First, the Yavneh Israel Institute constituted an uneasy marriage between an established yeshiva and an outside college group, each having its own agenda. In part because of Yavneh's own sense of independence within the yeshiva, the latter never quite warmed to the Yavneh boys, who were tolerated but not truly integrated. Second, the atypical yeshiva centerpiece courses—Jewish philosophy and *mahshevet Yisrael*, so crucial to Greenberg's religious-intellectual design—were in fact not taught as specified in the advertised brochure. Instead, Rabbi Drori taught the Maimonides's *Sefer ha-Mada* and the philosophy of Rabbi Abraham Isaac Kook, but, unfamiliar with intellectually-oriented American youth, did so in a non-academic style that was uncongenial to many of them. Anticipating this situation, Greenberg had negotiated with the yeshiva for professors of philosophy from Hebrew University to teach the boys *mahshevet Yisrael* in the afternoon, an idea categorically rejected by Merkaz Harav. Rabbi Druckman insisted that the Yavneh Institute was to be a totally self-contained program that was fully consonant with the yeshiva ethos and style of thinking. It was forbidden, he stressed, even to create the impression that classes in Talmud and halakhah belonged to the yeshiva whereas classes in other disciplines of Torah belonged to the university. This bifurcation of valid Jewish learning to his mind was unacceptable. He conceded, however, that although Nehama Leibowitz and Yehoshua Bachrach were outsiders to Merkaz Harav Kook, their great religious scholarship and traditionalism rendered them appropriate for inclusion in this yeshiva program.[36]

An alternative proposal—that Yavneh students be allowed to attend Hebrew University classes in the afternoon—was similarly dismissed. Nonetheless, in the second year, one Yavneh student did routinely attend a weekly afternoon philosophy seminar at the Hebrew University (he later himself became a prominent professor of philosophy in the United States) despite Rabbi Drori's strongly-worded remonstrations against his behavior and despite the Yavneh brochure's explicit statement that "attendance at the Hebrew University will not be permitted under this program." Both the yeshiva and the Department of Torah Education of the Jewish Agency were quite upset.[37] And when Rabbi Drori subsequently perused the Institute's third year promotional booklet, which featured a picture and statement of yeshiva purpose by the revered former Chief Rabbi of Palestine and yeshiva founder, Rabbi Abraham Isaac Kook, but which also promised the study of "Samson R. Hirsch, Martin Buber and Franz Rosenzweig" at the yeshiva, he furiously demanded the deletion of these references in future editions of the brochure. Pilzer tried to allay his anger by informing him that delays in printing resulted in the brochure not being used in the advertising of the program. Moreover, he reassured him, any copies distributed in the future "will have the names of Buber and Hirsch blacked out with a special mark."[38] In sum, the conceptual chasm between yeshiva self-understanding and Yavneh mission was wide indeed, and, even in the best of circumstances, would have militated against the realization of Greenberg's pioneering vision. Samuel Pilzer stated the obvious when in Spring 1966 he informed Eliezer Eliner of the Jewish Agency in Jerusalem of Yavneh's decision not to renew its Israel Institute at Merkaz Harav Kook: "The desired aims and goals of accomplishment for the Program as seen by the yeshiva and Yavneh are in conflict."[39]

Finally, pragmatic issues during all three years contributed to the program's demise. First, the boys who participated were a heterogeneous lot. Some were postgraduate students, whereas others were undergraduates; two of the students were married. In addition, their wildly disparate levels of Hebrew language and abilities to parse, prepare, and understand Talmudic texts on their own undermined the coherence and effectiveness of the Yavneh year of study. Some were deficient in one area, some in both. Those who were relatively proficient in both were understandably bored and dissatisfied with the discourse and analysis, which they sometimes disparaged as remedial Talmud. A number of students were graduates of the intensive Hebrew language instruction of the Yeshiva of Flatbush or Ramaz, while others were enrolled in the beginner's courses of the Jewish Studies Program at Yeshiva University. To be sure, Rabbi Drori, who was in charge of this situation, tried valiantly to address it with special introductory courses in both Hebrew and Talmudic vocabulary and logic, and these were of some value. And, in fairness to him, he was not apprised of the differences in student educational backgrounds much in advance, even though he had requested such information. As late as August 18, 1963, he was still inquiring whether all the Yavneh boys had yeshiva background.[40] In the course of the Institute's first year, he and the Yavneh Institute committee agreed that boys in subsequent programs should study in an Israeli ulpan in the summer months prior to attending the yeshiva. Students, subjected to a Yavneh application process and interview, were subsequently cautioned to address their deficiencies in language and text skills. Yet nothing quite solved the dilemma of these disparities. Indeed, in all three years some students left the Yavneh *shiur* and tried to integrate into the Israeli yeshiva *shiur*; others left the Yavneh program and Merkaz Harav altogether and found more appealing learning environments in other American-sponsored or Israeli yeshivot in Jerusalem. Ultimately, this issue too played a major role in the program's cancellation. As Pilzer wrote Eliner on April 19, 1966, "The problem of a lack of common background could not be overcome."[41]

Differences in educational background, age, and life experience took their toll on group cohesiveness. But cultural disagreements between American youths and Israeli adults and differences in practical expectations—complaints *against* the boys of excessive clothes washing and complaints *by* the boys of poor food, poor accommodations, especially in the first year when the new yeshiva dormitory had not been ready (requiring temporary housing), and the lack of central heating—proved equally troublesome; they led to frequent misunderstandings and lack of mutual empathy between the Yavneh students and Drori, the yeshiva-appointed Israel Institute Director. Many in the Yavneh program over the years felt him to be too inflexible, and believed that his way of handling problems tended too often to exacerbate rather than resolve them. Not unexpectedly, one reads that Yavneh had thoughts of trying to replace him with the Jerusalem-based Rabbi Gabriel Cohen of Machon Greenberg and Machon Gold. Irving Greenberg even mused that perhaps Adin Steinsaltz could teach Talmud to the Yavneh boys.[42] These alternatives were never acted upon, and some students continued to be unhappy. Already in the first year, a few dissatisfied students left the program early and returned home; others followed suit in the second and third years.[43]

In the second year, the Program almost collapsed. It had only eight students to begin with, but two transferred to another yeshiva; another got engaged to an Israeli girl so his mind was elsewhere. Rabbi Drori feared that the Jewish Agency would not honor its financial commitment to the program—which would have had dire economic consequences for him as well. Moreover, he was very upset with what he considered inappropriate behavior of the boys. He felt two were doing too much socializing with girls from the university, a fact made easier by virtue of the cars which they had purchased. Moreover, some of the Yavneh boys caused disturbances in the bet midrash, listening to transistor radios while Israeli students were busy preparing for *shiurim*. And he found some of the books and newspapers in the boys' rooms objectionable and totally inconsistent with the values of the yeshiva.[44] All of this led him to suggest that if the Yavneh program were to continue, the yeshiva might have to separate it and the boys physically from the yeshiva premises. This new development precipitated a twofold reaction by Irving Greenberg. First, he personally wrote to the *rosh yeshiva* of Merkaz Harav, Rabbi Zevi Yehuda Kook, admitting foolish behavior on the part of some boys, promising that the next batch would be better, and beseeching him, for the sake of the religious needs of the American boys, not to separate them from the spiritually uplifting yeshiva environs. At the same time, he arranged for prominent Orthodox Rabbi Herschel Schachter, president of the Religious Zionists of America, to pen a very strong letter—the text of which Pilzer and Greenberg had written for him—praising the incredible importance of Yavneh and soliciting continued support of the Jewish Agency for its Israel Institute. Both Greenberg and Schachter received positive responses.[45]

During the third year, which found thirteen boys at Merkaz Harav and seven girls at Machon Gold, the heterogeneity problems resurfaced in both institutions, as did the general dissatisfaction experienced by some of the participants. The girls found Machon Gold stifling and over-regimented, a far cry from the independence they were used to at home. Two of the seven left by mid-year. Some of the boys also had difficulty adjusting. At least three went home early, and Pilzer was periodically writing response letters to the students and to Yavneh contacts in Israel trying to ascertain what the sources of unhappiness were and how to tackle them. By the end of the third year, all three institutions—Yavneh, Merkaz Harav and the Torah Education Department of the Jewish Agency—had become disillusioned. All acknowledged that the lack of common backgrounds ultimately made the program unworkable. In addition, from the Israeli perspective, the poor student caliber and what they perceived to be the diminished commitment of the Yavneh students proved most disappointing. From the Yavneh perspective, however, it was clear that Yavneh and Merkaz Harav Kook/Machon Gold in religious orientation, accustomed social habits, and world view were incompatible. The Yavneh Israel Institute at both places was therefore terminated with the conclusion of the Spring 1966 term.

The ultimate failure of the program should not discount Yavneh's various administrative attempts to have it succeed. For example, during all three years the Institute committee provided students with access to more culturally congenial Americans in Israel—to advise them, to lend a welcome ear when necessary, and to address their various concerns as they arose. These individuals also acted as official liaisons between the students and the national Yavneh office, furnishing vital information to the student chair of the Israel Institute and the Institute's Educational Advisory Council.[46]

During the first year, Rabbi Yecheskel Hartman of St. Louis, an advisor to the Yavneh chapter at Washington University on sabbatical leave from his synagogue, agreed to serve as official American *madrich* to the boys in the yeshiva, and he spent many hours talking with them.[47] In the second year and third years, Rabbi Gabriel Cohen, who taught at both Machon Chaim Greenberg and Machon Gold and who had been appointed to the Educational Advisory Council, occupied that role, advising the girls at Machon Gold in 1965-66 as well. In intermittent correspondence, he recorded his impressions of Institute conditions to Institute Committee chair, Samuel Pilzer.

Yavneh also responded to student complaints. In addition to taking up student issues in long-distance correspondence with Rabbi Drori and Jewish Agency personnel, on two occasions it sent representatives to Israel to investigate the facts on the ground and to recommend policy directions. In the summer of 1965, Lawrence Kobrin, member of Yavneh's National Advisory Board and of the OU's National Executive Committee and Chair of its Campus and Torah Tour Commission, was sent to Israel by Yavneh to discuss the status of the Israel Institute and to explore with staff from both the yeshiva and the Jewish Agency possible administrative, pedagogic and social improvements in the program. Charged with writing a confidential report for Yavneh, he submitted an eight page text on August 17, 1965, which, however, had no appreciable impact on shaping the third and final year of the Institute. But the report's comments on Machon Gold specifically foreshadowed the problems Yavneh's young women would experience in the following academic year with that institution's overbearing supervisory control. As it observed, "The Machon Gold discipline and educational framework is very rigorous and perhaps even a restricting one. This is due basically for two reasons: first, the discipline problem is considered to be a serious one in the case of a coeducational institution, and second, there is the desire to create an adequate religious atmosphere for those coming from countries where they cannot obtain it." But as Kobrin noted, Yavneh at this time had little choice but to work with that institution, "because there is very little alternative to continued participation in the Machon Gold," which, he remarked, was testimony to "the inadequacy of girls' education in Israel."[48]

In January 1966, Rabbi David Eliach, a member of the Yavneh NAB and of its Israel Institute's Educational Advisory Council, travelled to Israel seeking teachers for his Yeshiva of Flatbush high school. But he also fulfilled the mandate given him by the Israel Institute Committee and Yavneh National Executive Board to probe the state of the program. He spent much time during that month talking to students and seeing for himself the structure of the boys and girls programs at their respective institutions. Upon his return, he filed a report at the February 13, 1966 National Executive Board meeting, which judged the viability of the program and which spelled out the following recommendations and information:

1. both the girls and boys program should be discontinued
2. Yavneh should act as a clearing and referral agency only, recommending individual students to the Jewish Agency, which would then handle their suitable placement
3. the flaws in the girls' program was that it took six months for the girls to adjust to the "somewhat ghettoized" life at the Machon, which kept them on a very tight leash
4. the Machon was uncooperative in not providing Yavneh with needed information or working to finding a *madricha* for its students
5. the boys program was a *"kishalon harif,"* an utter failure: the heterogeneity of the students, the lack of ahavas Yisrael at Merkaz Harav [an ironic twist, since this characteristic was considered one of its strong points in 1963], and its narrow world views made it a poor fit for Yavneh. Indeed Kerem B'Yavneh was a more apt venue for such a yeshiva program, were it to be attempted in the future

The report contributed decisively to Yavneh's decision to terminate the program at both Israeli institutions. But it also echoed what by now everyone around the Yavneh leadership table already knew: "The crux of the problem is the philosophy of the yeshiva, which, in general, is opposed to that of the students whom we have sent to learn there. Therefore, even if we could change our *madrichim*, who have not been satisfactory, it would not remedy the basic problematic issue."

Despite the problems that ultimately doomed the Yavneh Israel Institute, several of the Yavneh participants in the Merkaz Harav program claim to have gained much from their participation in the Yavneh Israel Institute. Those who forwarded letters to the national office depicted both specific and general features of their experience as enjoyable and laudable.[49] They recalled with great fondness the intensely inspirational yeshiva prayer services during the high holidays, the deep immersion in Talmud study, particularly in the months immediately following the Sukkot holiday, the superb courses in halakhah within the yeshiva by Rabbi Chaim Steiner and *parshat ha-Shavua* with Rabbi Yehoshua Hadari, and the courses they took outside the yeshiva with Nehama Leibowitz and Yehoshua Bachrach of Machon Gold. In fact, some time at the end of the first year program, students were requested to fill out a questionnaire that probed their feelings, positive and negative, about their year at the yeshiva, and which asked for concrete suggestions for improvement. Apart from highly specific questions, two general ones were posed: Have your experiences contributed to your personal religious growth? To that, seven answered yes, one answered no, and two chose not to reply. A second broad question queried whether the objectives of the Yavneh Israel Institute had been realized: Nine answered yes, and only one responded with a no. Nonetheless, it is clear that any fair assessment of the program must admit that the Yavneh Israel Institute did not elicit the transformative intellectual and religious experience conceived by the idealistic vision of Irving Greenberg.[50]

In the course of the 1960s and early seventies, Yavneh continued to seek appropriate Israeli educational frameworks for its students. Already in 1964 and again in 1965, dissatisfied with Machon Gold's unforthcoming attitude in negotiating a women's program, Yavneh approached Rabbi Yehuda Copperman of the Michlalah-Jerusalem College for Women for a possible collaborative venture that would insert a Yavneh program into his school. He was not enthusiastic, because his school had just recently opened and had not yet graduated its first class. He wanted first to discern whether his fledgling institution had stability and a serious future before expanding it in other directions. He also feared negative pedagogic repercussions if a foreign program sent girls to study in his institution for only one year, commenting that such a program "could arouse serious and weighty educational and religious problems." His Israeli students attended the school for three years and received a B.A. degree upon completion of their studies. He did selectively accept qualified Americans who had committed to three years of study or who thought it likely they would stay for three years, but he did not open the Michlalah to foreign students coming for only one year of study until 1969, when those admitted studied *his* curriculum, not one that was imposed from without.[51]

Yavneh also attempted partnerships for full-year study with Bar Ilan University during 1967-68 and again in 1968-69. Fifteen applications were received in the first year. The program was to be led by Gerald Blidstein, but rescission of promised rank and salary scuttled the initiative.[52] In 1969, however, 38 students did go on a Yavneh-Bar Ilan Summer program. In the years after the exhilarating Israeli victory of the 1967 Six Day War, which galvanized a mass movement of Orthodox one-year post-high school study in a newly expanded and territorially-unified Israel, Yavneh still tried to arrange its own Israel programs. For three years, 1970-71, 1971-72, and 1972-73, it established the only existing joint religious and secular studies program for women in Israel, arranging with Machon Gold and Hebrew University to have its students spend morning hours in the former and afternoon hours in the latter, an arrangement not too dissimilar from Eliach's proposal (see note 52) except that in these instances Yavneh did not run its own religious institute. Thirteen girls participated in the first year, but only a handful did so in the two subsequent years. In 1971-72 an analogous men's program was created, headquartered in Beit Midrash L'Torah (BMT) and Hebrew University. Again, here too only a handful of men participated.[53] And so, despite the organization's persistence in soliciting Israeli settings for year-long study in the 1970s, it is apparent that the farsighted course of study enunciated by Irving Greenberg in the early 1960s was but a distant memory, as these religious schools offered their own curricula and the opportunity to earn American college credit for work done at Hebrew University.

Although the Yavneh Merkaz Harav Kook program did not quite succeed as imagined and was short-lived, it nevertheless testifies to the inspired vision of Irving Greenberg and the college organization to which he was spiritually and intellectually dedicated in the 1960s. Yavneh was the willing incubator for the gestation of his splendid ideas— on how to overhaul Jewish education and uplift the spiritual and intellectual levels of modern Orthodox Jewry, on how to integrate the best of Western thought with a fully lived committed Orthodox Judaism—and both the student organization and its rabbinic mentor benefitted enormously. History does not always unfold the way social revolutionaries and intellectual dreamers intend; sometimes ideas and ideals just cannot be realized. But that in no way should hinder us from acknowledging the dreams and admiring the dreamers, those who aspire to fresh realities, who envision a more religiously fulfilled, passionately engaged, and spiritually enthused Jewish people. Among them were members of Yavneh; among them is Irving Greenberg.

NOTES

1. It is with an abiding sense of *hakarat hatov* that I contribute this essay on Yavneh to a Festschrift honoring Rabbi Irving (Yitz) Greenberg. During my undergraduate collegiate years, this very special organization and this most singular personality decisively influenced my intellectual and religious maturation. Truth be told, in so many profound ways their influence endures to this very day, and I delight in publicly acknowledging my indebtedness to them.

2. I express my deep appreciation to Barbara Selya, Professor David Shatz, and Dr. Joel Wolowelsky for their helpful critical comments on the draft of this text.

3. In the early and late 1960s and again in the early 1970s, graduate students served as national presidents of Yavneh (Louis Dickstein, Yosef Blau, Richard Mandelbaum, Harvey Blitz, Henry Horwitz, Aaron I. Reichel, Matthew Hoffman), and the subject of how best to involve them periodically was discussed. In 1961, 1963, and 1973, the issue of whether or not to establish a post-graduate Yavneh association of alumni or some graduate structure was raised at national board meetings. That idea was never acted upon, but special programs specifically for post-graduates were planned during 1963-64, 1975-76, and 1978.

4. This was not true for national Hillel and its campus branches; nor was it the case for student Zionist groups as the Student Zionist Organization (est. 1954), Massada (1956), and Mizrachi Hatzair (1952), or synagogue and denominationally-based student and youth organizations such as NCSY (Orthodox; 1956), NFTY (Reform; 1939), ATID (Conservative; 1960) and USY (Conservative; 1950).

5. Reaffirming its autonomy, Yavneh continuously and successfully resisted the attempts by the Union of Orthodox Jewish Congregations of America (OU) and its Campus Commission to have it become, or merely even be listed as, an OU project, as the latter's college arm supplementing its high school NCSY organization.

6. In addition to Greenberg, the first board listed in January 1961 consisted of Rabbis Mordechai Pinchas Teitz and Norman Lamm, and Professors A. Leo Levin, Marvin Fox and Yitzchak Twersky. Soon thereafter, Rabbis Emanuel Rackman and Israel Wohlgelernter and Professor Michael Wyschogrod were added. Over the years, the board expanded and contracted; new names were appointed while other members were not renewed.

7. Rabbi Menachem Mendel Schneerson, the Lubavitcher Rebbe, author Herman Wouk, and religious Zionist leader Zevi Zinger all took note of and expressed great support for Yavneh. Their comments appear in the Yavneh archives which are in my possession. As well, academic Charles S. Liebman, wrote appreciatively of Yavneh. See his remarks, "Orthodoxy in American Jewish Life," *American Jewish Year Book* 66 (1965): 57.

8. Norman E. Frimer, "Telling It Like It Is," *The Jewish Horizon* (March-April 1968): 5. For Frimer's more extensive views on the situation of Jewish students on campus, see his *A Jewish Quest for Religious Meaning* (Hoboken, NJ, 1993), unit 3, "American Jewish Youth on Campus," pp. 187ff. He also served as regional Director of all metropolitan New York Hillel chapters, and subsequently as Dean of Yeshiva University's Stern College for Women (1967-68) and Director of International Hillel (1975-79).

9. Marshall Sklare, in his earliest edition of *Conservative Judaism: An American Religious Movement* (Glencoe, IL, 1955):43, limned Orthodox Judaism in America "as a case of institutional decay." So too Nathan Glazer, *American Judaism* (Chicago, 1957), held out little long term hope for it. Sklare famously changed his mind about Orthodoxy in his book's updated 1972 edition.

10. See the approving and appreciative comments on Yavneh by Rabbi Joseph Grunblatt, "Leadership in Jewish Life," *Jewish Life* (May/June, 1964):11 and Rabbi Ralph Pelcovitz, "The Challenge of College," *Jewish Life* (July/August, 1963):19, 21.

11. All of this is fleshed out in great detail in my forthcoming "Yavneh: The Greening of American Orthodox Judaism in the 1960s."

12. In addition to Joel Levine and Rivkah Teitz Blau, other students who participated in organizing this first conference included: Daniel Greer, Princeton University; Arnold Olshin, Cornell University; Steven Levinsohn and Moshe Meiselman, Harvard University; Eli Passow, MIT; Marilyn Lefkowitz, Rutgers University; Emanuel Landau, Michael Hochstein, Robert Levine, Columbia University; Linda Lieberman, Elona Meiselman, Sara Serchuk, Lori Wilner, Barnard College. Rivkah Teitz Blau, *Learn Torah, Love Torah, Live Torah: Harav Mordechai Pinchas Teitz: The Quintessential Rabbi* (Hoboken NJ, 2001), 239.

13. An insightful example of these problems at Yale University is discussed by Dan Oren, *Joining the Club: A History of Jews at Yale* (New Haven, 1985), 229-248.

14. This discussion is much expanded upon in my forthcoming comprehensive work on Yavneh. See note 11 above.

15. The source of this biographical material on Greenberg is a personal interview I held with him in Spring 1993. The tape is in my possession.

16. Citation of Greenberg comes from Yavneh's paper, *The Jewish Collegiate Observer* 2,1 (1964):1.

17. Letter of Shaul Hochstein to Yavneh members, May 27, 1964. All future references to letters pertaining to the Yavneh Israel Institute come from files by that name in the Yavneh archives, which are in my possession.

18. Joel Levine, first Yavneh national president, is noted as having called for a Yavneh Israel program in Yavneh's newspaper, *The Jewish Collegiate Observer*, December, 1962, p. 2. His fellow Columbia University student Ralph Dessau did so as well. See letter by Yavneh national president Zvi Gitelman to Irving Greenberg, June 14, 1962, in which he writes, "Ralph Dessau is pressing the idea of sending college students to learn in Israel."

19. Rabbi Chaim Druckman, later a prominent Knesset member of the Mafdal political party, was initially earmarked to be *madrich* [guide or coordinator] of the Yavneh program but he became appointed *rosh yeshiva* of Ohr Etzion in Merkaz Shapira, near Ashkelon, in August 1963.

20. Greenberg, "Yavneh: Looking Ahead, Values and Goals," *Yavneh Studies* 1 (1962): 50.

21. Introductory comments by Irving Greenberg in the third booklet promoting the Yavneh Israel Institute, 1966. In his June 3, 1965 letter to Yavneh student Samuel Pilzer, Chair of the Israel Institute at that time, he noted that this introductory letter to the booklet "is a bit more hard sell than I am used to giving and perhaps more than is wise for college students. But I felt strongly and it came out that way." Ironically, this third and most impressive of the booklets produced to market the program was printed too late for maximal mass distribution in Spring 1965 to promote the 1965-66 Israel Institute.

22. Ibid.

23. Thirteen students participated in 1963-64, eight in 1964-65, and eleven in 1965-66. Their names: 1963-64—Jerry Barach (who came with his wife Norma, who joined Machon Gold classes), Herbert Basser, George Brown, Jacques Gorlin, Abner Groff, Joel Iskowitz, Daniel Jacoby, Stanley Kandel, David Koenigsberg, Samuel Pilzer, Aryeh Routtenberg, Alan Shapiro, and Glen Stengel. (On this group, the archives contain clear information about their college affiliation. Students from the first year program came from: Harvard, Northwestern, University of Pittsburgh, UCLA, NYU, City College of New York, Yeshiva University and Columbia University.) 1964-65—Allan Cohen, Richard Fiedler (came with his wife), Melvin Genauer, Dale Gottllieb, Alan Grossman, Harvey Makovsky, Ronald Roness, and Fred Levi. (Among the schools represented by boys from the second group that I have been able to determine were Brandeis, McGill, University of Maryland, Yeshiva University.) 1965-66—Charles Brand, Donald Davis, Edward Fritz, Samuel Johnson, Norman Kravetz, Moshe Poupko (came with his wife), Stanley Raskas, Joseph Rine, Roy Rosenbaum, Steven Schneid, and Ellis Sultanik.

24. The seven student participants included: Maxine Frank, Esther Ingber, Deborah Gellis, Edna Kreiser, Sheila Kolitch, Sue Ellen Samet, and Marcia Wilen.

25. Coincidentally, his co-founder was Yerah Glatter, Yavneh shaliah from 1971 to 1974.

26. Costs to the students were minimal; tuition and board was defrayed by the Department of Torah Education and Culture of the Jewish Agency, and the boys had to pay only airfare and sundry expenses.

27. Until the late sixties, Machon Gold was a coeducational teacher training institute for international students who would return to their countries of origin and enter the Jewish educational profession. Students came there from North and South America, Europe, Asia and Turkey. In the sixties, students enrolled in the B.Ed. degree program at Yeshiva University's Teachers Institute for Women were strongly encouraged to spend six months at Machon Gold as part of their teacher training; most went, as many as ten to twenty per year. The vast majority of expenses for students pursuing a teacher training certificate at Machon Gold was underwritten by the Department of Torah Education of the Jewish Agency. Other Israeli venues open to Americans at that time were: Machon Greenberg, AZYF's Summer Institute for College and Young Adults, SZO's High School for Summer Institute, Jewish Educators' Seminar in Israel, and Camp Ramah in Israel. None shared Yavneh's goals. See *A Guide to Israel Programs, 1966* published by the Information Department, Jewish Agency for Israel—American Section, 1-20.

28. See the June 17, 1965 letter of Rabbi Zevi Tabory of the Department of Torah Education and Culture of the Jewish Agency, New York to Samuel Pilzer, the June 28, 1965 letter of Eliezer Eliner of the Department of Torah Education and Culture of the Jewish Agency, Jerusalem to Pilzer, and the minutes of Pilzer's orientation session to Yavneh applicants to the women's program, March 14, 1966.

29. The Torah Education and Culture Department of the Jewish Agency in New York promised $1000 per student for groups of at least ten men and ten women. Additional subsidies per student were offered by its Jerusalem office to the two participating Israeli institutions directly to cover their costs of student board and their administrative and teaching staff.

30. See the letters from Druckman to Greenberg, February 19, 1963 and May 19, 1963. See too letters from Chamiel to Greenberg, October 3, 1962, January 1, 1963, January 8, 1963, March 17, 1963, April 13, 1963, April 18, 1963, and May 19, 1963. Since we do not have Greenberg's letters to them, we must infer from the various replies what Greenberg must have requested or proposed.

31. Letter of Chaim Druckman to Shaul Hochstein, August 15, 1963.

32. Students pursuing a teaching certificate, however, received substantial reductions in cost. That was one of the unappealing features for potential Yavneh students who by and large were uninterested in the teaching certificate curriculum. Had they joined that educational track, they would have been eligible for scholarships of over $400 each, which they did not receive as mere "non-educational" students in the Machon program. See the letter of national Yavneh president, Louis Dickstein to Phyllis Render, May 24, 1963, explaining the cancellation of the first year women's program. See too the letter of Samuel Pilzer to Dr. Shmuel Borenstein of the Jewish Agency's Torah Education Department in Jerusalem, December 23, 1964, asserting the principle that the cost of the girls' program should be equal to and not exceed that of the boys.

33. It is interesting that the first two brochures classified these *shiurim* under the rubric "Jewish Studies" rather than, say, *Limudei Kodesh*, and set them apart as a distinctive category from the subject classification of Talmud. The third and final booklet made no such bifurcation and categorized each subject of study under its own heading.

34. The second and third brochures for 1964-65 and 1965-66 offered a bit more candor about what actually took place with respect to Talmud: four hours each morning, plus two additional hours each day that students were expected to prepare on their own.

The rest of the curricular outline pretty much followed the first booklet text. The third booklet, however, was unique in other respects. It included a picture of Rabbi Abraham Isaac Kook, founder of the yeshiva, with a quotation of his providing the mission of the yeshiva; a signed introductory statement by Irving Greenberg; a picture of former Yavneh boys studying in the yeshiva; a listing of the faculty, with Dr. Nehama Leibowitz's name separated and excluded from the alphabetical listing of the teaching personnel (this had to do with gender—Rabbi Yehoshua Bachrach, who was not a faculty member of the yeshiva was nonetheless incorporated in the appropriate place in this list); and a comprehensive list of the Educational Advisory Council established by Yavneh president Jacques Gorlin in late 1964. See note 46 below. All of this was intended to professionalize the marketing of the Institute with a more attractive brochure.

35. Greenberg, "Yavneh: Looking Ahead," 51.

36. Letter of Chaim Druckman to Irving Greenberg, February 19, 1963.

37. The first two Yavneh brochures couched that statement within a broader context, stipulating right after that prohibition that "this program has been arranged so as to free both summers for attendance of [Hebrew University] summer sessions." In light of this student violation in year two and the upset it caused, in reply to the anger of the Israeli hosts the Yavneh Institute committee had its brochure announcing the third year of study delete this last statement. In a visibly pronounced page placement that no reader could miss, there appeared a simple stand-alone sentence declaring that Hebrew University attendance is not permitted.

38. See Pilzer's letter to Drori, June 3, 1965. Why Pilzer chose these two names and did not include Rosenzweig is not clear. Why Drori objected to the study of Hirsch is also not clear.

39. See Pilzer to Eliner, April 19, 1966.

40. He was upset to learn that they were not. See the letter of Rabbi Yecheskel Hartman to Shaul Hochstein, August 18, 1963. Hartman, having met Drori for the first time, wrote that "he is quite a guy and would like to plan a top-notch program for our students." Hartman's role is discussed in the text below.

41. Student letters make that point repeatedly. See, for examples, the letters of David Koenigsberg to Shaul Hochstein, November 28, 1963; Danny Jacoby to the Yavneh national office, December 5, 1963; and Richard Fiedler to Samuel Pilzer, March 24, 1965.

42. See letter by Pilzer to Gabriel Cohen, May 21, 1965. In Spring 1965, rumors reached New York that Drori himself was thinking of quitting his position. See Samuel Pilzer to Gabriel Cohen, May 20, 1965.

43. Students who cut short their stay faced an additional problem. Yavneh had written letters to their local Selective Service Boards requesting on their behalf draft deferments and permission to leave the country because of their participation in the Israel Institute. Pilzer notified those who sought an early return that he would have to inform the Selective Service of their departure from the program, thus making them eligible to be drafted.

44. How he came to be familiar with their rooms' contents was not spelled out.

45. Greenberg to Rabbi Zevi Yehuda Kook, July 5, 1965; Herschel Schechter to Chaim Chamiel, July 23, 1965.

46. An official Educational Advisory Council to the Israel Institute established in late Winter 1964 by national president Jacques Gorlin, who himself had been on the first program along with Pilzer. See *The Jewish Collegiate Observer*, February, 1965,

announcing the Council. Other members of this Council included: Rabbi Gabriel Cohen, teacher in Israel's Machon Greenberg and Machon Gold; Rabbi David Eliach, principal of the Yeshiva of Flatbush High School; Martin Golding, professor of philosophy, Columbia University; Rabbi Steven Riskin, Jewish Studies Program, Yeshiva University; Michael Shmidman, professor of Political Science, Brooklyn College; Rabbi Zevi Tabory, Department of Torah Education and Culture, Jewish Agency; and Rabbi Zephania Drori, Israeli Director of the Yavneh Israel Institute. The ostensible mission of this Council was to advise students interested in participating (which Riskin, in particular, did—some of his JSP students joined the Yavneh program) and to help in the planning of courses. In reality, not much changed from year to year on the courses, so that the Council, as a body, for the most part was a paper organization lending more visibility and status by its name to the program literature. Individual members, however, such as Cohen and Eliach, played some important roles. See text below on the special investigative report of David Eliach.

47. Refer to the April 26, 1963 letter of Ranon Katzoff, Yavneh Midwest Regional Vice-President and a member of the Israel Institute Committee, to Yecheskel Hartman. See too Hartman letters to Shaul Hochstein, August 19, 1963 and October 27, 1963.

48. See the Lawrence Kobrin report, August 17, 1965, pp. 3-4. The coeducational aspect of the institution became so untenable, that by 1968-69 the Torah Education Department of the Jewish Agency spun off a separate school for young men, Beit Midrash L'Torah (BMT), and, in consequence, transformed Machon Gold into an exclusively women's institution. In reality, there was one other potential women's institution with which Yavneh could have worked out a joint program, the Michlalah Jerusalem College for Women, founded by Rabbi Yehuda Copperman. And Yavneh did attempt to make arrangements with him. See text below. Kobrin's report reaffirmed what Yavneh Institute officials in New York had previously learned from correspondence with Copperman, that he was not interested in a large number of foreign students who would come to study only for one year.

49. See letters to the national office of first-year students Jacques Gorlin, *The Jewish Collegiate Observer*, February 1964, David Koenigsberg, November 28, 1963, Jay Iskowitz, October 23, 1963, and of second-year students Harvey Makovsky, *The Jewish Collegiate Observer*, November, 1964, Ronald Roness, September 14, 1964, Allan Grossman, April 8, 1965, and of third year student Edward Fritz, February 24, 1966.. Then too one must recall the herculean efforts of Samuel Pilzer as Chair of the Israel Institute after having spent the first year there; he would hardly have invested the time and effort if he had not enjoyed a positive experience or if he thought the program not worthwhile.

50. In addition to taped interviews with several of the participants on these various Yavneh Merkaz Harav programs that are in my possession, one can consult the personal website of Dale Gottlieb, formerly professor of philosophy at Johns Hopkins, and now Dovid Gottlieb, rabbi/educator at the Ohr Sameach Yeshiva in Jerusalem, for reactions to his year of study as a Yavneh Merkaz Harav student. See www.dovidgottlieb.com/comments/coming_h.htm. My thanks to Professor David Shatz for this information.

51. See letters of Rabbi Copperman to Samuel Pilzer, December 23, 1964 and April 10, 1965.

52. A full file-folder tracing the negotiations between Yavneh and Bar Ilan exists in the archives. It should be noted that Dr. Eliach's report of February 13, 1966 to the

National Executive Board enthusiastically endorsed partnering with Bar Ilan University. He thought that Yavneh could open its own institute in Israel, as a combination of a yeshiva and a university. It could create a *machon*, provide *shiurim* and find a qualified *rosh yeshiva* who would give morning classes, and then Yavneh students would join the Bar Ilan academic program in the afternoon. He further suggested that if the program succeeded in the first year for American students, then it could be opened to Israeli high school graduates. He stressed that such a program would be organized as a university, not bet midrash, and that Yavneh should strive for an opening date of 1967 or 68. He had one other intriguing thought. Politically in Israel the yeshivot and Bar Ilan stood opposed in outlook. Perhaps, he mused, the Yavneh program outlined above would bridge the gap somewhat. Finally, he remarked that at the university it would be possible to join both the girls' and boys' programs together, and that subjects such as Torah and Shulhan Arukh would be taught by instructors who had secular as well as religious backgrounds and who felt that there could be a synthesis between Torah and *madda*.

53. In February 1976, Yavneh announced a study program for the forthcoming year at the David and Fela Shapell College of Jewish Studies in Jerusalem. By May, 1976, eight students had been accepted into the program: Suzi Dostis, Joyce Herman, Ann Morgendstern, Allen Samson, Robin Schwartz, Gary Sherwood, Sheldon Wayman, and Leon Weitz. See the letter of May 20, 1976 from Yavneh Shaliah Yehoshuah Ben-Meir to Rabbi Galinsky of the Jewish Agency in New York. Unlike the material on the Israel Institute of 1963-66, however, the archives are silent about this program, and, indeed, whether it actually took place or not, and, if it did, with what results. On the other hand, there is a sharply worded mailgram sent by Yavneh national president Mory Korenblit to Rabbi Elefant of Yeshivat Itri expressing shock that the head of Shapell College, renowned educator Rabbi Chaim Brovender, had resigned. Korenblit appeals to Elefant to have Brovender reconsider. "We are very concerned," Korenblit stated, "that the new administration should continue the same type of program with the atmosphere and *hashkafah* of *ahavat am yisrael vieretz* [sic] *yisrael*. ...[Yavneh] will reevaluate the program based on these developments. We hope that Shapell will continue to be a yeshiva that Yavneh and American Orthodoxy can be proud of." Whether the departure of Brovender from Shapell's had an impact on the Yavneh's participation in 1976-77 I can not say from the documents available.

14

The Message of the Gog Pericope, Ezekiel Chapters 38-39

Jacob Milgrom

My friendship with Yitz began when our children moved from California to Riverdale. Till then I knew of Yitz only through his writings, Now I could meet the man. Whenever we were in New York a visit with Yitz and Blu accompanied our visit with our children. Happily, this continues when the Greenbergs are in Jerusalem.

What was said of King Saul applies to Yitz, *wayyigbah mikkāl- hā-ām miššikmô wāmā̆ălâ,* "he rose head and shoulders above all the people."(ISamuel 10:23). We are talking not of height, but of stature. Our Torah dialogues together made me realize how his students could say "I majored in Yitz Greenberg". He enabled his students to recognize the possibility of synthesizing the lessons of Jewish history with the challenges of Jewish commitment in our own age.

Ezekiel 38-39 deals with the demolition of Israel's surrounding hostile nations, which invade the land of Israel and are buried there. These chapters have been inserted in between the miraculous return of exiled Israel to their homeland (36-37) and the description of Ezekiel's visionary sanctuary (40-46). A chronological, if a historical, picture emerges: the resurrection, redemption and resettlement of all twelve tribes of Israel (47-48).

A major question concerns Ezekiel's theology. As a priest he is the scion of the Holiness School, which projects the following blessing for Israel, "I will grant peace in the land, so that you shall lie down, and no one shall make you afraid; I will eliminate vicious beasts from the land, and *no sword shall traverse your land*" (Leviticus 26:6).[1] This means that the enemy will be stopped at the border; God will not permit his land to be penetrated by any hostile force. Why then were Gog and his fully armed hordes permitted to enter? Moreover, considering that subsequent to Gog's annihilation on the mountains of Israel

(Ezekiel 38:8; 39:4) the Israelites would have to expend unlimited energy and time (at least seven months, 39:12) in burying the strewn enemy corpses and in purifying the land (39:16). Instead, in keeping with Leviticus 26:6, let the enemy be held at bay at the land's borders, and no sooner is Israel resettled (miraculously) in its land (Ezekiel 36-37), it can engage in learning the architecture and laws of the visionary sanctuary which YHWH has revealed to Ezekiel (chaps. 40-46), followed by the fecundation of the barren parts of the land and the division of the land equally among the twelve tribes (chaps. 47-48). In other words, according to the view of the redactor(s) of Leviticus, Ezekiel 38-39, the Gog chapters, would be entirely superfluous!

The answer lies in the explicit objective of the divine intervention in 38-39. Not only does it propose to rescue Israel from its avowed enemies, but also to enlarge and sanctify the name of YHWH among the nations (38:23). These nations have witnessed YHWH inviting the Babylonians, (or lacking the ability to prevent the Babylonians) to enter the land, raze its temple and exile its inhabitants (chaps. 1-10). Now, YHWH will again enter the land, but this time to destroy the very nations that have invaded the land to plunder its inhabitants (38:12). The divine principle of "measure for measure" is in operation. The nation(s) that entered the land to devastate it will now be devastated on Israel's mountains. Indeed, chaps. 38-39 are quintessentially the heart of the Gog pericope.

There is yet another message devolving from the placement of chaps. 38-39. Ezekiel is telling his progeny that Israel's settlement on its land cannot be secure unless the hostile nations that surround it are neutralized or destroyed, a lesson that informs zionist history to this very day.

The Gog pericope terminates with the claim of YHWH *'ăšer šāpaktî 'et-rûḥî 'al-bēt yiśrā'el*, *for I have poured out my spirit on the house of Israel* (39:29). What does this mean? The *rûaḥ YHWH*, 'Spirit of *YHWH*' represents the divine power, which is metaphorically an independent force: On earth, the Spirit takes the form of the wind; in creation, *'ōśeh mal'ākāyw rûḥôt*, 'he made the winds his agents', to blow the waters to their assigned place (Psalms 104:4, 8). The *rûaḥ* can be a lying spirit (*šeqer*) and deceive all the king's prophets (1Kings 22:22). This Spirit, moreover, has the power to effect the nature of man: as an artist, Bezalel is endowed with *rûaḥ 'ĕlōhîm bĕḥōkmâ ûbitĕbûnâ ûbĕda'at ûbĕkol-mĕlā'kâ*, 'divine spirit or skill, ability and knowledge in every craft' (Exodus 31:3); as a warrior, *wattiṣlaḥ rûaḥ-'ĕlōhîm 'al-šā'ûl*, 'the Spirit of God gripped Saul' (1Samuel 11:6); as a prophet, *wayyā'ṣel min-hārûaḥ 'ăšer 'ālyāw wayyittēn 'al šibě'îm hazzĕqēnîm*, ' he [God] drew upon the Spirit that was in him and put it upon the seventy elders' (Numbers 11:25); *mitnabbě'îm bammaḥăneh*, 'acting the prophet in the camp' (Numbers 11:27); as a leader, *wĕnāḥâ 'ālāyw rûaḥ YHWH rûaḥ ḥokmâ ûbînâ rûaḥ gĕbûrâ rûaḥ 'ēṣâ ûda'at wĕyir'at YHWH*, 'the Spirit of YHWH shall alight upon him: a

Spirit of wisdom and insight, a Spirit of counsel and valor, a Spirit of devotion and reverence for YHWH' (Isaiah 11:2). The divine Spirit is unstinting in its endowment, *ki 'eṣṣāq-mayim 'al ṣāmê wěnôzělîm 'al-yabbāšâ 'aṣṣōq rûḥî 'al zar‘ēkā* 'Even as I pour water on thirsty soil, and rain upon dry ground, so I will pour my Spirit on your offspring' (Isaiah 44:3).

The editor(s) of chaps. 38 and 39 graded the Gog invasion and annihilation so that in chap. 38, it was predicted for the far off future *miyyāmîm rabbîm*, 'after a long time' (38:8); *bě'aḥărît haššānîm* 'in the distant future' (38:8); *bě'aḥărît hayyāmîm*, 'in the distant future' (38:16). But in chap. 39, the advent of Gog successively narrows in time. At first, Gog and his horde are turned towards and brought to the mountains of Israel, *wěšōbabtîkâ...wahăbi'ôtîkâ 'al-hārê yiśrā'ēl*, 'I have turned you around...and brought you to the mountains of Israel' (39:2); the day of the annihilation of Gog and his horde has come: *hinnē bā'â wěnihyātâ* 'it has come' (39:8). The victory banquet: *'emōr lěṣippôr kol-kānāp*, 'proclaim to every kind of scavenger bird' (39:17). The immediate consequence:: *'attā 'āšîb 'et-šěbî[û]t ya‘ăqōb*, 'NOW[2] I will return the fortunes of Jacob' (39:25), for the restored people of Israel was showered with YHWH's spirit: *wěšāpaktî 'et-rûḥî 'al-bêt yiśrā'ēl*, 'for I have poured[3] out my spirit on the house of Israel' (39:29).[4]

Ezekiel avers that the divine Spirit has already been poured out over the house of Israel. He is not referring to the gift of life which was endowed upon Israel by YHWH's *rûaḥ* (37:14). It seems clear that he alludes to the spirit of prophecy, in answer to the challenge enunciated by Moses, *ûmî-yitten kol-‘am YHWH někî'îm kî-yitten YHWH 'et-ruḥô 'ălēhem*, 'Would that all YHWH's people were prophets, that YHWH put his Spirit upon them' (Num 11:29). The prophet Joel prophesies that Moses' fervent hope will be fulfilled in the future "I will pour out my Spirit on all (Israelite) flesh; your sons and daughters shall prophesy; your men shall dream dreams, and your young men shall see visions. I will even pour out my Spirit upon male and female slaves in those days" (Joel 3:1-2). Such is a distant eschatological vision, but Ezekiel is bestowing the gift of prophecy *on his own generation*.

By what measure do they merit it? Ezekiel has good reason to presume that his (exiled) generation is worthy of responding to the Mosaic challenge. First, like the Mosaic generation, it experienced exile and redemption and is poised upon entering, possessing and allocating the Promised Land (Ezek 48). Second, unlike the Mosaic and every other generation, it is *incapable of sinning*. It has been purified and given a new heart and a new Spirit, *'ăšer-běḥuqqay tēlēkû ûmišpāṭay tišměrû wa‘ăśîtem*, 'I will cause you to follow my laws and faithfully to observe my rules' (Ezekiel 36:25-27; cf. 11:17-21). Ezekiel had already inherited Jeremiah's prophecy that exiled Israel will be restored to its land and will be given "a single heart and a single nature to revere me [YHWH] for all time...

and I will put into their hearts reverence for me so that they do not turn away from me" (Jeremiah 32:39-40); "I will make a new covenant with the house of Israel and the house of Judah. Not like the covenant that I made with their fathers...which covenant of mine they violated... But this is the covenant that I will make with the house of Israel...*I will put my teaching inside of them and write it on their hearts* (Jeremiah 31:31-34 [30-33]).[5]

Ezekiel both incorporates and expands Jeremiah's prophecy. "I will sprinkle pure water upon you and you shall be clean...and I will give you a new heart and I will put a new spirit into you...Then I will cause you to follow my laws and faithfully to observe my rules" (Ezekiel 36:25-27). What Jeremiah and Ezekiel prophesied, Ezekiel sees fulfilled. The exiles will have been restored to their land (Ezekiel 38:8, 11, 14) and its enemies will have been destroyed. (39:1-21). YHWH then promises "Never again will I hide my face from them, for *I have poured out my Spirit*[6] upon the house of Israel" (39:29). Just as *miyyāmîm rabbîm* 'after a long time' and *bě'aḥărît haššānîm* 'in the distant future' (38:8) turn out to be an imminent NOW (39:8), so the final chorus of the Gog oracle moves the action forward. Possessing a new heart (36:25), meaning that Israel is unable to sin, renders it eligible to receive *rûaḥ YHWH*, the ability to prophesy.

Ezekiel also maintains that the redeemed Israel will be governed by an egalitarian principle. All superior offices and office holders will be abolished. Thus, there is no king; his duties will be reduced to that of the civil leader called *nasi* 'prince' (Ezekiel 44:15.31). There will be no high priest; his duties and prohibitions will be shared by all the priests (45:15.27). The promised land will be divided equally among all the tribes. Every resident, including the alien, will receive inheritable landed property, (47:22-23); chap.48 et passim). The capitol city will be accessible to all Israel and its maintenance the equal responsibility of all the tribes (48:30-35).

The egalitarian doctrine also holds for the prophetic office; Ezekiel is slated to be the last messenger prophet. Henceforth every Israelite, men as well as women, (note, *bêt yiśrāʾel* 'the house of Israel', not *běnê yiśrā el,* ' sons of Israel', 39:29) will be a "prophet" (cf. Joel 3:1-2,above), able to receive the divine word directly, because all intermediaries between Israel and God will disappear. In the post-Gog world, every Israelite, suffused by *YHWH's ruaḥ* 'spirit', will be directed by the will of *YHWH*.

The yearning of Moses to be the founder of a nation of prophets is therefore predicted by Ezekiel to occur in his own generation.

NOTES

1. See J. Milgrom, *Leviticus* 23-27(New York: Doubleday, 2001), 2295-9

2. Ezekiel frequently updates his prophecies by use of 'attâ 'NOW': 7:3, 8; 19:13; 23:43; 26:18; 43:9.

3. The distinction must be carefully made between *nātan rûaḥ* and *šāpaq rûaḥ* in Ezekiel. The former is used when the divine spirit placed (*nātan*) in the heart provides life to the carcass (37:14) or prevents the human being from sinning (36:27). As indicated above, when the divine spirit is poured (*šāpak*) on a person, he is elevated to prophetic status.

4. Cf. D.I. Block, "Gog and the Pouring Out of the Spirit," *Vetus Testamentum* xxxvii (1987) 257-68.

5. For further details, see M. Greenberg, *Ezekiel 21-37* (New York: Doubleday, 1997), 735-40.

6. *'ăšer šāpaktî 'et-rûḥ î* is so rendered by New American Bible; cf. Revised English Bible, taking account of the perfect.

15

The Fate of Hope in a Time of Renewed Antisemitism

Alvin H. Rosenfeld

I

"Jewish history affirms hope." These words appear at the end of Irving Greenberg's seminal essay on religious faith after Auschwitz, "Cloud of Smoke, Pillar of Fire."[1] Readers who encounter them within this study, subtitled "Judaism, Christianity, and Modernity after the Holocaust," might find the note of optimism surprising and, given the context, even discordant. In fact, Greenberg is able to sound it only after a torturous intellectual and spiritual confrontation with Jewish history at its most tormented. Such encounters are risky, for they expose one's most deeply-held beliefs to an order of human experience that can readily subvert them. As a scholar of the Nazi period, Greenberg has taken those risks, knowing that as a consequence his previous understandings of both God and man might be radically altered. His text is an unsettling one, for he presents in restrained but wrenching detail some of the Holocaust's most gruesome atrocities, including the burning alive of Jewish children in the fire pits of Auschwitz, a horror that is clearly seared into his consciousness. A faithful Jew, he remains committed to Judaism's fundamental affirmations of life, but the massive counter-testimony of the Nazi genocide of the Jews brings him to the edge of silence. In a memorable formulation, he concludes that "no statement, theological or otherwise, should be made that would not be credible in the presence of the burning children."[2]

If one takes this proposition literally and faces up to the challenge it poses, one is also brought to the point of silence. For it is difficult, if not impossible, to think of *any* positive statements one might plausibly make about life in the presence of such savagery. If "Jewish history affirms hope," it is, after the Shoah, a tenuous hope, constantly undermined by the human capacity for evil. In the author's cautionary words, "After Auschwitz one must beware of easy hope....Any hope must be sober, and built on the sands of despair, free from illusions."[3]

As Greenberg sees it, then, hope sits in dialectical tension with its opposite, and affirmations can be had only by acknowledging events that threaten to negate them. Greenberg seems to recognize as much when he writes: "If there is any imperative at all that bursts forth from the hell of Auschwitz and Treblinka...it surely must be: Never again!"[4]

To the degree that feelings of intense moral revulsion can be expressed in a single short phrase, "never again" does that, registering in two simple words absolute recoil from the Nazi crimes. The phrase also conveys an impassioned resolve to oppose anything remotely like a repeat of those crimes. In using this language, Greenberg expresses sentiments that are broadly shared by other Jews and, presumably, people of conscience everywhere. And yet, contrary to the assumption that unconditional opposition to anti-Jewish hostility has been universally embraced in the post-Holocaust period, recent events indicate that antisemitism is once again resurgent. Greenberg could not have foreseen these developments when he wrote his essay some four decades ago; but, in the words of Sir Jonathan Sacks, the Chief Rabbi of the United Kingdom, in our days "never again [has] become ever again."[5]

As evidence, consider the following. In 2006, the British parliamentarian, Denis MacShane, chaired a high-level commission appointed by Tony Blair to examine the growing problem of antisemitism in today's Britain. Here are a few of his conclusions:

> Hatred of Jews has reached new heights in Europe and many points south and east of the old continent....Synagogues [are being] attacked. Jewish schoolboys jostled on public transportation. Rabbis punched and knifed. British Jews feeling compelled to raise millions to provide private security for their weddings and community events. On campuses, militant anti-Jewish students fueled by Islamist or far-left hate seeking to prevent Jewish students from expressing their opinions.
>
> More worrisome was what we described as anti-Jewish discourse, a mood and tone whenever Jews are discussed, whether in the media, at universities, among the liberal media elite or at dinner parties of modish London. To express any support for Israel or any feeling for the right of a Jewish state to exist produces denunciation, even contempt.[6]

The hostility that Mr. MacShane describes has not abated since he and his colleagues filed their report. Indeed, it has grown within his own country. Nor are antisemitic utterances and antisemitic acts confined to Great Britain.

Especially with respect to Israel and its supporters, we are witnessing *more* openly expressed hostility, not less. In some cases aggressive anti-Zionist attitudes toward Israel have broadened into a generalized denigration of Jews as such. Such vilification is pervasive in much of the Arab and Muslim world, where "Zionist" and "Jew" are often coterminous references, but one finds it among European intellectuals as well.

Here is but one example of many that might be cited. In November, 2003, the famed Greek composer Mikis Theodorakis used the occasion of a public address in Athens to denounce the Jews and deride Judaism. Among other extravagantly abusive charges, he leveled this one: "Today it is possible to say that this small nation is at the root of evil." Expanding on his views a year later in an interview in the Israeli newspaper *Ha'aretz* (August 27, 2004), Theodorakis accused the Jews of being "arrogant and aggressive" and said they "hold world finance in their hands. This gives them a feeling of superiority." They dominate in the cultural sphere as well. Nor does their power stop there. "The international Jewish community...appears to control the big banks. And often the governments....And certainly the mass media." George Bush is beholden to them and "the war in Iraq and the aggressive attitude toward Iran is greatly influenced by the Israeli secret services." Israel itself, controlled by a leader [at the time, Ariel Sharon] who "is going to lead the Jews just as Hitler led the Germans," "is very much connected with Nazism," and Israeli behavior is 'similar to Nazi behavior."

Until recently, such extreme allegations have been propagated chiefly by those on the margins of society. Today, however, they are employed by people in elite segments of Western educational, political, and cultural life, who are introducing into mainstream discourse charges about undue Jewish "power" and "influence" that hitherto have been considered beyond the pale. Some of the people who use this abusive language are, like Theodorakis, figures of prominent, even elevated national and international standing. The toxicity of their rhetoric behooves us to ponder the consequences of chronic language contamination and to reflect on the peculiar language of anti-Semitism.

II

Of the 70 or so ancient Semitic languages, most died out long ago or have little currency today as vernacular forms of speech. The same cannot be said for the antisemitic languages. Muffled for a time in the post-Holocaust years, they have regained their voice and today resound on a global scale across the media of popular and elite cultures. Depending on who is employing them and the aims they are meant to serve, the antisemitic languages may be differently inflected, sounding at times like gutter speech and, at other times, using the more elevated style of academic discourse or the higher journalism. At bottom, though, all are alike in the animus they express and the people against whom they direct their antagonism. To understand how they function and the nature of their appeal is no simple task, and to figure out how to combat them is harder still. Nevertheless, we need to try, for in its volume and reach the rhetoric of hostility to Jews and, especially, the Jewish state is greater today than it has been for decades.

The speech codes that I am referring to as antisemitic languages have a variable focus and a shifting emphasis. In the past, they tended to be organized along predominantly religious or racial lines, for their principal aims were to malign Judaism as an obsolescent as well as a pernicious religion and to attack Jews as a decadent but also threatening people. Jews were hated within Christendom because they were branded guilty of deicide and of stubbornly refusing to recognize the truths proclaimed by the Gospel. For these purported sins they were at various times detested, persecuted, and massacred. To proponents of the racial gospel, they became targets of contempt as a people of "bad blood," a decidedly inferior human type on the ladder of racial hierarchies, who should be marginalized or even murdered in large numbers, lest they contaminate the purer or higher types. Political and economic aims have also been implicated at times in arguments against Judaism and the Jews. These factors may retain a residual presence in some circles still today, but inasmuch as the primary target of anti-Jewish hostility has switched to the Jewish state and its supporters, antisemitic discourse has taken on a largely ideological or political character. As the latest language of invective and abuse reveals, it is now the "Zionist," and not primarily the Jew as a religious or racial type, who attracts suspicion, fear, and loathing. Sharon the alleged murderer of Palestinian children and not Shylock seeking his pound of flesh has been chosen as the figure to be reviled and hated.

Rarely innovative or creative, the people who employ these negative speech codes draw on a well-established archive of inherited motifs, which portray the Jews as a conniving, corrupting, manipulating, and malicious presence. In projecting the Jew in these demeaning, sometimes even demonic, terms, antisemitic languages show themselves to be chiefly emotive or symbolic in character. While they have a logic of their own, it is not one that lends itself to developing reasonable, verifiable arguments or relies on empirical evidence in support of its truth claims. When the current President of Iran, for instance, declares the Holocaust to be a myth or insists that the "Zionists" blew up the revered Shiite mosque in the Iraqi city of Samarra, he is not speaking rationally or credibly about matters rooted in the facts of the real world. Rather, his language, which stirs strong feelings in his domestic listeners, even as it baffles and repels those on the outside, opens the gates to a fantasy realm where the Jew resides as a menacing figure capable of doing immeasurable harm.

In the past, most of the Jews' alleged victims were said to be Christians. Today, they are imagined to be chiefly Muslims. Thus far, though, the real victim of the fulminations and falsifications of a Mahmoud Ahmadinejad and others like him is language itself, which, as George Orwell clarified decades ago, is vulnerable to corruption and can end up making lies sound truthful and murder respectable. Through its manifold distortions and deceptions, that is precisely what antisemitic language is likely to do if it is allowed to proceed unchecked.

How it achieves its odious ends is no mystery. By repeating a series of biased and frequently inflammatory statements about the Jews, antisemitic rhetoric impedes a lucid apprehension of reality and instead encourages its auditors to hear and see what is not there. Moreover, through its evocative power and appeal, it can incite gullible, deluded people to act on the basis of these paranoid perceptions, with destructive consequences that are too well known to warrant retelling here.

What begs for attention today is linked to the past but has a currency that most people, including many Jews, probably did not expect to encounter again in their lifetimes–the open expression of anti-Jewish sentiment and, accompanying it, a resurgence of hostile activity against Jews and Jewish institutions in countries throughout the world. Episodic outbreaks of this kind have occurred before in the post-Holocaust period, but anti-Jewish aggression of the kind we have been witnessing over the past several years was generally not foreseen a decade or so ago. Given antisemitism's long and irrepressible history, though, its reappearance in our own day perhaps should not be so surprising.

Today's antisemitism often draws on the same repertoire of negative stereotypes that have shaped anti-Jewish prejudices in the past. There are some exceptions, most notably stereotypical images of the Jewish state as an implacably belligerent country, singularly wicked in its behavior if not in its very essence, and of Israelis as exceptionally brutal and pitiless aggressors. Otherwise, though, many of those who express hostility to Jews today see them, as they have been seen and reviled over the ages, as plotters and poisoners, agents of subversion and manipulation, who act on a global scale to conspire, corrupt, and control. One of the most striking things that an observer of contemporary antisemitism soon discovers, in fact, is its lack of freshness or originality. The rhetorical codes it employs are essentially derivative, little more than recyclings of old and long-discredited myths. These myths are potent, however, and refuse to disappear. They comprise the figurative core of what I am calling antisemitic languages.

A few examples will suffice to illustrate. While largely absent in today's Europe,[7] the blood libel charge is routinely heard in the Arab world. In November, 2003, Al-Manar, Hizbollah's Syrian-based satellite television channel, which is viewed worldwide, aired a 30-part television series on "the criminal history of Zionism," which depicts a cabal of Jewish leaders draining the blood of a murdered child for the preparation of matza.[8] Some years earlier, in a popular book entitled *The Matza of Zion* (1985), Mustafa Tlas, Syrian defense minister, also featured the blood libel. Similar accusations of Jewish ritual murder have been made in Egypt, Saudi Arabia, Abu Dhabi, and elsewhere. For centuries a staple of Christian antisemitism, the image of the bloodthirsty Jew is now a constituent feature of Muslim antisemitism.

Despite the fact that not a single case of this kind has ever been historically established, large numbers of people in Arab countries evidently believe that Jews ritually drink or otherwise use the blood of murdered non-Jews.[9]

When Jews are not committing these horrendous acts, they are said to be carrying out other equally barbaric outrages. Without any proof to support his claim, Yasir Arafat more than once accused the Israelis of employing depleted uranium to suppress the Palestinian people, just as his wife, Suha Arafat, charged them with poisoning Palestinian water supplies. Reports of a Zionist plot behind the destruction of the World Trade Center on September 11, 2001 have circulated widely alongside accounts of Jewish collusion in the war against Iraq. A Syrian writer, Zbeir Sultan, recently exposed what he claimed are "the dirty satanic methods employed by the Zionist entity to destroy Egypt's society and economy, as well as its military, spiritual, and cultural powers." To further these ends, the Jews are allegedly using HIV-positive Zionist prostitutes to infect Egyptian youth with AIDS, providing Egyptian children with candies that will cause them to become sterile, and supplying Egyptian university students with chewing gum laced with chemical agents to arouse sexual lust in them.[10]

With only a slight change here and there, such tropes of the Jew as contaminator and destroyer have a lineage that traces back centuries. By now they have taken on something like folkloric status and in many places have become part of popular understanding. And if it is not these particular accusations that one encounters anew, it is material lifted from *The Protocols of the Elders of Zion* alleging Jewish plots to subjugate the nations and dominate the world. Not so long ago this fraudulent text had no more contemporary resonance than *Mein Kampf*, but of late *The Protocols* is enjoying a vigorous second life (as is *Mein Kampf* itself). Among its many other appearances, it is enshrined in the Hamas Charter, where *The Protocols* is cited as an authoritative source to prove Jewish ambitions for global supremacy. "Our struggle against the Jews is extremely wide-ranging and grave," the Charter says. With their "huge and influential material wealth," it continues, "they take over control of the world media such as news agencies, the press, publication houses, broadcasting, and the like....They stood behind the French and the Communist Revolutions and behind most of the revolutions we hear about here and there....There was no war that broke out anywhere without their fingerprints on it...." The Charter includes both WWI and WWII in this list of Jewish-inspired wars, the first "so as to wipe out the Islamic caliphate," the second to "prepare for the establishment of their state." It also claims the Jews founded the League of Nations "in order to rule the world by means of that organization" and then created the United Nations for the same purposes. "Through [their] secret organizations, [the Jews] act for the interests of Zionism and under its directions, strive to demolish societies, to destroy values, to wreck answerableness, to totter virtues, and to wipe out Islam." The leaders of Hamas deny being antisemites, even as they repeatedly cite that most notorious of antisemitic texts, *The Protocols of the Elders of Zion*, as an authoritative source for exposing what they insist are age-old Jewish plots for war and world domination.

Baseless as they are, these notions disseminate broadly throughout the Muslim world. Within the last two years, dramatic versions of *The Protocols* have been prominently featured on both Egyptian and Syrian television; the text is available over the internet and at sidewalk bookstalls; and in an exhibition (October, 2003) opening the Alexandria Library, in Egypt, *The Protocols* was given pride of place next to the Torah as "a Jewish sacred text."[11] The tale it tells of clandestine Jewish efforts to seize power on a global scale evidently remains compelling to sizable numbers of people.

The same is unfortunately true with respect to other anti-Semitic myths. Jews alleged to be crafty money manipulators may no longer be called Shylock, but under the names of George Soros and Lord Levy they are still said to be up to their nefarious tricks. Similar accusations are made against imagined Jewish media czars and those who supposedly manipulate political power on behalf of "Zionist interests" through influential Jewish lobbies and "cabals." In this climate, perhaps it should have come as no surprise that the former Malaysian Prime Minister Mahathir Mohamed felt free to declare before a world gathering of Muslim leaders, in October, 2003, that the Jews now "rule the world by proxy."

In short, much of today's antisemitism is easily recognizable as a reprise of former antisemitisms, fueled as it is by the same feelings of contempt, envy, fear, resentment, and suspicion that have given rise to anti-Jewish passions in the past. The rhetorical figures employed to describe the Jews as a malign and threatening power are familiar, so much so that one wonders how an intellectual legacy this dull and with a history so notoriously destructive can possibly enjoy renewed vitality. And yet accusations against the Jews of the most impassioned sort *are* being heard once again, and not only on the margins of society. As these examples and numerous others like them clearly indicate, antisemitic speech codes have been revived and reenergized. Especially when seen in the service of anti-Zionism, they now comprise a popular language of global reach.

Languages are not automatically self-perpetuating, but they are assured of continuity and even longevity if enough people employ them on a regular basis. Vernacular forms of speech stay alive through steady use, and the more they are used, the more tenacious and durable they become. Their vitality, in sum, is owing to their functionality and their ubiquity. Symbolic languages work somewhat differently. Their aim is not so much to meet the practical needs of daily communication as it is to satisfy emotive or ritual ones. They offer access into the imaginative centers of people's minds and provide a means to release feelings and fantasies they otherwise cannot readily express and may not even know they have. In their most highly developed forms, as in art and prayer, symbolic languages enrich our individual and social lives as little else can. In cruder, less benign forms, as in the verbal codes that give voice to hate speech, they can become obsessive and destructive.

Among the antisemitic languages that served past generations of Jew-haters, those that focus on the purported religious errors and racial inferiority of the Jews have faded, although by no means are they altogether gone. In recent years, visual representations of the Jew as Christ-killer, for instance, have appeared as popular newspaper cartoons in several different countries. In addition, antisemitic web sites continue to draw on and propagate some of the older anti-Jewish myths, at times on a new level of sophistication. Have a look, for example, at www.jewishtribalreview.org, and you will find all you could possibly ever want to read on Jewish usury, Jews and slavery, Jews and crime, etc. But to find such invective today at its most potent one needs to turn to the language of anti-Zionism.

Now regularly accessible to many millions of people throughout the world, anti-Zionism as a popular speech code emerged in the 1960s largely as a result of Soviet and Arab efforts. Spoken in several different registers, ranging in tone from the vituperative, eliminationist rhetoric of Muslim preachers and political leaders to the more coolly expository and analytical discourse of academicians and political commentators, the tongue of anti-Zionism is versatile. It is also flexible and has proven itself adaptable to expression in a broad range of cultural genres. On an almost daily basis, one encounters anti-Zionism's verbal and visual vocabulary in international news broadcasts and journalism, political speech and propaganda, theater, cinema, television, poetry, fiction, poster-art, painting, cartoons, and more. Given its currency, popularity, and ubiquity, it is no exaggeration to say that this multi-faceted discourse has become the lingua franca of present-day antisemitism.

Some question whether anti-Zionism is always to be regarded as anti-Semitic, but there is no doubt that, in its present forms, anti-Zionism is the most virulent manifestation of contemporary anti-Jewish hostility. It often carries well beyond reasonable criticism of particular Israeli actions or policies to level the most severe indictments of the Israeli national character and even to question the state's fundamental legitimacy and right to continued existence. For many, the very term "Zionist" is one of contempt, equivalent in its negative connotations to "Nazi." In the rhetoric of European anti-Zionism, the Israeli-Nazi equation has become ubiquitous and, on some level, seems to be an attempt to displace unwanted guilt over the Holocaust onto the victims of the Holocaust and their descendants. The frequently heard description of the Palestinians as today's Jews and Israelis as their Nazi overlords is symptomatic of this effort at transference. In Muslim countries, by contrast, the Israeli-Nazi identification is often accompanied by expressions of Holocaust denial, as the rhetoric of Iran's current President demonstrates. As the Nazi epithet and its numerous variations–"racist," "colonialist," "imperialist," practitioner of "genocide" and "apartheid," etc.--indicate, in most cases anti-Zionism has little, if anything, to do with Zionism itself and is, rather, a symbolic means of expressing anger and other aggressive passions.

In some quarters, opposition to "Zionism" is considered a political and moral virtue and even a religious and national duty. At its most extreme, such opposition has produced a heretofore unanticipated but now all-too familiar type: the person who will act out his or her anti-Zionist convictions in homicidal fashion by becoming a human bomb and blowing up in the presence of Jews, murdering and maiming as many of them as possible. "It was always my wish to turn my body into deadly shrapnel against the Zionists and to knock on the doors of heaven with the skulls of Zionists," proclaimed Reem al-Reyashi, a 22-year old Palestinian mother of two young children before she killed herself and four Israelis at the Erez Crossing, in Gaza (January 13, 2004). The videotape on which she anticipates and celebrates this gruesome event has since become a graphic addition to the archives of anti-Zionism. In this case and countless others, the term "Zionist" has become a poisonous epithet for millions of people and, as they understand it, gives some of them the license to kill. To be branded a "Zionist" by radicalized Muslims, in short, is to live under a death sentence, as was borne out in the most revolting fashion with the videotaped butchering of Daniel Pearl, the *Wall Street Journal* correspondent decapitated by his kidnappers in Pakistan for being a Zionist and a Jew–that is to say, a person deemed eligible for ritual slaughter.

The "new antisemitism" is still an evolving phenomenon, and no one can predict for sure how much destructive force it is likely to unleash. A few particularly troubling aspects of it, though, are already apparent, and these are likely to remain with us for years to come. One is what the historian Robert Wistrich calls the "Islamicization" of antisemitism, which he sees correctly as "by far the most serious contemporary manifestation" of Jew-hatred. Anyone aware of the rhetoric employed in the Muslim world against "Zionism" should have little trouble recognizing both its inflammatory character and its genocidal aims.[12] In political rhetoric as well as in religious preaching, radical antisemitism--where *Zionist* and *Jew* are reviled terms employed interchangeably--has become commonplace, and the most violent denunciations of Israel and the Jews are standard fare. Listen to Sheikh Hassan Nasrallah speaking in the summer of 2006: "If we searched the entire world for a person more cowardly, despicable, weak, and feeble in psyche, mind, ideology, and religion, we would not find anyone like the Jew. Notice I do not say 'the Israeli.' "[13]

As here, an essential part of this dehumanizing rhetoric, and not only in the Muslim world, is the debasement of the Jew as a figure worthy of normal respect. Another of its core components is the steady demonization of the Jewish state as a thoroughly contemptible entity undeserving of inclusion in the family of nations. These hostile projections seem to be generated from two sources: one involves a return to the old repertoire of anti-Semitic stereotypes, portraying the Jew as a fearsome presence, bent on controlling and destroying; the other is the aforementioned demonization and delegitimization of Israel, which draw on some of these same stereotypes and newly align them with visual images of the Israeli as brutally tough, if not downright savage. Cartoons portraying the Jew as Christ-killer, alluded to earlier, feature not just any Jew, after all, but, specifically, Israeli Jews, sometimes portrayed as carrying out the crucifixion of the Palestinian people.[14]

Such images may have reached their high point in Dave Brown's celebrated cartoon of Ariel Sharon eating a Palestinian child, which first appeared in the London *Independent*. This work, which was awarded the British Political Cartoon Society's first prize, in November 2003, is as graphic an illustration as one can imagine of the transformation of the figure of the Jew from passive victim to voracious cannibal. It joins the widely-circulated but now discredited image of Mohammed al-Dura, the Palestinian boy allegedly shot by an Israeli marksman while crouching in fear behind his father, which exemplifies to millions an image of the Israeli as child-killer and wanton murderer.[15] Add to these images that of the American Rachel Corrie accidentally crushed by an Israeli bulldozer, and the transmutation of the Israeli Jew from a figure to be admired for building and defending his land to a figure of unrestrained cruelty is complete. Call this newly emergent type by the now-hostile epithet "Zionist" and associate the hated "Zionists" with the supposedly omnipotent and conniving Jews around the world who actively support "Zionist aggression," and you will arrive at the heart of today's antisemitism.

   Antisemitism is, of course, a more-than-linguistic fact, but, as I hope to have demonstrated, it rests on a strong linguistic base, which both articulates and incites anti-Jewish prejudices of a damaging and, ultimately, destructive kind. For a number of years in the post-Holocaust period, the words and images used to express suspicion, denigration, and hatred of Jews had been under a strong taboo. No longer. Particularly with regard to the Jewish state, the taboo has been lifted and, with its removal, the post-Holocaust era is effectively over. Through the articulation of an increasingly aggressive anti-Zionism, Israel is being steadily criminalized and those who support it disparaged and denounced as allies of an exceptionally deviant country, one fast on its way to being seen as a rogue state or outlaw nation. At their furthest extreme, the rhetoricians of anti-Zionism condemn Israel as a reprise of Hitler's Germany, as exhibited in Theodorakis's words quoted earlier, or a "disgraceful blot" that "should be wiped off the map," to cite the flamboyantly belligerent wish of the President of Iran. Few others will go that far, although in his polemical book, *The Myths of Zionism*, the British writer John Rose identifies Zionism as murderous as well as meretricious by nature and calls for its "removal," along with the state it created; in her equally impassioned book, *The Question of Zion*, the British scholar Jacqueline Rose sets out to expose Zionism as a form of lunacy and claims that Israel's "soul was forfeit from the day of its creation"; and the historian Tony Judt, who earlier found Israel in its present configuration as a Jewish nation-state merely "anachronistic," has progressed in his thinking and now likens the country to Franco's Spain as a repellent "symbol of oppression" and a "land of shame."[16] Innumerable others have spoken and written in a similar vein, routinely denouncing Zionism as the most pernicious of ideologies and reducing the Zionist state to Nazi-like status.

   It doesn't take much imagination to project beyond vilification of this sort to Israel's total delegitimization and wished-for demise. What will happen if we reach the point of still broader rejection is impossible to predict with any certainty. But if present trends persist and the purveyors of the new antisemitism succeed in turning Israel into a universally reviled state, unworthy of sympathy or support, what may lie ahead is not easy to contemplate.

III

In the face of these developments, what, then, of "never again?" And what of Irving Greenberg's insistence that "Jewish history affirms hope?" How well do these propositions hold up if one situates them within the context of contemporary events that implicate the Jews? Antisemitic utterances are wont to give rise to antisemitic deeds, and over the past decade dozens of Jewish synagogues, schools, and other institutions have been attacked in Europe and elsewhere, Jewish cemeteries have been repeatedly desecrated, Holocaust memorials defaced, and individual Jews beaten on the streets and in their shops. In addition, as has already been demonstrated in the preceding pages, the Jewish state has been routinely condemned and steadily criminalized, its very legitimacy undermined by an anti-Zionist rhetoric that questions its right to continued existence. This gathering hostility does not by itself invalidate the integrity of Greenberg's pleadings on behalf of Holocaust memory and Jewish hope, but it does pose severe and growing challenges to them.

One of this generation's earliest and most influential exponents of the transforming potential of Holocaust awareness, Greenberg has written that "memory [of the Holocaust] becomes a shield for the Jewish people and a profound confirmation of the necessity and moral-spiritual significance of the state of Israel."[17] Among people who take the Nazi crimes against the Jews seriously, he is surely right, but in an age of resurgent antisemitism, the protective powers of Holocaust memory inevitably lose some of their force, and the Jews once again become vulnerable to an all-too-familiar aggression. To recognize as much is not to call into question the value of Greenberg's important teachings, which have always stressed Judaism's fundamental commitments to the triumph of life, but it is to observe that his redemptive vision is seriously contested by what he has called the "powerful forces of death...in this world."[18]

Greenberg is not without allies, and people of conscience will look to join him in spreading a Jewish discourse of hope *despite* the Holocaust. They have their work cut out for them, no small part of which is to oppose newly emergent anti-Jewish discourses that minimize, distort, and deny the Holocaust and seek to turn its moral power *against* the Jews. How the contest turns out will be critical for the future in general, including the future of hope.

NOTES

1. Irving Greenberg, "Cloud of Smoke, Pillar of Fire: Judaism, Christianity, and Modernity after the Holocaust," in Eva Fleischner, ed., *Auschwitz: Beginning of a New Era? Reflections on the Holocaust* (New York: Ktav Publishing House, 1977), p.55.

2. Ibid., 23.

3. Ibid., p. 55.

4. Ibid., p.20.

5. Jonathan Sacks, "The New Antisemitism," *The London Jewish Chronicle* November 2007.

6. Denis MacShane, "The New Anti-Semitism," *Washington Post* September 4, 2007.

7. Europe is not entirely free of such accusations, as became clear in the Russian city of Novosibirsk in March, 2008, when hundreds of anti-Semitic pamphlets were circulated, "warning residents of the supposed Jewish practice of kidnapping children to

use their blood for Passover matza." The pamphlet carried this warning: "Beware Russian parents. Keep watch over your children before the coming of April, 2008, the Jewish holiday of Passover. These disgusting people still engage in ritual practice to their gods. They kidnap small children and remove some of their blood and use it to prepare their holy food (matza). They throw the bodies of the children out in garbage dumps." See Yael Branovsky, "Russian blood libel: Jews use children's blood for matzot," *Ynet News* March 19, 2008. http://www.ynetnews.com/articles/0,7340,L-3521307,00.html.

8. For a report on this 30-part television series, entitled "Al-Shatat" ("Diaspora"), see MEMRI's special dispatch no. 623, "Arab Antisemitism Documentation Project/ Syria," www.memri.org December 8, 2003.

9. For a study of the popularity of the blood libel charge in both Christian Europe and the Muslim Middle East, see Marvin Perry and Frederick M. Schweitzer, *Antisemitism: Myth and Hate from Antiquity to the Present* (Palgrave Macmillian, 2002), pp. 43-72.

10. See Douglas Davis, "The Jews Did It," *Jerusalem Post*, November 20, 2003.

11. See MEMRI special dispatch no. 619, "Egypt/Arab Antisemitism Project" December 3, 2003.

12. Robert Wistrich, "Letters from Readers," *Commentary*, vol. 117, no. 2 (February, 2004), 3.

13. Cited in Michael Gove, "Antisemitism is finding new allies on both Right and Left," *Times Online* (April 1, 2008).

14. See Michele Giannelli, "Non Resurrexit," Cartoon, *Il Corriere della Sera* March 31, 2002, and Giorgio Forattini, "Tanks at the Manger," Cartoon, *La Stampa* April 3, 2002; cited in Emanuele Ottolenghi, "Neither Auschwitz not the Brotherhood of Mankind: Some Reflections on European Anti-Semitism," an unpublished paper.

15. Although the Israeli army has been condemned throughout the Muslim world for this shooting, there is a serious dispute about who actually did kill the young boy. For a thorough analysis of the incident, see James Fallows, "Who Shot Mohammed al-Dura?" *The Atlantic Monthly* (June 2003).

16. See John Rose, *The Myths of Zionism* (London: Pluto Press, 2004), p.2; Jacqueline Rose, *The Question of Zion* (Princeton: Princeton University Press, 2005), p.72; and Tony Judt, "The Country That Wouldn't Grow Up," *Ha'aretz* May 26, 2006.

17. Shalom Freedman, *Living in the Image of God: Jewish Teachings to Perfect the World: Conversations with Irving Greenberg* (Northvale, N.J.: Jason Aronson, Inc.: 1998), p.231.

18. Ibid., 233.

16

It Is 2010: Are We One Jewish People?

Jacob B. Ukeles

INTRODUCTION

In 1985, Rabbi Irving ("Yitz") Greenberg crystallized the concerns of many American Jewish leaders in a brilliant four-part essay: "Will There Be One Jewish People by the Year 2000?"[1]

In the first part, "The Demographics of Separation," Yitz focuses on conversion, patrilineal descent, and halachically illegitimate children (*mamzerim*) as causing the Jewish people to split into two. He argues that, "If sociological forces are left to operate unchecked, the result will be predictable. Within two decades, the Jewish people will split apart into two, mutually divided, hostile groups who are unable or unwilling to marry each other."[2]

In the second part of the essay, "The Denominational Politics of Separation," he chastises Orthodox, Conservative, and Reform leaders for assuming the "other" will disappear. "In the past, anti-Semites built their plans on the expectation and hope that the Jews will disappear. We have come to a tragic situation where good and committed Jews are predicating their survival strategies on the disappearance of other Jews."[3]

In the third part of the essay, "A Critique of Separation," Yitz invokes the specter of "a Jewish civil war," as each denomination delegitimizes the other.

2000 has come and gone, and it is appropriate — 10 years after that milestone and 25 years after the essay was written — to take a fresh look at the state of the American Jewish community. What has happened? Did Yitz's worst fears materialize?[4]

In many ways, events that have unfolded represent two paradoxes:

First, the American Jewish community remains both remarkably unified and highly fractionalized; and

Second, all of the issues relating to personal identity that Yitz cogently laid out have remained unresolved. Yet the Jewish community has not split in two, nor, by the way, is it disappearing.

THE FIRST PARADOX: "WE ARE ONE" AND "WE ARE MANY"

Centripetal forces — how are we alike and what is pulling us together? [5]

The vast majority of American Jews say that being Jewish is important, and of these, typically more than half say being Jewish is very important to them.

The vast majority of American Jews continue to identify with a religion, and that religion is Judaism. Five to twenty percent of adults who self-identify as Jews, depending on the community, say that they have no religion and 1% to 4% say that their religion is Judaism and something else.[6]

Despite all of the rhetoric of post-denominational, trans-denominational, and non-denominational Judaism, in study after study, most American Jews still identify with a denomination. Only 10%% to 20% of Jews who say that their religion is Judaism do not identify with a denomination (just Jewish).

These shared commitments — to the importance of being Jewish, to Judaism, and to a denomination — suggest there may be a basis for building intra-Jewish relationships in the United States.

At another level, there have been some reasonably successful efforts to build bridges across the denominations:

CLAL & Jewish Federations: Yitz himself played a significant role in breaking down barriers between the denominations. CLAL, especially in its early days pioneered in bringing Orthodox, Conservative, Reform, and secular lay leaders together. But far more important than convening, Yitz brought Jewish learning and experience into the heartland of Jewish civic religion – the world of Federations. Orthodox Jews and observant Conservative Jews were "lone rangers" at General Assemblies in the 60's and 70's – hard-pressed to find a room for services, or to assemble a Minyan. Younger Orthodox and Conservative Jews active in Federations today are incredulous at these tales from the "dark ages."

The Wexner Foundation's Graduate Fellowship Program: Over the past ten years, the Wexner Graduate Fellowship program has provided financial support to hundreds of graduate students in cantorial studies, communal service, Jewish studies, and Rabbinics. While not its intent, an important byproduct of the program has been the creation of a trans-denominational community of future professional leaders of the American Jewish community. Each annual retreat of Wexner fellows and alumni is an intensive three day experience involving very bright, self-confident, committed Jews with diverse interests, background and sexual orientation – focusing on Jewish ideas and practice. Participants develop feelings of mutual respect for difference. When Wexner alumni talk about the Wexner community — it is not mere rhetoric.

To a lesser extent other programs, such as the Wexner Heritage Leadership Program, the Melton mini-schools, and the Meah program based in Boston, have also been bridge-building processes involving Jewish adults across the denominational spectrum in shared learning experiences.

Many people believe that Orthodoxy itself is a significant barrier to positive cross- denomination relationships.[7] In this context, the emergence of institutions committed to an open or progressive Orthodoxy, — the Chovevei Torah Yeshiva, the Bat-Ayin Yeshiva in Israel (a neo-Hasidic, "modern" Orthodox institution), Drisha, the Center for a Jewish Future at Yeshiva University, and JOFA — is itself a positive sign.

For those who have believed that Reform Judaism is the major roadblock to cross-denomination relationships,[8] the emergence of a Reform rabbinate more attuned to Jewish ritual and historic tradition is a positive steps toward reducing barriers.

Centrifugal Forces: how are we different and what is making us fly apart?

In almost every way, each of the three major denominations marches to its own drummer. For example, each of the three largest movements has recently made separate major policy decisions with regard to the issue of conversion. The Reform and Conservative movements have each put the issue of conversion at the center of their platforms during recent national conventions. In the year following these initiatives, the Orthodox community also was forced to address the issue of conversion, in light of the Israeli Chief Rabbinate's further curtailing its acceptance of conversions performed by Orthodox rabbis in North America. [9] The only serious effort to do inter-denomination conversions — the Denver experiment — failed even before Yitz's article appeared.[10]

The Orthodox community seems to be growing more insular,[11] the Conservative movement is struggling with its own survival and the Reform movement is focused on its own internal debates and struggles between classical and neo-traditional elements.

In fundamental ways, Orthodox and non-orthodox Jews live increasingly different lives. For example, most Orthodox adults under 30 are married (71%); most non-Orthodox adults under 30 are not (80%).[12]

To many American Jews the wars between the denominations are irrelevant to their lives. Even though most American Jews still identify with a denomination and most believe being Jewish is important, in many communities intermarriage, along with a concomitant disconnect from Jewish life is the dominant pattern among American Jews under 40. And there is growing evidence that most intermarried households have little or no interest in conversion.[13]

Since all of the issues of difference in the approach to personal identity remain exactly where they were in 1986 why have we not split into two (or more) communities?

THE SECOND PARADOX: WE CAN'T SEEM TO AGREE ON WHO IS A JEW AND IT DOESN'T SEEM TO MATTER

As Jack Wertheimer has pointed out, "From one perspective — perhaps the dominant one — the current climate of public amity is healthier than was the period of friction and conflict between the movements a decade and more ago. There is much evidence of overt cooperation, and where there are differences, everyone is more polite and eager to cover them over. Consensus has seemingly returned to the Jewish community... Certainly, this remains the case when it comes to matters of personal status. The question of "Who is a Jew" is no more resolved in the U.S. than it is in Israel. There is no agreement among American Jews on patrilineality. There is no agreement on what ought to be expected of potential converts to Judaism. There is no agreement on what is required to obtain a religious divorce. And there is no agreement on the status of children born to Jewish parents who did not obtain a Jewish bill of divorce, a *get*, from a previous marriage. On all these matters, the denominations are divided. As increasing numbers of people come of age who are patrilineal Jews or whose mothers did not obtain a *get*, questions of marriageability inevitably will propel ever more Jews into opposing camps and will engender resentment...The further damage caused by the current effort to paper over differences is that hardly anyone is working domestically on resolving these issues for the betterment—and unity—of the Jewish people. "[14]

Why are we in the paradoxical situation where all the causes of schism are in place, but the schism has not taken place?

Jews continue to be heavily influenced by American society. Diversity is celebrated and Americans of all types invent their own identity. To a significant extent these factors affect Jewish life as well. For most American Jews, issues of personal status are irrelevant. The open-ness of American society translates also into increasingly porous boundaries around Jewishness, Judaism, and the Jewish community. Whereas most people used to respond "yes" or no to a question, "Are you Jewish," more and more people will respond, "I think so," "partially," "somewhat," "in some ways," or "I am not sure." People will even relate differently to Jewish self-identification at different stages in their life.

The real impact of divisive practices and behaviors such as the establishment of patrilineal descent or the abandonment of historic Jewish requirements for divorce is at the personal, not the communal level. The consequences can be tragic – but for relatively few. The baal teshuva who learns that he is a mamzer and cannot marry the observant person he loves; the Reform Jewish NFTY leader who has a non-Jewish mother who has to undergo the indignity of a conversion to meet the Halachic standards of a fiancé and his family; the *agunah* whose husband doesn't believe that *Get* is important and won't be bothered.

Ironically, despite all the talk of "Orthodox" and "non-Orthodox", and the so-called "liberal movements" (Conservative, Reform and Reconstruction), the real divide on issues of personal status is between Orthodox and Conservative on the one hand and Reform on the other. On matters of personal status — *Get*, matrilineal descent and requirements for conversion – the differences between Conservative and Orthodox are trivial and between Reform and Reconstructionist are immense. The tendency to blur the distinction between Reform and Conservative Judaism is often made by people who literally do not understand the differences between the two movements. The Conservative movement embraces an essentially Halachic definition of who is a Jew; the Reform movement does not.

Looking forward: where can we go from here?

Most people who have quoted or responded to Yitz's seminal article, have focused on his dire prediction of a schism within the American Jewish community developed in the first three parts of his essay.

People tend not to focus as much as Yitz's two-part prescription for avoiding disaster. In the fourth part of the essay, Yitz prescribes the antidote: "American Jewry must establish a systematic religious dialogue among the Jewish denominations on the scale of the Jewish-Christian dialogue of the past fifty years."[15] "[We need to] assert the principle and the priority of *Clal Yisrael* (the unity and totality of the Jewish people). I would call upon all Jews to put pressure — peer pressure, moral judgment, even economic pressure — on the leadership of all the denominations."[16]

It is safe to say that in the main, his dire prediction of a division of the Jewish people in the USA into two groups has not happened, nor does it appear likely that it will happen in the next twenty years. Even the *Haredi* world, with strong separatist elements, also includes Chabad, with strong connections to non-observant Jews, as well as a variety of right-wing Rabbis and *Kolelim* serving Jewish communities.

The Jewish community in the United States has not split in two, nor do I believe it will. At the same time all of the challenges Yitz described 25 years ago exist today.

The fact that we have not literally become two peoples, that we have not reenacted the Karaite-Judaism schism, does not mean that the issues of personal identity and inter-denominational ignorance and contempt are not deeply disturbing issues. And I believe that both of Yitz's prescriptions remain as relevant today as they did 25 years ago.

In an unpublished study commissioned to assess the need for intra-Jewish dialogue about ten years ago, I interviewed 17 key informants. The interviews were aimed at eliciting the views of communal professionals and lay leaders on the need for dialogue in North America, the audience or "consumer" for such dialogue, the range of activities available, a possible program design, and the inherent roadblocks to such a program.

Key informants included: lay and professional leaders from Jewish federations, organizations and foundations; people with different denominational affiliation; professionals at different stages in their careers in the Jewish communal world and some communal professionals active in the field of dialogue or Jewish formal and informal adult education. Here are some findings:

Pluralism and Jewish Unity

Most of these key informants — some of the most thoughtful observers of the Jewish community in the United States — believed that pluralism and Jewish unity are among the most pressing issues facing the Jewish community in the United States today. A minority believed that the issue of pluralism and unity is vastly overshadowed by the issue of the decline in Jewish commitment and engagement among the majority of American Jews. And some believed that the pluralism/unity issue is an issue that concerns the elite; especially the fund-raising leadership of the community but that it hardly touches the "rank and file".

Intra-Jewish Dialogue

Of those who believe that the issue of pluralism and Jewish unity is an extremely pressing issue, most (but not all) believe that intra-Jewish dialogue can be an effective tool for enhancing Jewish unity. To the extent that the lack of mutual respect reinforces divisions, and to the extent that ignorance breeds contempt, bringing people with different views together may help improve the climate, even if people "agree to disagree." Some (a minority) believe that the divisions are so deep and the solutions so elusive that dialogue will not make a significant dent in the real issues.

While there have been a number of efforts in recent years to organize intra-communal dialogue, these have been relatively small-scale and localized. It appears that the Jewish communal system in the United States is not meeting the need for dialogue within the Jewish community.

There is today no institutional driver in the United States with a central focus on pluralism and Jewish unity OR on promoting dialogue.

Yitz's second prescription — a focus on *Clal Yisrael* — is even more pressing in my judgment than the need for inter-denominational dialogue.

Pluralism is a crucial precondition for implementing *Clal Yisrael* —you cannot implement a vision of *Clal Yisrael* without respect, without inclusion, without active engagement with other Jews who are different. You can't implement a commitment to *Clal Yisrael* without active engagement with Orthodox, Conservative, and Reform Jews and committed trans-denominational Jews

In 2003, I wrote, "A commitment to *Clal Yisrael* means accepting the ultimately mystical idea that in some fundamental, mysterious way the Jewish people is one organism. In the final analysis, *Clal Yisrael* is an ideal. There are those who argue that since the Jews are clearly not unified, *Clal Yisrael* is no longer relevant. This is like saying that freedom or love or wisdom should be discarded as human ideals because they are not easily attainable."[17]

I have argued, and continue to believe, that the most dangerous schism in the Diaspora, and in Israel as well, is between those who believe in the vision of *Clal Yisrael* and those who do not — far more dangerous than the schism among denominations. Judaism's strength is in its boundless variety of Jewish expression. So many people do not fall neatly into one category or another: secular Jews studying Talmud, Orthodox Jews on the cutting edge of science and the arts; Reform, Conservative and Progressive Orthodox Jews for whom the religious and secular strands of Jewish life are inextricably woven.

While differences over the relevance and nature of Halacha are often cited as impenetrable barriers to implementing a pluralistic vision of *Clal Yisrael*, there is a powerful model for pluralism imbedded in classical Judaism that we can and should use.

The oft-cited, classic model for Jewish pluralism is found in the Talmud, Tractate *Eruvin*, page 13, side B. "Rabbi Abba said in the name of Samuel: for three years, the House of Shammai and the House of Hillel differed [about a series of laws].These said, the law is according to our view, these said, the law is according to our view. A Heavenly Voice spoke, and said, 'These and these are the words of the living God.'"[18]

But the truth is, that this is not a good model for pluralism — The House of Shammai and the House of Hillel agreed on so much, that the range of disagreement was minute compared with the difference that exist between different kinds of Jews in America.

But there is another model for pluralism that I believe is a much better model: In the fifth chapter of the Ethics of the Fathers, the seventeenth Mishna, "Any dispute which is for the sake of Heaven shall in the end be of lasting worth, but that which is not for the sake of Heaven shall not in the end be of lasting worth." [19]

We can call this model of Jewish pluralism, "sustainable controversy," which implies that controversy is to be expected. So what is the meaning of "for the sake of Heaven"? It means that the parties to the dispute are honorable people who are true to their own definition of the highest ideals of Judaism. In Rabbi Samson Raphael Hirsch's words, "When in a controversy both parties are guided solely by pure motives and seek noble ends, and when both parties seek solely to find the truth...both views will have permanent value." [20]

Anyone who has had contact with active Orthodox, Reform, Conservative or Reconstructionist Jews, understands that they all meet this test — serious Jews in a serious exploration of being Jewish.

What is the difference between these two models? The standard of "these and these are the word of the living God," implies a value judgment in which each side believes that the views of the other are legitimate and valid. On the other hand, an argument for the sake of Heaven does not imply a judgment about the intrinsic merits of each point of view, but rather a sense of respect for the holders of those views. In the Talmudic story of the arguments between the House of Hillel and the House of Shammai, the final resolution — that the Law is according to the House of Hillel — comes from a Heavenly voice – only the divine can confer legitimacy. Conferring or taking away the legitimacy of a position is not a human task. Pluralism and a commitment to Clal Yisrael do not require a value judgment about the intrinsic merit or value of another Jew's position. As free human beings, we can agree to engage in debate and dialogue with those whose views are honest, who seek the truth as they see it, and who are willing to engage without either accepting or rejecting another's views. [21]

At a more practical level, we need an American analogue to the Kinneret Agreement. Drafted in 2002 by several dozen Israeli intellectuals and communal leaders, the Kinneret Agreement was a thoughtful effort to restate the social contract among the Jewish people, with a focus on Israel.

Clal Yisrael used to occur naturally, and today it is needs to be re-created. The challenge of building *Clal Yisrael* requires a compact, like the Kinneret agreement, followed by an intensive and extensive educational process.

A group of American Jewish intellectuals and community activists, spanning the denominations and the trans-denominational foci of Jewish energy need to come together to draft a Clal Yisrael covenant for American Jewry. An American version of the Kinneret agreement would remain on the shelf, an interesting piece of paper, unless it becomes the basis for an ongoing, sustained effort to spread the understanding of *Clal Yisrael*, the commitment to *Clal Yisrael* and to model behavior based on *Clal Yisrael*. A covenantal process, as opposed to a covenant, is ongoing, not a one-time event. Second, a covenantal process is action-oriented. The goal of a process is to generate change. Very few documents generate change by themselves.

The *Clal Yisrael* Process should focus heavily on education at all levels. Here are just some of the ideas that might emerge from such a process:

- Curricula on Jewish unity to be used in Jewish schools and for adult education.
- Study Groups to study and disseminate the texts about Jewish unity –including *Clal Yisrael* and *Araivut*.
- A children's video series with a focus on the themes of *Clal Yisrael*

The best tribute to Yitz Greenberg's life work would be a serious effort to restore the centrality of *Clal Yisrael* — in all its marvelous diversity, complexity and even contentiousness.

BIBLIOGRAPHY

Beck, Pearl *Addressing the Needs of Intermarried Families in Cleveland: An Exploration of Decision-Making Regarding Jewish Educational Experiences among Parents of School-Age Children* (Cleveland: Jewish Community Federation, 2008).

Freedman, Samuel G. *Jew vs. Jew: The Struggle for the Soul of American Jewry* (New York: Simon and Schuster, 2000).

Greenberg, Irving "Will There be One Jewish People by the Year 2000." *Perspectives* (New York: The National Jewish Center for Learning and Leadership). The essay originally appeared in June 1985 and in a revised version in February 1986.

Heilman, Samuel C, *Sliding to the Right: The Contest for the Future of American Jewish Orthodoxy* (Berkeley: University of California Press, 2006).

Kleinberg, Darren. "Getting Pluralism Back on Track: Conversion and the Challenge of Jewish Peoplehood." Judaism: A Quarterly Journal of Jewish Life and Thought, (Sept 2006).

Perspectives, CLAL: The National Jewish Center for Learning and Leadership, n.d. The essay originally appeared in June 1985 and in a revised version in February 1986.

Ukeles, Jacob B. "The Kinneret People: Can there be One Jewish People?" Renewing the Jewish Social Contract, Bridging the Religious-Secular Divide, a publication of the AJC, (August, 2003), pg. 44-47.

Ukeles, Jacob B., Ron Miller and Pearl Beck *Young Jewish Adults in the United States Today* (American Jewish Committee, 2006).

Wertheimer, Jack. "All Quiet on the Religious Front." American Jewish Life, a publication of the AJC, (April 2005), pg. 1-33.

NOTES

1. Irving Greenberg, "Will There be One Jewish People by the Year 2000." *Perspectives* (New York: The National Jewish Center for Learning and Leadership). The essay originally appeared in June 1985 and in a revised version in February 1986.

2. Ibid., p.1

3. Ibid., p.4

4. In his original essay, Yitz seems to be focusing on the American Jewish community, and I will do the same. Israel and the Diaspora outside of the USA each represent a different complex reality.

5. These data are drawn from seven major Jewish community studies carried out by Ukeles Associates, Inc. (Atlanta [2005]; Baltimore [1999]; Denver [2007]; New York [2001]; Philadelphia [1996]; Pittsburgh [2002]; San Diego [2003]. All data files are available at the North American Jewish Data Bank.

6. This excludes Messianic Jews, who are typically not included in Jewish community studies.

7. Darren Kleinberg, "Getting Pluralism Back on Track: Conversion and the Challenge of Jewish Peoplehood." *Judaism: A Quarterly Journal of Jewish Life and Thought*, (Sept 2006).

8. Ibid.

9. Ibid., p. 2

10. See the description of the Denver conversion process in Samuel G. Freedman, *Jew vs. Jew: The Struggle for the Soul of American Jewry* (New York: Simon and Schuster, 2000), pp. 80-114.

11. Samuel C. Heilman, *Sliding to the Right: The Contest for the Future of American Jewish Orthodoxy* (Berkeley: University of California Press, 2006)

12. Jacob B. Ukeles, Ron Miller and Pearl Beck *Young Jewish Adults in the United States* Today, (American Jewish Committee, 2006), p. 58.

13. Pearl Beck, Addressing the Needs of Intermarried Families in Cleveland : An Exploration of Decision-Making Regarding Jewish Educational Experiences among Parents of School-Age Children (Cleveland: Jewish Community Federation, 2008).

14. Jack Wertheimer, "All Quiet on the Religious Front? Jewish Unity, Denominationalism, and Postdenominationalism in the United States" (New York: American Jewish Committee, 2005) p. 22-24.

15. Irving Greenberg, "Will There be One Jewish People by the Year 2000." *Perspectives* (New York: The National Jewish Center for Learning and Leadership), pg. 7.

16. Ibid, p. 8

17. Jacob B. Ukeles, "The Kinneret Agreement: Can there be One Jewish People." *Renewing the Social Contract: Bridging the Religious-Secular Divide* (New York: The American Jewish Committee, 2003), p. 45.

18. *Tractate Eruvin, Babylonian Talmud*, page 13b.

19. *Ethics of the Fathers*, Chapter 5, Mishna 17. The Mishna goes on to cite the argument of Shammai and Hillel as an example of an argument for the sake of Heaven.

20. Rabbi Samson Raphael Hirsch *Siddur, commentary on Ethics of the Father*, p. 502.

21. Based on a presentation by the author at the Edah Conference in New York, October, 2005.

17

Rebbe Israel of Kozhenitz

Elie Wiesel

To Yitz, my old friend and colleague of more than five decades: Teacher, Scholar, Theologian, Philosopher, Social Guide: you have influenced generations of students and Jewish activists. They owe you much. Personally, were it not for you, my entire academic life would not have been what it is. So let this essay be an act of gratitude.

> And it came to pass that when the great Rebbe Elimelekh of Lizensk felt that he was about to depart from this world, he summoned to his bed his most beloved disciples to offer them his farewell gifts.
>
> He gave his sight to the Seer of Lublin, his mind to Reb Mendel of Rimanov, his wisdom to the Rebbe of Apt, and his heart to Rebbe Israel, the Maggid of Kozhenitz.

A story: A woman, a simple peasant woman, came to the celebrated Maggid Rebbe Israel Hoftstein of Kozhenitz and poured her heart out to him. She had been married for many, many years to a good man, a pious Jew. In the beginning, they were happy. They still were—how could it be otherwise? They had bread and milk for their daily meals—they had wine and fish for the Sabbath. God is, after all, the father of his people—of all people. It would be sinful not to feel happiness," except that we are also unhappy," said the woman, "for we are childless." "I see," said the great Tzaddik, "I see." And, after a while: "Tell me, woman, what are you willing to *do* about all this?" The woman didn't understand what he meant, so she kept quiet. "My mother," continued the Maggid with a smile, "had the same problem. She was getting old—in fact she was old—and still she had no child. She wept, she cried, she

277

tried fasting—and still nothing happened. One day she heard that the Besht—the Besht himself—was in town. She ran to his inn and pleaded with him to intercede in heaven on her behalf." "What are you willing to do about all this?" he asked her. "What can I do?" she replied. "I can do nothing. My husband is a poor bookbinder, and I am his wife. We have nothing but ourselves. No...we do have something. A kaftan, a cape—I will give it to you." She ran home, fetched the cape and hurried back to the inn—too late. The Besht had gone back to Medzebish. So she set out to follow him on foot. She walked from town to town, from village to village, until she reached Medzebish. She eventually found the right street, the right house. When she found the Besht, she handed him the cape and waited. The Besht took the cape, hung it on the wall and said: "Now all is well." Whereupon my mother walked back to Apt. I was born one year later. "Thank you, thank you," shouted the woman excitedly. "Now I know what to do. I am going to bring you the best and most expensive cape in town..." "No," said the Maggid. "Don't. It won't work. You see, there is a difference between my mother and you. *You* know the story."

Amusing and beautiful as it may sound, this anecdote does present some difficulties and warrants some comments.

First of all, it does not sound Hasidic. No, it doesn't because the woman in the story does *not* receive help. How is that possible? One woman becomes pregnant because of a story—and another one does not, all because of the same story? Isn't everybody entitled to the Rabbi's sympathy and intercession?

Really, is that why the woman came to the Maggid? To hear a funny story? What about her problem? What about her pain? Her solitude? Her anguish, what about her anguish? Why did he allow her to leave unconsoled? Because he had told her the story? So what! If not knowing Hasidic stories is a virtue— why are they told in the first place? Why *did* he tell her his story in the first place? And why are we repeating it?

At this point we cannot but sympathize with the woman and take issue with the Holy Master for not empathizing with her enough. But we are only at the beginning of our story. Wait for a few more stories, legends, anecdotes, sayings. Perhaps our attitude will change and—who knows?—our criticism of him may turn into admiration.

One cannot evoke Hasidism without feeling attracted to Rebbe Israel. Because of his wisdom? Others may well have been wiser. Because of his erudition? Others may well have been more learned. Because of his wonders and miracles? Greatness is not necessarily measured by miracles. No—he was great for different reasons, on different levels. And we intend to elaborate on that later, as we dedicate this essay to his personality, to his life and work.

We shall tell stories by him and about him—for what would Hasidism be without stories? It even offers us stories to diminish the importance of stories . . . When this occurs—what does one do? One waits before passing judgment.

The Maggid of Kozhenitz was born in the city of Apt, near Sandomir, in the year 1737—which creates yet another problem with our earlier story which had to have taken place a year earlier, in 1736—the year of the Besht's revelation. Is it possible that the Maggid's mother had already heard of his miracles—so soon? He revealed himself in the neighborhood of Brody and settled in Medzebish much later—and yet the story tells us that the Maggid's mother followed him to Medzebish.

How is one to solve these problems of chronology and geography? Fortunately Hasidism chooses to pay attention to neither. But there are other difficulties as well; there are different versions—better yet, different stories—about the Maggid's mother being helped by the Besht.

Listen: It was Friday evening and the Besht, surrounded by his close disciples, was celebrating the holiness and purity of Shabbat. Suddenly, the Master fell silent, sinking into a meditation which lasted for hours. No one dared make a move for fear of disturbing him. Finally he seemed to awaken, for he burst into laughter. When the Sabbath was over, Reb Zeev Kitzes timidly asked the Master why he had laughed. "Come with me, " he told his disciples. "I want you to meet someone special." The coach was ready, the horses were impatient. "We are going to Apt, " said the Besht to his faithful coachman Alexey. It was far? Not for the Besht's horses. They arrived in Apt before dawn. "Fetch a bookbinder named Shabtai," the Besht ordered his disciples. They found him and brought him to their Master. "Tell us what you did on the Sabbath eve," the Besht demanded. And the bookbinder replied: "Since you mention it, this Sabbath was indeed special. You see, Rebbe, until now I worked hard throughout the week and made just enough to allow my wife, Perele to go to the market and buy candles, wine, fish and meat and challah for Shabbat. This week I earned nothing; I am too old, my customers are leaving me. So, I told my wife: "If this is God's will, so be it. We must not borrow money, nor shall we accept charity. Better to fast and stay in darkness than to depend on someone else's money." As always, I went to shul, said the usual prayers, and came home ready to sit down and fast. But, to my surprise, there was light in my house and the table was covered with the finest dishes and the best wines. I did not wish to pain my wife, so I did not ask why she violated our pact and borrowed money. But she had not. She told me so during the meal. What had happened was that she had discovered, on an old jacket, some golden buttons and she had sold them for enough money to buy what she needed to prepare the Shabbat meal. When I heard that I felt such joy, such ecstasy, that I took my wife and began dancing with her..." The Besht nodded and said: "I saw you dancing and I could not help laughing, for the entire community of angels, in heaven, joined in your dance." And in spite of their advanced age, the old bookbinder Reb Shabtai and his wife Perele had a child one year later—the future Maggid of Kozhenitz.

Another version: It was Kol Nidre eve and, all of a sudden, in the old synagogue of Apt a quarrel broke out about "Nusah"—which tradition to follow in saying the "piyutim", which ones to say and when. The two sides fought with such conviction and vigor that all the prayer-books were torn apart. At the end of the evening, someone turned to the bookbinder Shabtai and said jokingly: "With all these damaged prayer-books, you, at least, are bound to have a good new year." But the bookbinder did not know what the man was talking about, so concentrated had he been in the prayer. As a reward for his pious concentration, his new year *was* a better one: his wife Perele gave birth to a son—and what a son!

And there is yet a fourth version: it happened during the winter—and the winters are brutal in Apt. Perele, Reb Shabtai's wife, went, as was her custom, to the river for her obligatory ritual immersions. When she found the river frozen, she went back for a hatchet and cut a hole into the ice, and performed the ritual of tvila. That night, she told her husband, "I almost died while immersing myself in the icy waters, so, my husband, please: tonight, let your thoughts fly higher." And so, according to this story, it was thanks to her zhut—her virtues and spirit of devotion and self-sacrifice—that seven months later the future Maggid of Kozhenitz was born unto them.

One thing is clear: Reb Shabtai and Perele were old—very old—when they had their son, the future Maggid. No wonder then that, in due time, Reb Israel involved himself with miracles, and especially with those helping barren parents.

A boy in such a situation is usually spoiled, but he was not. He himself often recalled a painful episode from the time he was seven. Even then he loved to study, while some of his companions did not. During Chanuka evenings, Yeshiva students often played cards, and one particular Chanuka evening he promised his father that he would not join them. Instead, he would stay only until three small candles remained lit. But they lasted until late into the night. "You played cards!" scolded his father, and gave him what he thought was an educational spanking. "He was wrong," the Maggid said later. "I was studying. Had I said so, my father would have believed me. But I didn't want to *use* study of Torah, not even for the sake of avoiding pain." That he was a good student is clear from the fact—recorded in the official Pinkas of Apt—that he was admitted as a full-fledged member of the Scholarly Association of "Ner Tamid" when he was only seven. He had to pay dues, and his father paid them for him: three silver coins.

When—at what age—did he develop his attraction for Hasidism? Late—very late. He visited the Great Maggid of Mezeritch, who had succeeded the Besht, and was impressed. But why did he wait so long? Why didn't he go to see the Besht himself, if only to say thank you? He surely knew the story with the cape since he was the one who revealed it.

He was 22 or 23 when the Besht died. Why wasn't he curious enough to meet him? Medzebish is not that far from Apt: why didn't he go there? A possible explanation—not a very good one—is that he was too busy studying. He did travel a lot, but only to Yeshivot. He went through Vholnia and Poland, and studied with the men whom Eastern European Jewry considered its most prestigious teachers. One of them was Rabbi Shmelke of Nicholsburg, who was known both as a Talmudic scholar and a Hasidic master. Young Reb Israel probably sought him out, and the scholar befriended him. The Maggid remembered having spoken on the topic of Chanuka in the presence of Reb Shmuel and, "All the dignitaries were ready to swallow me up alive. But Reb Shmuel remarked: 'Good, good', and they all remained mute." The young student also befriended Reb Shmuel's brother, the famous Reb Pinhas, the author of the "Haflaa." The two brothers were faithful followers of the Maggid of Mezeritch. Under their influence Reb Israel decided to go to Mezeritch and see for himself. Legend has it that he worked hard to save money to purchase a horse and coach, and to hire a coachman. The journey lasted many weeks. When at last he arrived in Mezeritch, he met Reb Shneur-Zalmen of Ladi, the founder of Habad, who in turn introduced him to the Maggid. "Young man, where are you from?" inquired the Maggid. "From Kozhenitz, not far from Warsaw." "Good," said the Maggid, "I am glad you came. I need you. I have in my possession a Lurianic prayer-book in manuscript. You will proof-read it." Reb Israel stayed there twelve weeks. If one is to believe a Hasidic legend—and who would dare not to believe Hasidic legends?—then the Maggid of Kozhenitz had finished reading eight hundred books on Kabbala *before* he came to Mezeritch; but when he saw the old Master he understood immediately that he knew nothing, nothing at all.

Why did he leave Mezeritch? He had to. He had a wife, Reizele, and a son, Reb Moshe. A wife? His second. The first was Reb Aharon Brisker's daughter. Something went wrong—we do not know what. All we know is that the marriage did not last long. Reb Israel remarried. The family grew: two sons and two daughters. He had to make a living. As a rabbi? No, not at first. At first, he did what most Hasidic masters had done before him: he became a Melamed, an instructor, a teacher. Then he became a preacher for Kozhenitz. Since the community was poor, unable to offer decent salaries, Reb Israel also had to preach in neighboring villages such as Magnishov and Greitza.

His father, Reb Shabtai, died in 1761 and the Maggid went every year to visit his grave in the town of Apt. So, naturally, local dignitaries invited him to preach in their synagogue, and he usually complied. One year he refused, explaining: "Did I accomplish anything with my last year's sermon? So why do it again?" Nobody protested, but that day hundreds and hundreds of Jews gathered in front of the inn where the Maggid stayed, waiting in silence for him to appear. When he did, they lowered their heads, still waiting. Suddenly, a man of the forest said aloud: "Rebbe, I wish to speak to you alone." They went inside. "Rebbe," said the man, "in my case you did accomplish something. You spoke last year of the necessity for every Jew to have God before him. Well, since last year I do. I constantly see His name before me; it is written with black fire on white fire; and it is you who made me see it."

Then the Maggid preached another sermon.

From local chroniclers we learn that he was a good preacher. In contrast to his colleagues, he rarely invoked fire and brimstone but spoke with tenderness instead. He advocated love, not fear. The Torah must be obeyed, not because of Hell and its punishments, but because of its own infinite measure of gratification. Only once a year would he speak of sin and its consequences: on Yom Kippur-eve, when the entire community of Israel, and indeed the whole world, pass before the Almighty for sentencing. Penitence and repentance are then prerequisites. "Let us atone for our sins," the Maggid would say to his congregation. "But my sins are greater and heavier than yours; I am a worse sinner than you." One of his friends once asked him whether he truly believed what he had said. "Of course, I do," replied the Maggid. "Impossible," objected the friend. "Why?" asked the Maggid. "Just think about it. We are all about to enter the holiest day of the year, ready to fast and pray and do penitence. Don't you know, my friend, that in matters of Teshuva a 'hirhur'—a thought—is sufficient?" His friend said nothing, so the Maggid continued: "Really, my friend. Do you really think that when I, Israel son of Perele of Kozhenitz, speak to my community, on the eve of Yom Kippur, I see in them sinners? No, they are all good Jews, loyal to their people, faithful to their ancestors. Only I am a sinner, only I."

A preacher he was—a preacher he remained. Unlike some of his close friends, such as the Rav of Ladi or of Berditchev, he never occupied a pulpit. He was not a Rabbi, but a Rebbe. After the death of the Maggid of Mezeritch, he chose Rebbe Elimelekh of Lizensk as his Master. Of his teacher and friend Rabbi Elimelekh of Lizensk, he said: "I know more than he in matters of Kabbala and even in Talmud, but when it comes to "m'sirat nefesh"—dedication and fear and love for God—I learn from him." He helped him and others strengthen and enrich the Hasidic experience among the hungry and despairing Jewish masses from the Dniepr to the Vistula, and beyond.

How did he become a Rebbe? One day he visited his friend Reb Levi-Itzhak. It was winter and the Maggid was dressed in a warm overcoat. Reb Levi-Itzhak accompanied him outside, forgetting to put on his own caftan. "Lend me your coat," he said to his visitor. They walked and walked. Finally Reb Levi-Itzhak returned the Maggid's coat, saying: "Now it's *your* turn to be warm." And that, according to legend, is how the Maggid became a Rebbe.

Like Reb Levi-Itzhak, the Maggid of Kozhenitz suffered greatly from the "Mitnagdim." The movement's adversaries picked both of them as their favorite targets. When Reb Levi-Itzhak was chased from his home, he sought refuge in Kozhenitz; and when the Maggid was driven out of Kozhenitz, he fled to his friend in Zelichov.

David of Makov, Hasidism's fiercest enemy, hated the Maggid most of all. Was it because the Maggid had tried to prevent the publication of his vitriolic anti-Hasidic pamphlet? The pamphlet was a personal smear attack against all Hasidic masters, but particularly against the Kozhnitzer Maggid who stood accused of being "so busy performing miracles that he has no time left for study."

Let us now briefly examine the context. The second part of the eighteenth and the early part of the nineteenth centuries—during which Hasidism attained its consummate expression both religiously and socially—have never ceased to fascinate me. So much violence on the one hand, so much naiveté on the other. Washington and Lafayette fought for American independence, while the holy Maggid and his disciples established new Hasidic kingdoms for the sake of Heaven. French revolutionaries introduced the word "terror" into our vocabulary while proclaiming the reign of reason and liberty, while in Eastern Europe the question for Jews was whether, in the Mussaf-service, "Naaritzakh" or "Keter" was to be sung. Napoleon altered the national physiognomy and the cultural landscape of Europe and beyond, but what mattered to Hasidism was the outcome of the dispute between Lizensk and Lublin, and later between Lublin and Pshiskhe. Danton and Robespierre, Bach and Beethoven, Kant and Goya, Mozart and Goethe were all contemporaries of Reb Shneur-Zalmen of Ladi, Reb Shmelke of Nicholsburg, Reb Zusia of Onipol, Reb Mendele Rimanover and the Maggid of Kozhenitz. They lived in the same period—was there no similarity in the way they reacted to its impact? Was Jewish history so separate from other people's history? Occasionally there were contacts—mostly hostile. Whenever nations went to war, Jews were among the first to suffer. On the other hand, when emancipation imposed itself as the latest fashion, Jews were its victims as much as its beneficiaries. Forced conversion was followed not by cultural freedom, but by forced assimilation—that is why Jews resisted both with equal passion. If the Maggid and his friends opposed compulsory military service for Jews, it was not out of fear for their lives but for their souls. When equal rights were granted to all citizens, some Hasidic leaders, including the Maggid, wanted them delayed as far as Jews were concerned. They were apprehensive. They thought Jews might be affected by their newly won freedom in ways that would not make them better Jews, but more distant Jews.

However, on a higher mystical level, attempts were made—as we shall see later—by some Hasidic masters to merge Jewish history with general history and redeem both at the same time. That endeavor, known in Hasidic literature as "the messianic conspiracy," was the work of three great masters: Rebbe Mendel of Rimanov, the Seer of Lublin, and the Maggid of Kozhenitz.

Redemption was their common obsession—redemption was the obsession of all Masters and all their followers; it remains the obsession of all Jews, though the word may mean a different reality—or lack of reality—to different people. Having concluded that most solutions to problems usually brought forth new problems, they opted to pray for the ultimate remedy: the Messiah. Said the Maggid of Kozhenitz: "Master of the Universe, I plead with you on behalf of the people Israel: send us the redeemer. If for reasons known to you alone you should be unwilling to do so, then redeem all the peoples around us."

This beautiful prayer is characteristic of the man. Of his total faith in prayer. Of his concern for his brethren. And for people in general. His mission on Earth? To offer help and hope. Whoever needed help knew where to turn. There exist innumerable legends about his "powers" to heal the sick, comfort the poor, encourage the forsaken. They called him the "second Baal-Shem Tov." There was an element of the supernatural in his life-style. His younger sister had died at a young age, but the heavenly tribunal gave her permission to dwell in her brother's house; and, according to legend, the Maggid would consult her in matters of charity. But, so the story goes, she loved to watch the servants and report on their misdeeds to her brother. The Maggid, however, disliked informers and told her to keep quiet. She felt hurt, and left the house forever.

His house was a busy house, always full—full of wandering beggars and melancholy innkeepers in need of something. Childless couples, abandoned wives, children of imprisoned parents: all came to Kozhenitz in quest of miracles. Few Hasidic Masters are reputed to have performed as many miracles as he did for as many supplicants.

Why did they all come to him? Perhaps because he had an aura of saintliness. Thin, emaciated, weak, unable to walk, he had to be carried to the House of prayer. Physicians marveled at his ability to stay alive; medically, they said, he was beyond their reach. He would spend days and nights in bed, rising only for services. But once inside the *shtibel*, he would jump to his place near the ark. Once, when he was invited to a circumcision ceremony, his disciples wanted to help him into his carriage, but he angrily rejected their assistance: "Naronim"—silly ones, he said, "It is written: 'Vakavei adoshem yakhlifu koach'—I borrow God's strength, and he has more strength than you." And the Maggid walked from the carriage to the circumcision. If he could perform miracles for others he could, for the sake of a mitzvah, accomplish them for himself as well.

Were miracles his trademark, his distinctive sign? No. Prayer was. Said he: "I love to pray. Nothing is as gratifying to me—nothing gives me as much joy. Nothing offers me as much fulfillment." Nothing?

What about study? Study too, naturally. But, to him, prayer and study were totally compatible; one enriched and completed the other. And, in fact, that is what I like most about him. Had he chosen one or the other, one against the other, he would have remained a marginal figure in the Hasidic tradition. But he combined both.

So learned was he that even the Gaon, Reb Hayim of Volozhin, praised his erudition. "When I, as a wanderer, came to Kozhenitz," he said, "I discussed Talmud with the Maggid and found him to be erudite in the Babylonian and Palestinian treatises, which he knew by heart as well as the Tosafot." He wrote about Halakha and Aggada, Nigla and Kabbala, about Maimonides and the Maharal of Prague, about Mitzvot and philosophy, about Rabbi Itzhak Lurie and Rabbi Bahye Ibn Pekuda. His knowledge was profound and all-encompassing, but for him, unlike for many others, it constituted no obstacle to prayer. "Man must be consumed by his prayer," said the Maggid. Often he lost consciousness during services. Once, in the middle of "Keter," he fainted and only when someone called his name did he regain consciousness. To his son, he said: "There is not an alien thought that did not come to me while I prayed, but I restored every one of them to its origin."

Legend has it that when his son, Reb Moshe, fell ill, desperately ill, the Maggid was overcome with sadness. In the morning, while getting ready for prayer, he exclaimed: "It is said of Haggar that she 'cast the child under the shrubs'. The shrubs, the shrubs, oh yes, the shrubs of prayer. She cast the child under the shrubs so that one word of prayer might be uttered with joy." When Reb Levi-Itzhak of Berditchev, who at that time was still living in the neighboring village of Zelikhov, heard of the Maggid's comment, he went to the Mikva and prayed to Heaven to influence the Maggid's trend of thought so that he would pray for the recovery of his son instead of reflecting on Haggar, and he succeeded. The Maggid prayed for his son and his son recovered. But, stipulates Hasidic legend, that night his son was not the only child to recover from his illness; all the sick children did. Everywhere.

Rabbi Levi-Itzhak of Berditchev was one of his closest friends. When he was thrown out by his opponents, on Hoshana-rabba, in the middle of the holiday, he came to seek refuge in Kozhenitz. Later, when the Berditchever was "deprived of his mystical powers" and went into depression and solitude, he again sought and found comfort and companionship in the home of the Maggid. We are told that, for six months, he could do nothing but pray from a small "siddur," not understanding what he was saying.

We have mentioned this disquieting phenomenon on other occasions. Most Hasidic Masters had such periods of depression. But they usually emerged from them stronger. By helping their followers they helped themselves.

Jews and non-Jews flocked to him. Princes, generals, noblemen—all had faith in him. Prince Poniatowski, Prince Chartoritzky, Count Potocky swore by him. Prince Chartoritzky had no sons, so he pleaded with the Maggid to give him his blessing and pray for him; the Maggid did. He said to God: "Master of the Universe, you have so many gentiles in this world of yours; let there be one more—why should you mind?"

He did, in fact, have an exquisite sense of humor. A woman came to him weeping: her husband had left her. "Why?" asked the Maggid. – "He claims that I am old." "Well, maybe you are," said the Maggid. – "Yes, but I used to be young and pretty." "Master of the Universe," the Maggid exclaimed, "isn't this the story of your people too? Maybe today, after centuries of exile and hardship, we have grown old and ugly—but remember? In the beginning, when we first met, 'Knesset Israel' was young and fervent and radiant with singular beauty."

A wealthy Hasid boasted before him of eating bread and drinking water all week long. "Why do you do that?" the Maggid asked him. "I am modest and my desires are modest," said the man. "Don't be!" the Maggid shouted. "I want you to eat roast meat and drink wine." And to his Hasidim he explained: "If rich people eat meat, at least they realize that poor people need bread; if rich people eat bread, they will think that poor people can live on stones."

A villager and his wife cried their heart out before him: they wanted a son. They were desperate. "All right," said the Maggid, "I shall give you my blessing, but it will cost you fifty-two gulden, for 52 is the numerical value of BEN, the Hebrew word for son." "No, 30," said the villager. "No." "No?" shouted the villager. "Then we don't need you. Come, woman," he said to his wife, "let's go home. God will help us without his blessing." "He has already helped you," smiled the Maggid.

Once he was told by one of his followers that an elderly couple, not of Hasidic background, had just had a child. "See?" the Maggid commented with tongue in cheek, "God wanted to show that He too can perform miracles."

A couple was on the brink of divorce. The Maggid wanted to know the reason. Said the husband: "I work hard all week. I long for the Sabbath. I love the Sabbath. Above all, I love kugel on the Sabbath. The problem is that the meals in our home are rich. I eat fish and meat and cholent. When the time for kugel arrives I am no longer hungry. So I plead with my wife: serve kugel first. She says that in her father's home it was customary to serve kugel at the end of the meal." "You are both right," said the Maggid. "Therefore I order you to have two kugels on the Sabbath, one at the beginning, one at the end." And ·man and wife stayed together.

Some of the stories had less happy endings. Constantin, Prince Adam Czartoritzky's brother, refused to give credence to the stories about the Maggid's mystical powers. "You want proof?" he said to his brother, "come, I will give it to you." They both went to the Maggid and Constantin asked him to pray for his sick son who was not sick at all. The Maggid did not respond. Laughing, Constantin insisted. Finally the Maggid said to him: "Go home, go quickly. You may still find him alive." He didn't.

But many of the other legends deal with reward, not punishment. And many of the other legends deal with prayer. Kozhenitz *means* prayer, the importance of prayer, the richness of prayer, the passion for prayer. Remember: Hasidism saw in prayer the shortest way to Heaven. The easiest as well. Some Masters spent more time preparing for prayer than praying. Reb Levi-Itzhak of Berditchev was one of them. When he came to visit the Maggid of Kozhenitz, the Maggid asked him to make an exception and do what people did in Kozhenitz: daven on time. Reb Levi-Itzhak promised. And tried. And failed. In his ecstasy, he forgot time.

Kavana, Dvekut, Hitlahavut—concentration, fusion, fervor—are key-words in the Hasidic vocabulary. It is not what one says but how one says it that matters. A simple "Shma Israel" on the lips of a shepherd is worthier than a litany uttered by a sage.

"Turn my tales into prayers," said Rabbi Nahman of Bratzlav. What is prayer if not an expression of man's need to transcend himself and turn ordinary words into a ladder leading up to the Heavenly throne? "The fact that I am a descendant of Abraham, Isaac, and Jacob is enough to make me drunk and go around dancing, dancing, dancing in the streets," said the Maggid of Kozhenitz. "Just imagine," said he, "I, a speck of dust, but a descendant of Abraham, can speak to God Almighty and address Him as Thou." What is prayer if not a dialogue—a dialogue with God? All of a sudden you are no longer alone, yet you are alone—alone with God who listens, and at times even responds.

Prayer draws its fire and meaning from a most obscure zone in our being—a source where sound becomes word and word becomes melody and melody turns into offering.

Prayer is an encounter with memory and God—with God's memory?—and with oneself. A moment of grace, of abandonment, of affirmation, of recognition. If art is man's way of saying no, prayer is his way of saying yes. Yes to creation and creator, yes to life and its meaning, yes to faith, to hope, to joy. A beacon to the lost wanderer in the forest, a presence to dreamers in search of dreams, a window to the soul: prayer is what is most indispensable in man's passage on Earth. If Torah kept us alive, prayer kept our hope alive. God himself needs prayer—ours and his own. What is His prayer? The Talmud tells us: "she'ekhbosh kaassi va'arrakhem al banai," may I contain my anger and have pity on my childen. When everything else seems lost, prayer still exists—and thanks to it, everything else becomes possible.

The Maggid used to study and daven in a sing-song; that is how he would speak too. All his words were melodious. And Hasidim believed that his tune was special: he had heard it from the lips of angels. Other disciples maintain the opposite: that the angels had learned the tune from him. Still others claimed that the angels were created by his tune.

Kozhenitzer Hasidim explain how their Master had acquired a beautiful melody which he alone would sing for Lekha dodi on erev-Shabbat.

Once, at midnight, he heard a voice calling him, moaning: "Holy teacher, help me." "Who are you?" "A wandering soul; all gates are closed to me." "Who are you?" "I used to be a musician; I belonged to a troupe of minstrels and troubadours; I sinned. A lot." "Why did you come to me?" "I played at your wedding. You liked the tune. You made me play it again and again." "You still remember it? Play it." And the dead musician did.

The following Friday evening the Maggid sang that melody for Lekha-dodi. Nobody could join in. And nobody ever remembered it.

Like Rebbe Pinhas of Koretz, the Maggid of Kozhenitz loved singing. When he was ill and weak, his friend, the "Jew of Pshiskhe," sent him two disciples to sing for him, and his health improved with every hour, with every song. "The Jew of Pshiskhe," said he, "knew that I had not managed to penetrate the "Olam haniguna," the world of melody. That is why he sent you to me. Now I shall try."

Said he: "Every man leaves Egypt every day, and every day we must receive the Law. The Torah speaks of today—of today too. Its tales are for and about now. Cain and Abel? A story about jealousy. The tower of Babel? Vanity. The floods? A story about lust."

Said the Kozhenitzer Maggid: "God is my witness that what gives me true pleasure is a fervent prayer. God grants me this pleasure as a reward for the few good deeds that I may have performed. But it makes me worry: for me, there may be no further compensation in the other world."

Remember the unhappy woman in our first story? She was ready to buy the Maggid a caftan. Did the Maggid help her? Yes, he taught her a lesson: that it is possible to be heard in Heaven without spending money on gifts and presents, without coming to the Rebbes and Masters with pleas and supplications. He taught her to rely on her *own* prayers.

What the Maggid of Kozhenitz sought to achieve with prayer was not only individual improvement for his fellow Jews, but redemption on a cosmic scale. Together with his two friends and associates, the Seer of Lublin and Reb Mendel of Rimanov, they conspired to hasten the coming of the Messiah. They saw in the Napoleonic wars that ravaged Europe a heavenly sign that the times were ripe: those wars, to them, symbolized the apocalyptic upheavals of Gog and Magog. Who should win and who should be defeated? The Hasidic community at large was divided. Reb Shneur-Zalmen sided with the Czar, Reb Mendel with Napoleon. The Maggid, in the beginning, agreed with Reb Mendel but then yielded to Reb Shneur-Zalmen. Hasidic legend has enough information—or call it imagination—to give us the background: Reb Shneur-Zalmen and the Maggid agreed that whoever would blow the shofar first would win the argument, so, on that Rosh-Hashana, the Maggid urged his followers to pray fast, faster, still faster—but when he reached the Tkiat-Shofar he stopped and said: "Reb Shneur-Zalmen has outwitted me, his people have blown the shofar before services." And so the Maggid too turned against Napoleon, which, of course, is the reason for the Emperor's defeat at Waterloo. And if you think that Napoleon didn't know it, you are wrong. He did know it—there are Hasidic legends to prove it. The Emperor himself came to see the old Maggid, who received him lying in bed. Napoleon pleaded with him. To no avail.

Had the Masters agreed on whom to support, the Messiah might have come. But then, as today, unanimity is not the most obvious Jewish virtue.

We know that the three conspirators met often—usually at the home of the Kozhenitzer Maggid who, for health reasons, could not go anywhere. They had their secret discussions and prepared their secret moves for the next battles. Determined to bring the Messiah even if it meant using force, they worked on it relentlessly. It appears that they were close to success but then Satan, as always, used his own arguments up there in Heaven, and the project was sabotaged. The three participants died the same year: 1815.

The first to die was the Kozhenitzer Maggid. It was erev Sukkot. He was close to eighty. Old, weak, sick—he fought valiantly to the end.

To his daughter, Perele, he once remarked: "If I so wished, I could bring the Messiah." "Then father," she said, "why don't you?" "The price of redemption would be high, too high. Jewish blood would be shed in the streets. People would search with candles for a Jew who had remained alive, and they would not find him." "Then don't," said his daughter. "The life of even a single Jew would be too high a price to pay."

A variation on the same theme is told about the Besht. He too sought redemption. Once, when he was about to utter the mysterious names and thus break the chains holding the Messiah a prisoner, he suddenly perceived the crying of a hungry child and he immediately hurried away to feed it. "The Messiah can wait," he said, "a hungry child cannot."

Perele was a strong personality in her own right. She would often don a talit, a prayer shawl, and she would fast Mondays and Thursdays. Hasidim considered her a "Rebbe" and brought her *kwitlekh* soliciting her blessings.

She was close to her father. Their relationship was reminiscent of the relationship that existed between the Besht and his daughter, Odel. But Perele's life was filled with tragedy. All her children died young, except the one who became the "Seraphin" of Magelnitza.

The Maggid of Kozhenitz died on the eve of Sukkot, in the year 1815—and Kozhenitz itself died during Sukkot 1942. The ghetto was evacuated, liquidated on the first day of Hol-hamoed. People had felt the end was near, before the holiday. On the first day of Sukkot parents and children recited their prayers and bid farewell to each other. "Our life ends tomorrow," they said to one another, according to survivors. Most were sent to Treblinka, the others to a nearby labor-camp. One of them, a survivor named Leah, daughter of Yankel Sherman, tells of four Kozhenitzer Jews whom the Germans hanged publicly in the square: "They were hanging," says the eyewitness, "And the wind was moving them back and forth, back and forth, not like human beings but like laundry, yes, like laundry."

As for the great-grandson of the Maggid, who had succeeded him on the throne, Rabbi Aharon-Yehiel, he was away from Kozhenitz. He had left his hometown before the outbreak of the war. He was active among young Jews, especially the assimilated, trying desperately to bring them back to Judaism. He was known to be charismatic and artistic. Often he would play the violin and sing, and thus attract the youth. The war found him in Otwock, near Warsaw. One day, in 1942, as he was studying Talmud, a messenger came to tell him the tragic news about what was happening in Treblinka. For a while he remained motionless, bent over his books. Then, it is told, he whispered to himself: "In this case, why go on living? It is too much to bear." He stood up, went into another room, settled into a chair—and died.

Once the holy Maggid of Kozhenitz whispered:

"Master of the Universe, I beseech you to send us the redeemer. If you need a high-priest, I will show you the holy Rebbe of Apt. If you need a prophet, look at the Seer of Lublin. If you need a Tzaddik, take Reb Levi-Itzhak of Berditchev or Reb Mendel of Rimanov. If you need a penitent, take me: I repent, I repent for all the sins I have committed—for all the sins I could have prevented others from committing, I repent."

To the Rebbe of Apt who found him lying in bed on Shavuot, he said: "I am like a soldier. The five pebbles that David used against Goliath, I have them: they are in *my* bed. I am a soldier, Apter Rebbe. I must fight."

Then, on Yom Kippur, lying on his stretcher facing the Holy Ark, he stopped before the prayer "Vayomer adoshem salakhti kidvarekha"—and the Lord has said I forgive you—and he whispered: "Master of the Universe, you alone know how great and powerful you are. I do not. But you also know how weak I am, for I too know that. And yet, throughout the month of Elul I have been here, in this place of worship, and I have prayed to you day after day, hour after hour, not for my own sake but for the sake of your people, the people of Israel. And I am asking you, Master of the Universe: Do you think it is easy for an old man of my age to take upon himself the burdens of a community? And yet I took them on myself. In exchange, Lord of creation, God of Abraham, Isaac, and Jacob, do something which, for you, is less difficult. Say two words, just two: "Salakhti kidvarekha," I have forgiven."

Then he fell quiet. He waited a minute, another one. He waited a long while. Suddenly he burst into song, a song of joy. And he said: "God has answered our prayer. He has said that He forgives our sins."

Legend has it that the Kozhenitzer Maggid, during that last Yom Kippur service, was determined not to resume his prayer until he himself would hear God's answer.

Was it too much for him? Too great an effort? He died four days later.

But the Messiah has not come.

Bibliography —
Writings of Yitz Greenberg

"On the Divine Plan and the Human Role in Development of Religion: A Response to Tom Idinopulos," in JOURNAL OF ECUMENICAL STUDIES, Vol. 42 Issue 3 (Summer 2007), pp. 458-462.

"Theology After the Shoah: the Transformation of the Core Paradigm," MODERN JUDA-ISM, vol.26, no.3 (2006), pp. 213-239.

"Section 1: Reflections on the Film: A Review of Mel Gibson's Passion of the Christ," in Zev Garber, editor, MEL GIBSON'S "THE PASSION": THE FILM, THE CONTROVERSY, AND ITS IMPLICATIONS (IN: Purdue University Press, 2006), pp. 7-12.

FOR THE SAKE OF HEAVEN AND EARTH: THE NEW ENCOUNTER BETWEEN JUDAISM AND CHRISTIANITY (New York: The Jewish Publication Society, 2004).

"Judaism, Christianity, & Partnership After the Twentieth Century" in Tikva Frymer-Kensky, David Novak, Peter Ochs, David Fox Sandmel & Michael A Signer, editors, CHRISTIANITY IN JEWISH TERMS (Boulder, Colorado: Westview Press, 2000), pp. 25-36.

"Judaism & Christianity: Covenants of Redemption" in Tikva Frymer-Kensky, David Novak, Peter Ochs, David Fox Sandmel & Michael A Signer, editors, CHRISTIANITY IN JEWISH TERMS (Boulder, Colorado: Westview Press, 2000), pp. 141-158.

"Pluralism and Partnership" in ICCJ UNITY WITHOUT UNIFORMITY: THE CHALLENGE OF PLURALISM, Martin Buber House publication, Number 26 (Spring 1999), pp. 68-81.

"Jewish Denominationalism Meets The Open Society" in Marjorie Garber & Rebecca L. Walkowitz, editors, ONE NATION UNDER GOD (New York: Routledge, 1999), pp. 32-59.

LIVING IN THE IMAGE OF GOD-JEWISH TEACHINGS TO PERFECT THE WORLD: CONVERSATION WITH IRVING GREENBERG, Co-Author with Shalom Freedman, (New Jersey: Jason Aronson, 1998).

"Seeking the Religious Roots of Pluralism," in JOURNAL OF ECUMENICAL STUDIES, vol. 34, no. 3 (Summer 1997), pp. 385-94.

"Covenantal Pluralism," JOURNAL OF ECUMENICAL STUDIES, vol. 34, no. 3 (Summer 1997), pp. 425-36.

"Yitzhak Rabin and the Ethic of Jewish Power," PERSPECTIVES (National Jewish Center for Learning and Leadership, 1995).

"Judaism and Christianity: Their Respective Roles in the Divine Strategy of Redemption," in Eugene J. Fisher, editor, VISIONS OF THE OTHER, Jewish and Christian Theologians Assess the Dialogue (Mahwah: Paulist Press, 1994), pp. 7-27.

"The Ethics of Jewish Power," in R.R. Reuther and M.W. Ellis, editors, BEYOND OCCUPATION: AMERICAN JEWISH, CHRISTIAN AND PALESTINIAN VOICES OF PEACE (Beacon Press, 1990), pp. 22-64.

"The Ethics of Jewish Power," (abridged version) in Elliot N. Dorff and Louis E. Newman, editors, CONTEMPORARY JEWISH ETHICS AND MORALITY, A READER (Oxford University Press, 1995), pp. 403-422.

"The Dialectics of Power: Reflections in light of the Holocaust," in Daniel Landes, editor, CONFRONTING OMNICIDE JEWISH REFLECTIONS ON WEAPONS OF MASS DESTRUCTION (NJ: Jason Aronson Inc. 1991), pp.12-35.

"The Challenge to the Jewish Community: Religion, Life and the State of Israel," in Yehudah Baur, editor, REMEMBERING FOR THE FUTURE (Oxford: Pergamon Press, 1989), pp. 2903-2930.

THE JEWISH WAY: LIVING THE HOLIDAYS (New York: Summit Books, November 1988).

THEODORE ROOSEVELT AND LABOR: 1900-1918 (New York: Garland Publications, 1988).

"Will there be One Jewish People by the year 2000? Further Reflections," in Steven M. Cohen, editor, CONFLICT OR COOPERATION: PAPERS ON JEWISH UNITY (New York: AJC, 1989), pp.9-18.

"Toward a Principled Pluralism," in Ronald Kronish, editor, TOWARDS THE TWENTY-FIRST CENTURY: JUDAISM AND THE JEWISH PEOPLE IN ISRAEL AND AMERICA (KTAV Publishing, 1988), pp. 183-205.

"Toward a Covenantal Ethic of Medicine," in Levi Meier, editor, JEWISH VALUES IN BIO-ETHICS (New York: Human Sciences Press, 1986), pp. 124-49.

"Will There Be One Jewish People By the Year 2000," PERSPECTIVES (National Jewish Center for Learning and Leadership, June 1985).

"The Relationship of Judaism and Christianity: Toward a New Organic Model," in Eugene Fisher, James Rudin, and Marc Tanenbaum, editors, TWENTY YEARS OF JEWISH/CATHOLIC RELATIONS (New York: Paulist Press, 1986), pp. 191-211.

"Religious values after the Holocaust: A Jewish View," in Abraham J. Peck, editor, JEWS AND CHRISTIANS AFTER THE HOLCAUST (Philadelphia: Fortress Press, 1982), pp. 63-86.

"Teaching of the Holocaust," in Bernard Rosenberg and Ernest Goldstein, CREATORS AND DISTURBERS REMINISCENCES BY JEWISH INTELLECTUALS (New York: Columbia University Press, 1982), pp. 227-233.

"Voluntary Covenant," PERSPECTIVES (National Jewish Center for Learning and Leadership, October 1982).

"The Third Great Cycle of Jewish History," PERSPECTIVES (National Jewish Center for Learning and Leadership, September 1981).

"New Revelation and New Patterns in the Relationship of Judaism and Christianity," JOURNAL OF ECUMENICAL STUDIES, vol. 16, no. 2 (Spring 1979), pp. 249-67.

"Orthodox Judaism and the Holocaust," GESHER, no. 7 (1979), 55-82.

CONFRONTING THE HOLOCAUST: THE IMPACT OF ELIE WIESEL, Irving Greenberg and Alvin Rosenfeld, editors (Indiana University Press, 1978).

"From Modernity to Post-Modernity: Community and the Revitalization of Traditional Religion," RELIGIOUS EDUCATION, vol. 73, no.4 (1978), pp.449-469.

"Cloud of Smoke, Pillar of Fire: Judaism, Christianity and Modernity After the Holocaust" in Eva Fleischner, editor, AUSCHWITZ: BEGINNING OF A NEW ERA? (New York: KTAV, 1977), pp. 7-55, 441-446.

"The Interaction of Israel and American Jewry After the Holocaust", in Moshe Davis, editor, WORLD JEWRY AND THE STATE OF ISRAEL (New York: Arno Press, 1977), pp. 259-282.

"Historical Events & Religious Change," in Stanley, Kazan and Nathaniel Stampfer, editors, PERSPECTIVES IN JEWISH LEARNING, vol. 1 (Chicago: Spertus College Press, 1977), pp. 43-63.

"The End of Emancipation," CONSERVATIVE JUDAISM, vol. xxx, no. 4 (Summer 1976), pp. 47-63.

"Interpreting the Holocaust for Future Generations," in INTERPRETING THE HOLOCAUST FOR FUTURE GENERATIONS: PROCEEDINGS OF A SYMPOSIUM (New York: 1975), pp. 18-40.

"Judaism and Christianity After the Holocaust," in JOURNAL OF ECUMENICAL STUDIES, vol. 12, no. 4 (Fall 1975), pp. 521-51.

"Scholarship and Continuity: Dilemma and Dialectic" in Leon Jick, THE TEACHING OF JUDAICA IN AMERICAN UNIVERSITIES (New York: KTAV/Association for Jewish Studies, 1970), pp. 113-31.

"The Jewish College Youth," in Gilbert S. Rosenthal, editor, THE JEWISH FAMILY IN A CHANGING WORLD (New York: T. Yoseloff, 1970), pp. 201-230.

"Toward Jewish Religious Unity: A Symposium," in Peter I. Rose, editor, THE GHETTO AND BEYOND: ESSAY ON JEWISH LIFE IN AMERICA (New York: Random House, 1969), pp. 150-172.

"Jewish Survival and the College Campus," JUDAISM, vol. 17, no. 3 (Summer 1968), pp. 42-74.

"Jewish Values and the Changing American Jewish Ethic," TRADITION, vol.10, no1 (1968), pp. 42-74.

"The New Encounter of Judaism and Christianity," BARAT REVIEW, vol. 3, no. 2 (June 1967), pp. 113-25.

"The Cultural Revolution and Religious Unity," RELIGIOUS EDUCATION, vol. 62, no. 2 (March 1967), pp. 98-104.

"Toward Jewish Religious Unity," JUDAISM, vol. 15, no. 2 (Spring 1966), pp. 133-39, 152-63.

"Judaism and the Dilemma of War," in Henry Siegman, editor, JUDAISM AND WORLD PEACE (New York 1966), pp. 17-25.

"Adventure in Freedom or Escape from Freedom: Jewish Identity in America," AMERICAN JEWISH HISTORICAL QUARTERLY, vol. 55, no. 1 (September 1965), pp. 5-22.

Contributors

Steven Bayme serves as Director of the Contemporary Jewish Life Department and of the Koppelman Institute on American Jewish-Israeli Relations at the American Jewish Committee. Dr. Bayme is Visiting Associate Professor of History at the Jewish Theological Seminary and author of *Understanding Jewish History: Texts and Commentary* and *Jewish Arguments and Counter-Arguments*.

Eugene B. Borowitz is Distinguished University Professor, the Sigmund L. Falk Distinguished Professor of Education and Jewish Religious Thought at the New York School of Hebrew Union College-Jewish Institute of Religion. His most recent books are: *The Talmud's Theological Language-Game: A Philosophical Discourse Analysis* and, with Frances W. Schwartz, *A Touch of the Sacred: A Theologian's Informal Guide to Jewish Belief*.

Alice L. Eckardt is a Protestant theologian and a pivotal figure in Jewish-Christian relations. In books such as *Long Night's Journey into Day*, written with her husband Roy, she helped re-conceive Christianity's relationship to Judaism in light of the Holocaust.

Arnold M. Eisen is the seventh Chancellor of The Jewish Theological Seminary. He previously served as the Koshland Professor of Jewish Culture and Religion at Stanford University. Chancellor Eisen's publications include four scholarly works about Judaism in the modern world as well as a personal essay, *Taking Hold of Torah: Jewish Commitment and Community in America*.

David Ellenson is President of Hebrew Union College-Jewish Institute of Religion (HUC-JIR) and I.H. and Anna Grancell Professor of Jewish Religious Thought. Dr. Ellenson's publications include, *After Emancipation*, which was the 2005 National Jewish Book Award winner in the category of Modern Jewish Thought.

Immanuel Etkes is Professor Emeritus of Modern Jewish History at the Hebrew University of Jerusalem. His books include *Rabbi Israel Salanter and the Mussar Movement*; *The Gaon of Vilna: The Man and His Image*, *The Besht: Magician, Mystic, Leader*.

Sylvia Barack Fishman is Professor of Contemporary Jewish Life in the Near Eastern and Judaic Studies Department at Brandeis University and Co-director of the Hadassah-Brandeis Institute. Her books include, *The Way Into the Varieties of Jewishness*, and *Double Or Nothing? Jewish Families and Mixed Marriage*.

Lawrence Grossman, is Editor of the American Jewish Year Book and is Associate Director of research at the American Jewish Committee. Dr. Grossman has published numerous essays and reviews on American Jewish life most recently, "The Organized Jewish Community and Evangelical America: A History."

David Hartman is the Founder of the Shalom Hartman Institute in Jerusalem. Rabbi Hartman received the Avi Chai Prize in 2000, the Guardian of Jerusalem Prize, and The Samuel Rothberg Prize for Jewish Education. His numerous books include *Maimonides: Torah and Philosophic Quest* and *A Living Covenant: The Innovative Spirit in Traditional Judaism*, both winners of the National Jewish Book Award.

Steven T. Katz is Director of the Elie Wiesel Center for Judaic Studies at Boston University where he is the Alvin J. and Shirley Slater Professor in Jewish and Holocaust Studies. He is the editor of *Modern Judaism*, and his many publications include *Post-Holocaust Dialogues*, which won the National Jewish Book Award in 1984.

Reuven Kimelman is Professor of Classical Judaica at Brandeis University. He recently issued three new audio books and is the author of *The Mystical Meaning of 'Lekhah Dodi' and 'Kabbalat Shabbat.'* And the forthcoming *Rhetoric of Jewish Prayer: A Historical and Literary Commentary on the Prayerbook*.

David Kraemer is Joseph J. and Dora Abbell Librarian at The Jewish Theological Seminary, where he has also served as Professor of Talmud and Rabbinics. His books include *The Mind of the Talmud, Responses to Suffering in Classical Rabbinic Literature,* and *Jewish Eating and Identity Through the Ages.*

Benny Kraut was, until his unfortunate death in 2008, Professor of History and Director of the Jewish Studies Program and the Center for Jewish Studies. He published widely in the fields of modern and American Jewish history and Judaism. His books include *From Reform Judaism to Ethical Culture: The Religious Evolution of Felix Adler,* and he wrote more than three dozen scholarly essays and book chapters.

Jacob Milgrom is Professor Emeritus of Biblical Studies at the University of California, Berkeley, and past chair and founder of its Jewish Studies Program. He is the author of numerous books including, *The JPS Torah Commentary: Numbers,* and most recently *Leviticus: A Book of Ritual and Ethics.*

Alvin H. Rosenfeld is Professor of English and Jewish Studies and Director of the Institute for Jewish Culture and the Arts at Indiana University. Dr. Rosenfeld is the author and editor of numerous books including, *A Double Dying: Reflections on Holocaust Literature* and *Imagining Hitler.*

Daniel Septimus is the Editor-in-Chief of MyJewishLearning.com. He hosts the 92nd Street Y's Jewish Literary Exchange and, for several years, was the Books columnist for the *Jerusalem Post.*

Eliyahu Stern is Junior Research Fellow at University of Oxford in Modern Jewish Eastern European History. He writes regularly for beliefnet and is a term-member on the Council on Foreign Relations. In Fall 2010 he will assume the position of Assistant Professor of Modern Jewish Intellectual and Cultural History at Yale University.

Jacob B. Ukeles is the President of Ukeles Associates Inc (UAI), a New York-based planning, policy research, and management consulting firm. Prior to establishing UAI, Dr. Ukeles served as director of community services at the UJA-Federation of New York. Dr. Ukeles was the founding Chair of the Graduate Department of Urban Policy of the New School for Social Research.

Elie Wiesel is the Andrew W. Mellon Professor in the Humanities at Boston University. He received the Nobel Peace Prize in 1986. He has written numerous books and is the recipient of numerous literary awards as well as honorary degrees from more than one hundred and twenty colleges and universities in America, Europe and Israel. His latest novel, *Le cas Sonderberg*, was published in France in 2008.